Traditional Practices
Reproductive Health i   Using Human Rights

SCHOOL OF HUMAN RIGHTS RESEARCH SERIES, Volume 13

A commercial edition of this dissertation will be published by Intersentia under ISBN 90-5095-226-7

The titles published in this series are listed at the end of this volume.

Using Human Rights to Change Tradition

Traditional Practices Harmful to Women's Reproductive Health in sub-Saharan Africa

Mensenrechten als instrument om tradities te veranderen
Traditionele praktijken die schadelijk zijn voor de reproductieve
gezondheid van vrouwen in sub-Sahara Afrika
(met een samenvatting in het Nederlands)

PROEFSCHRIFT

ter verkrijging van de graad van doctor
aan de Universiteit Utrecht
op gezag van de Rector Magnificus, Prof. dr. W.H. Gispen
ingevolge het besluit van het College voor Promoties
in het openbaar te verdedigen
op woensdag 5 juni 2002 des middags te 2.30 uur

door

Corinne Angeline Agnès Packer
geboren op 7 april 1967, te St. Boniface, Manitoba, Canada

INTERSENTIA
Antwerpen – Oxford – New York

Promotores: Prof. dr. C. Flinterman
              Prof. dr. R.E. Howard-Hassmann

CRC prepared by: G.J. Wiarda Instituut, Utrecht

ACKNOWLEDGEMENTS

I am especially grateful to five persons who were most closely associated with me in the writing of this doctoral thesis. First, to Professor Cees Flinterman, who encouraged me to pursue this research from our first meeting some years ago and very graciously agreed to be my supervisor, offering positive support and input all the way through. His optimism was infectious and helped me remain committed to the task. Second, to Professor Rhoda Howard-Hassmann, who came for a sabbatical to SIM in Utrecht in the hope of catching up on a variety of her own research projects but left with an additional charge as my second supervisor. Her constant encouragement and keen challenges helped me develop, refine and, ultimately, defend my arguments. Third, to John, my husband, who never seemed to have a doubt that I would finish the research, was always willing to listen to me ramble on about it, and put his English editing skills to work in the final days. Finally, to Sébastien and Nicholas, my children, who tolerated my absence as I went to 'school' to 'sing songs'… or so they seemed to think! They put my thesis to good use, making beautiful drawings on the early drafts.

I would also like to express my appreciation to the members of my reading committee (Dr. Augustine Ankomah, Professor Abdullahi An-Na'im, Professor Bas de Gaay Fortman, Professor Jenny Goldschmidt and Professor Titia Loenen) for examining the thesis. Many friends and colleagues furnished me with valuable comments on various chapters, in particular: Juan Amaya-Castro, Zdenka Machnyikova, Wambui Mwangi, Rolanda Oostland and Bahia Tahzib-Lie. As if they didn't have enough work on their desks already! An additional word of thanks goes to Rolanda and Juan for their careful translation of the summary into Dutch.

Present in these pages are the people who otherwise supported me along the way, in particular: my fellow researchers and the staff at SIM, my parents, my friends outside of university and my sons' babysitters, particularly Petra Kulhankova and Martha Wanjiku. A final word of thanks goes to Irnsje Veerman for her professional layout of this book.

TABLE OF CONTENTS

Acknowledgements — v

Glossary of Acronyms and Abbreviations — xiii

Chapter I
Introduction — 1
1 The Purpose of the Study — 1
2 Defining the Parameters of the Study — 2
2.1 The Socio-Cultural Determinants of Women's Reproductive Health — 2
2.2 Human Rights as a Tool for Social Change — 2
2.3 Women, Reproductive Health and Harm from Traditional Practices — 3
2.4 The Region of Sub-Saharan Africa — 5
3 The State of Challenges to Harmful Traditional Practices — 9
4 The Structure of the Study — 13

Chapter II
The Harmful Traditional Practices in Question and Supporting Customs and Norms — 17
1 Introduction — 17
2 Traditional Practices Harmful to Women's Reproductive Health — 18
2.1 Female Circumcision — 18
2.2 Early Marriage (Early Sexual Activity and Pregnancy) — 25
2.3 Dietary Taboos during Pregnancy and Lactation — 28
2.4 Practices Relating to Childbirth — 29
2.5 Incisions in Pregnant Women — 30
2.6 Female Religious Bondage — 31
3 Customs and Norms Bolstering Traditional Practices Harmful to Women — 31
3.1 Authority of the Husband and Spousal Violence — 31
3.2 Extended-Family-Household Structure — 32
3.3 Kinship Influence and Intervention in the Name of Lineage — 34
3.4 Son Preference — 35
3.5 Polygyny — 36
3.6 Extra-Marital Sexual Activity — 38
3.7 Brideprice (Bridewealth) — 40

3.8	Levirate (Wife Inheritance) Marriage	41
3.9	Abduction for Purposes of Rape, Impregnation and Marriage	42
4	Norms Influencing Fertility	42
4.1	Universal Marriage	43
4.2	Ideal Family Size	43
5	The Culture of Silence and Superstition	44
6	Combined Customs Contributing to HIV/AIDS Infection	46
7	Conclusions	48

Chapter III
The Rights in Question — 49

1	Introduction	49
2	Situating Harmful Traditional Practices within the Framework of International Human Rights Law	49
2.1	The Obligations of the State in General	49
2.2	The Obligations of the State Particular to Harmful Traditional Practices	53
3	Determining Human Rights Violations by the Nature of the Practice	57
3.1	The Right to Health	58
3.1.1	The Inseparability of the Rights to Life and Health	59
3.1.2	Grey Areas	60
3.2	The Right to Freedom from Discrimination on the Basis of Gender	61
3.2.1	Grey Areas	62
3.3	The Right to Freedom from Violence	63
3.3.1	Grey Areas	67
3.3.2	Moving Away from the Blanket Gender-Violence Approach	69
3.3.3	A Word on 'Global' Ideologies on Gender and Feminism	70
3.4	The Rights to Freedom of Thought, Belief, Opinion and Expression	74
3.4.1	Grey Areas	75
3.5	The Right to Education	77
3.6	The Right to Choose One's Spouse	78
3.7	The Right to Found a Family	78
4	Conclusions	79

Chapter IV
The Theoretical Value of the Human Rights Approach — 81

1	Introduction	81
2	Over Two Millennia of Theorizing on Human Rights and Moral Wrongs	84
2.1	The Debate in Antiquity	84

2.2	The Debate in the Era of Enlightenment	86
2.3	Contemporary Relativist Arguments	88
3	Other Factors Influencing Relativism	89
4	Resolving the Differences	94
4.1	The Pluralist Perspective	96
5	Have We Over-Theorized?	97
6	Cross-Cultural Normative Judgements	99
6.1	Inevitable Cultural Evaluations	100
6.2	A Model for Understanding	102
7	Closing the Circle	107

Chapter V
Assessing the African Charter as a Tool for Social Change 109

1	Introduction	109
2	Deriving Insight from the *Travaux Préparatoires*	110
3	Deriving Insight from the African Commission	111
4	Deriving Insight from the African Charter on the Rights and Welfare of the Child	114
5	Deriving Insight from Scholarly Argumentation and Interpretation	115
5.1	The General Situation of Women's Rights	115
5.2	Clauses Protecting the African Family, Morals and Traditional Values	116
5.2.1	Clauses on the Protection of the Family	117
5.2.2	Clauses on the Protection of African Morals and Traditional Values	120
6	Deriving Insight from the Unique History and Outlook of the African Region	123
7	Special Measures to Improve the Protection of Women's Rights	123
7.1	Draft Additional Protocol on Women's Rights	124
7.2	Special Rapporteur on the Rights of Women	127
7.3	Considering Alternative Measures	127
8	The Verdict	129

Chapter VI
Practical Limitations on the Human Rights Approach 131

1	Introduction	131
2	Commonly Recommended Strategies and Their Presumed Influence	132
3	Re-evaluating the Impact of Human Rights Education	134
4	Questioning the Empowering Force of Human Rights	137
5	Women's Groups and Power	139
5.1	Theories on Women's Groups and Empowerment	139

5.2	Some Challenging Evidence	139
6	Formal Education and Social Change	143
6.1	Theories on Education, Reproductive Health and Empowerment	143
6.2	Some Challenging Evidence	144
7	Critical Assessments of the Value of Law and Rights in Africa	149
7.1	Structural Impediments in the Use of Law	149
7.2	Cultural Impediments in the Use of Law	150
7.3	Psychological Impediments in the Use of Law	151
7.4	Recognizing the Limitations of Legislation	153
8	Conclusions	155

Chapter VII
Drawing Lessons from Successful and Failed Challenges to Traditional Practices — 157

1	Introduction	157
2	Chinese Footbinding	158
2.1	The Practice	158
2.2	Its Demise	159
3	*Sati* (Widow Burning) in India	161
3.1	The Practice	161
3.2	Its Demise	163
4	Some African State Initiatives to End Female Circumcision	165
4.1	Egypt	165
4.2	Kenya	165
4.3	The Sudan	167
5	Lessons Drawn	168
5.1	Positive Lessons	168
5.1.1	The Importance of Local Leadership and Support of Opinion Leaders	168
5.1.2	Gaining Public Support for Eradication as the Primary Measure	169
5.1.3	The Role of Outsiders	170
5.2	Negative Lessons	170
5.2.1	Prioritizing Legislation as a Measure	170
5.2.2	Admissibility under Certain Forms or Circumstances	171
5.2.3	Penalizing Those Already Penalized	172
5.2.4	The Persistent Potential of Regression	173
6	Some Key Differences and Their Possible Implications	173

Chapter VIII
Key Agents of Change and the Role of the African State — 175

1	Introduction	175

2	Determining the Most Appropriate Role for the State	175
3	Indigenous Mechanisms	180
3.1	Customary (Family) Law	180
3.2	Religion and Traditional Indigenous Belief Systems	182
3.2.1	Alternative Initiation Rites and the Role of Ceremonial Leaders	186
3.3	The Relationship between the State and Indigenous Mechanisms	188
4	The Media and Other Mechanisms of Communication	189
5	The Roles of Other Actors	190
5.1	Local Interest Groups and Concerned NGOs	190
5.2	Ordinary men	191
5.3	The Monitoring Bodies of the International Human Rights Treaties	194
5.4	Donors	194
5.5	Women's Rights Advocates, Legal Aid and the Legal Profession	195
6	Conclusions	196

Chapter IX
Summary and Conclusions 199
1	Summary	199
2	Conclusions	205
2.1	The Utility and Effectiveness of the Human Rights Approach	205
2.2	General Recommendations	208

List of Figures, Tables and Boxes
Figure I	Sub-Saharan African Countries Where Female Circumcision is Practiced and Percentage Performed on the Total Female Population	19
Figure II	Harmful Traditional Practices and the Rights Violated	59
Figure III	How Practices Become Targeted for Global Human Rights Action	103
Figure IV	The Framework of Relations among Strategies	133
Table I	Percentage of Girls Married Prior to Age 19 Years and Under in Senegal, According to Ethnic Group	26
Table II	Percentage of Children Living in Extended-Family-Household Structures in a Sample of Sub-Saharan African Countries	34
Table III	Percentage of Children Living in Polygynous Households in a Sample of Sub-Saharan African Countries	38
Table IV	Express Treaty Obligations Relevant to the Eradication of Harmful Traditional Practices	55
Table V	The Legal Literacy Paradigm	135
Box I	Pregnancy and Childbirth in a Traditional Rural Setting	29
Box II	Lessons from Rural Ghana	187

Annexes

Annex A: Relevant Excerpts of Interpretations by Treaty Bodies — 211
I. CEDAW's General Recommendation No. 14 concerning Harmful Traditional Practices (1990) — 211
II. CEDAW's General Recommendation No. 19 on Violence against Women (1992) — 212
III. CEDAW's General Recommendation No. 21 regarding Equality in Marriage and Family Relations (1994) — 214
IV. The Committee on Economic, Social and Cultural Rights' General Comment No. 14 on Health (2000) — 216

Annex B: Relevant Excerpts of Statements and Strategies from Declaratory Documents — 217
I. Declaration of Mexico on the Equality of Women, World Conference on the International Women's Year (United Nations, 1975) — 217
II. Nairobi Forward-Looking Strategies for the Advancement of Women, World Conference on the United Nations Decade for Women (United Nations, 1985) — 217
III. Vienna Declaration and Programme of Action, World Conference on Human Rights (United Nations, 1993) — 218
IV. Declaration on the Elimination of Violence against Women (United Nations, 1993) — 218
V. Cairo Programme of Action, International Conference on Population and Development (United Nations, 1994) — 219
VI. Copenhagen Declaration, World Summit for Social Development (United Nations, 1995) — 222
VII. Beijing Declaration and Platform for Action, World Conference on Women (United Nations, 1995) — 222
VIII. Draft Addis Ababa [African] Declaration on Violence against Women (1997) — 225

Annex C: Excerpts from the Initial Report of the Central African Republic to the Committee on the Rights of the Child (2000) — 229

Selected Bibliography — 231

Index — 249

Samenvatting — 253

About the Author — 259

Glossary of Acronyms and Abbreviations

BDPA	Beijing Declaration and Platform for Action
CCPR	International Covenant on Civil and Political Rights
CEDAW	Committee on the Elimination of Discrimination against Women
CESCR	International Covenant on Economic, Social and Cultural Rights
CRLP	Center for Reproductive Law and Policy
HIV/AIDS	Human Immunodeficiency Virus/Acquired Immunodeficiency Syndrome
IAC	Inter-African Committee (on Traditional Practices Affecting the Health of Women and Children)
ICPD	International Conference on Population and Development
NGO	Non-governmental organisation
OAU	Organization of African Unity
PRB	Population Reference Bureau
STD	Sexually transmitted disease
TFR	Total fertility rate
UDHR	Universal Declaration of Human Rights
UN	United Nations
UNFPA	United Nations Population Fund [formerly United Nations Fund for Population Activities]
VDPA	Vienna Declaration and Programme of Action
WHO	World Health Organization

CHAPTER I
INTRODUCTION

1 THE PURPOSE OF THE STUDY

The ultimate purpose of this study is a practical, albeit admittedly ambitious, one – to help change traditional practices and socially condoned behaviours which place the reproductive health of girls and women in sub-Saharan Africa (SSA) at risk. Human rights standards and discourses (which combined are understood herein as forming the 'human rights approach') are examined as a means advanced and employed to facilitate such change. The study seeks to establish the strengths and weaknesses of the human rights approach in the context of sub-Saharan Africa with regard to women as a group and reproduction and health as issues. In so doing, the real potential and ideal application of the human rights approach is to be determined.

The two most significant facts inspiring this study are that the practice of female circumcision (as one of the most documented, harmful, and widespread traditional practices experienced by women in sub-Saharan Africa), and the spread of HIV/AIDS (as a rapidly spreading disease and one of the harmful outcomes of practices and behaviours condoned in the socio-cultural environment of the region) continue relatively unabated, despite numerous efforts by, *inter alia*, the women's and human rights movement to stop them. But female circumcision is not the only traditional practice which potentially threatens the health and lives of women, and HIV/AIDS is not the only outcome of these practices. Adolescent pregnancy, taboos in child delivery, and restrictions on the consumption of nutritious foods during pregnancy also place women's reproductive health and lives (as well as the wellbeing of their babies) at risk. Vaginal incisions in pregnant women and the enslavement of young girls to deities (the 'virgin slave' phenomenon) are lesser known practices specific to certain communities in the region which also threaten women's reproductive health. Infections to the reproductive tract, obstructed childbirth and anaemia are some of the numerous harms potentially resulting from these practices. Restricted access to skilled medical professionals (and their sterile environments) as prescribed by some of these practices (such as in the case of some traditional birthing practices and the virgin slave phenomenon) prevent women from avoiding or remedying these specific harms.

2 DEFINING THE PARAMETERS OF THE STUDY

2.1 The Socio-Cultural Determinants of Women's Reproductive Health

The status of our reproductive health is partly the outcome of processes (both behavioural and biological) that involve a series of individual decisions and actions taking place within a social and cultural context. This study is solely concerned with the social and cultural context within which African women and men must pursue their reproductive health and human rights. For many, this context is a major determinant of vulnerability to preventable diseases, disability, and premature death,[1] although other political, geographical or economic determinants also come into play. It is a firm position throughout this study that traditional practices throughout sub-Saharan Africa which are harmful to women's reproductive health cannot be understood – never mind ended – without taking into consideration the socio-cultural context within which individuals are influenced by powerful and deeply-embedded attitudes, norms and beliefs. In this light, the most effective and decisive way to modify or put an end to those traditional practices which harm women is to modify the socio-cultural attitudes, norms and beliefs which fundamentally maintain them.

2.2 Human Rights as a Tool for Social Change

One strategy used to effectuate such socio-cultural change has been the campaign and discourse of human rights, often in association with a campaign for better health. Championed in particular by the women's human rights movement, the philosophy and language of human rights have been advanced as offering a framework to stimulate societal change both at the level of policy and normative behaviour. Mann, a pioneer in the health and human rights approach, notes that '…recognition of human rights will help define the direction and nature of societal change needed to promote public health.'[2] This is particularly so because the philosophy and language of human rights offers a framework for analysis which is both universal and accommodating of particularities, including respect for cultural differences. The potential of the human rights approach in general, and human rights provisions in international instruments and plans of action in particular, to carry out this objective thus forms the crux of this study.

Two facts require acknowledgement. The first is that human rights standards aim to protect individuals, including the state of their health. The second is that the socio-cultural (unlike economic) determinants of health lie fairly directly within the control of people. Generally speaking, every individual may make a cognitive and independent

---

1 J.M. Mann *et al.*, *Introduction*, in J.M. Mann *et al.*, eds., HEALTH AND HUMAN RIGHTS (1999), p. 2.
2 *Id.*, p. 3.

decision to ignore customs and norms which threaten their health and act otherwise, and every State theoretically should be able to influence behaviour. Both of these considerations are important to keep in mind when theorising on the role of human rights in securing reproductive health. Ultimately, it is the girl or woman who otherwise conforms her behaviour to customs who is expected to use the language of human rights to free herself from those which may harm her. The human rights approach seeks to describe – and then to protect and promote – the societal-level prerequisites for human well-being. Recognition of the dependency of health on societal factors, and of the linkages between these factors and the fulfilment of human rights, must occur in monitoring governmental responsibility and accountability for respect (or non-respect) of rights affecting health.[3] This study thus attempts to inform us of the societal context in sub-Saharan Africa and its relationship to human rights, using harmful traditional practices as a subject of special concern and as an example.

In grappling with this task, three fundamental questions arose as underscoring the entire study. These are:

1. Why have we come to use the human rights approach to tackle harmful traditional practices?

2. Whether, and to what extent, the human rights discourse may be meaningful in the context of achieving reproductive health, especially in sub-Saharan Africa?

3. Whether women and men in sub-Saharan Africa are able to assert their rights within the framework of gender relations and the social and cultural norms and traditions which influence their daily lives? For instance, on the basis of their knowledge of their human rights, are women able to negotiate real or perceived opposition of parents, husbands, male figureheads, religious authorities and medical providers when it comes to traditional practices?

2.3 Women, Reproductive Health and Harm from Traditional Practices

The scope of this study is limited to examining only those practices that are traditional (understood herein to mean longstanding, resistant to change, and embedded within the cultural fabric of a community) and that carry potential harm to women's reproductive health. Other traditional practices occurring in sub-Saharan Africa, such as facial scarring, elongation of the neck, or widowhood (mourning) practices are thus excluded since they do not bear influence on a woman's reproductive health. There are several reasons for this focus. Women, as a group, are commonly considered to be less empowered and therefore to have more to gain from human rights. Reproductive health

---

3   See id., pp. 2-3.

(especially as regards pregnancy and childbirth) is essentially limited to women. It also introduces another dilemma in the application of human rights since our understanding of the function of reproduction and sexuality and related behaviours are strongly influenced by societal prescriptions which, it is argued, fall within the realm of privacy. Reproductive health, therefore, tends to be a difficult form of health to influence through the human rights (or any other) approach. Finally, practices rooted in the socio-cultural traditions of a community add a deeper challenge to the human rights approach.

Health concerns the physical, mental, and social wellbeing of individuals the world over. *Reproductive health* is a specific aspect of health which is crucial to securing a good quality of life. For men it may mean the prevention or treatment of sexually transmitted diseases. For women, it may mean carrying a pregnancy safely to term. Whatever the reasons, almost every human being will at one time or another be concerned with at least one aspect of reproductive health.

According to the definition by the World Health Organization (WHO), reproductive health implies that people have the ability

> ... to reproduce, that women can go through pregnancy and child birth safely, and that reproduction is carried out to a successful outcome, i.e. infants survive and grow up healthy. It implies further that people are able to regulate their fertility without risks to their health and that they are safe in having sex.[4]

At the International Conference on Population and Development (ICPD) held in Cairo in September 1994, the definition was further developed, as follows:

> Reproductive health is a state of complete physical, mental and social well-being and not merely the absence of disease or infirmity, in all matters relating to the reproductive system and to its functions and processes. Reproductive health therefore implies that people are able to have a satisfying and safe sex life and that they have the capability to reproduce and the freedom to decide if, when and how often do so.[5]

Hence, the term 'reproductive health' throughout this study refers to several elements at once, notably:
– family planning;
– the causes and consequences of unwanted pregnancies (e.g., unmet need for contraception and induced abortions);

---

4 World Health Organisation, REPRODUCTIVE HEALTH: A KEY TO A BRIGHTER FUTURE (1992), p. 3.
5 United Nations, REPORT OF THE INTERNATIONAL CONFERENCE ON POPULATION AND DEVELOPMENT, CAIRO (1994), para. 7.2, and United Nations, REPORT OF THE FOURTH WORLD CONFERENCE ON WOMEN, BEIJING (1995), para. 94.

- the prevention and treatment of sexually transmitted diseases (STDs), including HIV/AIDS;
- infertility;
- sexual health (including issues such as female circumcision);
- child survival; and
- safe motherhood.

2.4 The Region of Sub-Saharan Africa

The study at hand is limited to the region of sub-Saharan Africa, both because the level of women's reproductive health is the poorest in the world and because the content and significance of human rights is claimed by some to be diminished or altered by the region's socio-cultural environment. For the purposes of this study, sub-Saharan Africa is understood to include all countries South of the Sahara (which closely follows the Tropic of Cancer), with the exception of Southern Africa.[6] It can otherwise be understood to consist of Eastern, Middle and Western Africa. Southern Africa is excluded because it is usually recognised as a region of its own, the practice of female circumcision is near-to-absent throughout the region, and because indicators of reproductive health are notably different from the remainder of the African continent. For example, the average rate of fertility in the region of Southern Africa (3.1 children per woman)[7] is significantly lower than in the remainder of sub-Saharan Africa. The Republic of South Africa stands out particularly in opposition to other countries in Africa, with a considerably higher rate of gross national product (GNP), a more lenient policy on abortion, and a more developed policy on reproductive health care than any other country in the African continent.[8] This region is therefore of less immediate concern and applicability.

Of all the regions in the world, sub-Saharan Africa is in greatest need for improved reproductive health. Indeed, the region fares worst in all categories of general indicators of reproductive health. To begin, the rate of maternal mortality is highest in sub-Saharan Africa. An average of one in every 16 women in Africa dies as a result of childbirth, representing the highest risk in the world and a disheartening one by comparison to rates in other regions of the world.[9] The socio-cultural situation of women has a direct impact on safe motherhood. This can be witnessed in their poor

---

6 The region of Southern Africa is understood to be comprised of Botswana, Lesotho, Namibia, South Africa, and Swaziland.
7 *See* Population Reference Bureau (PRB), 2001 WORLD POPULATION DATA SHEET 2 on website: http://www.prb.org/Content/Naviga...1_World_Population_Data_Sheet.html.
8 For greater detail, *see* Center for Reproductive Law and Policy (CRLP), WOMEN OF THE WORLD: LAWS AND POLICIES AFFECTING THEIR REPRODUCTIVE LIVES (1997), pp. 90-112.
9 The lifetime risk of maternal death in Asia is one in 65, and one in 130 in Latin America. Rates in developed countries range from one in 4,000 to one in 7,000. *See* UNFPA, MATERNAL MORTALITY UPDATE 1998-1999 on website: http://www.unfpa.org/tpd/mmupdate/hilites.htm.

health and nutritional status before, during and after pregnancy, limited knowledge and awareness of health, lack of decision-making power and resources for seeking health care, weak negotiating power, heavy physical workloads regardless of pregnancy status, and exposure to violence.[10] Finally, the 'Safe Motherhood' or 'Mother-Baby' Packages which are clinical guidelines developed by the WHO consisting of antenatal care, normal delivery care, essential obstetric care (including care of complications arising from abortion) and family planning services are often incomplete in this region. A number of reasons for this are cited, the primary one being insufficient financial resources.[11] In reviewing allocations for projects in the area of reproductive health in 1996, UNFPA recognised that 82% of countries in the sub-Saharan region could be categorised under 'priority need', representing the largest number (proportionately) of countries in need of assistance to realise the goals of the 1994 International Conference on Population and Development (ICPD).[12] Certainly, the great majority of least developed countries are found in the sub-Saharan region.[13] This implies that they are the countries least able to cope with the resource demands of reproductive health. However, this is also a matter of choice regarding allocation of State funds throughout the public sector.

Second, the rates of fertility in this region are consistently among the highest in the world. The average total fertility rate (TFR)[14] is 5.7 in Eastern Africa, 6.6 in Middle Africa and 5.8 in Western Africa.[15] By comparison, the TFR in South East Asia is 2.8 and 2.6 in South America, whereas in Western Europe and North America it is 1.6 and 2.0 respectively.[16] Most of the countries concerned which have been surveyed by the United Nations consider their rates of population growth too high yet demand for family planning is still low.[17] For the most part, the modern contraceptive prevalence rate remains alarmingly low, falling below 20 per cent in many countries in the region.[18]

---

10 W.J. Graham and S.F. Murray, *A Question of Survival: A Review of Safe Motherhood in Kenya*, Reproductive Health Matters, Special Issue (1999), p. 106.
11 C. Lissner and E. Weissman, *How Much Does Safe Motherhood Cost?*, World Health, No. 1 (1998), p. 11.
12 UNFPA, ANNUAL REPORT 1996 (1997), Appendix C, p. 50.
13 14 of the world's 16 least developed countries are located in the sub-Saharan region. These are: Angola, Burundi, Burkina Faso, Chad, Congo, the Democratic Republic of Congo, Ethiopia, Liberia, Malawi, Mali, Niger, Somalia, Sierra Leone and Uganda. *See* UNFPA, POPULATION ISSUES BRIEFING KIT 2001 on website: http://www.unfpa.org/modules/briefkit/05.htm.
14 The 'total fertility rate' indicates the average number of childen a woman would have, assuming that current age-specific rates remained constant throughout her childbearing years (usually considered to be ages 15 to 49). As defined in PRB, *supra*, n. 7.
15 *Id.*
16 *Id.*
17 *See* PRB, 2001 WORLD POPULATION DATA SHEET 5, on website *supra*, n. 7.
18 The average per cent of married women aged 15-49 using contraception in the region of sub-Saharan Africa is 19 per cent as compared to 73 per cent in highly industrialised countries. *See* PRB, 2001 WORLD POPULATION DATA SHEET 4, on website *supra*, n. 7.

Third, the African continent has been worst affected by the AIDS pandemic.[19] No African country is exempt. Whereas one AIDS case in 17 in the region concerned a woman in 1986, this proportion has risen to one in two.[20] Four out of five HIV-positive women in the world live in Africa.[21] The area of highest HIV prevalence in the region forms a belt stretching East-West across the continent along the equator, with the highest levels of infection are found among the people living around Lake Victoria, including the countries of Rwanda, Burundi, the Democratic Republic of the Congo, Uganda and the Congo.[22] Figures of HIV infection are lower for the West African coast but significant enough to be of great concern.[23]

There is also a concern for teenage women as a critical group. The sub-Saharan African region boasts the highest rate of births to very young mothers worldwide: three out of four female teenagers in Africa are mothers, 40 per cent of whom are aged 17 or under.[24] Pregnancy too early and too often, and exposure to STDs (because of the relative absence of safer sex practices) pose risks to the reproductive health of these young women.[25]

Sub-Saharan Africa is also the least urbanised of all regions of the world.[26] This fact has implications on reproductive health since health posts and medical staff are greater in number and better equipped in urban centres. Because individuals in rural areas are typically poorer, the costs to travel to health posts or to obtain medical attention can be prohibitive

Of course, each sub-Saharan African country is unique in its social and cultural frameworks and composition of religious beliefs. One, therefore, cannot easily speak and write about sub-Saharan Africa as a single and homogeneous society. In spite of this pluralism, however, it is possible to discern certain common characteristics and recurrent elements. This may be attributed to the extraordinary flexibility and absorbing nature of traditional African societies, which through history have exchanged ideas and practices over wide areas.[27] Although the family community may be defined differently in different societies throughout Africa, the family is typically considered the basic component of the social structure: to use the words of one sociologist, '[i]t

---

19 8.6 per cent of the population in sub-Saharan Africa aged 15-49 has HIV/AIDS. The world average is 1.1 per cent. *See id.* for further statistics.
20 UNAIDS, WORKSHOP REPORT ON HIV/AIDS AND REPRODUCTIVE HEALTH (1998).
21 *Id.*
22 *Id.*
23 *Id.*
24 UNFPA, MEETING THE POPULATION CHALLENGE (1996), p. 12.
25 *See* L.S. Zabin and K. Kiragu, *The Health Consequences of Adolescent Sexual and Fertility Behaviour in Sub-Saharan Africa*, Studies in Family Planning, Vol. 29, No. 2, 1998.
26 Only 30 per cent of the population lives in cities, compared to an average of 40 per cent in all other developing regions and 75 per cent in the most developed regions. *See* PRB, *supra*, n. 17.
27 A. Shorter, *Concepts of Social Justice in Traditional Africa* in AFRICAN TRADITIONAL RELIGION on website: http://isizoh.net/afrel/atr-socjustice.htm.

is difficult to exaggerate the importance of family community in traditional Africa'.[28] The strict hierarchy of authority within the family is also unfailing.[29] A compilation volume on African families and social change similarly paints a picture of commonality throughout the region. As one author in the volume notes:

> The family in Africa... is connected by blood, marriage, adoption, and *shared cultural, economic and psychosocial tools for adaptation* [emphasis in original]. The role of families in social support, moral judgements, and economic exchanges and as the unit carrying important values and practices being used by communities today is clear... Furthermore, our African colleagues talk of families in these ways... The African *family* [emphasis in original], where African values and traditions are reproduced and transmitted, is one that is very real...[30]

Within this commonality of social and cultural values and parameters, one finds that social and cultural customs which negatively impact upon reproductive health are very much alive and thriving throughout the sub-Saharan region. It follows that the region experiences common reproductive health problems, as indicated above. While harmful customs in the region may differ somewhat in nature and intensity from country to country, their root in social and cultural beliefs and pressure to conform have the same hold on individuals throughout the region.

Another commonality throughout the region which is of particular importance to the study at hand is the strength and prevalence of customary law. Common or civil law traditions generally govern in all realms except one – family law – in which case African customary law and religious laws based on Islamic, Christian, indigenous traditional religions and other religions usually apply.[31] This is of particular relevance to this study since issues of gender discrimination and reproductive customs and behaviour usually fall within the scope of this law.[32]

Finally, in many sub-Saharan African countries, religion or belief systems (such as indigenous value systems or rituals) play an important role in all facets of life, including reproduction and gender roles. In many, if not most cases, religious customs are so deep-rooted and steadfast that they have come to influence social and cultural customs and become one of the same. As a result, it is usually difficult to examine strictly the influence of religious customs on reproductive health and rights, since social customs and cultural beliefs usually fall under the same realm.

---

28 *Id.*
29 *Id.*
30 C. Bradley and T.S. Weisner, *Introduction: Crisis in the African Family*, in T.S. Weisner *et al.*, eds., AFRICAN FAMILIES AND THE CRISIS OF SOCIAL CHANGE (1997), p. xxvi.
31 Center for Reproductive Law and Policy, WOMEN OF THE WORLD: LAWS AND POLICIES AFFECTING THEIR REPRODUCTIVE LIVES (1997) p. 154.
32 *Id.*

3 THE STATE OF CHALLENGES TO HARMFUL TRADITIONAL PRACTICES

There have been numerous activities undertaken within, and outside of, Africa to challenge harmful traditional practices in the region. Since the mid-1980s, the Inter-African Committee on Traditional Practices Affecting the Health of Women and Children (hereafter 'IAC'), an NGO based in Geneva and Addis Ababa with 26 national branches throughout sub-Saharan Africa is by far the largest African NGO working to eliminate these practices in the region.[33] Although not confined to female circumcision, the practice is the focus of the greater part of its work. The organisation specifically seeks to influence change in social values at the grassroots level and, with this understanding, largely aims its information campaigns at health professionals (particularly traditional birth attendants), government officials, media specialists and opinion leaders. In taking a position on harmful traditional practices, the IAC has consistently called for a human rights approach to the issue and regularly reports to the UN Commission on Human Rights and UN agencies (e.g. WHO, UNDP and UNFPA) involved in some shape or form with the elimination of these practices. Other interest groups and NGOs work either in combination with the IAC or independently in target communities. Most of these and the IAC have reported various degrees of success in their activities.

The adoption of legislation against harmful traditional practices in specific countries is commonly considered to be among their successes. The IAC, for instance, has attributed recent legislative measures adopted in Burkina Faso, Côte d'Ivoire, Djibouti, Egypt, Ghana, Guinea, Senegal, Tanzania and Togo to sustained lobbying by its National Committees together with other NGOs.[34] For the most part, the other successes reported by these organisations have been that their activities have 'resulted in notable consciousness-raising.'[35] For instance, in Benin, a televised debate on female circumcision was organised.[36] In Burkina Faso, large street demonstrations against female circumcision were organised.[37] Consciousness-raising is indeed a crucial first step for any campaign to end harmful traditional practices, along with acquiring data on the nature and scope of these – activities which local and foreign interest groups as well as governments have undertaken in earnest in most countries of sub-Saharan Africa. Consciousness-raising efforts generally have been formulated in order to create a maximum 'snowball' effect, such that key individuals within a community are trained to train and educate others of the facts concerning harmful traditional practices. For

---

33 Two branches, or 'committees' as they are termed by the IAC, are currently inoperative. These are in Sierra Leone and Côte d'Ivoire.
34 Inter-African Committee on Traditional Practices Affecting the Health of Women and Children (IAC) ACTIVITY REPORT 1999 (1999), p. 1.
35 *Id.*
36 IAC, FOURTH REGIONAL CONFERENCE/GENERAL ASSEMBLY (1997), p. 47.
37 *Id.*, p. 49.

instance, in Guinea Conakry, a team of university and secondary school students was formed along with school directors and teachers to be campaigners against female circumcision. This team was trained to intervene in different places during the school vacations since a study found that 85 per cent of girls in the country were excised during the school vacations.[38] Measures such as these are expected to mobilise grass-roots popular support to end harmful traditional practices.

In sum, many organisations and States are claiming success in their efforts to sensitise people to the issues, while accepting that many more such efforts must be made. While there is a degree of success achieved in simply co-ordinating and carrying out these sensitisation campaigns, their significance lies in the number of people who claim to have changed their views on these traditional practices as a result of such initiatives. A review of the literature to date reveals only one statistical survey conducted to demonstrate such success. From Burkina Faso, we learn that 70 per cent of participants in such an initiative carried out by IAC 'changed attitude to be against [female circumcision], while the control group showed a variation on attitude of only 3%'.[39] In Sudan, it is reported that there has been 'indications of positive change within urban and rural communities' as reflected by the creation of four indigenous groups campaigning against female circumcision.[40] The IAC also reports generally a 'positive attitude towards the cause to end [female circumcision] especially amongst the school children reached in sensitisation seminars.'[41] It can only be hoped that other sensitisation campaigns have been as successful. There has also been modest success in the conversion of circumcisers, with some of these women ceremoniously 'laying down their knives' and given training in other areas.[42]

Several more steps need to be taken before one may claim success, if by this we mean the veritable elimination of harmful traditional practices affecting reproductive health. The next steps would seek to ensure:
a. that trainers trained maintain the momentum, i.e. diffuse the information and proceed with sensitisation efforts;
b. that there is a notable change in attitudes by the general populace; and
c. that a community actually changes behaviour, i.e. alters the tradition and abandons the harmful practice.

With very few exceptions, these phases have yet to be achieved. This is arguably because not enough time has elapsed since the campaigns against harmful traditional

---

38 IAC, ACTIVITIES REPORT 1999, *supra*, n. 34, p. 21.
39 *Id.*, p. 15.
40 IAC, FOURTH REGIONAL, *supra*, n. 36, p. 111.
41 *Id.*, p. 122.
42 Notably in Guinea Conakry and Mali. In the latter case, 10 women stopped their practice and retrained in poultry production. Some have come to work on the campaign against female circumcision and are said to be excellent advocates against the practice. Reported in IAC, ACTIVITIES REPORT 1999, *supra*, n. 34, pp. 22 and 26.

practices first began and because the organisations involved have not been able to return to do field work and collect data on the continued diffusion of information and changes in attitudes, inadequate resources being a key factor in the latter cases. Hence, we have scant evidence of nurses, opinion leaders, traditional birth attendants, youth peer counsellors, influential women, etc., trained by these organisations to be trainers actually carrying out their designated tasks.

The few success stories of changes in attitudes towards female circumcision are accompanied by even fewer reported cases of communities that have abandoned the practice. While the number of *documented* cases of abandonment can be easily counted, they are important to acknowledge. In Mali it has been reported that nine villages targeted by the national branch of the IAC have decided to abandon female circumcision: '[i]n three of the villages (Solefara, Makono and Baala) ceremonies were organised in recognition of their desire to abandon the practice… Further ceremonies are envisaged for the remaining 6 villages, pending funding.'[43] While a celebration is a good idea to mark the *desire* and *decision* of the villagers to abandon the practice, it may still be too early to count this case as a success; the challenge is actual abandonment.

It has also been reported by Tostan, an international educational NGO working in Senegal, that female circumcision has been ended in 31 villages. The first village to do so was Malicounda Bambara. Here, women were reported to have made the decision together with their husbands, the village chief, and religious leaders after attending health and education workshops offered by Tostan. Following sessions on female anatomy in which the women were able to discuss sexuality, the subject of female circumcision was raised. Intially the women appeared uneasy and reticent to speak of the matter and so only began to be addressed some three sessions later. Eventually they began to discuss the negative health consequences of the practice outside the workshops with their women friends and husbands. They then sought the advice of the Imam and village chief on the issue, both of whom reportedly surprised the women by expressing their support to end the practice. The Imam, in stressing his own opposition to the practice, further explained that the *Qu'ran* did not require Muslims to practice the rite. The women then created a play and performed it in front of their own village and others in the hope of raising awareness of the benefits of ending the practice. By June 1997, the village chief endorsed the women's decision to end the practice and, since enough people in the village were convinced of the dangers of female circumcision, no circumcision ceremonies were held that year. Publicity surrounding Malicounda Bambara's decision prompted other villages in the area to reconsider the practice. Recognising the significance of the opportunity, the Imam of Malicounda Bambara voluntarily committed three months to visiting these and other villages in the area urging them to end the practice. Interest in the issue spread and prompted a united

---

43 IAC, FOURTH REGIONAL, *supra*, n. 36, p. 27.

community meeting on the issue. Religious, health and government representatives were included in the meeting and after much discussion and information sharing, a declaration (known as the Diabougou Declaration) was produced which pledged the commitment of these communities to end female circumcision. By 1999, a total of 31 Senegalese villages had signed the declaration and publicly declared an end to the practice. To ensure that the community's pledge was enduring and enforceable, a committee was elected to guard against breaches of the agreement.[44]

Another case of reported success comes from Uganda. A first attempt to curb female circumcision as a rite of passage was made among the Sabini people in the Kapchorwa district of Uganda in the early 1990s.[45] Attempts to enforce compliance with the declared effort to abandon the practice provoked indignation and resistance. Another attempt was made with the same community by a foreign-headed NGO named REACH. Extensive health awareness-raising in the community reportedly led local women gradually to express (without prompting) their concerns over the negative health effects of circumcision.[46] With the assistance of REACH, the community eventually decided to replace the rite of passage with a symbolic ceremony of gift-giving, while the singing, dancing and other traditional festivities which marked a girl's initiation as a full-fledged member of the community were preserved.[47] Heralded as a great success by human rights and feminist groups everywhere, it was later reported that girls who had been spared circumcision the year in which the alternative rite was instituted were circumcised the next season.[48] This has been attributed to the fact that few within the community maintained the pressure for change, particularly since the NGO was no longer present. A similar alternative initiation rite followed in Kenya, led this time by a domestic women's group called *Maendeleo Ya Wanawake*, with numerous parents reportedly adopting the alternative initiation rite. [49]

Unconnected with independent initiatives such as these, it has also been reported, although without statistical evidence, that urbanisation has also contributed to some degree to the decline in female circumcisions. Hosken, for instance, observes that there has been 'a marked decrease in the number of mutilations close to Nairobi and other urban centres.'[50] It is difficult to establish whether this purported trend is associated with increased education for girls, increased household wealth, or increased distance from rural settings and kin, both of which maintain strong commitments to traditions.

As regards other harmful traditional practices, there are hardly any successful stories of abandonment to be found. In the cases of harmful traditional birthing

---

44   *See* Tostan, BREAKTHROUGH IN SENEGAL – ENDING FEMALE GENITAL CUTTING (1999).
45   Reported by E. Eliah, *REACHing for a Healthier Future*, Populi, March 1996.
46   *Id.*
47   *Id.*
48   CRLP, *supra*, n. 31.
49   Reported in IAC, FOURTH REGIONAL, *supra*, n. 36, pp. 151-152.
50   F.P. Hosken, STOP FEMALE GENITAL MUTILATION (1995), p. 60.

practices, dietary taboos, vaginal incisions in pregnancy, and enslavement of virgin girls in the Volta region of Ghana, this may be explained by the fact that their practice has only recently been properly studied and documented, and placed on the agenda for international action. As such, it is perhaps too early to find successful changes. The practice of early marriage (encompassing early sexual activity and pregnancy), however, has been the focus of international attention for decades. Few initiatives have been taken to end this practice other than adopting domestic legislation banning marriage under a fixed minimum age and consciousness-raising efforts. These bans and sensitisation efforts, however, have yielded virtually no change. Rather, where there has been a slight rise in age at first marriage for girls, these have usually been explained by urbanisation, increased education for girls, or increased household wealth. In the case of the latter, for instance, some parents are less dependent on brideprice to boost the family income.

This review of successful change in harmful traditional practices is a useful exercise in that it helps situate the study of these practices. Since we are evidently still in the process of developing strategies, the time seems ripe to evaluate the role which human rights may have in these. It is with this in mind that this study was undertaken.

4 THE STRUCTURE OF THE STUDY

The study essentially consists of three parts or tasks:
1. establishing a theoretical framework by defining and analysing the harmful traditional practices and human rights in question and the means by which the human rights approach may be expected to influence tradition (Chapters II through IV);
2. identifying and resolving problem areas in the use of human rights instruments, discourses or strategies (Chapters V and VI); and
3. drawing lessons from these and real initiatives to end harmful traditional practices, and applying these to the framework of human rights, particularly as regards the role of the African State and its obligations under international human rights law (Chapters VII and VIII).

In Chapter II the traditional practices in the region recognized as potentially causing harm to women's reproductive health are identified and described, along with the reasons why they are practiced and the ways in which harm may be incurred. It is submitted that knowledge of the reasons behind the practices in each socio-cultural setting is essential to make appropriate connections between the practices and the human rights they may violate. Few human rights activists and campaigns undertake this task and so risk wrongfully asserting the bases for certain practices and consequently draw incorrect or inaccurate conclusions about the practice and human rights violations. In this respect, reasons matter – the reasons for the practices and the reasons supporting a purported violation of human rights. Norms and other practices which essentially support and maintain these practices, and the ways in which they do so, are also identified.

The specific rights which may be violated in the practice of each harmful tradition are identified in Chapter III along with the obligations of the State to protect, ensure and fulfill these rights in each instance. This exercise reveals a plethora of ambiguous scenarios where an apparently harmful practice may not necessarily result in a violation of a woman's rights. The particularly thorny issue of women's consent to these practices and its consequences on claims of violations of human rights is one example of such ambiguities. The common conception of harmful traditional practices as a form of gender-based violence is also scrutinized along with feminist claims of global gender ideologies. These, it is submitted, are problematic for campaigns to end harmful traditional practices and bring into question the credibility of human rights as universal and culturally unbiased.

Western challenges of certain traditions in sub-Saharan Africa have led to numerous African (and non-African) reactions which merit serious attention. Among the most prominent are claims that Western condemnations of harmful traditions as violations of human rights are unwarranted and even hypocritical. Human rights standards invoked in this regard are claimed to be irrelevant to, or simply inconsistent with, the socio-cultural context of sub-Saharan Africa. These claims, along with similar assertions over the last two millenia of bias in the evaluation of the customs of other peoples, are explored in Chapter IV. It is advanced that the framework of human rights is both universal and accommodating of particularities, including respect for cultural differences, with the firm understanding that human rights standards must be applied in a manner which works within the African social, cultural and religious setting. More specifically, the case is made that evaluations of cultural practices outside one's own culture are warranted and that human rights norms present a means by which to approach such cross-cultural evaluations.

The response to relativist claims that some African cultural values and traditions are so significant to, and play such important functions in, the cultural fabric of Africa that they override universal human rights norms continues in Chapter V. Attention is specifically focused on the African Charter on Human and Peoples' Rights and the standards relevant to the protection of women and the elimination of harmful traditional practices. Clauses within the Charter calling for the protection of the family and traditional values cause activists concern and are therefore specifically addressed. It is ultimately concluded that these concerns are without basis and that the Charter and its monitoring body can be used as tools to challenge harmful traditional practices.

Many strategies have been advanced, *inter alia*, in human rights treaties or by their monitoring bodies and in global platforms as means of challenging harmful traditional practices and behaviours. These include (either independently or in various combinations): human rights education for women; improving women's access to formal education; supporting the formation of women's groups and increasing women's participation in these; adopting domestic legislation against harmful traditional practices and increasing women's use of the law; and the empowerment of women. All have been advanced from a human rights perspective. In many instances, these measures are joined together under the banner of women's empowerment, with knowledge of human rights forming its backbone. In the case of each of these measures, diminished loyalty to harmful traditions is an expected by-product of their success. It is advanced in Chapter VI that, on the basis of survey findings and sociological commentaries, these expectations are difficult to extrapolate to the socio-cultural setting of sub-Saharan Africa and, therefore, may be misplaced. As such, strategies of women's empowerment (as welcome as they may be) should not necessarily or alone be relied upon as means to end harmful traditional practices.

In Chapter VII lessons are drawn from the eradicated harmful traditional practices of footbinding (in China) and widow burning (in India) which also affected only women. The ways in which eradication campaigns in these two cases initially failed and eventually succeeded are identified in order that lessons may be drawn and applied to the case of harmful traditional practices in sub-Saharan Africa. The initiatives of long-running and generally well-documented campaigns to eradicate female circumcision in three African countries are then considered. It is submitted that these campaigns are generally repeating the same mistakes made in China and India and that these and other sub-Saharan African countries could improve eradication efforts by applying, *mutatis mutandis*, the lessons learned in China and India to their own situations.

Perhaps the most fundamental lesson drawn in Chapter VII is the general incapacity of the State *per se* to challenge traditions, since the State does not typically have the cultural legitimacy to do so. This finding is particularly significant in that it is the State which, under international law, bears the responsibility to protect human rights and act accordingly to end harmful traditional practices. This being so, Chapter VIII endeavours to identify those agents and mechanisms which do have the legitimacy and power to challenge harmful traditional practices in the socio-cultural context of sub-Saharan Africa. The potential facilitating role of the State in relation to each of these is then examined as a matter of State responsibility in relation to international human rights obligations. General conclusions are made in the final Chapter of the study in which the basic question of the study – can human rights challenge tradition – is answered, the thesis being that human rights standards and discourses can contribute to changing traditional practices harmful to women's reproductive health if and to the extent the standards are applied and the discourses are formulated with due attention to the socio-cultural context. While in theory this may be so, the practical task remains substantial. The real challenge is to develop and implement effective strategies and programmes which will not only address the many obstacles to women's reproductive health but result in changes in behaviour which yield good health.

CHAPTER II
THE HARMFUL TRADITIONAL PRACTICES IN QUESTION AND SUPPORTING CUSTOMS AND NORMS

1 INTRODUCTION

Female circumcision (more commonly known in the Western world as 'female genital mutilation') is by far the most broadly documented and discussed of the so-called harmful traditional customs and practices. This is particularly true in the scholarly literature, international supervisory bodies and global fora addressing women and human rights. Indeed, most of these refer to 'female genital mutilation and *other* harmful traditional practices' without explicitly identifying what the 'other' practices are. In this Chapter, a number of harmful traditional customs and practices, including female genital mutilation, existing in sub-Saharan Africa are identified and described along with the ostensible reasons for them and the harm they may represent to the reproductive health of girls and women. While the harm done to girls and women is important to establish in order to advance such practices as potentially constituting or contributing to violations of women's human rights, it is submitted that the reasons behind these practices are particularly important if violations of certain rights are to be established.

It should be borne in mind that the list comprises customs and practices which take place throughout the sub-Saharan region of Africa, but do not necessarily take place in all countries represented in the region nor do they occur among all their populations. In most cases, the custom or practice is addressed from a general perspective, since there are various ways in which they may manifest themselves. For this reason, for instance, I refer to 'practices relating to childbirth' in general rather than addressing specific taboos, superstitions or behaviours in childbirth which potentially result in harm.

The list could not, and does not, purport to be exhaustive. For instance, the practice of introducing dehydrating substances into the vagina to enhance male pleasure[1] is less known and hardly researched and is therefore excluded from this study. Similarly, the practice of vagina prolongation (where the labia minora is elongated because it is believed to offer greater satisfaction to men) is said to be practiced in some communi-

---

1   On this practice, *see* IAC, SITUATION OF WOMEN IN AFRICA IN THE CONTEXT OF FAMILY HEALTH (1995), p. 4.

ties within Uganda.[2] However, little documentation was found on this practice and no evidence given of the harm it poses to women's reproductive health (which leaves aside other bases of criticism of the practice, and possible human rights violations it may constitute). Conversely, two practices which are limited to a very few communities are included because their risk to women's reproductive health has been established. It is important to remember that not all individuals in sub-Saharan Africa feel the same pressure to conform to traditional customs and practices, nor do they experience them to the same extent. In this sense, the list admittedly highlights the 'worst case scenarios'.

The list holds a dual purpose. On the one hand, it represents a form of 'checklist' for researchers and activists who must assess the customs and practices which exist in the region (and the reasons why they are maintained) against human rights standards. On the other hand, it enables us to understand the broad, plural, and overlapping nature of customs and practices harmful to health which are intricately embedded in African culture.

2 TRADITIONAL PRACTICES HARMFUL TO WOMEN'S REPRODUCTIVE HEALTH

2.1 Female Circumcision

Before entering into a description of female circumcision, it is necessary to note and consider the different terms used by commentators to describe the same practice in its various forms. Different communities and language groups in Africa use different terms to describe the practice, often conveying within the term the reason for the practice. For instance, the term *sunna*, ascribed to a certain form of female circumcision, means 'tradition' in Arabic. The term *Tahur* used in the Sudan means 'purity', conveying the notion of purification through the act of circumcision. It is when we come to translating the term into English that the problems arise. The term 'female genital mutilation' (frequently used in its abbreviated form 'FGM') is by far the most common term ascribed to this practice, particularly in the West. While the term certainly emphasises the possible extent and nature of the cutting, it is specifically employed to maximise the dramatic impact. It also conveys a strong (and not necessarily correct) value judgement about the intent of those who carry it out: the family and circumciser are 'mutilating' (a term synonymous with barbaric and senseless destruction). Needles to say, in no African community and by no person practicing female circumcision is the term 'female genital mutilation' employed as the name for the practice. Use of the term within Africa, particularly by foreign interest groups and human rights activists, conse-

---

2 As reported in C. Obbo, *What Women Can Do: AIDS Crisis Management in Uganda*, in D.F. Bryceson, ed., WOMEN WIELDING THE HOE: LESSONS FROM RURAL AFRICA FOR FEMINIST THEORY AND DEVELOPMENT PRACTICE (1995), p. 175.

quently conveys an assessment about the persons involved and potentially represents a large disservice to the campaign to end this practice. Another term used is 'female genital surgeries'[3] or 'female genital operations.'[4] Both terms recognise in their plural form that the practice takes many different forms and do not covey any value judgement or denounce the practice *a priroi*. However, they do evoke aseptic hospital settings (which are not usually where circumcisions take place) and suggest a medical reason for the cutting – surgeries and operations typically being carried out to remedy disease or ill-health. Instead, the term 'female circumcision' is used in this study. Admittedly, it, too, is not wholly accurate since the term 'circumcision' (from the Latin *circum* meaning 'around' or 'about' and *caedere* meaning 'to cut') is commonly used with reference to the practice where the prepuce of the penis of a boy is removed. This extent of the cutting of the male penis pales in comparison to the more extensive excisions and, in some communities, the complete removal of external genitalia performed on girls. It does, however, evoke the notion of cutting into (or away) the healthy tissues and sexual organs of girls and boys, which is common to all forms of the practice. For this reason, it is the term I have chosen to convey the practice in all its forms.

While female circumcision is known to be practiced in over 30 countries within the region of sub-Saharan Africa, the rates of prevalence have been officially recorded in approximately only 25 of these.[5] These are listed in Figure I below. The countries with the highest incidence of female circumcision are Somalia, Djibouti and the Sudan where 90 per cent or more of women are said to be infibulated.

Figure I
Sub-Saharan African Countries where Female Circumcision is Practiced and Percentage Performed on the Total Female Population[6]

Benin (30%)	Kenya (40%)
Burkina Faso (78%)	Liberia (55%)
Cameroon (15%)	Mali (80%)
Central African Republic (35%)	Mauritania (55%)

---

3   As employed, e.g., by C. M. Obermeyer, *Female Genital Surgeries: The Known, the Unknown, and the Unknowable*, Medical Anthropology Quarterly, Vol. 13 (1999).
4   As employed, e.g., by R. Howard, *Human Rights and Personal Law: Women in sub-Saharan Africa*, Issue, Vol. 12 (1982).
5   *See*: F.P. Hosken, STOP FEMALE GENITAL MUTILATION (1995); and N. Toubia, FEMALE GENITAL MUTILATION: A CALL FOR GLOBAL ACTION (1993).
6   As reported by IAC, SYMPOSIUM FOR LEGISLATORS ON THE DRAFTING OF AN AFRICAN DECLARATION ON VIOLENCE AGAINST WOMEN (1997), p. 50. Although the practice is known to take place in numerous other countries of sub-Saharan Africa, its prevalence is not recorded by the IAC. These other countries are: Angola, Burundi, Congo, Eritrea (estimated by Hosken at 90 per cent prevalence), Gabon, Malawi, Mozambique, Niger, Rwanda, Zaire (Democratic Republic of the Congo), and Zambia. *See*: Toubia, *supra*, n. 5; and Hosken, *supra*, n. 5, p. 26.

Chad (40%)　　　　　　　　Nigeria (55%)
Côte d'Ivoire (40%)　　　　Senegal (20%)
Djibouti (95%)　　　　　　Somalia (99%)
Ethiopia (85%)　　　　　　Sierra Leone (60%)
The Gambia (79%)　　　　Sudan (90%)
Ghana (20%)　　　　　　　Tanzania (15%)
Guinea (60%)　　　　　　　Togo (40%)
Guinea-Bissau (45%)　　　Uganda (20%)

There exist several different types of circumcision.[7] 'Pharaonic circumcision' or 'infibulation' is the most invasive and traumatic of these. It involves the complete excision of the clitoris and labia minora and the paring and stitching of the labia majora. 'Intermediate circumcision' includes a lesser degree of excision of the labia with milder or no infibulation. In a 'clitoridectomy,' the clitoris is removed. Finally, the least traumatic circumcision is the type known as *sunna*. It consists of removing the hood (prepuce) of the clitoris.[8] The type of circumcision performed on a girl is decided by her mother or grandmother, but typically follows the type which is traditional to her community. [9]

There are many reasons asserted for the performance of female circumcision.[10] These are principally:

1. Health and hygiene, e.g.:
– maintains cleanliness
  A girl who is excised is believed to be 'cleaner', hence the term *Tahur* used in the Sudan. A woman is considered dirty and polluted if she is not infibulated.
– prevents still-births *in primigravida*
  The clitoris is viewed as a dangerous organ that may kill the baby during childbirth and therefore must be removed.

---

[7] There is no uniform classification of types of female genital circumcision, so all descriptions are generalizations. *See* Obermeyer, *supra*, n. 3, for a discussion on various problems of discrepancies in such classifications in the literature on female circumcision.
[8] Summarized from *id.*, p. 82.
[9] United Nations, HARMFUL TRADITIONAL PRACTICES AFFECTING THE HEALTH OF WOMEN AND CHILDREN (1996), p. 9.
[10] Reasons listed have been compiled from various sources, notably: Hosken, *supra*, n. 5; Toubia, *supra* n. 5; O. Koso-Thomas, THE CIRCUMCISION OF WOMEN: A STRATEGY FOR ERADICATION (1987), pp. 5-9; F.N. Adjetey, *Reclaiming the African Woman's Individuality: The Struggle between Women's Reproductive Autonomy and African Society and Culture*, The American University Law Review, Vol. 44, No. 4, 1995, p. 1362; and WHO, FEMALE GENITAL MUTILATION: INFORMATION KIT (1994). These are categorised by this author.

- maintains good health and enhancement of fertility
  It is widely believed that a woman who is not excised is unable to have children. Excision is thus perceived as a method to increase a woman's fertility. Some communities also believe that the clitoris may damage the husband's genitalia during intercourse and injure him and make him infertile. The Bambara in West Africa believe the clitoris is the male equivalent of the penis and must be removed before childbearing is possible.

2. Physical necessity, e.g.:
- improves aesthetics
  A woman's external genitalia is considered ugly.
- prevents protrusion of the genitalia
  It is claimed by some that if the organ is not cut it will eventually protrude between a girl's legs.
- improves male sexual performance and pleasure
  Believed to be so because the opening of the vagina is reduced by circumcision and thereby increases friction.
- preserves virginity before marriage
- diminishes female sexual satisfaction
- purges the body of 'evil' and ill-health.

3. Social necessity, e.g.:
- as a rite of passage/puberty rite
  It is used by communities as a means of acknowledging a girl's coming-of-age. It is also believed by some that the clitoris connotes maleness while the prepuce of the penis represents femaleness. Hence both boys and girls have to be circumcised in order to be accepted as an adult in his/her sex group.
- promotes social and political cohesion and prevents female promiscuity
  There is a widespread belief that women are otherwise incapable of controlling their sexual urges. The operation therefore needs to be done to 'calm' a girl down and make her submissive. If she is not excised or infibulated she will be like a prostitute and bring disgrace to her family.
- ensures progeny
  Infibulation helps assure the husband that the children borne of his wife are his own.
- increases matrimonial opportunities
  A man may refuse to marry a girl who is not circumcised. Even if he accepts, he may refuse to pay brideprice.
- protects women against rape and sexual assault.

4. Religious proscriptions, notably as believed to be a requirement of the *Qu'ran* – infibulation is practiced mostly in areas with devout Muslims who seek visibly to guarantee chastity.

Circumcisions typically take place in a secluded location outside the village (such as near a river, under a special tree or in a secret bush). Girls living in the city are brought back to villages specifically to have the circumcision performed according to the tradition of their ancestors. The conditions under which these take place are often unhygienic and the instruments used crude and unsterilised: usually a razor blade, a piece of glass, a sharp stone, or a kitchen knife. Wounds are dabbed with a range of treatments including alcohol, lemon juice, ash, earth, herb mixtures or cow dung.[11] After the cutting, the wound may be sewn closed, again usually with primitive sutures, such as thorns. The girl's legs are then bound together until her wounds have healed, a process which may take up to 40 days. In West Africa, the raw edges of the labia majora are not sewn together after the operation. Instead, the girl's legs are tied together in a crossed position, and the same result is said to be achieved.

Because circumcision is generally performed under poor conditions and with primitive implements, there are many immediate and long-term physical and psychological health consequences. The potential damage to reproductive health alone includes:[12]

Immediate complications: haemorrhaging (uncontrolled bleeding), shock due to blood loss and pain (and since no anaesthetic is given), septicaemia (known in layman's terms as blood poisoning), infections of the wound (including tetanus, which is fatal), acute urinary retention (due to occlusion or because of pain when urinating), injury to adjacent tissues (such as the rectum or urethra), and urinary infection.

Intermediate complications: pelvic infection, dysmenorrhoea (absence of menstruation), cysts and abscesses, and keloid scarring (hardening of the scars).

Late complications: haematocolpos (closure of the vaginal opening by the scar tissues), infertility (due to chronic infection), recurrent urinary infection, difficulty in passing urine as well as menstrual blood and painful menstruation, and hypersensitivity.

Complications upon consummation: difficulty in penetration, painful penetration and 'false vagina' (failure of the circumcision scar to dilate). Where infibulation has been performed, the bride must be cut open before penetration can take place which causes injury and more infections. Excision may also result in an almost complete closing of the vagina and require cutting open.

---

11 See Toubia, *supra*, n. 5, p. 8.
12 Summarized from: Koso-Thomas, *supra*, n. 10, pp. 25-28; and Hosken, *supra*, n. 5, pp. 22-24.

Upon delivery: prolonged and obstructed delivery, unnecessary Caesarian sections, perineal laceration (due to baby's head being pushed through the perineum), and excessive blood loss and pain. Obstructed labour also brings risks to the baby (particularly the first born) who may suffer brain damage or die due to lack of oxygen.

Post-natal complications: prolapse and fistulae (rupturing of the vaginal wall). The latter is said to be common due to obstructed labour and causes incontinence in women for the remainder of their lives.

Sexual complications: lack of orgasm, frigidity and anxiety.

Superstitions ensure that the blame for a failed circumcision lies with the girl rather than the circumciser. If the child dies from complications, its death is attributed to evil spirits or fate which it has brought onto itself.[13]

If a girl lives within a community where the circumcision of females is a traditional practice, it is almost certain that she will undergo the procedure *as a matter of course*. Should she refuse the procedure, she would risk, *inter alia*, diminishing her chances of marriage, bringing injury to her family's honour, or being shamed and shunned by her community or labelled promiscuous.[14]

Overall, female circumcision is a traditional practice which has become synthesized over time from various values.[15] While acknowledging all of the reasons noted above as independent factors, the practice can be summed up as stemming initially from women (and men) strictly and unquestioningly complying with the dictates of tradition within their communities.[16] In other words, *tradition* exercises a powerful influence which obstructs efforts to limit or eradicate female circumcision. It is a catch-all notion for all the causes of circumcision and is, without further explanation, the predominant *reason* cited for maintaining it. This has been confirmed in the few social surveys which have been conducted on the practice. For example, a study in Sierra Leone on the reasons for which women submit to female circumcision found the procedure largely accepted 'for the sake of tradition.' More specifically, of the 369 women who participated in the study and were asked why they submitted to circumcision, the majority (56 per cent) attributed their decisions simply to 'tradition', 23 per cent cited the need for social acceptance, while only 11 per cent based their decisions on religion.[17] A similar finding was found in the Sudan.[18] In her review of the five countries for which Demographic Health Surveys data are available on women's opinions

---

13 United Nations, HARMFUL TRADITIONAL PRACTICES, *supra*, n. 9, p. 9.
14 *See* F.A. Althaus, *Female Circumcision: Rite of Passage or Violation of Rights*, Family Planning Perspectives, Vol. 23 (1997), p. 132.
15 United Nations, HARMFUL TRADITIONAL PRACTICES, *supra*, n. 9, p. 10.
16 Koso-Thomas, *supra*, n. 10, p. 69.
17 As reported by C. Chelala, *A critical move against female genital mutilation*, Populi, March/April 1998, p. 15.
18 *See* L. Williams and T. Sobieszczyk, ATTITUDES SURROUNDING THE CONTINUATION OF FEMALE CIRCUMCISION IN THE SUDAN (1996).

towards excision, Althaus similarly found *tradition* to be the most commonly cited reason for the practice to continue.[19]

The research findings of Obermeyer, a medical anthropologist working in the Department of Population and International Health at Harvard University, on the medical consequences of female circumcision may be significant to our understanding of why female circumcision continues and, consequently, how the human rights discourse should address the practice. As such they merit closer inspection. Obermeyer suggests that the prevalence of complications reported to arise from female circumcision are considerably exaggerated (indeed, few researchers evidence their claims of 'widespread medical complications' with statistics). Specifically, she notes that:

> … the rate of medical complications suggests that they are the exception rather than the rule. This should be cause to ponder, because it suggests a discrepancy between the forceful rhetoric, which depicts female genital surgeries as causing death and disease, and the large numbers of women who, voluntarily or under pressure, undergo these practices.[20]

Indeed, this may largely explain why so few African women contest the practice and refuse to undergo the procedure. However, no matter what the exact numbers of individuals suffering complications or the degree of severity of these, we (the 'international community') still evaluate the pain and suffering that accompany the intervention to be too high, and the cutting and removal of healthy tissue in a sensitive area of the female anatomy to be unnecessary (because it has no medical benefits) and cruel. However, these assessments are not universally shared. For instance, many African women evidently do not assess the practice as 'unnecessary.' As suggested in the list of reasons above, the practice may be considered necessary for reasons that have nothing to do with health but are crucial to the definition of a beautiful feminine body, the marriageability of daughters, the balance of sexual desires between the sexes or the sense of value and identity that comes from the traditions of a group.[21]

One important conclusion to be drawn from these considerations is that the reasons for which female circumcision is performed in a community must be known if a discourse of human rights is to be meaningfully applied. Arguments that the practice violates a woman's rights to freedom from discrimination and violence, or to health, will only be considered legitimate if the reasons for it being performed are truly perceived to be rooted in discrimination (i.e. to lack a relevant basis for the difference in treatment for men), if the practice is considered a form of violence within that culture, and if the risks of medical complications from the practice are perceived to be an issue of concern.

---

19   As concluded by Althaus, *supra*, n. 14, p. 132.
20   Obermeyer, *supra*, n. 3, p. 92.
21   Obermeyer further discusses these conclusions and suggests parallels with male circumcision, breast implants, nose jobs and other plastic surgeries; *id.*, p. 94.

2.2 Early Marriage (Early Sexual Activity and Pregnancy)

One of the most obvious traditional practices detrimental to reproductive health is the encouragement of marriage, and hence sexual activity, for girls at an early age. This is widely practiced across much of Africa. In Ethiopia, for instance, 34.1 per cent of girls enter into marriage before the age of 15 years and 75 per cent before the age of 18. In Ghana and Kenya 20 per cent of girls are married before 15 years of age and 80 per cent before 18.5 years of age.[22] The reasons given for early marriage include:

- protecting the virginity of the girls for the honour of the family;
- strengthening and enlarging family bonds (e.g. when marriage occurs between cousins or kin); and
- economic benefits (notably through dowry and reduction of family expenses).[23]

Africa has the highest rate of births to young mothers. Statistics vary from source to source but are consistently high enough to be alarming. The UNFPA, for instance, reports that three out of four teenagers in Africa are mothers, 40 per cent of whom are aged 17 years or under.[24] The IAC reports that approximately 50 per cent of first births in many sub-Saharan African countries are to women under the age of 19.[25] Culturally, it is often believed that a young woman is ready to be a wife once she has obtained puberty or shortly thereafter. As ill-prepared as their bodies may be, when girls are married before or soon after their first menstruation they may conceive almost immediately.[26] This natural risk is bolstered by social expectations which make many girls feel pressure to have children soon into marriage.[27] But this is not all. Research has further shown that women who start having children early generally have more children, at shorter intervals, than those who embark on parenthood later, resulting in a greater risk of reproductive ill-health.[28]

Women's rights activists stress that the practice of early marriage is rooted in women's subordination. In marrying at a young age, young women become the property of men (who are physically and psychologically dominant if not by the mere fact that they are older). Girls are commonly thought to be more valuable as young

---

22 Reported in IAC, SYMPOSIUM, *supra*, n. 6, p. 42.
23 *Id.*, p. 48.
24 UNFPA, MEETING THE POPULATION CHALLENGE (1996), p. 12.
25 IAC, SYMPOSIUM, *supra*, n. 6, p. 37.
26 IAC, SITUATION OF WOMEN IN AFRICA, *supra*, n. 1, p. 4.
27 *See* A. Odaga and W. Heneveld, GIRLS AND SCHOOLS IN SUB-SAHARAN AFRICA: FROM ANALYSIS TO ACTION (1995).
28 United Nations, HARMFUL TRADITIONAL PRACTICES, *supra*, n. 9, p. 19.

brides because they are sexually inexperienced virgins and they are more complacent and malleable in personality and likely to obey orders.[29]

Many sub-Saharan African countries recognise early marriage as a source of problems and have introduced legislation raising the legal age at which girls may marry. For many health and women's rights advocates, however, the minimum ages set by legislation remain too low. The Senegalese Red Cross, for instance, has advocated that the earliest age at which a woman would be sufficiently developed and ready to have her first baby and be safe in pregnancy and childbirth would be after 19 years of age. Taking this into account, it considers as early marriage all those marriages contracted before a woman has attained the age of 19. This is an important statement in light of the statistics on marriage in Senegal prior to the age of 19 and, more so, prior to the age of 14, as demonstrated in Table I. Despite lobbying the Government of Senegal to raise the minimum age for marriage for women to 19 years, the law remains fixed at 16 years.[30]

Table I
Percentage of Girls Married Prior to Age 19 Years and Under in Senegal, According to Ethnic Group[31]

Ethnic Group	Age at marriage (under 14 years)	Age at marriage (between 14-18 years)	Total (married prior to 19 years of age)
Wolof	8.69 %	36.36 %	45.05 %
Serere	4.75 %	37.53 %	42.26 %
Toucouleur	20.4 %	48.50 %	68.90 %
Peulh	19.46 %	58.38 %	77.84 %
Diola	8.03 %	28.57 %	36.60 %
Bambara	10.08 %	49.50 %	59.58 %
Socé	32.15 %	18.48 %	50.62 %
Sarakolé	20.68 %	46.55 %	67.23 %
Mandjack	9.23 %	29.23 %	38.46 %

Because they are physically under-developed and psychologically unprepared to cope with the demands of marriage, pregnancy, labour and nursing, married adolescents

---

29 *See*, e.g., S. Correa, POPULATION AND REPRODUCTIVE RIGHTS: PERSPECTIVES FROM THE SOUTH (1994), pp. 82-83.
30 As reported in F. Bathily, *Combat against traditional practices harmful to the health of the mother and the child: Activity report from the Senegalese Red Cross*, in IAC, REPORT ON THE REGIONAL CONFERENCE ON TRADITIONAL PRACTICES AFFECTING THE HEALTH OF WOMEN AND CHILDREN IN AFRICA (1991).
31 *Id.*, p. 236.

have higher lifetime risks to health and life.[32] Among numerous psychological and physical dangers, a major health risk associated with pregnancy among girls is obstructed or prolonged labour because the baby's head is too big for the underdeveloped pelvis. This can result in maternal death or serious complications, the most disabling of which are obstetric fistulas.[33] In one study of vesico-vaginal fistula (ruptures in the vaginal wall) in northern Ethiopia it was found that the mean age at marriage of fistula victims was 11.5 years.[34] A girl's underdeveloped body is also easily damaged by sex and is thus particularly vulnerable to disease, such as HIV. This is due to the fact that a young girl has an immature cervix and low vaginal mucus production.[35]

Furthermore, there is also a widespread belief in Africa that young girls are less likely than grown women to be infected with HIV and, as such, are considered safe sexual partners.[36] Of even greater concern is the dangerous belief in some communities (such as in Mozambique) that having sexual relations with a very young girl will cure or protect a man from AIDS. These beliefs add to the common phenomenon of men throughout Africa selecting brides significantly younger than themselves,[37] marrying girls even as young as 10 or 11 years old.[38]

Summing up, early sexual activity in young women exposes them to many risks. In terms of pregnancy, the health risks associated with pregnancy and childbearing are more pronounced than for older women. For instance, young women are more likely to suffer from pregnancy-induced high blood pressure, anaemia and haemorrhage, obstructed and prolonged labour and postpartum infections.[39] Because of their physiological constitution, sex at an early age also exposes girls to a greater risk of contracting sexually transmitted diseases, including HIV.[40] Moreover, declining age at menarche puts girls at risk of early pre-marital exposure to sexual activity even in societies with a tradition of early marriage, thereby extending the high-risk period over a girl's lifetime.[41]

---

32 IAC, SITUATION OF WOMEN IN AFRICA, *supra*, n. 1, p. 4. UNFPA reports that the risk of maternal mortality is 25 times higher for girls under 15, and two times higher for girls 15-19 years old. *See* UNFPA, MATERNAL MORTALITY UPDATE 1998-1999 on website: http://www.unfpa.org/tpd/mmupdate/hilites.htm.
33 IAC, SITUATION OF WOMEN IN AFRICA, *supra*, n. 1, p. 4.
34 *Id.*
35 *Id.*, p. 8.
36 As reported by: E. Ram, *Children and the Plague of AIDS*, International Herald Tribune, 29-30 November 1997, p. 6; and African Centre for Women, TRADITIONAL AND CULTUAL PRACTICES HARMFUL TO THE GIRL-CHILD (1997), p. 6.
37 World Bank, CONFRONTING AIDS: PUBLIC PRIORITIES IN A GLOBAL EPIDEMIC (1997), p. 124.
38 As reported in M. Owen, *The Bottom Line; Mozambique*, Population Parenthood Challenges, Nos. 1 and 2, 1997 p. 46.
39 *See* L.S. Zabin and K. Kiragu, *The Health Consequences of Adolescent Sexual and Fertility Behaviour in Sub-Saharan Africa*, Studies in Family Planning, Vol. 29 (1998), pp. 215-218.
40 *See* A. Lawson, *Women and AIDS in Africa: Sociocultural Dimensions of the HIV/AIDS Epidemic*, International Social Science Journal, Vol. 161 (1999), p. 395.
41 *See* Zabin and Kiragu, *supra*, n. 39, p. 213.

2.3 Dietary Taboos during Pregnancy and Lactation

Taboos on the foods consumed by African women are applicable particularly at certain times in life, notably during periods of pregnancy, nursing and bereavement. Food taboos specially targeted at pregnant and lactating women usually restrict the consumption of food high in essential nutrients. For example, taboos exist in societies of Sierra Leone where it is maintained, largely through superstitions, that a woman should not eat:[42]

– chicken or eggs
 If she does, it is believed her child will be afflicted with loose stools. In a region where dysentery and diarrhoea are killer diseases, the fear is a formidable one. Eggs are thought to cause hiccups in babies, induce children to steal and make a woman infertile.
– crayfish, crab or shrimp
 It is said that these will cause excessive salivation in a baby.
– pumpkins and plantains
 These are believed to stop the healing process of the cut umbilical cord.
– coconut or palmnut
 It is thought a woman's child will be plagued by constant vomiting.

Further discussion of nutritional discrimination appears under 'Son Preference' (Section 3.4) below.

Inadequate consumption of highly nutritious foods bearing vital vitamins, protein and iron at a period in a woman's life when she is most vulnerable leads to malnutrition and anaemia, especially in women who have too many pregnancies too closely spaced. Eggs, for instance, are a complete food, containing protein, iron and carbohydrates which are important nutrients in pregnancy helping to prevent anaemia and ensuring the well-being of the mother and foetus. It should be noted that commonly associated with taboos are economic arguments, since chicken, cashews, groundnuts and other foods are typically considered export (higher income earning) crops not to be consumed. Thus, persuading women they may and should eat these nutritious foods during pregnancy and lactation is not only a battle against superstition or misinformation, but also possibly against straightforward money matters – although this is to leave aside the economic costs of ill-health, disability and death of affected women and children.

---

42 *See* E. Hyde, *The African woman and nutrition* in IAC, REPORT ON THE REGIONAL CONFERENCE, *supra*, n. 30, p. 132; and S. Yilla, *African (Sierra Leone) women and nutrition*, in *id.*.

2.4 Practices Relating to Childbirth

Sub-Saharan Africa is riddled with cultural taboos, superstitions, and traditional beliefs regarding how childbirth should take place. Many reinforce unsafe childbirth. The examples of traditional beliefs and customs in rural parts of Ghana related in Box I offer a glimpse of the considerations at hand. In other regions of Ghana, a prolonged or difficult labour is thought to be caused by adultery on the part of the woman. The woman is looked upon with scorn and simply abandoned until she 'confesses'.[43] A similar belief and practice has been reported in Sierra Leone.[44] Another example of a harmful traditional birthing practice present in Sierra Leone requires herbs to be inserted into the vagina of a woman who is experiencing prolonged labour. Practices such as these pose one or several risks, ranging from infection or septicaemia to death to the mother, unborn or newborn baby.[45] It has also been reported that women who have been circumcised are encouraged to under-eat during pregnancy. This increases the likelihood that they will have smaller babies which are more easily delivered from the tightened, circumcised vagina.[46]

Box I Pregnancy and Childbirth in a Traditional Rural Setting

A Story from Kassena Nankana District, Northern Ghana[47]

A recent survey conducted in the Kassena Nankana District of Northern Ghana estimated the maternal mortality rate to be 813 per 100,000 live births, one of the highest in the country. The main causes of maternal deaths were found to be post-partum haemorrhage, infections, obstructed labour and severe anaemia, all preventable with good management.

The remoteness of most of the communities in the region has ensured that adherence to traditional practices and cultural belief systems, particularly those associated with pregnancy and childbirth, has remained strong. Traditionally, a woman is not recognized as being pregnant until the pregnancy is officially announced by *lingeru*, a complex and colourful ritual performed by the mother-in-law. This usually occurs after abdominal distension becomes evident (generally about 20 weeks into the pregnancy). The head of the compound is then informed and he consults the *vuru* (soothsayer) who, with the aid

---

43 See F. Azu-Billa Anaba, *Traditional practices, beliefs and taboos that affect the health and nutrition of women and children in the northern sector of Ghana*, in *id.*, p. 129.
44 See S. Yilla, *African (Sierra Leone) Women and Nutrition*, in IAC, REPORT ON THE REGIONAL CONFERENCE, *supra*, n. 30, p. 134.
45 *Id.*
46 See Toubia, *supra*, n. 5.
47 Excerpt from P. Allotey, *Where There's No Tradition of Traditional Birth Attendants: Kassena Nankana District, Northern Ghana*, Reproductive Health Matters, Special Issue 1999.

of ancestral and other spirits, foretells the development and outcome of the pregnancy. During pregnancy and childbirth the *vuru* offers advice about treatment of illness and the use of various health services, although he is not directly responsible for the intervention. It is not uncommon for women to cite edicts from the *vuru* as their reason for not attending ante-natal clinics.

Should a woman become ill during pregnancy, there is a range of *tindana* (traditional healers) to consult, each with a specific area of specialization, depending on the perceived cause of the illness. The *vuru* often provides advice on which particular *tindana* should be consulted.

Labour is recognized by the waters breaking and the appearance of the presenting part of the infant in the vagina. Contractions alone are not considered a definitive sign of imminent birth because they are thought to mimic a number of other conditions. This has implications on the time at which women call for assistance. Birth is considered the exclusive domain of women, who usually give birth on their own or assisted by one of the older women in the compound. Births usually took place in the area of the compound where the livestock are tended overnight – over a bed of evenly spread, dried cow dung which is soft enough to be comfortable but ensures that the placenta and other products of childbirth remain in the part of the compound that is considered unclean.

Two types of *tindana*, both of them men, are called in to manage difficult births: one specialized in the removal of retained placentae and the other in the management of obstructed labour. The principal role of the latter *tindana* is to perform ritual genital excisions (removal of the prepuce, clitoris and labia minora) at puberty. During prolonged second stage births, however, he also performs incisions to widen the vaginal opening.

2.5 Incisions in Pregnant Women

Among a few African communities, a practice known as '*Zur Zur*' is performed on women in the 34th or 35th weeks of their first pregnancy. The practice consists of making a deep cut in the anterior wall of the vagina. The wound is allowed to bleed and the woman rests for a while before being sent home to nurse her wound. It is thought that this practice prepares a woman for an easy delivery. However, the consequences can be shock, infection of the birth canal and vesico-vaginal or vaginal fistula, and death through excessive bleeding.[48]

---

48 United Nations, HARMFUL TRADITIONAL PRACTICES, *supra*, n. 9, p. 22; unfortunately, this report does not specify among whiich communities exactly the practice is performed..

2.6 Female Religious Bondage

A practice which can be found among some animists is that of 'virgin slaves' being offered to deities. Reported to date as occurring only in the Volta Region of Ghana, this practice involves young virgin girls given away as 'gifts' by their families to shrines (male oracles) in order to pacify gods for offences committed by other members of the families. The girls, often as young as ten years old, are forced into marriage with the oracles, and serve their husbands sexually with no access to health care. Once given to the shrine the girls are restricted from leaving the compound, even to go to clinics or health posts. It is believed that any girl breaking this rule is responsible for bringing on the wrath of gods.[49]

3 CUSTOMS AND NORMS BOLSTERING TRADITIONAL PRACTICES HARMFUL TO WOMEN

Numerous customs and norms act to support and maintain the harmful traditional practices identified above. In many instances, two or more mutually reinforce each other. For instance, the practice of polygyny (where one man has multiple wives) bolsters the practice of early marriage and the norm of son preference. The practice of female circumcision similarly reinforces harmful traditional birthing practices and helps maintain harmful dietary taboos in pregnancy. The practice of brideprice is found commonly to maintain the practice of both female circumcision and levirate marriage. The interdependent character of these practices and norms are described below. Ultimately, they converge to form a picture of the African woman as subordinate and unable to influence meaningfully decisions and patterns of behaviour which impact on her own health and well-being.

3.1 Authority of the Husband and Spousal Violence

Almost all societies in sub-Saharan Africa are patriarchal.[50] This translates into the norm of male authority. The authority and ultimate decision-making power of the husband, father or other male relative manifests itself in many ways, each potentially impacting on the action of a woman to prevent reproductive ill-health, or maintain or improve her reproductive health. Violence is commonly socially condoned when it is believed that a daughter or wife did not behave in a culturally approved manner,[51]

---

49 IAC, REPORT OF THE INTER-AFRICAN COMMITTEE ON TRADITIONAL PRACTICES AFFECTING THE HEALTH OF WOMEN AND CHILDREN (1994).
50 As reported, *inter alia*, by Koso-Thomas, *supra*, n. 10, p. 38.
51 *See* African Centre for Women, *supra*, n. 36, p. 5; and A.A. Bawah *et al.*, *Women's Fears and Men's Anxieties: The Impact of Family Planning on Gender Relations in Northern Ghana*, Studies in Family Planning, Vol. 30 (1999), p. 57.

reinforcing social norms of ultimate male authority and male decision-making, even with regard to reproduction. The following comment made by one male opinion leader in Northern Ghana reflects this understanding:

> *If a woman is not experiencing her menses and is not sick, she has no right to refuse sex, because we marry her to have children, and that is how we can get children. We don't marry women for their cooking. So if she refuses to have sex, why won't I want to beat her? I will beat her.*[52]

Research in sub-Saharan Africa to date suggests that authority structures in African families result in poor communication among couples.[53] For instance, an average of only one in four rural women in Southern Ethiopia are reported to discuss family size and family planning with their husbands.[54] Yet, communication between spouses is necessary in order for them to initiate discussion of topics about sexuality and for them to reach an agreement on matters important to their own reproductive health or that of their children, such as whether their daughter will be circumcised and at what age she may marry.[55] The reasons for poor inter-spousal communication regarding sex and reproduction are twofold. First, men are traditionally seen as the dominant decision-makers (bolstered by the likely older age of husbands).[56] In this light, women see discussion on the topic to be futile. Second, wives consider the subject of sexuality and reproduction difficult to broach (whether truly or perceived to be so) with their husbands.[57] This is largely due to the cultural taboo against speaking openly about sex (see 'Culture of Silence', Section 5 below).

3.2 Extended-Family-Household Structure

Within the extended-family-household structure, parents-in-law, and in particular mothers-in-law, have a significant say in decisions over, and the behaviour of, a daughter-in-law, including her use of contraception in marriage and what she eats

---

52 Cited in *id.*, p. 57.
53 *See*, e.g., D.P. Hogan *et al.*, *Household Organisation, Women's Autonomy, and Contraceptive Behavior in Southern Ethiopia*, Studies in Family Planning, Vol. 30 (1999), p. 305.
54 *Id.*, p. 308.
55 *Id.*, p. 305.
56 *See*: A.C. Ezeh, *The influence of spouses over each other's contraceptive attitudes in Ghana*, Studies in Family Planning, Vol. 24 (1993), pp. 163-174; A.J. Gage *et al.*, HOUSEHOLD STRUCTURE, SOCIOECONOMIC LEVEL, AND CHILD HEALTH IN SUB-SAHARAN AFRICA (1996); D. Meekers and M. Oladosu, *Spousal Communication and Family Planning Decision-Making in Nigeria*, POPULATION RESEARCH INSTITUTE WORKING PAPERS IN AFRICAN DEMOGRAPHY (1996); and S. Salway, *How attitudes toward family planning and discussion between wives and husbands affect contraceptive use in Ghana*, International Family Planning Perspectives, Vol. 20 (1994), pp. 44-47.
57 *See*, e.g., findings of Bawah *et al.*, *supra*, n. 51.

during pregnancy and nursing.[58] Grandmothers are particularly highly respected and their influence strong, especially on their granddaughters. Given the extended family structure, they have considerable control over whether and when a granddaughter will be circumcised, and when and whom she should marry.[59] Stories abound of grandmothers who defy their daughters and solve disagreements on the issue of circumcision by secretly taking their granddaughters to traditional circumcisers to be cut.[60] The hierarchy of influence and authority over most matters, including reproduction, in such a structure is clear. For instance, a recent study of the Kipsigis community of Kenya demonstrates the underlying understanding of young men to recognise the authority and wishes of their parents: when asked whether it was more important to maintain harmony with one's wife or parents, all placed parents first.[61]

Not surprisingly, it is less likely that traditional values regarding children and childbearing are supported in a nuclear household, a living structure which has proven to be more conducive, for instance, to the uptake of family planning.[62] This being said, in much of Africa, the influence of family members does not disappear when couples establish separate residence. Family contact is maintained even at long distances. Thus, even though couples may not live in the same household as their parents and in-laws, contact may be frequent enough to influence a couple's behaviour and decision-making.[63] The authors of an Ethiopian study on the subject of household structure admit that, while there is yet no empirical evidence to support this conclusion, the influence is so apparent that 'this reality must be acknowledged'.[64] Even if the norm is for couples to live in an extended-family household only in the early years of marriage, as is the case in Southern Ethiopia, it is precisely in this period that the roles and decision-making patterns of husbands and wives are set. Indeed, most couples throughout sub-Saharan Africa live in an extended-family-household at some point in their married life (see sample in Table II), especially in the early years of their marriage.

---

58   *See*, e.g., S. Castle *et al.*, *A Qualitative Study of Clandestine Contraceptive Use in Urban Mali*, Studies in Family Planning, Vol. 30 (1999), p. 232.
59   *See* Hosken, *supra*, n. 5, p. 86.
60   Peruse generally Hosken's report, *supra*, n. 5.
61   C. P. Edwards, *Morality and Change: Family Unity and Paternal Authority among Kipsigis and Abaluyia Elders and Students*, in T.S. Weisner *et al.*, eds., AFRICAN FAMILIES AND THE CRISIS OF SOCIAL CHANGE (1997).
62   *See* Hogan *et al.*, *supra*, n. 53, p. 304.
63   *Id.*, p. 313.
64   *Id.*

Table II
Percentage of Children Living in Extended-Family-Household Structures in a Sample of Sub-Saharan African Countries[65]

COUNTRY	RURAL	URBAN
Burkina Faso	43.3	65.6
Cameroon	54.6	68.8
Kenya	39.0	54.5
Madagascar	40.5	52.9
Namibia	78.4	81.6
Niger	47.0	55.5
Nigeria	33.9	38.6
Rwanda	21.8	50.9
Senegal	89.5	84.6
Tanzania	52.4	62.0
Zambia	51.1	67.6

3.3 Kinship Influence and Intervention in the Name of Lineage

It is not only husbands and their parents who maintain some form of control over the decisions and behaviours of women, but also the entire network of kin. In most of traditional Africa, community leaders are strongly concerned with intergenerational family unity and with upholding the authority of the male head of household.[66] The kinship lineage system emphasizes the importance of kin. It determines family governance and assigns roles and obligations.[67] A steady supply of children is viewed as essential in such a system as it ensures a strong lineage and enhances male authority and respect.[68] In return, women who have several children gain respect from relatives because they have continued their lineage.[69] As noted by a team of social science researchers on this subject, 'Women are seen as their husbands' property or as that of their husbands' families, submerged within a corporate identity where individual preferences have no place. Their major function in life is to produce children for their husbands and the lineage.'[70]

---

65 Data adapted and assembled by author from data provided in Gage *et al.*, *supra*, n. 56, p. 8.
66 *See* Edwards, *supra*, n. 61.
67 *See* M. Mhloyi, *Sociocultural Milieu, Women's Status and Family Planning*, in United Nations, FAMILY PLANNING, HEALTH AND FAMILY WELL-BEING (1996), p. 63.
68 *See* Bawah *et al.*, *supra*, n. 51.
69 *See* K.M. Fallon, *Education and Perceptions of Social Status and Power among Women in Larteh, Ghana*, Africa Today, Vol. 46 (1999), p. 71.
70 Bawah *et al.*, *supra*, n. 51, p. 60.

The situation observed among the Tiriki people, situated in the Western Province of Kenya, provides a good example. The Tiriki are very much connected with contemporary industrialised world culture. Many attributes of Western industrialised society are as commonplace as they are in less urbanised areas of Europe and America. The attributes include a large Christian following, Western medical and public health practices, British-and American-type schooling, Western clothing, prevalence of tape recorders and radios, not to mention the presence of a money market economy. Yet local life remains very different from the West, mostly as a result of the high status and respect generally accorded to the elderly.[71] Even a full generation after the inception of a family planning programme in Western Kenya, the social pressure by elders to fulfil the cultural ideal of having many children and then grandchildren has been identified as an important factor in maintaining the average fertility level of 8 children per woman.[72]

3.4 Son Preference

Son preference is prevalent in many parts of Africa, going hand-in-hand with patriarchy.[73] Where boys are more highly valued than girls, they may receive more preventive health care and timely attention at health institutions when they fall ill. Girls may receive less nutritious or smaller quantities of food than boys – owing to food taboos or discrimination – resulting in a higher prevalence of malnutrition in girls. For many girls, adulthood is entered into with poor health as a consequence of years of poor nutritional status and heavy work.[74] This leads to stunting in growth and a lack of reserve energy which, in turn, can lead to higher risks of complications during childbirth.[75] A malnourished woman is more likely to have a low-birth-weight baby, thus initiating a cycle of malnutrition and illness.[76] Discrimination in the feeding and care of female infants and girls has been reported to exist particularly in the countries of Cameroon, Liberia, Madagascar, Nigeria and Senegal.[77] The sad irony is that girls from communities where early marriage is customary are often also the victims of the norm of son preference. Their stunted growth will only contribute to a higher risk of ill-

---

71 As reported by W.H. Sangree, *Pronatalism and the Elderly in Tiriki, Kenya*, in AFRICAN FAMILIES, *supra*, n. 61, pp. 184-185.
72 *Id.*, p. 185.
73 IAC, SITUATION OF WOMEN IN AFRICA, *supra*, n. 1, p. 4.
74 Girls and women in Africa typically bear the heaviest burden of essential chores, including walking great distances collecting and carrying heavy loads of firewood and water, performing agricultural work, processing food, and caring for younger siblings. Indeed, women in the region on average work more hours than men. In Kenya, for example, it is estimated that women work 10 times the hours of men. *See* United Nations Development Programme, HUMAN DEVELOPMENT REPORT (1995), p. 92.
75 African Centre for Women, *supra*, n. 36, p. 3.
76 IAC, SITUATION OF WOMEN IN AFRICA, *supra*, n. 1, p. 4.
77 United Nations, HARMFUL TRADITIONAL PRACTICES, *supra*, n. 9, p. 14.

health and mortality in a situation which fuels early pregnancy and childbirth.[78] They are therefore doubly the victims of custom, each fostering risks to their reproductive health.

There are other reasons for son preference as illustrated in the Gusii society of Kenya. In this society, as in many others across Africa, a woman, through her sons' wives, acquires dependants who have to show her respect, obey her, and assist her in her daily chores. When a woman's son marries, she is gradually able to remove herself from her husband's authority. She becomes a member of her son's household and expects to receive services from her son, daughter-in-law and grandchildren. With increasing age, women expect their daughters-in-law and grandchildren to serve as 'extra pairs of hands' – to work with and for them.[79] In this case, a woman's comfort and security in old age depends on her sons. This is particularly so since a woman lacks easy access to money or control over the fruit of her own labour during her productive years. Daughters, on the other hand, offer no such security.[80] The view of one man interviewed in Northern Ghana sums up the sentiments at hand: ' ... *a daughter can't build my house. We feel it is only a son who can build a house.*'[81]

3.5 Polygyny

The practice of polygyny is a distinctive feature of sub-Saharan marriages.[82] As it is the prerogative of the husband to choose a polygamous marriage, the practice is commonly associated with women's low status and inequality within a marriage.[83] This is particularly true when combined with the young age at which a woman may be chosen and made a wife, and the older age of husbands. Young brides are not uncommon in polygamous marriages. This further contributes to poor husband-wife communication and perpetuates male dominance in marriage. Like extended-family-household situations, polygyny is often thought to weaken women's decision-making power and to make them dependent on a large number of sons.[84] Where there is competition among wives, women may seek to make themselves as sexually accessible as possible

---

78 *Id.*, p. 17.
79 As described by N.T. Hakansson and R.A. Le Vine, *Gender and Life-Course Strategies among the Gusii*, in AFRICAN FAMILIES, *supra*, n. 61, pp. 256-257.
80 *See* Sangree, *supra*, n. 71, p. 193.
81 Cited in Bawah *et al.*, *supra*, n. 51, p. 60.
82 *See*, e.g.: I. Nyamongo, *Anthropology: A Social Science in the Control of HIV Transmission in Africa*, African Anthropology, Vol. 2 (1995), p. 49; and J.C. Caldwell, P. Caldwell and P. Quiggin, *The Social Content of AIDS in sub-Saharan Africa*, Population and Development Review, Vol. 15 (1989).
83 *See*: A. Boye *et al.*, *Marriage law and practice in the Sahel*, Studies in Family Planning, Vol. 22 (1991); and, Ezeh, *supra*, n. 56.
84 As noted by Hogan *et al.*, *supra*, n. 53, p. 312, although their findings regarding Southern Ethiopia did not support these conclusions.

and bear many children to bring honour to their husbands.[85] A risk arising from the nature of a polygamous marriage is such that it results in increased sexual networks which, in turn, increases the risk of transmission of STDs where one of the partners is infected.[86]

Polygyny has somewhat declined in importance as a means of economic advancement, but continues to give a man prestige, expressed as 'becoming an important man in the clan'. The old ideal of attaining immortality by founding a large lineage still forms part of the motivations for polygamy.[87] The more a man has grandchildren, the more he can expect to be surrounded and cared for in old age. This said, there are at least two important factors that counteract polygamy: the fact that it conflicts with Christian ideology and that caring for the large number of children resulting from such unions is costly.[88] The practice has declined, in large part because of changing values and the attendant loss of social support for it,[89] but there still remains a significant enough population in polygamous marriages to maintain scrutiny. In Kenya, for example, 19.5 % of married women were reported in 1997 to be in polygamous unions,[90] while in Zimbabwe one in five married women are in polygamous unions.[91] In Southwest Nigeria, as in other parts of West Africa, almost half of all wives are in polygamous marriages.[92] Reports of high levels of polygyny have also come from the Horn of Africa (e.g. an average 31.2 % of unions in Southern Ethiopia are polygamous).[93] Further statistics appear in Table III.

---

85 See E.R. Fapohunda and M.P. Todaro, *Family structure, implicit contracts, and the demand for children in Southern Nigeria*, Population and Development Review, Vol. 14 (1988).
86 See Lawson, *supra*, n. 40, p. 394
87 As described by Hakansson and Le Vine, *supra*, n. 79, pp. 261-262.
88 *Id*, p. 262.
89 *See: Id*; and R.A. Le Vine and B.B. Le Vine, NYANSONGO: A GUSII COMMUNITY IN KENYA (1996).
90 CRLP, WOMEN OF THE WORLD: LAWS AND POLICIES AFFECTING THEIR REPRODUCTIVE LIVES (1997), p. 53.
91 *Id.*, p. 130.
92 As reported by J. Caldwell *et al.*, *The Construction of Adolescence in a Changing World: Implications for Sexuality, Reproduction, and Marriage*, Studies in Family Planning, Vol. 29 (1998), p. 138.
93 See Hogan *et al.*, *supra*, n. 53, p. 308.

Table III
Percentage of children living in polygynous households in a sample of sub-Saharan African countries[94]

COUNRTY	RURAL	URBAN	TOTAL
Burkina Faso	28.1	7.1	35.2
Cameroon	15.3	5.3	20.6
Madagascar	0.1	0.0	0.1
Namibia	0.4	0.3	0.7
Niger	15.8	13.7	29.5
Nigeria	20.6	10.1	30.7
Rwanda	0.1	0.0	0.1
Senegal	0.1	0.1	0.2
Tanzania	2.2	0.9	3.1
Zambia	2.8	0.5	3.3

Men oriented towards an agrarian lifestyle which requires large production of cash crops (which is the majority of people in sub-Saharan Africa) resort to polygamy to ensure large families to provide labour.[95] Hence, it is more commonly practiced in agrarian communities. In urban areas of sub-Saharan Africa, traditional polygyny has evolved into many forms of formal and informal marriages and consensual unions, often concurrent and long term.[96]

3.6 Extra-Marital Sexual Activity

Although the social norm in most sub-Saharan African countries tends to favour monogamy and mutual fidelity, it fails to provide sufficient protection for women, since society expects women to abide by this rule but tacitly excuses male infidelities. One example is the 'second office', where a man spends time with another woman.[97] This double standard contributes to a common scenario where a woman has a single sexual partner throughout her married lifetime, whereas men may have several partners and are even encouraged to do so.[98] African society appears to react to such male infidelities only when the multiplicity undermines the image of family unity.[99] Indeed, women who are themselves aware that their partners are intimate with other women tolerate their infidelities, particularly if they are dependent on the men and their needs are

---

94 Data adapted and assembled by author from data provided in Gage *et al.*, *supra*, n. 56, p. 8.
95 *See* P.L. Kilbride and J.C. Kilbride, *Stigma Role Overload, and Delocalization among Contemporary Kenyan Women*, in AFRICAN FAMILIES, *supra*, n. 61, p. 210.
96 World Bank, *supra*, n. 37, p. 124.
97 *See* Lawson, *supra*, n. 40, p. 393.
98 IAC, SITUATION OF WOMEN IN AFRICA, *supra*, n. 1, p. 8.
99 *See* Lawson, *supra*, n. 40, p. 394.

being met.[100] Ankomah reminds us that most women decry partnerships outside of marriage on the part of women not for reasons of health (e.g. fear of HIV/AIDS) but because of the risk of pregnancy by a man other than one's husband.[101] While African societies in general tolerate multiple sexual partners for men, they exert moral and social sanctions on women. Women's infidelities, which can consist merely of looks and touches, are commonly branded prostitution.[102]

The propensity of men to have extra-marital affairs is further bolstered by the custom of abstinence during a wife's pregnancy and post-partum – a custom which assures healthy child spacing. Abstinence is guaranteed by the traditional belief in the incompatibility of mother's milk with semen.[103]

As noted above, although formal polygamous marriages are on the decline, another form of union – regular multiple partnerships – are common and widely tolerated throughout sub-Saharan Africa.[104] These partnerships carry less social recognition but they often have the same characteristics of formal unions. A substantial explanation for the existence of these unions in Africa is the very high rate of labour migration, in some countries, affecting more than half the adult male population,[105] combined with weak conjugal bonds and the tacit acceptance of extra-marital relationships for men.[106] One comparative survey found as many as 36% and 55% of men in the Central African Republic and Lesotho, respectively, had more than one regular partner.[107]

STDs are likely to spread more widely where multiple, concurrent partnerships are the norm. This norm, therefore, is highly conducive to the rapid spread of HIV, which is another explanation why the disease has reached epidemic proportions in the region in so short a time span.[108] As summarised in a World Bank report, '[s]ocial norms and peer pressure that encourage men to use the services of prostitutes or that venerate men with many female 'conquests', while placing a high value on female chastity create the conditions for an explosive HIV epidemic.'[109]

---

100 A. Ankomah, *Sex, Love, Money and AIDS: The Dynamics of Premarital Sexual Relationships in Ghana*, Sexualities, Vol. 2 (1999), p. 297.
101 *Id.*
102 *See* Obbo, *supra*, n. 2, p. 176.
103 *See* R. Schoenmaeckers *et al.*, in H. Page and R. Lesthaeghe, eds., CHILD-SPACING IN TROPICAL AFRICA: TRADITIONS AND CHANGE (1981), p. 38.
104 *See* M. Caraël, *Sexual Behaviour*, in J. Cleland and B. Ferry, eds., SEXUAL BEHAVIOUR AND AIDS IN THE DEVELOPING WORLD (1995) p. 99.
105 *Id.*
106 *See* J. Caldwell, DISASTER IN AN ALTERNATIVE CIVILIZATION: THE SOCIAL DIMENSION OF AIDS IN THE SUB-SAHARAN AFRICA DEMOGRAPHIC CENTRE (1989), p. 5.
107 *Id.*
108 *See* National Research Council, FACTORS AFFECTING CONTRACEPTIVE USE IN SUB-SAHARAN AFRICA (1993).
109 World Bank, *supra*, n. 37, p. 124.

3.7 Brideprice (Bridewealth)

The practice of brideprice (also known as bridewealth) is found throughout many societies of sub-Saharan Africa. In patrilineal societies, the handing over of the brideprice represents the transfer from one family to another of the rights over the productive and reproductive capacities of a woman.[110] It is a deeply ingrained expectation on the part of families, husband and wives that in exchange for the husband's payment of brideprice, usually in the form of sheep and cattle, women must bear children for their husbands and the lineage.[111] The words of one man interviewed in Northern Ghana offer insight into these expectations:

> *[I]n this place we marry our women with cows. When my father pays the bridewealth, he does that for [her] to deliver children for me and build my house... I have... picked [her] to build my house, so [she] must deliver children to me. I know her father will support me.*[112]

Interrupting or stopping childbearing therefore risks being viewed as short-changing the husband and his family – as though he has not got his money's worth in children. Women in the same survey in Northern Ghana responded with a similar view. As one young woman commented:

> *If we give birth till the time the man's mind wants, he will then tell you to stop, for you have given birth to the time he wants and you have paid for all the cows.*[113]

A publication by a women's group in Nairobi explains the problems associated with this practice in Kenya:

> Brideprice operating in a money economy has come to acquire the qualities of a sale – it is now, more than ever before, the *price* of a woman. Greed and gain have led some parents to force their daughters to leave school, even if they are still very young, to wed rich elderly men for a fat brideprice... It is always argued by protagonists of brideprice that it protects the virtue of girls, and ensures stability of the marriage... But brideprice in reality is an anachronistic archaic custom that reduces women to merchandise and in an overtly polygamous society like Kenya it promotes inequality.[114]

---

110 Lawson, *supra*, n. 40, p. 393.
111 *See*, e.g. Castle *et al.*, *supra*, n. 58, p. 234.
112 Bawah *et al.*, *supra*, n. 51, p. 60.
113 *Id.*
114 As cited in Hosken, *supra*, n. 5, p. 61.

The brideprice for a girl will be higher if a woman's virginity has been preserved, forming a strong incentive for daughters to be circumcised.[115] Indeed, excision and/or infibulation are typically required by a husband-to-be who will not pay brideprice to the father otherwise.[116]

3.8 Levirate (Wife Inheritance) Marriage

Widows are notoriously among the most vulnerable of women in many African societies. In traditional patrilineal societies, the practice of levirate marriage (or wife inheritance) allows a male relative (usually a brother) of a deceased man to inherit his wife, along with his physical property such as land and house.[117] This occurs because of the belief that a woman and her children form part of her husband's property. In some instances, the woman (but not necessarily her children) may be released from the obligation if the payment of brideprice given to her family upon her marriage is paid back. In many cases, however, the family is unable or unwilling to do so.

Where the family of the deceased man also believes a widow's reproductive potential belongs to the family, widows may be expected to become the wife of the male relative in the physical sense.[118] Where this occurs, the practice of levirate marriage increases a woman's risk of rape and contracting and transmitting STDs,[119] never mind the fact that she is left with little choice to refuse sex, remain a widow, or eventually choose another partner. Should the widow refuse to honour the tradition, she risks becoming a victim of domestic violence[120] and/or is likely to be evicted from her home, particularly if she is living on what is regarded as family land.[121] Widows' daughters are also reported to be vulnerable to early sexual exploitation and rape because they lack a father to protect them.[122] In parts of Mozambique, the rules of levirate marriage are straightforward. Widows (who in some provinces constitute more than 60 per cent of adult female population owing to the civil war) must undergo the traditional custom known as 'ritual cleansing' through sexual acts. This custom requires a woman to sleep with one of her husband's male relatives and then be inherited by him.[123]

---

115 United Nations, HARMFUL TRADITIONAL PRACTICES, *supra*, n. 9, p. 18; and Hosken, *supra*, n. 5, p. 110.
116 *See* Hosken, *supra*, n. 5, p. 61.
117 *See* A. Mutua *et al.*, in A. Hardon and E. Hayes, eds., REPRODUCTIVE RIGHTS IN PRACTICE (1997), reports on this tradition in rural Kenya, p. 62.
118 *See* Lawson, *supra*, n. 40, p. 395.
119 Reported in IAC, SYMPOSIUM, *supra*, n. 6, p. 43.
120 *See id*, p. 47.
121 *See* E. Mayambala, WOMEN AND HIV TRANSMISSION IN UGANDA: AN EVALUATION OF SAFER SEX STRATEGIES (unpublished manuscript, 1994), p. 20.
122 *See id*, p. 47.
123 As reported in Owen, *supra*, n. 38, p. 47.

Chapter II

3.9 Abduction for Purposes of Rape, Impregnation and Marriage

In the Arsi region of Southern Ethiopia, a custom allows men to kidnap young girls and rape them until they become pregnant.[124] Once the girls are pregnant, the captor announces his 'victory' to the village elders and demands that the woman become his wife since she is carrying his child. The elders then negotiate a dowry with the girl's parents, which usually consists of oxen. Despite being illegal, this practice is so common in this region that the police commonly do little to stop it; it is usually left in the hands of the village elders to resolve cases where there are disputes.[125]

4 NORMS INFLUENCING FERTILITY

A woman's status in Africa, much like a man's, is often identified with her fertility, with greater respect being accorded to people who have many children.[126] While numerous traditional ancestral rites have been replaced by Christianity and Islam, the ideology of parenthood and social pressures on both men and women to have many children are so diffuse and pervasive that parenting many children and taking great pride in the birth of numerous grandchildren has continued.[127]

The status given to women upon childbearing is perhaps even more visible when viewed from the other side of the coin. Where fertility is praised so highly, infertility is perhaps among the worst social stigmas a woman must endure. Although the biological reasons for infertility are almost equally shared between the sexes,[128] the psychological and social burden of infertility falls heaviest upon the woman, and failure to have children can be seen as a social disgrace or cause for divorce.[129] Having one child does little to improve matters, as the respondent in one social survey explains:

> *If you have only one child, and even if you are well-to-do, nobody will respect you for your wealth, but they will think less of you with only one child.*[130]

Fertility is also important because of the concept of family lineage, which consists of all persons who trace their descent from a common ancestor. Thus the family consists

---

124 As reported by R. Jere-Malanda, *Wife by Abduction*, New Africa, No. 376, 1999.
125 *Id.*
126 *See* Bawah *et al.*, *supra*, n. 51, p. 60.
127 *See* Sangree, *supra*, n. 71, p. 193.
128 Infertility existing in the female with no demonstrable factor in the male occurs in 12.8 % of cases and infertility existing in the male with no demonstrable factor in the female occurs in 7.5 %, as cited in T.M.M. Farley, *The WHO Standardized Investigation of the Infertile Couple*, in S. Shan Ratnam *et al.*, eds., INFERTILITY: MALE AND FEMALE (1986).
129 As reported by M.F. Fathalla, *The Impact of Reproductive Subordination on Women's Health*, The American University Law Review, Vol. 44 (1995), p. 1188.
130 Bawah *et al.*, *supra*, n. 51, p. 60.

of the dead, the living, and the unborn, and women are considered the facilitators of the continuation of the family line.[131]

Women also gain social respect when they become mothers. The attainment of matronhood is necessary for a woman's acceptance as a peer among other young mothers. Those who are not yet mothers must show greater respect for those who are. Grandmothers similarly claim and receive deference from those who are not yet grandparents.[132] Essentially, one must be a grandparent to be a respected elder within the community, for it is only upon reaching this status that elders receive social responsibility and power.[133] Conversely, in some settings, a childless older man is treated with great circumspection because it is feared that envy may motivate him to use sorcery against fertile relatives and neighbours.[134]

4.1 Universal Marriage

Anthropological studies have generally examined marriage as an element of stability and social harmony. Few have studied marriage from a perspective of sexuality and sexual behaviour. Although it is not the only option for sexuality, it remains the pole around which sexual culture is organised and around which society shapes norms on sex and reproduction before, within and after marriage.[135]

Most Africans believe that children are the main reason for marrying and living. The fact that everyone marries (the phenomenon of 'universal marriage') ensures the continuance of the life cycle. Marriage is seen as 'a pact between two families and their wider clans and its ultimate objective is procreation: in short, the continuity of the clan.'[136] Within marriage, fertility is exploited to its fullest as numerous offspring imply a divine blessing to the couple and an insurance policy for old age.[137] Once a woman is married she effectively *belongs* to her new family and clan. Those who do not enter into marriage meet with the disapproval of the entire society.

4.2 Ideal Family Size

Ideal family size reflects the accepted societal norm for the number of children born to a couple. It does not necessarily mirror the actual total fertility rate of that society. This being said, an ideal family size which is low suggests a strong social motivation

---

131 *See* K. Wiredu, *An Akan Perspective of Human Rights*, in A.A. An-Na'im and F.M. Deng, eds., HUMAN RIGHTS IN AFRICA: CROSS-CULTURAL PERSPECTIVES (1990), pp. 243-248.
132 *See* Sangree, *supra*, n. 71, p. 188.
133 *Id.*, p. 192.
134 *See* Edwards, *supra*, n. 61.
135 *See* Caraël, *Sexual Behaviour*, *supra*, n. 104, pp. 75-76.
136 A. Kapinga, *Freedom for African Women?*, The Courier, No. 169 (1998), p. 77.
137 *Id.*

to control fertility.[138] In most countries in sub-Saharan Africa ideal family size remains high, and individuals accordingly face strong social pressures to comply with this ideal. As an example, in a Mozambican survey of ideal family size, most urban women responded that they believed women should have six children, while in rural areas, women believed the ideal to be seven or more.[139] It is interesting and very revealing to note that, despite the fact that all the women in the sample were using contraception, the 'ideal' which they reported was nevertheless very close to Mozambique's total fertility rate of 6.5 children per woman.[140] One researcher has reported on the considerable teasing, even disapprobation, couples endure when they appear to be falling behind the ideal.[141]

5 THE CULTURE OF SILENCE AND SUPERSTITION

Most African societies consider the discussion of sex-related issues to be taboo. Speaking with people about sexuality and sexual matters is very difficult and people feel 'ashamed'.[142] Indeed, sex is rarely discussed even with one's own husband.[143] Although this culture of silence is somewhat more relaxed in urban areas, it remains strong even in this setting.[144]

As may be expected, silence contributes to ignorance among women about their own bodies and reproduction. Such a culture, maintained under the cover of custom and tradition, keeps many of the hardships women suffer secret.[145] Most women have been brought up to suffer quietly and not complain of their discomfort or pain. This would be considered, as Adjetey describes, 'airing one's dirty linen in public.' A woman, therefore, is not likely to discuss rape or genital cutting, for instance, never mind the negative effects these have had on her health. When she does complain of ill-health, her condition is readily retraced to supernatural causes.[146] As related by Koso-Thomas,

> the tendency of the superstitious to blame all illnesses on witchcraft... [leads women] to treating themselves with unproven herbs and sometimes ultimately ruin their health and their chances of survival... Their traditional silence over their own personal welfare is a result

---

138 As reported by S. Amin and C.B. Lloyd, WOMEN'S LIVES AND RAPID FERTILITY DECLINE (1998).
139 Survey reported in Owen, *supra*, n. 38, p. 45.
140 *Id.*
141 *See* Sangree, *supra*, n. 71, p. 194.
142 As reported in Owen, *supra*, n. 38, p. 45
143 *See* Koso-Thomas, *supra*, n. 10, p. 13.
144 *See* Owen, *supra*, n. 38.
145 *See* Adjetey, *supra*, n. 10, p. 1357.
146 *See* Koso-Thomas, *supra*, n. 10, p. 13.

of ignorance about health matters in general, and this has made them unaware of what a feeling of 'wellness' is.[147]

More importantly, this culture of silence plays a considerable role in the continuation of harmful norms and practice, since silence is seen as a sign of acquiescence. The culture of silence which enshrouds rites of passage is iron-clad. Few dare to break the law of silence as they are well aware of the social repercussions which are likely to ensue if they do. For the majority of the people, there is a real fear of the consequences of not conforming to a system controlled by supernatural powers. These consequences, instilled into individuals since childhood, include misfortune, ill-health and death.[148]

Silence, secrecy and superstition typically surround initiation rituals as well. The entire organisation of female circumcision is particularly shrouded in secrecy and mystique. In Guinea-Bissau, for instance, girls must go through initiation rites locally called *Fanado*.[149] All that happens in the *Fanado* school concerning sex is taboo. The circumcised women cannot reveal to others anything about the kind of education they received at the *Fanado*. Those who dare transgress this taboo are exposed to punishments through several mechanisms of social constraint.[150] In Liberia, female circumcision is practiced as an initiation ritual during the attendance of *Sande* or 'bush' school.[151] *Sande* members must not reveal to non-*Sande* members. What they have learned This secret ritual is also common among the Bundu people of Sierra Leone. Bundu girls are forbidden to tell what happens in the secret bush where initiations are conducted and where the girls are circumcised as a group. All girls are sworn to secrecy. As such new initiates have no idea what awaits them and are afraid of the magic powers of the women who conduct the ceremonies. Each girl has to stay in the Bundu bush under the watchful eye of the Bundu chief and her helpers until they heal or die. The death of a daughter in the secret bush, however, is never blamed on the matron or the ritual conducted, but is attributed to evil spirits.[152]

The culture of silence makes it difficult to break existing norms because those who act differently and adopt other values often do so in a clandestine fashion. Thus the existing norms are not openly challenged. This is apparent, for example, in the clandestine use of contraception by women, which is not uncommon throughout sub-Saharan Africa.[153] Women keep these secrets for two reasons; the first is out of fear of reprisals,

---

147 *Id.*
148 *Id.*
149 *See* M. Lima da Costa, *Activity Report of the Union Démocratique des Femmes Guinéennes*, in IAC, REPORT ON THE REGIONAL CONFERENCE, *supra*, n. 30, p. 215.
150 *Id.*
151 *See* Hosken, *supra*, n. 5, p. 82.
152 *Id.*
153 *See*, e.g.: Bawah *et al.*, *supra*, n. 51; Castle *et al.*, *supra*, n. 58; A.E. Biddlecom and B.M. Fapohunda, *Covert Contraceptive Use: Prevalence, Motivations, and Consequences*, Studies in Family Planning, Vol. 29 (1998).

and the second for fear of ridicule. In the first case, the secret use of contraception and family planning services is a major coping strategy used by women to protect their interests and maintain peaceful family relationships.[154] In the second case, women fear embarrassment. As reported by one young woman in Northern Ghana:

> *People from this area feel embarrassed when they know that other people are aware they are using a method. So most of the time, they go secretly to do it, and you would not know. They do this because people laugh at those using family planning methods to prevent pregnancy.*[155]

Superstitions also add to the difficulty of practicing family planning. As another young woman explained:

> *Some women may want to do it but may not feel free to do so because there is the belief among many women that the ancestors are against such practices, and that one may die or may not get any blessing from the ancestors if she practices those things.*[156]

6 COMBINED CUSTOMS CONTRIBUTING TO HIV/AIDS INFECTION

Sexually transmitted diseases (STDs), including HIV/AIDS, highlight some of the most significant socio-cultural norms and practices that contribute to women's reproductive ill-health, particularly those related to unequal power between women and men. Caldwell, a renowned and widely respected scholar on Africa and sexual/reproductive norms, has focused on socio-cultural factors particular to Africa to explain the rapid spread of HIV/AIDS in the continent. His research has led him to conclude that 'the African model is more vulnerable to the spread of the HIV virus than the Eurasian one'.[157] He has noted that, in contrast to Western countries where the population at risk has been generally limited to male homosexuals and drug users, AIDS in Africa is spread more diffusely throughout the heterosexual population. He attributes the high incidence of AIDS in Africa to traditional African marriage systems, which includes weak conjugal bonds, polygyny, and few sanctions on premarital or extramarital sex and pregnancy. These practices considerably increase the risk of infection with HIV and other STDs. The fact that the husband is entitled, by custom, to treat and use his wife as he wishes, and very often neglects to inform his partner that he is HIV-positive, means that little attention is given to the possibility that he might pass on any disease to his wife.[158] Similarly, even when women are informed that they are HIV-

---

154 All cases were reported in Bawah *et al.*, *supra*, n. 51.
155 *Id.*, p. 59.
156 *Id.*
157 Caldwell, DISASTER IN AN ALTERNATIVE CIVILIZATION, *supra*, n. 106, p. 5.
158 *See* Kapinga, *supra*, n. 136.

positive, many choose not to inform their partners, but for a different reason: fear of rejection. This underlines the problem of their self-protection: even if a woman knows that her companion has other sexual partners, it is difficult for her to demand the use of a condom during sex, because her upbringing allows her no say in the matter.[159]

Some scholars have refuted Caldwell's argument that the African socio-cultural model is more conducive to the spread of HIV.[160] However, they are far outnumbered by those who support the theory that the special socio-cultural context of sub-Saharan Africa acts as the feeding ground of the disease. The IAC, for instance, pinpoints male resistance to safer sex practices, women's inability to negotiate safer sex, and the double standard of female monogamy and male infidelity as customs which place women at greater risk of HIV infection.[161] When women attempt to negotiate safer sex practices they are reported to face violence or abandonment, or threats thereof.[162]

As noted earlier, disease '...is never considered to be an accident but always believed to have a supernatural cause'.[163] For instance, when a husband is infected with HIV, it is the wife who is more commonly accused of bringing bad luck upon her family, especially if she is an outsider to the clan.[164]

Lore identifies a number of other practices which contribute to the spread of the virus in Africa. For example, the preference of many men that the vagina be dry for enhanced coital friction causes vaginal abrasions. These wounds, intercourse in polygamous or non-monogamous marriages (where one of the spouses is infected), as well as the sharing of instruments for the circumcision of girls, all contribute to the increased risk of HIV infection for women.[165]

Finally, women are also more likely to receive blood transfusions due to anaemia or childbirth complications. Where there is inadequate screening of blood (as is commonly the case throughout sub-Saharan Africa), the risk of transmission of the HIV virus through blood increases.[166]

---

159 See E.M. Ankrah, *The impact of HIV/AIDS on the family and other significant relationships: the African clan revisited*, AIDS Care, No. 5.
160 See G. Waite, *The politics of disease: The AIDS virus and Africa*, in N. Miller and R.C. Rockwell, eds., AIDS IN AFRICA: THE SOCIAL AND POLICY IMPACT (1988); and D. Brokensha, *Social factors in the transmission and control of AIDS in Africa*, in *id.*
161 IAC, SITUATION OF WOMEN IN AFRICA, *supra*, n. 1, p. 8.
162 *Id.*
163 See Lawson, *supra*, n. 40, p. 396.
164 *Id.*, p. 393.
165 See C.A. Lore, *Women and AIDS: Factors that Put Women at Risk of HIV Infection*, paper prepared for the African Regional Meeting on Reproductive Rights and Population, Nairobi, Kenya (1993), as cited by S. Correa, POPULATION AND REPRODUCTIVE RIGHTS (1994), p. 76.
166 IAC, SIUTATION OF WOMEN IN AFRICA, *supra*, n. 1, p. 8.

7 CONCLUSIONS

Harmful traditional customs and practices are most often deemed acceptable to women and men. Most serve (or are believed to serve) an important purpose, such as helping them and their families meet their practical daily needs, even if these practices may reinforce the subordination of women or deny women reproductive autonomy. A good example is that of early marriage. Parents too poor to care for all their children consider that both they and their daughters positively gain from marrying, even at a very early age: the parents obtain money from the brideprice and the daughters gain security, social status, and a home. The potential harm to the young girl's health is rarely considered. Another example is polygamy. Although this practice increases the risk of STD infection among co-wives, or may place the last wife chosen in a position of subordination within the household, the union enables co-wives to reduce their daily burdens by sharing the tasks of childrearing, household maintenance and farming.[167] These practices, enforced by tradition and maintained by superstition,[168] thus hold a great degree of legitimacy in the communities where they exist.

As is typical in most patriarchal societies throughout the world,[169] African men tend to have power over economic, political and reproductive aspects of life. A woman, on the other hand, is usually expected to be submissive, obedient and respectful of her husband.[170] This is even reflected in some tribal languages. Among the Kasaï, for example, the husband is called the *mfumu*, which translates as 'chief' or 'master'. The practice of brideprice reinforces the notion of servitude by the wife and ownership by the husband.[171] The core value of respect includes obedience to the decisions and desires of male figureheads with regard to women's sexuality and reproduction. Assuming women were convinced of the need for social change, their lower social and economic status reduces their ability to break with traditional norms and customs and behave differently.[172] Even when situations are not stark, a woman's lower status (with attendant lower literacy, lower incomes, economic dependency, reduced land and property rights, reduced access to information on, and treatment of, reproductive ill-health, and reduced ability to leave a bad relationship)[173] leaves her with little option but to accept the *status quo*, including the customs and expectations of the society in which she lives, regardless of the harm they may cause her.

---

167 *See* S. Diagne, *Defending Women's Rights - Facts and Challenges in Francophone Africa*, in J. Kerr, ed., OURS BY RIGHT: WOMEN'S RIGHTS AS HUMAN RIGHTS (1993).
168 *See* Koso-Thomas, *supra*, n. 10, pp. 13-14.
169 *See* K. Bhasin, WHAT IS PATRIARCHY? (1993).
170 *See* African Centre for Women, *supra*, n. 36, p. 5.
171 *See* Kapinga, *supra*, n. 136, p. 77.
172 *See* World Bank, *supra*, n. 37, p. 125.
173 Examples of low status of women listed in *id.*

CHAPTER III
THE RIGHTS IN QUESTION

1 INTRODUCTION

The campaign against harmful traditional practices may be better served if the link between each practice and the violated human right(s) were clearly established. Such an exercise would need to identify how the State is responsible for the violations of rights in the case of harmful traditional practices (including when committed by private persons) in general, and to clarify whether a particular practice necessarily results in a violation of a woman's human rights in every case.

As a first step, the obligations (both 'negative' and 'positive') of States under international law to respect, protect and fulfill the human rights of individuals are highlighted. The specific rights, which may be violated in the practice of each harmful tradition, are then identified. Such identification has been attempted in various UN documents (e.g., in human rights treaties, general comments of treaty bodies, and declaratory documents of UN conferences) as well as scholarly writings. For the most part, however, the relation between a particular practice and the violation of specific human rights has not been well established – often taken for granted or merely implied – or has been asserted without consideration of possible exceptions. However, these same sources stipulate or recommend numerous measures by which States are to eradicate negative norms, attitudes and stereotypes (and thereby the harmful traditional practices resulting therefrom), protect women's human rights and fulfil their obligations. These measures are summarized below according to the rights in question. The issues of consent, gender-based violence, and the gender experience in relation to harmful traditional practices are also considered.

2 SITUATING HARMFUL TRADITIONAL PRACTICES WITHIN THE FRAMEWORK OF INTERNATIONAL HUMAN RIGHTS LAW

2.1 The Obligations of the State in General

Under international law, States are responsible for the acts or omissions of their organs (e.g. law- and policy-making bodies, public medical clinics and schools) and agents (e.g. licensed medical professionals and the State police), even if these were not specifically instructed.¹ The State also may be responsible for acts or omissions of private individuals (third parties) who violate the rights and freedoms of another. This notion is known as *horizontalwirkung* (horizontal effect) or *drittwirkung* (third party effect). The notion of horizontal effect derives from the notion of vertical effect in which a State as duty-holder is bound to respect the rights of human beings who 'fall within' the State's jurisdiction; the State is conceived to be above and the individuals below. According to the vertical effect, the State is held responsible for acts impoted to it. However, international law also holds the State responsible for its omissions. It is these omissions which are likely to have horizontal effects relating to relations between individual human beings. For example, the rights to life and personal security entail considerable obligations on the State to *ensure* (as opposed to *respect*) them by protecting persons against assaults and possible homicide perpetrated by other individuals (i.e. not acting as or for the State). Concretely, the State is obliged to enact criminal legislation, establish a judicial system and place sufficient police protection in the streets. Failure to do so would be an omission which may have the horizontal effect of one private person assaulting or murdering another.² In short, the duties of a State Party arising from the relevant international human rights conventions to *ensure* the rights involved create horizontal effects. This implies that possible or actual interference with any of these rights by one individual against another requires a minimum of action by the State.

The realization of human rights thus depends on States acting with due diligence in respect of their specific obligations (or duties). These duties take the form of either forbearance or performance. Duties of forbearance are typically associated with the 'negative' human rights of individuals, meaning that States are required not to interfere. This is mainly a matter of the State *respecting* the individual's *freedom*. The obligation to respect³ requires the State, including all its organs and agents, to abstain or refrain from doing anything that violates the integrity of the individual or infringes

---

1 For discussion, *see* I. Brownlie, PRINCIPLES OF PUBLIC INTERNATIONAL LAW (1990), pp. 446-454.
2 For more on horizontal effects, *see:* M. Nowak, U.N. COVENANT ON CIVIL AND POLITICAL RIGHTS: CCPR COMMENTARY (1993), p. 412; and P. van Dijk and G.J.H. van Hoof, THEORY AND PRACTICE OF THE EUROPEAN CONVENTION ON HUMAN RIGHTS (1998), pp. 22-26.
3 The nature of obligations also have been summarized as consisting of three types: obligations to respect, to protect and to fulfil. This typology was first advanced by Asbjørn Eide when United Nations Special Rapporteur on the right to food in the mid-late 1980s with respect to social and economic rights and the minimum or 'core' requirements for them to be enjoyed regardless of circumstances. These were further elaborated in the Maastricht Guidelines on Violations of Economic, Social and Cultural Rights. While conceived in the framework of economic, social and cultural rights, the typology has been embraced as describing the nature of obligations arising from all human rights. See: A. Eide, *Realization of Social and Economic Rights and the Minimum Threshold Approach*, Human Rights Law Journal, Vol. 10 (1989), p. 37; T. van Boven *et al.*, eds., *The Maastricht Guidelines on Violations of Economic, Social and Cultural Rights*, SIM SPECIAL, No. 20, 1998, p. 4; and V. Dankwa *et al.*, *Commentary on the Maastricht Guidelines on Violations of Economic, Social and Cultural Rights*, in *id*, pp. 19-21. Definitions of these types of obligations in this study are derived from these sources.

on his or her freedom. For the most part, African States are not actively involved in encouraging, maintaining or enforcing harmful traditional practices. In fact, a good number of them have taken some form of action against such practices, including adopting legislation prohibiting female circumcision and marriage below a set age. Those that have certainly not adopted such prohibitive legislation have not adopted legislation requiring female circumcision or marriage at an early age. Very few have adopted laws or established administrative practices restricting or otherwise interfering with information necessary to ensure reproductive health. In this light, African States generally abstain from doing anything that violates the rights in question and thereby generally *respect* the human rights in question.

Duties of performance, on the other hand, require the State to engage through positive (active) action (hence the term 'positive' rights). Here, the State must take steps (i.e. develop, diffuse, adopt, prevent, furnish, facilitate or otherwise act upon matters) to ensure that individuals can enjoy their human rights and freedoms. The obligation to *protect* human rights requires the State to take measures necessary to prevent other individuals or groups from violating the human rights of individuals. For instance, where the State is directly engaged in health care or in a position to act directly, it should act to protect women's rights, e.g. by properly training traditional birth attendants and informing them of the harmful effects of incisions in a pregnant woman. In carrying out its duties to *protect* the right to health, the State must act to prevent its violation at the hands of an individual,[4] e.g. by stopping an excisor from circumcising girls or any individual from taking certain actions which will cause harm to a woman's health. Although harm to, or the death of, a woman is usually directly caused by the actions of a private individual, the responsibility for the violation of her human rights to health, life, etc., lies in this sense with the State. As one scholar explains:

> If a State facilitates, conditions, accommodates, tolerates, justifies, or excuses private denials of women's rights... the State will bear responsibility. The State will be responsible not directly for the private acts, but for its own lack of diligence to prevent, control, correct, or discipline such private acts through its own executive, legislative or judicial organs.[5]

The line between protection and fulfilment is fine. Indeed, in most cases, protection cannot be achieved without creating the conditions for fulfilment. For instance, the problematic issue of whether a woman's consent to a harmful traditional practice has been falsely or coercively obtained becomes less troublesome if the factors acting as

---

4 This duty is implicitly provided with regard to the right to health. According to the CESCR's General Comment on the Right to Health (*see* Annex A.IV), the State's duty to protect requires that States parties to the relevant human rights treaties take measures to prevent third parties from interfering with the guarantees of the right to health.

5 R.J. Cook, *State Accountability under the Convention on the Elimination of All Forms of Discrimination against Women*, in R. J. Cook, ed., HUMAN RIGHTS OF WOMEN (1994), p. 229.

restraints on consent are reduced or removed. In simple terms, a girl in sub-Saharan Africa cannot be protected fully from forcibly undergoing female circumcision if her status in society is not improved. The full protection can only be guaranteed if the improved and equal status of men and women is achieved. As an analogy, one cannot consider a fire extinguished if the cinders are still burning. With this in mind, it becomes evident that a practice rooted in custom or tradition may be difficult to stop without a change in the attitudes and beliefs of the community where it is widespread. Indeed, this logic stands for *any* practice which is harmful or discriminatory (such as racism, religious intolerance or xenophobia). This logic is clearly visible in international human rights law. The role of the State in changing 'negative' traditional beliefs and practices is framed as a significant obligation to promote human rights in numerous human rights instruments. Some provisions make an explicit call for the abolition of practices harmful to health, whereas others are implicit, calling for the elimination of discrimination, violence, or general customs and practices that bolster harmful traditional practices. Other provisions establish an obligation on the part of the State to delve deeper and tackle the norms, beliefs and behaviours which have given rise to traditional practices harmful to women and maintain their stronghold still today. These provisions call for changes so significant that most other forms of discrimination or prejudices against women should be eliminated concomitantly, including those which bolster harmful traditional practices.

When a State has committed an illegal act or omission, there has been 'injury' to an individual and the State is in breach of duty. Reparations may be required, including 'payment of compensation (or restitution), an apology, the punishment of the individual responsible, the taking of steps to prevent reoccurrence of the breach of duty, and any other forms of satisfaction.'[6] The State has an obligation to provide a remedy for any violation (which implies that it has failed to protect), even if the violation takes place between private persons in the privacy of the home.[7] For example, a woman who has been forcibly circumcised may demand that the State pay her compensation (particularly, but not only, if it has prohibited female circumcision by law) and/or ensure health services and costs to 'uncircumcise' her or deal with the consequences of circumcision. This type of obligation aims to *fulfil* a human right. This requires the State to take measures (be they legislative, administrative, budgetary or judicial) so that each person within its jurisdiction has the opportunity to enjoy his or her rights – to

---

6 Brownlie, *supra*, n. 1, p. 458.
7 The UN Special Rapporteur on violence against women notes 'a State that does not act against crimes of violence against women is as guilty as the perpetrators.' UN, Economic and Social Council, PRELIMINARY REPORT SUBMITTED BY THE SPECIAL RAPPORTEUR ON VIOLENCE AGAINST WOMEN (1994), para. 72. For further discussion on the State's obligation to investigate and punish such violations and a critique of the 'private sphere' argument, refer to the arguments advanced by various authors in R.J. Cook, ed., HUMAN RIGHTS OF WOMEN, *supra*, n. 5, and more generally by A. Clapham, HUMAN RIGHTS IN THE PRIVATE SPHERE (1993).

obtain satisfaction of his or her right-based needs or desires – recognized in the human rights instruments, which cannot be secured by personal efforts. It is required that the State use the maximum of its available resources to this end and that the relevant rights will be progressively realized.[8]

2.2 The Obligations of the State Particular to Harmful Traditional Practices

As noted in Chapter II, there are numerous norms and customs (such as universal marriage, high fertility, brideprice, dowry, son preference, the authority of male family figureheads, the extended-family-household structure, and the culture of silence and superstition) that contribute to, and result from, the poor status of women. However, establishing a direct cause-and-effect relationship between these norms and customs and violations of human rights is difficult, even if one argues that they contribute to the unequal treatment of women or cause discrimination against them. For instance, there is nothing necessarily contrary to a woman's human rights in the way her community treasures boys, encourages marriage and reproduction among all its members, or frowns upon speaking about sexual matters. Even when the association between these traditions and the subordination and disempowerment of women is argued and accepted, there remains another stumbling block: convincing African communities that these traditions represent violations of women's human rights and must be eradicated.

Although these norms and customs are not violations of human rights in and of themselves, this does not imply that human rights discourses are of no interest or use. Rather, the fact that it is the status of these widespread and popular norms and customs that must be changed, rather than individual actions that must be prevented or stopped, implies a need to alter the emphasis and direction of human rights discourses. For instance, it is arguably more straightforward to prevent a person from expressing his racist beliefs than to change the racist beliefs of an entire community. Similarly, it is a rather more simple matter to outlaw under-age marriage but altogether more difficult to alter a community's belief that such a union is bad and must be stopped. Hence, eradicating harmful traditional practices should be seen to require tackling more broadly the beliefs that effectively bolster them. The campaign thus becomes a larger challenge of prevention through changes in attitudes and perceptions. Such changes, it is submitted later in this study, can only be achieved through social, cultural and religious introspection within a community, thus requiring wider participation.

---

8   Regarding the notions of achieving progressively the full realisation of rights and the use of available resources, *see* Eide, *supra*, n. 3, and the Limburg Principles paras. 21-28 with commentary on the scope of these by E.V.O. Dankwa and C. Flinterman, *Commentary by the Rapporteurs on the Nature and Scope of States Parties' Obligations*, Human Rights Quarterly, Vol. 9 (1987), pp. 125-126 and pp. 139-140. *See also* Maastricht Guidelines 9 and 10 in Dankwa *et al.*, *Commentary on the Maastricht Guidelines on Violations of Economic, Social and Cultural Rights*, in T.C. van Boven *et al.*, eds., THE MAASTRICHT GUIDELINES ON VIOLATIONS OF ECONOMIC, SOCIAL AND CULTURAL RIGHTS (1998).

Chapter III

Human rights standards provide both a basis on which to *evaluate* the norms and customs of one's society and to *modify* its socio-cultural behaviours and beliefs which cause or sustain human rights violations. Evaluation may begin with some form of inter- or intra-cultural reflection and airing of concerns. Through this process, the ways in which certain norms and customs contribute to violations of human rights are identified. Changing these norms and customs, however, requires a more proactive approach. Here, the framework is in the language of *obligations on the part of the State* rather than the *rights of individuals*. This is an important difference which reflects the difficulty of the challenge at hand. For instance, the obligation (even if expressly provided) of a State to undertake to modify socio-cultural patterns of conduct between men and women and to counteract practices which sustain the idea of the superiority of one sex[9] is significantly different from, and arguably less substantial than, an express right not to be submitted to patterns of conduct, customs and practices based on the idea of the inferior status of women.[10] In other words, the undertaking is of a softer character than a legal claim. Unfortunately for women in Africa who do not wish to conform to harmful traditional practices, this 'softer', more murky, realm is the realm of the entire discourse.

The texts of the provisions which are particularly relevant to the issue of harmful traditional practices and customs (and the treaties in which they are stipulated) are cited in Table IV. In my view, the most significant of these treaties is the African Charter on Children's Rights[11] because it is specific to the African region, relates only to children and most directly addresses the problem of harmful traditional practices. Provisions in a human rights treaty specific to the Americas (the Inter-American Convention on Violence against Women[12]) are also identified as they demonstrate both that harmful traditional practices are not limited to Africa and that these practices are equally considered contrary to human rights standards in another, clearly non-Western, culture.

---

9 As provided in Art. 5(a) of the Convention on the Elimination of All Forms of Discrimination against Women, and Article 8(b) of the Inter-American Convention on Violence against Women.
10 Indeed, such a right does not, and most likely would never, exist.
11 Full title: African Charter on the Rights and Welfare of the Child, adopted at Addis Ababa, Ethiopia, on 11 July 1990; Organization of African Unity; full text in United Nations, HUMAN RIGHTS, A COMPILATION OF INTERNATIONAL INSTRUMENTS; VOLUME II, REGIONAL INSTRUMENTS (1997), pp. 347-365.
12 Full title: Inter-American Convention on the Prevention, Punishment and Eradication of Violence Against Women, adopted at Belém do Pará, Brasil, on 9 June 1994; Organization of American States treaty A-61; full text at http://www.oas.org/juridico/english/Treaties/a-61.htm [checked on 26 January 2002] and in *id.*, pp. 62-70.

Table IV   Express Treaty Obligations Relevant to the Eradication of Harmful Traditional Practices

	Obligation to eliminate customs and practices harmful to health specifically
African Charter on Children's Rights	States… shall 'take all appropriate measures to eliminate harmful social and cultural practices affecting the welfare, dignity, normal growth and development of the child and in particular: a) those customs and practices prejudicial to the health or life of the child; and b) those customs and practices discriminatory to the child on the grounds of sex or other status' (Article 21.1).
Children's Convention[13]	'States Parties shall take all effective and appropriate measures with a view to abolishing traditional practices prejudicial to the health of children' (Article 24.3).
	Obligation to modify/eliminate customs and practices which implicitly include traditional practices harmful to health
African Charter on Children's Rights	'Child marriage and the betrothal of girls and boys shall be prohibited and effective action, including legislation, shall be taken to specify the minimum age at marriage to be 18 years…' (Article 21.2).
Women's Convention[14]	States Parties shall undertake '[t]o take all appropriate measures, including legislation, to modify or abolish existing laws, regulations, customs and practices which constitute discrimination against women' (Article 2(f)).
Inter-American Convention on Violence against Women	States shall 'take all appropriate measures, including legislative measures, to amend or repeal existing laws and regulations or to modify legal or customary practices which sustain the persistence and tolerance of violence against women' (Article 7(e)).
	Obligation to change socio-cultural behaviour and beliefs which implicitly maintain harmful traditional practices
Women's Convention	'*Aware* that a change in the traditional role of men as well as the role of women in society and in the family is needed to achieve full equality between women and men' (Preamble).
	States Parties shall '… modify the social and cultural patterns of conduct of men and women, with a view to achieving the elimination of prejudices and customary and all other practices which are based on the idea of the inferiority or the superiority of either of the sexes or on stereotyped roles for men and women' (Article 5(a)).

---

13 Full title: Convention on the Rights of the Child, adopted by United Nations General Assembly resolution 44/25 of 20 November 1989; full text in United Nations, HUMAN RIGHTS, A COMPILATION OF INTERNATIONAL INSTRUMENTS; VOLUME I (FIRST PART), UNIVERSAL INSTRUMENTS (1994), pp. 174-195.
14 Full title: Convention on the Elimination of All Forms of Discrimination against Women, adopted by United Nations General Assembly resolution 34/180 of 18 December 1979; full text in *id.*, pp. 150-163.

Chapter III

	States Parties shall ensure '[t]he elimination of any stereotyped concept of the roles of men and women at all levels and in all forms of education by encouraging co-education and other types of education which will help to achieve this aim and, in particular, by the revision of textbooks and school programmes and the adaptation of teaching methods' (Article 10(c)).
Inter-American Convention on Violence against Women	States Parties agree to undertake 'to modify social and cultural patterns of conduct of men and women, including the development of formal and informal educational programs appropriate to every level of the educational process, to counteract prejudices, customs and all other practices which are based on the idea of the inferiority or superiority of either of the sexes or on the stereotyped roles for men and women which legitimize or exacerbate violence against women' (Article 8(b)).

Aside from these 'hard law' (i.e. legally binding) treaty provisions which specify measures to challenge beliefs and behaviours which maintain harmful traditional practices, an abundance of recommendations have been made to States in 'soft law' instruments, including consensus documents.[15] These include, for example:
- CEDAW's General Recommendation No. 14 which recommends, for instance, that States should include in their national health policies the training of specialized health personnel to explain the harmful effects of female circumcision (see Annex A.I);
- CEDAW's General Recommendation No. 19 which recommends States take preventive measures, including public information and education programmes to change attitudes concerning the role and status of men and women (Annex A.II);
- The United Nations Declaration on the Elimination of Violence against Women which suggests developing national plans of action to promote the protection of women against any form of violence (Annex B.IV); or the
- Plan of Action of the Beijing World Conference on Women which suggests, *inter alia*, collecting data and encouraging research on the causes, nature and consequences of violence against women (Annex B.VII).

Most sub-Saharan African States have attained the stage of *respect*. For instance, few, if any, interfere with campaigns to end harmful traditional practice. None have adopted legislation favouring or enforcing harmful traditional practices. A good deal of States have also taken some steps towards *protection*. For instance, numerous States have adopted legislation against harmful traditional practices. Police and medical professionals, as agents of, or licensed by, the State are required to uphold this legislation in the mandate of their professions. All sub-Saharan States, however, are very far from

---

15 In simple terms, 'soft law' refers to the body of instruments (e.g. declarations and resolutions) and documents (e.g. plans of action agreed upon by States through consensus) which do not have the 'hard' (i.e. legally binding) character of the body of law arising from ratifications by States Parties of human rights treaties.

fulfilment. As argued hereabove, this will ultimately require that States actively seek to change attitudes, norms and customs which bolster harmful traditional practice.

3 DETERMINING HUMAN RIGHTS VIOLATIONS BY THE NATURE OF THE PRACTICE

A harmful traditional practice may violate several rights at the same time. This is because, as noted by Cook, '[w]omen's health interests often cross the boundaries that separate one legally described right from another.'[16] The rights *potentially* violated by each of these practices are indicated in Figure II and examined here below. The qualification of 'potential' is necessary as recognition that harmful traditional practices may not automatically or always contribute to the violation of a woman's human rights. Possible exceptions are considered within this section under the rubric of 'grey areas'.

There is no express right to freedom from harmful traditional practices provided in any human rights treaty. Even the human rights treaties specific to children (the only treaties to make express mention of the need to eliminate socio-cultural practices harmful to health and life) frame the issue as a State's obligation to undertake measures rather than as an individual's right to be claimed. The absence of such a specific right makes the tasks of informing individuals of their rights in this regard or formulating claims that harmful traditions constitute a violation of their human rights more complex. Moreover, only the two instruments specific to children's rights obligate the State to change those socio-cultural customs and practices *harmful to health*. As such it is a challenge to bring States to understand that their obligation to change discriminatory attitudes and beliefs as stipulated in numerous provisions (see Table IV) also includes those attitudes and beliefs which maintain and condone harmful traditions. In other words, the causal relationship in the cases of both the rights of the individuals not to be harmed by traditional practices and the obligations of the State to remove this harm may not be immediately evident and may have to be reasoned. Even when reasoned, it may not be convincing. Even if convincing, it still may be discredited as culturally irrelevant.

Given that there is no express right to freedom from harmful traditional practices and that human rights instruments speak more of a State's obligation to ensure individuals the best attainable state health and protect against discrimination in this respect and in a general sense, it is necessary to construct claims that harmful traditional practices violate human rights on the basis of interpretations of one or several rights. Already in the 1970s, practices such as child marriages were condemned as violations of human rights, although, the rights in question were not spelled out (see, e.g., Declaration of Mexico, Annex B.I). In the 1979 Convention on the Elimination of All Forms of Discrimination against Women (hereafter the 'Women's Convention'), it was recognized that changes in traditional male and female roles and attitudes were needed

---

16 R.J. Cook, WOMEN'S HEALTH AND HUMAN RIGHTS (1994), p. 19.

to ensure women the fulfillment of their human rights in general. The importance of attitudinal changes to eliminate inequality was further stressed in the 1980s (see, e.g., Nairobi Forward-Looking Strategies, Annex B.II), although there was still no discussion of harmful traditional practices as a concept nor of the human rights violations such traditions constituted. Some independent commentators, however, were already building up cases against specific harmful traditional practices and in favour of deep social change.[17]

3.1 The Right to Health

General Comment No. 14 on the right to the highest attainable standard of health was adopted by the Committee on Economic, Social and Cultural Rights in May 2000 (see Annex A.IV for relevant text). It lays to rest many queries as to the meaning and scope of this right provided in Article 12 of the International Covenant on Economic, Social and Cultural Rights.[18] In terms of the subject at hand, it recognizes that the right to health includes the right to control one's health and body, including sexual and reproductive freedom, and the right to be free from interference, such as the right to be free from torture or non-consensual medical treatment (para. 8). The Committee has interpreted the right as an inclusive right extending not only to timely and appropriate health care, but also to the underlying determinants of health. Access to information and education on sexual and reproductive health is recognized as one of these determinants (para. 11). A core element of the right is prevention of ill-health. This requires 'the establishment of prevention and education programmes for behaviour-related health concerns such as sexually transmitted diseases, in particular HIV/AIDS, and those adversely affecting sexual and reproductive health, and the promotion of social determinants of good health' (para. 16). As noted earlier, the *prevention* of ill-health and the *promotion* of socio-cultural determinants of good health are two sides of the same coin. As such, socio-cultural factors causing and maintaining ill-health are addressed within the General Comment as obstructions to the full realization of the right to health. The risks to health that certain traditional practices pose and the need to abolish them for these reasons is also acknowledged.

All six harmful traditional practices addressed in this study potentially contribute to violations of the right to health. Female circumcision, early pregnancy, incisions in pregnancy, some traditional birthing practices, and dietary taboos during pregnancy

---

17 *See*, for example: Nawal el-Saadawi's early books: WOMEN AND SEX (1972) and THE HIDDEN FACE OF EVE (1980); J. Nichol's, *The Clitoris Martyr*, World Health, May 1969; and Awa Thiam's BLACK SISTERS, SPEAK OUT: FEMINISM AND OPPRESSION IN BLACK AFRICA (1986) originally written in French under the title LA PAROLE AUX NÉGRESSES (1979).
18 Various interpretations of the scope of the right to health have been advanced. An overview of these interpretations and their controversial aspects is provided by B. Toebes, THE RIGHT TO HEALTH AS A HUMAN RIGHT IN INTERNATIONAL LAW (1999), particularly pp. 16-26.

and lactation all carry the real potential of risk to a woman's reproductive and general well-being. The type of harm to a woman's reproductive health posed by each practice, whether individually or in combination, has been established in Chapter II. The fact that all these harmful traditional practices, by their very definition, threaten a woman's health implies that they (or rather the person and State which causes, assists in, or allows the harm to take place) potentially violate her right to health. In the case of the practice of religious bondage, the violation of the woman's right to health is of a different kind, since she is denied access to health care by her husband, but the effect remains harm done to her health.

Figure II Harmful Traditional Practices and the Rights Violated

	Rights to health and life	Freedom from discrimination	Freedom from violence	Based on: Right to liberty and security; Freedom from cruel, inhuman and degrading treatment; and/or Freedom from slavery	Freedom of thought, belief, opinion and	Right to education	Right to choose one's spouse	Right to found a family
Female circumcision	●	●		●	●			●
Early marriage/ Early pregnancy	●	●			●	●	●	●
Incisions	●				●			
Birthing practices	●				●			
Dietary taboos	●				●			
Religious bondage	●	●			●	●	●	●

3.1.1 The Inseparability of the Rights to Life and Health

A woman's right to life is grouped in this study with her right to health because, although none of the practices aim to endanger the woman's life, egregious harm caused by certain practices can, and sometimes does, result in death. Countless numbers of women have died as a result of unhygienic or unassisted traditional birthing procedures, complications in labour owing to their immature bodies, or from excessive bleeding or infection caused by genital circumcision. The right to life comprises not only life in a biological sense (such as the opportunity to survive) but also in a protective (personal security) sense. Hence, as examples of the first condition, a State which does not make clinics available or accessible to women suffering ill-effects of circumcision may be in breach of its obligations to ensure a woman's right to life in the biological sense. This would also be true for a State which fails to ensure that licensed medical practitioners inform their patients that certain practices (e.g. circumcision, incisions or dietary restrictions) have no medical basis and in fact have deleterious effects on health. More immediately, all midwives, traditional birth attendants, and other medical practitioners of the State must refrain from further performing these practices; in this sense, the State is obliged to refrain from causing (through its agents) such harm. For instance, under all circumstances, the midwife who performs traditional incisions in a pregnant woman (regardless of whether the woman consequently suffered ill-health, lost her foetus, or died) can be held responsible for the harm to, or death of, that woman. The State, in allowing the midwife to practice is ultimately responsible for the violation of this woman's rights to health and life. This is especially so where such professions are licenced by the State, but is also true where the State is simply aware such persons are acting and yet fails to intervene. If the midwife was unaware of the contra-indications potentially arising from such an operation and that such an operation had no medical basis on which to be performed, then the case of violation by the State would be even stronger since it would have failed to perform its duty to provide the midwife the necessary training or ensure that she was competent to carry out her professional functions.

With regard to the second, protective, element of the right to life, a State may be deemed responsible for violating a woman's right to life when it has failed to communicate to its population the risk of HIV infection arising from the sharing of non-sterilized circumcision or birthing instruments (such as razor blades). HIV infection leads to AIDS which hastens death. In this sense, the State would have failed to protect the individual's rights to health and life. Similarly, a State which fails to challenge harmful traditional practices, most notably by addressing the socio-cultural norms and values which maintain them, has failed to protect a woman's right to life. The means by which a State can best address these norms and values in order to eradicate harmful traditional practices and thereby fulfil its international obligations are considered in Chapter VIII.

3.1.2 Grey Areas

The responsibility of the State for the violation of a woman's rights to health and life is not always immediately evident. Let us begin with examples where there is no party which can be held accountable for the harm done. For instance, a woman who adheres to dietary taboos during pregnancy and lactation usually does so of her own accord.

Unlike female circumcision, no one is performing a harmful act on her. It is also very likely that no one is forcing her, or possibly even telling her, that she must abide by these taboos. It is simply a long-standing tradition of the women of her community to avoid certain, all be they nutritious, foods while pregnant or breastfeeding. Superstition stops her from breaking away from this taboo. The same can be said of some traditional birthing practices. There have been numerous reports of women being given information on the dangers of some traditional methods of giving birth and being encouraged to use a midwife, but refusing to do so (see Box II in Chapter VIII). Instead, women opt to keep with tradition, e.g. by giving birth in the barn by themselves or simply with the help of a female relative.[19] In such cases, it may even be that the State has made efforts to inform women of the dangers of certain practices and made safer alternatives available. And yet, these women may independently and without apparent coercion choose to adopt or continue the harmful practice because of its traditional status and their fear or dislike of changing this tradition. This undeniable stronghold or trump card of tradition is, in essence, the real dilemma at hand. A State may legislate against harmful traditional practices. It may instruct medical professionals, or any other individual, not to perform the practices in question. It may engage the police to assist in the eradication effort. It may proceed with information campaigns – possibly with little or no effect on the practices in question. Under these circumstances, the State may have made a genuine effort to fulfil its obligations with regard to the rights to health and life. Its failure in such circumstances, however, merely reinforces the argument that the fundamental obligation (and failure) of the State here must be seen as that of challenging *tradition* itself. In short, the State must, as a priority, seek effectively to challenge socio-cultural norms and customs if it is to ensure women's rights to health and life and thereby fulfil its legal obligations. This, it is submitted in Chapters VII and VIII, can better be achieved by engaging the help of those persons and institutions capable of reformulating traditions in the socio-cultural environments unique to sub-Saharan Africa.

3.2 The Right to Freedom from Discrimination on the Basis of Gender

The State has violated a woman's right to freedom from discrimination if it has not sought to prevent or punish an act between private individuals which has the purpose

---

19   *See*, e.g., P. Allotey, *Where There's No Tradition of Traditional Birth Attendants: Kassena Nankana District, Northern Ghana*, Reproductive Health Matters, Special Issue (1999).

or *effect* of nullifying or impairing equality of treatment.[20] The Women's Convention defines discrimination as:

> ... any distinction, exclusion or restriction made on the basis of sex which has the effect or purpose of impairing or nullifying the recognition, enjoyment or exercise by women, irrespective of their marital status, on a basis of equality of men and women, of human rights and fundamental freedoms in the political, economic, social, cultural, civil or any other field (Article 1).

It is commonly concluded that all traditional practices harmful to women's reproductive health constitute violations of this kind.[21] Two reasons are usually given. First, these harmful practices are targeted solely at women and as such are indicative of an inferior status attributed to them. Second, some practices function to keep women in a state of subordination (as in the cases of female circumcision, early marriage and religious bondage). By these reasons, women are treated in distinctive and sometimes restrictive ways which impair or nullify the enjoyment of various of their human rights.

3.2.1 Grey Areas

It is submitted that the status of the three remaining practices – incisions, traditional birthing practices and dietary taboos in pregnancy and lactation – as violations of a woman's right to freedom from discrimination is not always self-evident. One reason is because of the nebulous cause-and-effect relationship. To be more specific, one must establish how these practices distinguish, exclude or restrict women, and that such distinctions, exclusions or restrictions impair or nullify other rights, such as their right to health. This can certainly be attempted, but is not as evident as is often assumed. Indeed, the link between these particular practices and discrimination is tenuous. A process of simple questioning helps to make the point. For instance, are incisions, which are believed to ease delivery in a first pregnancy, restrictive? Exclusionary? A consequence of the subordinate position of women in African society? Are dietary taboos surrounding pregnancy intended to cause harm to women? And is the manner in which they cause harm sufficiently well and broadly understood? Finally, is the way in which a woman traditionally gives birth in sub-Saharan Africa construed to denigrate women or to place them at physical risk? The lack of action by the State to end these practices is not necessarily motivated or intentional, but it arguably has the effect

---

20 For a general discussion of intent or motive in discrimination, *see* W. Mckean, EQUALITY AND DISCRIMINATION UNDER INTERNATIONAL LAW (1983), pp. 286-287. For a discussion of express and unintended discrimination in government policies, *see* R.A. Sedler, *The Role of 'Intent' in Discrimination Analysis*, in T. Loenen and P.R. Rodrigues, eds., NON-DISCRIMINATION LAW: COMPARATIVE PERSPECTIVES (1999).
21 *See*, e.g.: CEDAW's General Recommendation No. 21 (Annex A.III) and Declaration on Mexico on the Equality of Women (Annex B.I).

of discrimination in that their existence and the social pressures on women to maintain them as traditions leads to the impairment or nullification of their other rights, principally their rights to health and life.

This being said, the fact remains that in all of these practices the crime appears to be more one of ignorance and non-communication (by and between State policy-makers, health professionals, and women themselves) than of discrimination. In fact, vaginal incisions in first pregnancies and dietary taboos are practiced precisely because they are believed (albeit wrongfully so) to be beneficial to the health of mother and child and not as an act of discrimination. Traditional birthing practices are deeply rooted in beliefs and superstitions that childbearing by nature is supposed to be this way. While it can be convincingly argued that these practices carry the risk of physical harm to women (and States knowledgeable of this are ultimately in breach of their obligations), the argument that these also constitute discrimination against women is: a) much more difficult to establish; and b) difficult for Africans to accept (especially since they are effectively carried out in the belief that they protect women). The fundamental impetus behind these three practices is therefore arguably very different from female circumcision, early marriage and religious bondage which are typically carried out to control women's sexuality and maintain women in a subordinate position – all evidencing of an inferior status attributed to women and all strong bases on which to establish discrimination.

3.3 The Right to Freedom from Violence

There is no express right to freedom from violence. Rather, the right to freedom from violence is a composite (constructed) right comprised of several expressly provided rights which act individually or jointly. Specifically, these are the right to liberty and security and the right not to be subjected to torture or cruel, inhuman or degrading treatment or punishment. In certain cases these rights are particularly meshed with the rights to health and life. Cook, for instance, asserts:

> In its widest sense, the right to security is equal to the right to well-being and coincides with the WHO understanding of health. Health contributes to security and security is a major component of health... Insecurity reflects not just a lack of health and resources but vulnerability to become disadvantaged.[22]

In its General Recommendation (No. 19) on Violence against Women, the Committee on the Elimination of All Forms of Violence against Women (hereafter 'CEDAW') recognized gender-based violence as a form of discrimination within the meaning of Article 1 of the Women's Convention (see paragraphs 1 and 6 of the General Recom-

---

22 Cook, WOMEN'S HEALTH AND HUMAN RIGHTS, *supra*, n. 16, p. 29.

mendation in Annex A.II). This form of discrimination is acknowledged in paragraph 7 of the Recommendation to seriously inhibit, impair or nullify a woman's ability to enjoy other rights and freedoms. The 1993 UN Declaration on Violence against Women (see Annex B.IV) follows up on this reasoning. It describes violence against women to be a manifestation of historically unequal power relations between men and women, which has led to domination over and discrimination against women. Violence against women is defined as:

> any act of gender-based violence that results in, or is likely to result in, physical, sexual or psychological harm or suffering to women... whether occurring in public or in private life... Violence against women... encompasses... physical, sexual and psychological violence occurring in the family, including ... female genital mutilation and other traditional practices harmful to women...[23]

In making a blanket reference to 'other traditional practices harmful to women' (a reference repeated in many other relevant documents[24]), the category of harmful traditional practices constituting violence against women is acknowledged to be much broader than female circumcision. Since her preliminary report in 1994,[25] the UN Special Rapporteur on violence against women has been singularly influential in solidifying this approach which I label the 'blanket gender-violence approach' (whereby all harmful traditional practices are claimed to constitute violence against women). Most human rights scholars, reports and UN documents have adopted wholeheartedly this perspective.[26] Few have sought to clarify which other rights, beyond those protecting against violence, may be drawn upon.[27] For instance, the UN Special Rapporteur on traditional practices affecting the health of women and children,[28] the Commission

---

23 Articles 1 and 2.
24 *See*, e.g.: CESCR General Comment No. 14 (Annex A.IV); BDPA (Annex B.VII); and the draft African Declaration on Violence against Women (Annex B.VIII).
25 UN, Economic and Social Council, PRELIMINARY REPORT, *supra*, n. 7.
26 One exception is General Assembly Resolution 52/99 on traditional or customary practices affecting the health of women and girls which briefly notes that '... *certain* traditional or customary practices affecting the health of women and girls constitute a definite form of violence against women and girls and a serious violation of their human rights...' [emphasis added], UN doc. A/RES/52/99.
27 Instead, this task has been left to independent commentators. *See*, e.g.: Cook, WOMEN'S HEALTH AND HUMAN RIGHTS, *supra*, n. 16; L.P. Freedman, *Reflection on Emerging Frameworks of Health and Human Rights*, in J.M. Mann *et al*, eds., HEALTH AND HUMAN RIGHTS: A READER (1999), and some UNFPA publications.
28 The Special Rapporteur on traditional practices affecting the health of women and children has so far made no mention of the violation of any rights, choosing in all her four reports to focus instead on the identification of practices and initiatives for change in all of her four reports. *See* UN documents: E/CN.4/Sub.2/1995/6; E/CN.4/Sub.2/1996/6; E/CN.4/Sub.2/1999/14; and E/CN.4/Sub.2/2000/17. This being said, the Sub-Commission on the Promotion and Protection of Human Rights (to which the Rapporteur, as a Member, reports) has recalled the principle that no one shall be subjected to torture or to cruel, inhuman or degrading treatment or punishment in its four resolutions on traditional practices affecting the health of women and the girl child (resolutions 1997/8, 1998/16, 1999/13 and 2000/10).

of the Status of Women,[29] and the Secretary General's report on the matter[30] have not sought to define the relationship any further. Instead, they and others have accepted the broad definition of the Declaration on the Elimination of Violence against Women and the preliminary associations advanced by the Special Rapporteur on violence against women of harmful traditional practices, violence and freedom from discrimination, and worked from this basis.

A recently drafted regional declaration maintains the focus on harmful traditional practices as forms of gender violence. Indeed, the 1997 draft Addis Ababa [African] Declaration on Violence against Women is deceptive in its title given that it mostly emphasizes harmful traditional practices, and 'female genital mutilation' in particular, rather than violence against women in general. The Declaration was the result of a symposium held at the headquarters of the OAU in Addis Ababa, with the joint participation of IAC and a variety of United Nations agencies (see Annex B.VIII for full text).[31] The declaration remains to be adopted by the OAU.

The UN Special Rapporteur on violence against women has in fact argued, albeit briefly, that harmful traditional practices constitute more than a simple violation of the principle of non-discrimination. She explains:

> Many international legal instruments dealing with human rights include the protection of women from violence in their provisions... Article 3 of the Universal Declaration provides that 'everyone has the right to life, liberty and security of person'. Article 5 provides that 'no one shall be subjected to torture or to cruel, inhuman or degrading treatment or punishment'. The non-discrimination clause, taken together with article 3 and 5, means that any form of violence against women which can be construed as a threat to life, liberty or security of person or which constitute torture or cruel, inhuman or degrading treatment is not in keeping with the Universal Declaration and is therefore a violation of the international obligations of Member States.[32]

---

29 Specific recommendations with regard to traditional and customary practices affecting the health of women and girls were made in the Commission's Agreed Conclusion on Violence against Women, where violence was defined to include harmful traditional practices against women. In its Agreed Conclusion on the Human Rights of Women, customary or traditional practices harmful to, or discriminatory against, women and girls were recognised as violations of human rights of women and girls. Neither Conclusion spells out the link between a particular harmful tradition and the violation of a specific human right. *See* UN, Economic and Social Council, OFFICIAL RECORD OF THE ECONOMIC AND SOCIAL COUNCIL, 1998, Supplement No. 7.

30 The report reaffirms that '... such practices constitute a definite form of violence against women and girls and a serious form of violation of their human rights...' No further specification is offered. UN, General Assembly, TRADITIONAL OR CUSTOMARY PRACTICES AFFECTING THE HEALTH OF WOMEN (1998), para. 2.

31 IAC, SYMPOSIUM FOR LEGISLATORS ON THE DRAFTING OF AN AFRICAN DECLARATION ON VIOLENCE AGAINST WOMEN (1997).

32 UN, Economic and Social Council, PRELIMINARY REPORT, *supra*, n. 7, para. 80.

Chapter III

She further states:

> ... [I]t seems painfully obvious that violence against women manifests itself in its possibly most blatant form through traditional practices affecting the health of women and children. These culturally conditioned practices are not only dangerous to women's health, at times even resulting in their death, but also violate the basic human rights of women and seriously impair their dignity. Through the infliction on them of different forms of physical and mental violence throughout their life span, girls and women are denied their human right to be free and independent, and to live in a secure environment within their families, homes and communities.[33]

These statements by the Special Rapporteur in her reports are so far the best available description of the association between harmful traditional practices and human rights in any document at the international level, with the exception of CEDAW's General Recommendation No. 19 on Violence against Women, which simply lists the 'other relevant rights and freedoms' (see paragraph 7 of the Recommendation in Annex A.II). Notwithstanding the limited nature of the argument, the association of harmful traditional practices with violence against women is repeated in almost every instance of international reporting. While such repetition arguably solidifies the consensus (at least at the international level) against harmful traditional practices – a no doubt positive development, this fails to elaborate in precise terms *why* such (apparently all) practices constitute violations of human rights.

This blanket gender-violence approach has influenced our conception of harmful traditional practices and is the dominant, if not only, human rights discourse on the subject. Most human rights scholars and activists working on the subject of harmful traditional practices have adopted the approach, with a few exceptions. This has accumulated over time into a self-confirming argument in each instance of usage: each global conference, UN resolution and Rapporteur's report, reconfirming the previous assertions of the earlier documents and authors without critical analysis.[34] But, in the absence of clarification concerning the point(s) of violations, it is difficult both to convince the skeptical and to devise practical strategies and programmes to effect changes of behaviour. It also fails to provide or indicate any criteria by which important distinctions might be made among various traditional practices, some of which might not always be harmful or, even if harmful, not in all cases violent or, ultimately, human rights violations.

---

33 UN, Economic and Social Council, PRELIMINARY REPORT, *supra*, n. 7, para. 169.
34 For instance, General Assembly Resolution 52/99 of 12 December 1997 on traditional or customary practices affecting the health of women and girls reads like a paper chase, listing all the UN documents addressing such practices, beginning with the reports of the two Special Rapporteurs. UN, General Assembly, A/RES/52/99, 9 February 1998.

3.3.1 Grey Areas

It is submitted in this study, that only some harmful traditional practices constitute forms of violence against women. Those that do, do so for reasons that are largely self-evident. The most obvious case is that of the forced circumcision of young girls without their consent. The brute force with which an unwilling young initiate of female circumcision is pinned down, and the excruciating pain she endures when a blunt instrument is used to cut her genitalia without any anaesthetic relief is surely violence in its crudest form. The fact that initiates are often unaware that they will be circumcised and have not consented to the operation heightens the element of violence. However, it is much less clear that circumcision sought by an older, informed and consenting woman within a health clinic constitutes violence and such a claim requires establishing one or several matters: a) that she was somehow 'coerced' or 'subjected' (to use the term of Article 5 of the UDHR), an issue discussed under Section 4.4.1 below; b) that her consent reflects a larger level of tolerated and/or fostered societal violence against women; and/or c) that the *intention* behind the practice of female circumcision is itself a form of violence.

Not all 'early marriages' (i.e. where the woman is less than 18 years of age) may be said to constitute violence; not all such marriages are coerced or in any other sense necessarily harmful. More importantly, in many (but not necessarily all) cases of early marriage, girls are coerced by their spouses into having sex and lack the social and physical power to refuse. In these instances of forced intercourse, their rights to freedom from violence can be said to be violated.[35] A girl is given into enslavement to a deity with no possibility of obtaining freedom suffers violations of her rights to liberty and security, to freedom from cruel, inhuman and degrading treatment, and to freedom from slavery. As illustrated in Figure II, these rights together form the core rights of the composite (and non *expressis verbis*) right to freedom from violence. But while the practice of religious bondage constitutes violations of these core rights, it does not *ipso facto* constitute a violation of the right to freedom from violence. The only exception would be if it could be proven that, by the very nature of this practice, a girl would have an increased risk of marital rape. These examples show the importance of differentiating cases and of establishing violation. In particular, the non-differentiation between violence and harm should be critically analyzed, along with the implications of such non-differentiation for the human rights discourse.

---

[35] One may further consult J. Fitzpatrick, *The Use of International Human Rights Norms to Combat Violence against Women*, in R.J. Cook, ed., HUMAN RIGHTS OF WOMEN, *supra*, n. 5.

Chapter III

Let us examine more closely the practice of early marriage. This practice often seriously diminishes a young woman's full development and potential as a human being. It commonly results in a shortened period of education and an early initiation into the burdens of domestic life. Since especially women marry young with consequent effects, it is a clear manifestation of gender discrimination. The element of potential 'harm' enters into the equation when early marriage results in early pregnancy with its attendant physical risks. There is also a potential of psychological harm arising from early marriage in that the young bride may find herself in a low bargaining position within the couple and her extended family, and, thereby, becomes subjugated. But violence does not have a direct correlation with early marriage, beyond the fact that *some* girls may suffer physical abuse or rape by their older, dominant husbands and that such abuse or rape is often socially condoned. With this understanding, to assert that early marriage *equates* violence would be highly contentious among the African populace and invites suspicion of cultural bias in the human rights discourse.

Consider another example – the practice of dietary restrictions (nutritional taboos) in pregnancy, which is recognized as a gender-based form of violence (manifested in a traditional practice), *inter alia*, in CEDAW's General Recommendation No. 19 on Violence against Women and the Special Rapporteur on violence against women's preliminary report.[36] Is this practice truly or always form of *violence*? In fact, there is very little socio-cultural research on why this practice has come to exist and become embedded into the traditions of a community. Yet when reasoned, it is more than likely that this practice – usually involving the restricted consumption of eggs, chicken and other sources of essential protein and iron during pregnancy – arose from something other than an attempt to place women in submission or to cause them harm. More than likely, incidents of food poisoning from these foods caused a myth to be created around their consumption during pregnancy, since the life of a foetus may be threatened by food poisoning. Such a belief, therefore, may have spawned a 'traditional practice.'[37] The example of the Sabini tooth-pulling practice, which evolved from a myth spawned for positive purposes but with negative implications in the longer term, supports this argument. Formerly, the Sabini people of Uganda practiced a traditional custom which involved the removal of two incisor teeth of boys some time around the age of puberty. The ancient practice once served a purpose. In the time before antibiotics and immunization, tetanus and its resultant condition (lock-jaw) were common.

---

36 UN, Economic and Social Council, PRELIMINARY REPORT, *supra*, n. 7, paragraph 166.
37 As another example of food taboos, a popular interpretation of the Jewish faith's decree against the consumption of pork has it that the taboo arose because the pig was considered an unsanitary animal. Religious historians, however, have further argued that individuals had most likely become ill or died from consuming pork. Vilifying the pig as a dirty animal was an easy way to dissuade the Jewish population from consuming pork. The likely truth was, however, that illness or death had resulted from the unhygienic conditions under which the pork had been prepared or stored which resulted in food poisoning. The myth, created to preserve the health of the Jewish people, remains a traditional practice today.

The Sabini discovered they could sometimes save a life by knocking out a few teeth and using the opening to force-feed the patient. Routine tooth-pulling became a preventive measure and then another milestone on a young Sabini boy's road to adulthood. But with the advent of immunization and the spread of information, the practice has all but disappeared.[38] The fact of the matter is that both dietary restrictions and tooth-pulling are traditional practices and may cause harm but they should not be construed as forms of violence. As an analogy, would Westerners consider tonsillectomy, which had become a largely routine preventive surgical practice, a 'harmful traditional practice'?

Another indirect claim conveyed in the blanket gender-violence approach is that only women are the victims of harmful traditional practices. Traditional practices harmful to men, such as the circumcision of men[39] and scarification (performed as a boy's rite of passage among some communities) are very rarely acknowledged in human rights discussions on such practices. The question which naturally follows is whether these practices also constitute forms of violence – violence against men? In failing to recognize that men also undergo harmful traditional practices and suffer violence, we are in fact acting in the very manner we are criticizing: we are discriminating. The response of many feminists against this argument is that, if we place traditional practices harmful to men on par with those harmful to women, we would minimize the systemic and socialized discrimination against women in Africa and elsewhere and its serious effects on their lives. But the two need not be mutually exclusive in the discourse of human rights. The practice of male circumcision among the Xhosa can, and should, be framed as a violation of a man's human rights to health, freedom of belief and liberty and security. This does not diminish the severity and magnitude of the violations which women-specific harmful traditional practices, and the broader discrimination on which they are based, constitute.

3.3.2 Moving Away from the Blanket Gender-Violence Approach

If the above reasoning is accepted, the blanket gender-violence approach should be reconsidered. An alternative campaign against harmful traditions may be better approached from an 'egalitarian' perspective. In this way, for instance, both those practices endured by women and men would be placed under the human rights micro-

---

38 As reported in [no author], *Examining a tradition*, Populi, March 1996, p. 16.
39 For instance, the ritual circumcision of all young men is a traditional rite of passage among the Xhosa-speaking people in South Africa. Young men are required to undergo this ritual before they are allowed to marry, have property rights and attend and speak at gatherings. Much like female circumcision, the ritual is performed by persons without adequate medical knowledge, using crude instruments and under unhygienic conditions. As reported by G. Meintjes, *Challenge to Tradition: Medical Complications of Traditional Xhosa Circumcision*, Indicator, Vol. 15 (1998).

scope for evaluation.⁴⁰ Indeed, the egalitarian approach might better serve most human rights campaigns on most subjects. There are reasons, however, why the egalitarian approach is particularly suited to the sub-Saharan context. These are cultural sensitivity and effective strategy. In addressing harmful traditional practices from a broad perspective of gender discrimination and violence, an entire social system is condemned with African men (including spiritual, community and political leaders) marked as the oppressors of women and advocates of harmful traditional practices. Such an approach has numerous faults, starting with some incorrect premises. Aside from all harmful traditions being incorrectly thrown into the basket of violence, research has shown that women are equally, and in some cases more forcefully the defenders of these harmful traditions.⁴¹ The response by some feminists to this fact is that these women are victims – unaware of the extent to which – they have been socialized into accepting gender violence as the norm and are (as agents of men) presumably acting on the basis of a sub-consciously imbedded threat against them too.⁴² The proliferation of African feminist thought has responded in various ways to this counter-statement. While some accept the argument, others take offense at 'Western' feminists and human rights campaigners, arguing that they do not need to be rescued by those applying theoretical paradigms foreign to African society; as remarked by one such commentator, '... we are not collectively sitting about in bondage waiting for other people to lift our veils or keep the knives away from between our legs.'⁴³

3.3.3 A Word on 'Global' Ideologies on Gender and Feminism

Engaging in a discourse on feminism in Africa has its challenges and pitfalls.⁴⁴ To illustrate this, one commentator observes with regard to Kenya that the country '... is caught up in a war against the demands of women spirited through feminism. While change in gender relations is inevitable with time, the feminist project in Kenya is up

---

40 Howard, for instance, warns of the threat to the liberal notion of the universality of human rights, social democracy and the community if rights abuses suffered by men as well are presumed to be endured only by women; R.E. Howard, *Women's Rights, Group Rights and the Erosion of Liberalism*, in C. Levitt *et al.*, eds., MISTAKEN IDENTITIES (1999), p. 136.
41 Refer to the summary of female circumcision in Chapter II.
42 Support for this position draws on a very broad notion of violence. It may be noted that the Special Rapporteur on violence against women also uses a broad definition, as follows:
Violence against women is defined in the Declaration as including, but not being limited to, physical, sexual and psychological violence that occurs in the family... The definition ... appears, therefore, to be a broad one whereby violence is not strictly construed as meaning only the actual use of physical force, but implies the right to inquire against all forms of action which disempower women because of the fear of violence, whether the fear is instilled by the state, actors in the community or member of the family.
UN, Economic and Social Council, PRELIMINARY REPORT, *supra*, n. 7, para. 98.
43 A.P.A. Busia, *Foreword*, in Center for Women's Global Leadership, GENDER VIOLENCE AND WOMEN'S HUMAN RIGHTS IN AFRICA (1994), p. iv.
44 The term 'feminism' used here refers to that branch of knowledge that identifies the systematic discrimination against women on grounds of gender and the subsequent commitment to changing that reality.

against very tough opposition nurtured through masculinity...'[45] One problem, she notes, is that 'instead of substantiating to the general population the central purpose of feminist ideology that seeks to establish gender equity, many of the leaders of Kenya's women's organisations have tended to present feminism as an 'anti-men' project.'[46] This hardly creates enthusiasm among men who are expected to change behaviour. Consequently, knowledge that meetings may be discussing women's legal rights and mixing in the political arena women's lived and emotional anxieties tends to make opposition worse.[47] Another risk is that concerns labeled as 'women's issues' are trivialized and set apart from the 'real' issues of men's concerns and politics.[48]

Feminist theorizing in Africa is finding its own feet, formulating its own framework of understanding and concepts that have evolved from the experiences of African women. A good deal of space within African feminist literature is spent precisely on emphasizing that African women are 'not simply waiting to be rescued by outside feminists and practitioners.'[49] The literature illustrates that African women, now and throughout history, have developed their own analyses and strategies for action to take control of their lives in those areas that *they* have collectively determined to need redress.[50] While it is admitted that women around the world essentially suffer the same subordination for the same reasons, the assumed authority and universal validity of the theoretical paradigms from the West in the face of other systems of thought, social constructions, modes of practice, negotiations and lived experiences angers African women, which see this feminist praxis as another form of neo-colonialism, despite all of its good intentions.[51] Halim highlights the negative repercussions of global feminist assumptions and actions:

> African women sometimes feel racism in the way their problems are tackled in the west. Most of the time they feel betrayed because what western women, and even some of their African sisters, have decided is African women's number one issue is not exactly a priority in their lives.[52]

The time is therefore very much ripe for Western aid establishments and Western feminist organisations to 'be guided in their activities in Africa by requests for assis-

---

45 M.G. Ntarangwi, *Feminism and Masculinity in an African Capitalist Context: The Case of Kenya*, SAFERE *(South African Feminist Review)*, Vol. 3 (1998), p. 19.
46 *Id.*, pp. 26-27.
47 See F. Butegwa, *Challenges of Promoting Legal Literacy Among Women in Uganda*, in Margaret Schuler and Sakuntala Kadirgamar-Rajasingham, eds., LEGAL LITERACY: A TOOL FOR WOMEN'S EMPOWERMENT (1992), p. 151.
48 *See* Ntarangwi, *supra*, n. 45, p. 26.
49 Busia, *supra*, n. 43, p. iii.
50 *Id.*
51 *Id.*, p. iv.
52 A.M.A. Halim, *Tools of Suppression*, in Center for Women's Global Leadership, GENDER VIOLENCE, *supra*, n. 43, p. 29.

tance made by African actors themselves, oriented to projects that African women deem to be a priority.'[53] Whether the projects address violence against women, discrimination against women or women's health, in terms and priorities established by them, must be left for African women to decide.

African feminist theorizing has arisen partly because of rapidly evolving political, economic and cultural awareness and capabilities within the developing world, and their ability to envision and move towards a future which is not merely an imitation of the present in the West.[54] African literature and feminist theory shows how issues in feminism, such as victimhood, agency, sisterhood, etc., are recast in different, complex and interesting ways, particularly in works by African women writers. Nnaemeka, an expert on African feminism and literature, emphasizes 'the importance of cultural literacy to any valid feminist theorizing,'[55] confirming the necessary relation between the cultural environment and our expressions and understanding of feminism and its fundamental assumptions.

On this basis, some African literature on feminism expressly rejects the fundamental assumptions of Western theories on gender. For instance, the idea that gender is socially constructed (and thus that differences between men and women are to be located in social practices rather than in biological facts) is a cornerstone of Western feminist scholarship. The notion is particularly attractive because it has been interpreted to mean that gender differences are not ordained by nature, and thus are changeable. At the same time, another fundamental assumption of feminist theory has been that women's subordination is universal. The African feminist theorist Oyewumi, however, takes issue with these assumptions:

> The universality attributed to gender asymmetry suggests a biological basis rather than a cultural one, given that the human anatomy is universal whereas cultures speak in myriad voices... [T]he categorization of women in feminist discourses as a homogenous, bio-anatomically determined group which is always constituted as powerless and victimized does not reflect the fact that gender relations are social relations and, therefore, historically grounded and culturally bound. If gender is socially constructed, then gender cannot behave in the same way across time and space. If gender is a social construction, then we must examine the various cultural/architectural sites where it was constructed, and we must acknowledge that variously located actors (aggregates, groups, interested parties) were part of the construction.[56]

---

53 R.E. Howard, *Women's Rights and the Right to Development*, in R. Cohen *et al.*, eds., HUMAN RIGHTS AND GOVERNANCE IN AFRICA (1993), p. 133.
54 *See* J. Dator, *Loose Connections: A Vision of a Transformational Society*, in E. Masini, ed., VISIONS OF DESIRABLE SOCIETIES (1983), p. 44.
55 O. Nnaemeka, *Introduction: Imag(in)ing Knowledge, Power, and Subversion in the Margins*, in O. Nnaemeka, ed., THE POLITICS OF (M)OTHERING (1997), p. 7.
56 O. Oyewumi, THE INVENTION OF WOMEN: MAKING AN AFRICAN SENSE OF WESTERN GENDER DISCOURSES (1997), p. 10.

From a cross-cultural perspective, the significance of this observation is that one cannot assume the social organisation of one culture (the dominant West) as universal or the interpretations of the experiences of one culture as applicable to another. This puts in doubt the exportability of Western conceptual categories to other cultures that have a different cultural logic.[57] Oyewumi concludes that the potential value of Western feminist social contructionism is relatively little and recommends that we refrain from using the Western gender framework on non-Western cultures and projecting it as 'universal.'[58] As a final attack on the false notion of 'global' feminism, Oyewumi observes that '[t]hough feminism in origin, by definition, and by practice is a universalizing discourse, the concerns and questions that have informed it are Western (and its audience too is apparently assumed to be composed of just Westerners).'[59] As such, feminism, despite its radical stance, 'exhibits the same ethnocentric and imperialistic characteristics of the Western discourses it sought to subvert. This has placed serious limitations on its applicability outside of the culture that produced it.'[60] The well-known feminist theorist Nancy Chodorow is similarly concerned by the focus on sexual difference in Western feminist theory:

> For our part as feminists, even as we want to eliminate gender inequality, hierarchy, and difference, we expect to find such features in most social settings... We have begun from the assumption that gender is always a salient feature of social life, and we do not have theoretical approaches that emphasize sex similarities over differences.[61]

Consequently, the assumption and deployment of patriarchy and gender as universal elements in most feminist scholarship risks being seen as ethnocentric and a demonstration of the hegemony of the West over other cultural groupings,[62] as though to say that Western experiences define the human. Higgins strikes at the heart of the problem noting that, while the central commitment of feminist project is the respect for difference, it imposes a Western concept of equality and thereby imposes standards in much the same was that feminists have criticized States for imposing male-defined norms on women.[63]

In sum, the approach which the current international human rights campaign against traditional practices has generally embarked upon may be construed as culturally paternalistic and strongly antagonistic, fueling a largely unsought and unsupported battle of the sexes in Africa. While this approach may work in some contexts

---

57 *Id.*, pp. 10-11.
58 *Id.*
59 *Id.*, p. 13.
60 *Id.*
61 N. Chodorow, FEMINISM AND PSYCHOANALYTIC THEORY (1989), as cited in *id.*, p. 15.
62 *Id.*
63 T. Higgins, *Anti-Essentialism, Relativism, and Human Rights*, Harvard Women's Law Journal, Vol. 19 (1996), pp. 89ff.

with regard to other issues, it is questionable whether it can be successful in the African setting where women not only do not have access to traditional systems of power and, thereby, lack the means to push through change (see Chapter VI.5 for related discussion), but also may conceive their experience and condition as women differently from that suggested by the 'global' feminist project. This observation invites interested scholars and advocates at the international level to reflect upon the validity and, thus, effectiveness of their discourses in Africa.

3.4 The Rights to Freedom of Thought, Belief, Opinion and Expression

The United Nations Human Rights Committee's General Comment No. 22 on Article 18 of the International Covenant on Civil and Political Rights (CCPR)[64] elaborates the scope of the right to freedom of thought, conscience and religion (which includes the freedom to hold beliefs).[65] It specifically recognizes in paragraph 4 that '[t]he observance and practice of religion or belief may include not only ceremonial acts but also such customs as the observance of dietary regulations … [and] participation in rituals associated with certain stages of life.' However, it similarly recognizes in paragraph 9 that a religion or belief '… shall not result in any impairment of the enjoyment of the rights under the Covenant.' This reinforces Article 5.4 of the 1981 United Nations Declaration on the Elimination of All Forms of Intolerance and of Discrimination Based on Religion or Belief which stipulates that '[p]ractices of a religion or belief in which a child is brought up must not be injurious to his physical or mental health or his full development'.[66] In light of these provisions it is evident that the invocation of religious justification does not excuse or give reason to tolerate harmful traditional practices. The rights to freedom of thought, belief, opinion and expression further guarantee that African women must be able to form their own views on the practices in question, be able to express these views and acting on them, whether or not such views or action runs counter to religious tenets or customs.[67]

Inextricably linked to the rights to freedom of thought, conscience, religious belief, opinion and expression is the right to seek and obtain information, since it is through information that one begins to formulate an opinion of one's own. It has been noted earlier that a culture of silence permeates much of sub-Saharan Africa with regard to anything related to sex and reproduction. This makes it difficult for individuals to

---

64 UN doc. CCPR/C/21/Rev.1/Add.4 (1993), reprinted in Human Rights Law Journal, Vol. 15, pp. 233ff, 1994.
65 For a discussion on these and the other paragraphs of this General Comment, *see* B.G. Tahzib, FREEDOM OF RELIGION OR BELIEF: ENSURING INTERANTIONAL LEGAL PROTECTION (1995), pp. 307-370.
66 G.A. Res. 36/55 of 25 November 1981, UN GAOR, 36th Session, reprinted in International Legal Materials, Vol. 21, 1982, pp. 205ff.
67 For a specific discussion in relation to female circumcision, *see* B.G. Tahzib-Lie, *Dissenting Women, Religion or Belief, and the State: Contemporary Challenges that Require Attention*, in T. Lindholm *et al.*, eds., FACILITATING FREEDOM OF RELIGION OR BELIEF: A DESKBOOK (2002).

speak out against a tradition, never mind act outside of it. And yet these rights must be protected and promoted if women are to give valid consent to undergo female circumcision, have incisions made in their genitalia during pregnancy, or are to marry at an early age. The basic elements required of consent are:

1. being informed of both the benefits and the harms of a practice;
2. consequently being able to form and hold a *belief* or formulate an *opinion* on the practice and express it, even if it is contrary to the belief or opinion held by one's community or religion;
3. eventually *expressing* one's consent or non-consent to the practice;
4. giving this consent without undue influence or coercion; and
5. being able to act accordingly.

This thorny issue of consent merits further elaboration.

3.4.1 Grey Areas

If we placed the concept of free and informed consent in a sterile social and cultural environment it would be relatively easy to establish whether a woman has
- been given all the necessary information concerning a practice (such as the reasons why it is considered important and the possible consequences of the practice on her reproductive health);
- been informed that she has the ability to choose whether she will undergo the practice or not; and
- agreed or disagreed to undergo the practice.

Yet for most African women, social prescriptions and cultural norms work against free and informed consent. Women often lack the necessary information to make a considered choice and the power (including information) to act outside of the tradition. Moreover, there is no social safety net on which to fall back should they choose to break with tradition. In such a socio-cultural setting, it is possible that consent, even if it is given, is obtained under duress.[68] The question which ensues is, if it is evident that a woman's 'consent' to undergo a practice is not wholly free and informed, have her human rights necessarily been violated?

In the case of female circumcision, most activists and scholars firmly assert that the 'issue of consent' does not mask the element of violence. Where women submit to genital mutilation, they argue, the same human rights issues as those involved in

---

68 In fact, no individual in any society is completely 'free' in his or her consent since we all live within a social, cultural, religious and economic environment which will influence our consent on different matters to some degree.

domestic violence against women arise.[69] For instance, it is commonly argued and accepted that these women are dependent on their batterers and can therefore hardly be said to be able to act freely according to their own wishes. The same arguments of deep-rooted societal violence against women are given with respect to religious bondage or early marriage. Others, particularly African women, believe such an unequivocal position to be wrong. They posit, for instance, that a good number of African women make a cognizant and independent decision, even as adults, to have themselves circumcised. While admitting that they do so because it is a tradition within their community, they scoff at any suggestion that they are being *pressured* and they reject that there is any violation of their human rights. Under these circumstances, African female circumcision, some argue, is not dissimilar to breast augmentation procedures in the West which are never scrutinized for consent or asserted to be violation of a woman's human rights. Others conclude that where consent has been given freely and is informed, the practice should be considered to be in conformity with human rights and women should be allowed to undergo the procedure and not incur any penalties.[70]

Although the majority of women tacitly consent to these practices, the reality remains that their option *not* to consent is essentially non-existent. This is particularly true in the case of female children. For instance, the ability of a young girl to refuse her parents' choice of husband or their decision that she undergo circumcision is often fictive. Culturally, they lack the power to decide and demand otherwise. If they do insist otherwise, domestic violence or ostracism may result. They have few, if any, meaningful alternatives to, or escape from, such sever results.

The role and rights of parents, and their ability to act on behalf of their daughters (as so-called minors under the protection and welfare of their parents), are especially relevant in such situations. In this relation, children-specific human rights instruments advance two conflicting concepts: the right of parents to act in the best interests of their child; and the child's right to decide matters independently according to her evolving capacities. The two are never easy to combine or reconcile, but particularly so with regard to practices embedded in tradition. Where these practices are common and non-conformity severely socially penalized, most parents believe that, in having their daughters marry early or circumcised according to tradition, they are acting in their daughter's best interests. The girl's ability to reflect on these interests, much less give consent, is not a matter of concern for her parents, and her capacity to appreciate fully the consequences of non-conformity may arguably not be sufficiently evolved. Ironically, this results in a situation where a girl is considered mature enough to marry, but not mature enough to formulate an opinion and act independently, including in a

---

69 *See*, e.g., Fitzpatrick, *supra*, n. 35, p. 541.
70 As suggested in CRLP, FEMALE GENITAL MUTILATION: A MATTER OF HUMAN RIGHTS (1995), p. 30.

manner which carries less risk to her own reproductive health.[71] Even if provided the opportunity to give her consent, her dependence on her family and her socio-cultural milieu place enormous constraints on her ability to act otherwise. In such a situation of limited real choices, fully informed and (relatively) free consent may well result in the perpetuation of the practice(s). This appear to be the African reality.

Regardless of the rights of parents to decide matters of their child's upbringing, international human rights law clearly places a duty on the State to ensure that the best interests and well-being of the child remain the primary consideration.[72] The 1990 African Charter on the Rights and Welfare of the Child is even more resolute providing in its first article that '[a]ny custom, tradition, cultural or religious practice that is inconsistent with the rights... in the present Charter shall... be discouraged'. Hence, regardless of parental wishes and rights, the well-being and rights of the child should prevail in the event of conflict. Bearing these provisions in mind, recognition of a girl's evolved capacities and her right to health could and should be better considered and advocated within a campaign against harmful traditional practices, taking into account and formulated with regard to the whole African socio-cultural context.

3.5 The Right to Education

In general, the expectation and unspoken rule in much of sub-Saharan Africa is that young women who marry and young women who become pregnant out of wedlock while in school will not carry on their education. In the first case, the young bride will be expected to take on her new duties as wife immediately following marriage. Her schooling therefore must end and, indeed, is usually considered unnecessary for fulfilling her new duties as wife and homemaker. The widespread practice of early marriage means that many girls have to stop their education at a young age regardless of their wishes. In the second case, girls who become pregnant out of wedlock must terminate their schooling. These girls are often labeled a prostitute and a bad example to the other pupils. Commonly, they are greatly shamed and find themselves incapable of caring for a baby while attending school, both factors leading them to choose to drop out of school. Hence, formal expulsion is often not needed. These firm societal expectations obstruct a young girl's right to pursue education and thereby contribute to violation of the right to it. Education being important for the digestion of information, the development of independent thought and the formulation of opinions, violations of the right to education are arguably related to other violations of rights which

---

71 For more discussion on the conflict between the two concepts with regard to adolescent pregnancy, *see* C. Packer, *Preventing adolescent pregnancy: the protection offered by international human rights law*, International Journal of Children's Rights, Vol. 5 (1997).
72 Article 3 of the 1989 Convention on the Rights of the Child and Article 4 of the 1990 African Charter on the Rights and Welfare of the Child.

depend upon informed consent. This may be true with regard to issues of harmful traditional practices.

3.6 The Right to Choose One's Spouse

Early marriage and religious bondage have been identified in Figure I as constituting violations of a woman's right to choose her spouse. Because the very practice of religious bondage entails that a girl is handed over to a spiritual man (otherwise known as a deity) as penitence for the sins of a male within her family, a girl is *ipso facto* not able to exercise choice over marriage. The denial of her right to choose freely her spouse (if any) is therefore evident, particularly where the man chosen for her is specifically against her will.

3.7 The Right to Found a Family

It is the right in its negative form, i.e. the right *not* to found a family, which is more likely to apply in the case of harmful traditional practices. The United Nations Human Rights Committee, in its authoritative interpretation of the right to found a family (General Comment No. 19 of 1990), has interpreted the right to imply that individuals, with the exception of special circumstances such as mental disability, shall have the freedom to start a family without coercion or restriction.[73] But this does not imply an *obligation* to establish a family.[74] Rather, the right merely infers that individuals must not be coerced or forced to establish a family. Persons should be free to choose if and when to start a family (i.e. to initiate, delay or forego childbearing), and neither the State nor another individual may interfere with this choice. Coercive pro-natalist population policies are commonly condemned on this basis as contrary to international human rights law.[75] The same can be argued in the case of traditional practices which coerce women into establishing a family. Specifically, the harmful traditional practices which may violate a woman's right to found a family are:
- female circumcision, insofar as some forms control a woman's ability to have children until a specific time[76] – usually beginning from the night of nuptuals. The control is imposed even after the first birth since once she has given birth she may

---

73 For the text of General Comment No. 19, *see* UN doc. HRI/GEN/1/Rev.3 of 15 August 1997 at pp. 29-31; General Comment No. 19 addresses Article 23 of the ICCPR concerning the family and marriage with para. 2 stipulating the right to found a family and para. 3 stipulating the right to marry on the basis of 'the free and full consent of the intending spouses.' For more discussion on the right to found a family and especially its relation to reproductive health and rights, *see* C. Packer, THE RIGHT TO REPRODUCTIVE CHOICE (1996), pp. 43-54.
74 *See* Packer, *id.*, pp. 88-91.
75 For more discussion, *see*: *id.*, pp. 98-101; and K. Tomaševski, HUMAN RIGHTS IN POPULATION POLICIES (1994), pp. 25-32.
76 Particularly the infibulation form where the labia majora is stitched closed.

be recircumcised until the post-partum period has passed and the husband desires engaging once again in sexual relations. The cycle may continue;[77]
- early marriage, as customs in communities which practice early marriage usually encourage the marriage to be immediately followed by pregnancy; and
- religious bondage, as young girls are sexually enslaved to the deity and are typically without access to contraception.

It should also be noted that the option of obtaining an abortion is not available in much of sub-Saharan Africa either because it is illegal or not accessible. Thus, even if a young woman wished to end her pregnancy she would rarely be able to do so in a safe manner.

4 CONCLUSIONS

The problem of consent to harmful traditional practices in sub-Saharan Africa illustrates that the challenge of State action to change deep-seated norms, values and beliefs must be understood in context and fully appreciated. The conclusions of various treaty monitoring bodies, and international programmes and plans of action, much like the provisions in some human rights treaties, indicate this as an obligation to be undertaken seriously by the State. They also suggest ways in which to achieve change. Some are concrete and targeted (e.g. using role models in popular media to encourage delayed pregnancy, proper nutrition in pregnancy, or organizing co-education classes). Others are much more general, suggesting improved and longer education for women and empowering of women, e.g. by increasing their numbers in political organs. The limitations of some of these measures in light of the socio-cultural context of sub-Saharan Africa are considered in Chapter VI.

It has been submitted that some practices are unquestionable manifestations of gender violence. Others, however, may result in harm to a woman's health, but do not inherently represent forms of violence and are not solely targeted at women whether and to what extent a particular traditional practice constitutes a violation of a specific human right is to be established in each case. This is a matter of careful and sensitive application of international standards according to established international norms of interpretation. In terms of discourse, however, the matter is more complex. Of concern is this regard is the blanket gender-violence approach which has informed the entire campaign against harmful traditional practices throughout the 1990s until now and has been intertwined with Western-led feminist ideologies (often associated with 'radical' discourses). As a result, the campaign against harmful traditional practices has been less than effective, not because it has failed to be picked up and supported within

---

77 While a large majority of women would not seek to establish a family out of wedlock in sub-Saharan Africa, the timing of one's first pregnancy should not be controlled by another individual or the State. Women who seek to be defibulated prior to marriage are often denied the procedure and are treated with disdain.

Chapter III

Africa, but because the premises on which it has been actively advanced (discrimination, violence, and gender/feminism) appear to have failed to resonate for socio-cultural reasons and, moreover, because the premises have met with some basic challenges. However, this does not mean that human rights discourses are in general inappropriate or ineffective for the elimination of harmful traditional practices. Rather, it implies that harmful traditional practices, customs and norms must be better understood by human rights advocates and that the human rights they are deemed to violate (or more specifically *how* specific human rights are violated) must be better established. In completing this exercise the need to reorient our human rights discourse and approach on these issues will become more evident.

CHAPTER IV
THE THEORETICAL VALUE OF
THE HUMAN RIGHTS APPROACH

1 INTRODUCTION

It is perhaps necessary to affirm from the start that traditional practices which negatively affect reproductive health cannot realistically be altered by reference to human rights *alone*. What is somewhat more contested, or at least less apparent, is whether these negative affects can be altered *at all* by reference to human rights. Indeed, for a non-lawyer or non-human rights activist, human rights may well not be the most apparent source for a solution to end harmful traditional practices in sub-Saharan Africa. The health practitioner would likely turn to medical ethics and make appeals to his/her patients and community of care. A practitioner who is particularly active may even seek to influence State policy or legislation relating to harmful traditional practices. Local women's groups or NGOs working on development projects may think it best to address harmful practices through their general strategies to improve the overall well-being (health and development) of a community.

In fact, we have witnessed in recent years a growing number of professions and disciplines expand their traditional perspectives and embrace human rights discourses as an additional source of inspiration and tool for challenging harmful practices within their domains. This development suggests that the framework of human rights is considered flexible and accommodating enough that it can be applied not only across cultures but also across professions and disciplines,[1] and not only within the traditional

---

[1] The examples of the cross-disciplinary use of human rights discourses in this domain are too many to mention. However, among the health professions at the global level, the WHO's adoption of a health and human rights approach is indicative of this trend, while in Africa the work of Dr. Irene Thomas within the framework of the pan-African NGO Inter-African Committee on Traditional Practices Affecting the Health of Women and Children stands out. Fran Hosken, who worked in urbanisation and housing projects in Africa, also turned to human rights to assist her in her work against female circumcision (*see* note 7 below).

Chapter IV

constraints of mandated humanitarian[2] and development efforts but more broadly.[3] This 'cross-polination' is also evident within the work of NGOs whose traditional mandates would certainly include human rights but would not normally extend to the issue of harmful traditional practices.[4] The trend also suggests a strategic evaluation by these and other actors that international human rights standards provide a universal legal framework which speaks in terms applicable to all and which confirms the legitimacy of their aims. Hence, the doctor is not only arguing against pre-natal incisions for health reasons, but because such incisions are contrary to the female patients' human rights to health, to dignity and to freedom from violence. Similarly, the director of a gender-based development NGO is not only advocating against early marriage because it reinforces the cycle of poverty and reduces a girl's lifetime opportunities, but because it contributes to violations of her rights to education, health and dignity. To this extent, the 'rights' argument strengthens the 'health' and 'welfare' arguments. Thus, from the perspective of those invoking human rights, the discourses may strengthen the legitimacy of their work and make their recommendations more compelling.[5] From the subjects' perspective, human rights discourses may legitimise their concerns and 'empower' them.[6]

Ultimately, if we expect – or if most of our hopes lie in – human rights discourses and law to help prompt changes in harmful traditional practices, it is worthy asking how this is to be achieved in theory and in practice within the social, cultural, religious, political and economic realities of sub-Saharan Africa. Prior to analysing the practical utility and effectiveness of human rights law and discourses to bring about changes in traditional practices affecting women in sub-Saharan Africa (Chapter VI), it is impor-

---

2   E.g., the United Nations High Commissioner for Refugees (UNHCR) has stepped beyond its traditional framework of refugee law and mandate of refugee protection to advocate against some harmful practices under the framework of international human rights law: *see* UNHCR, SEXUAL VIOLENCE AGAINST REFUGEES (1995); and UNHCR, HANDBOOK ON REPRODUCTIVE HEALTH IN REFUGEE SITUATIONS (1996).
3   For instance, almost all gender-based projects, ranging from micro-income generation for women to women in conflict resolution, now incorporate a component of training in human rights for their constituents.
4   Amnesty International, for instance, which has long dealt with torture in the traditional understanding (i.e. in terms of State-sponsored violations of civil rights) addressed both early marriage and female circumcision in its 2001 report *Broken Bodies, Shattered Minds: The Torture of Women Worldwide*. Minority Rights Group International has also taken a step beyond traditional human rights interpretations, addressing female circumcision as a minority rights issue since 1990 and producing a 42-page report on the practice FEMALE GENITAL MUTILATION: PROPOSALS FOR CHANGE (1996).
5   Those of a more pessimistic nature might argue that many NGOs and governments incorporating human rights advocacy into their work do so on false pretences, e.g. to please donors and precisely to legitimise their work because the international community has deemed human rights advocacy as a requisite of legitimacy. In short, these organisations are thought to be 'using' human rights. Nonetheless, the effective incorporation of human rights in the work of NGOs is certainly not to be derided.
6   For an assessment of the empowering force of human rights, *see* Chapter VI.

tant to examine the theoretical or presumed value of human rights in tackling such practices. Although this value can take various forms, I have chosen two specific characteristics which I believe to be the most significant.

The first value, as alluded to above, lies in the universality of human rights – the understanding that all human rights apply to all persons equally, regardless of, among other things their culture, religion or geographical situation. This assertion carries across disciplinary and humanitarian interests globally. Idealistically, the language of the universality of human rights conveys a sense of global justice thought to be needed in addressing an array of human behaviour, including harmful traditional practices, across cultural and religious divides. In this light, the argument that human rights are relative – and thus do not apply to all persons equally or are conditioned, *inter alia*, by culture, religion or geographical situation – poses a serious threat. Accepting relativist arguments does not simply mean accepting an academic theory of little consequence. It means repudiating the basis on which African women can understand human rights to be *rights* that they too possess, regardless of their poverty, sex, social class or circumstance. It means rejecting the basis on which evaluations of customs and practices are made across cultures. In short, it implies that some peoples' practices, harmful traditional practices included, are not to be condemned by others. It also means that the asserted universal relevancy of human rights is rejected and we must return to relying primarily on arguments of health and development as the basis for eradicating harmful traditional practices. A review of historical universalist/relativist positions on rights and justice, morality and customs leads this chapter. A liberal and pluralist vision of the universality of human rights is advanced in contemporary terms as convincing on divisive points and potentially reconciling vis-à-vis some relativist stances, and therefore a highly suitable standpoint from which to consider issues with regard to Africa, women and traditions. It is also suggested that we have under-evaluated the practical, religious, and political motivations fueling the relativist discourses which have been insulated by theoretical discussions over many decades. Even more regrettable, genuine voices and opinions on the matter at the grassroots level have not been sufficiently sought or heard.

The second proposed theoretical value of human rights also relates to legitimacy, only this time the legitimacy of cross-cultural normative judgements. This is a very important value indeed. Increasingly, non-Africans working to end harmful traditional practices in sub-Saharan Africa are challenged by Africans, even those sensitive to the issues and active in campaigns to end these practices, to explain their authority and motives.[7] 'Who are you to say such practices are bad and that they should be banned?'

---

[7] For instance, despite being recognised as a leading activist and key source of information for the campaign against female circumcision for over 25 years, Fran Hosken still endures much questioning as to the legitimacy of her involvement in the campaign because she is a white American. One may refer

Chapter IV

'What do you know about the daily realities of African women?' These are valid questions[8] that require clear and honest answers. In this light, notions such as our shared consciousness of vulnerability and moral judgements based on human rights are reviewed. At the same time, it is suggested that such questioning of authority and motives should be cause for concern, potentially further revealing that the human rights campaign against harmful traditional practices employed to date may not have been appropriate in its tone, content or delivery – thus partly explaining its relative lack of success.

2 OVER TWO MILLENNIA OF THEORIZING ON HUMAN RIGHTS AND MORAL WRONGS

2.1 The Debate in Antiquity

Debates over concepts of man's very essence of being, the relationship between man and society, and laws of nature existed as far back as Antiquity. Indeed, it is not terribly difficult to trace the origins of contemporary theories on the nature of human rights to this period.[9] Sophocles (496-406 B.C.), in his play *The Tereus*, already introduced notions of equality among all human beings.[10] Hippias (born approximately 450 B.C.) wrote of a similar principle of non-discrimination. Rather humourous today, he argued that all individuals were to be considered in the same way, even barbarians and Greeks.[11] Pericles (495-429 B.C.), on his part, wrote of unwritten laws which were applicable to all, even ordinary, mortals. These works introduced the notion that rights

---

to Hosken's celebrated work on FGM, STOP FEMALE GENITAL MUTILATION (1995), now in its fourth edition.

8   An entire stream of feminist theory questions precisely the standpoint, and hence the objectivity/subjectivity, of the social and cultural anthropologist studying foreign customs and practices. *See generally* J. Grant (ed.) FUNDAMENTAL FEMINISM (1993). Or *see specifically*: D. Haraway, *Situated Knowledges in Feminism and the Privilege of the Partial Perspective*, Feminist Studies, Vol. 14 (1988); and S. Harding, THE SCIENCE QUESTION IN FEMINISM (1986). The issue of standpoint is significantly less addressed within the study of international human rights law, and when addressed it is usually by cultural relativists or proponents of critical legal studies. Universalists typically assert that any evaluation of a custom or practice under the terms of international human rights law guarantees the greatest objectivity possible, and thus simply dismiss penetrating critiques.

9   Gillespie offers an excellent and concise overview of the human rights notions in Antiquity. The present summary is largely derived from this work. *See* A. Gillespie, *Ideas of Human Rights in Antiquity*, Netherlands Quarterly of Human Rights, Vol. 17 (1999).

10 Fragment 532 reads: '…there is a single human race. A single day brought us all forth from our father and mother. No man is born superior to another…' as noted in M. Cleve, THE GIANTS OF PRE-SOPHISTIC GREEK PHILOSOPHY (1969), pp. 527-530.

11 A passage in *Protagoras* reads: '…by nature (…) are all constituted alike in all things which are essential by nature to all men (…) In these things no barbarian is set apart from us, nor Greek…', cited in B. Jowett, THE DIALOGUES OF PLATO (1931), pp. 321-324.

existed for all people, irrespective of whether they were officially acknowledged in texts. These and other philosophers in Antiquity, such as Socrates (470-399 B.C.) and his pupil Plato (427-347 B.C.), belonged to the school of philosophy which espoused the existence of universal values which were unchanging and eternal – unchanging and eternal because they resided in the inherent dignity of every member of the human family. Plato's *Republic* is considered the first attempt at setting out the rights and responsibilities which individuals and communities possess. His master plan was designed to maintain the greatest possible unity within and equality among all 'the Republic's' citizens. Aristotle (384-322 B.C.), a pupil of Plato, similarly believed in rights. However, he did not believe in such things as self-evident truths arising from nature, existing outside and independently of social considerations[12]. Rather, he deemed the State natural and essential for the creation of justice and the source of rights. Finally, proponents of Stoicism, the last school of Antiquity, believed that there was a family of humanity and that all members within this family were essentially equal. The principles of humanism included the idea that there were rules and rights for all people at all times, an idea which later resurfaced in Christianity[13] and which features centrally in the universalism of today.

The counter-school of relativism also existed as far back as 2,500 years ago. This school of thought countered existing social philosophy and the notion of universal values. Of particular interest to the subject at hand, early relativists, beginning with the Sophists and later the Skeptics, considered social customs in particular to be a discriminating factor among men. For instance, Herodotus' *The Histories*, reads:

> [I]f one were to put before all men the suggestion that out of all customs they should choose the best, each people would examine them and then pick their own; so accustomed are they to think that their own customs are far the best... There are many proofs to show that all men customarily hold this attitude towards customs.[14]

Herodotus (484-424 B.C.) and others, such as Pindar (518-438 B.C.), showed that for every socially justifiable practice, there was an opposing one elsewhere. Herodotus went so far as to create a small catalogue of social customs that varied between different peoples. According to the Sophists and Skeptics, this would necessarily preclude

---

12 As explained by F. Miller, *Aristotle and the Origins of Natural Rights*, Review of Metaphysics, Vol. 49 (1996), pp. 879-880.
13 Gillespie, *supra*, n. 9, p. 258.
14 Book III, part 38, of Herodotus' THE HISTORIES (reproduced in 1954). Nearly 2,500 years later Melville Herkovits echoes this very same sentiment, stating:
    ...nonrelativists say that some moral judgments are valid for everyone, but when asked to state them they always list the rules of *their* culture. They label as 'right' the habits of their own people, and condemn as 'wrong' the habits of others. [emphasis in original]
    M.J. Herkovits, CULTURAL RELATIVISM: PERSPECTIVES IN CULTURAL PLURALISM (1973), p. 50.

any possibility of universality in values. In this manner, they proclaimed, no one man or race was or should be made competent to judge which custom was better than the other. Sextus described an example:

> ...we oppose (...) the habit (...) of the Egyptians who tattoo their children (...) and whereas the Indians have intercourse with their women in public, most other races regard this as shameful (...) among Persians it is the habit to indulge in intercourse with males (...) with us adultery is forbidden. [15]

From the Skeptics point of view, Herotudus' claim that 'social custom was King over all' rang true.

Although the arguments may have become more refined and complex, the cultural relativists of today would still find much consolation and reinforcement in the Sophist and Skeptic schools of thought. Universalists would find solace in the philosophies of the Stoics.

2.2 The Debate in the Era of Enlightenment

There is no doubt that the vernacular of 'rights' arose from Western Enlightenment. It was in this period that the philosophical doctrine, known as *natural law*, was born, which stated that there is a natural moral law, irrespective of time and place. Man knew this law through his own reason. Originally a product of early rational thought, the Christian form of the doctrine[16] was first defined by Saint Thomas Aquinas (1225-1274).[17] Dating back to the 18th Century, rights ideology became embedded in the European convictions that human beings were inherently endowed with inalienable fundamental rights and freedoms and that they were entitled to defend these rights and have them defended.[18] A number of basic human rights, such as freedom of speech and religion, were derived from natural law doctrine, as later developed by the English philosopher Locke. Locke (1632-1704), together with his successors, the Swiss Romand philosopher Rousseau (1712-1778) and his German counter-part Kant (1724-1804), were well aware that they were not just discussing the moral relationship between ruler and ruled, but dealing with matters of great contemporary political

---

15 Sextus in *The Tenth Mode* as noted in J.L. Saunders, (ed.), GREEK AND ROMAN PHILOSOPHY AFTER ARISTOTLE (1966), pp. 177-181.
16 For a concise description of the influence of Christian thought on natural law (especially as conceived by Locke) and human rights, *see* D. Little, *A Christian Perspective on Human Rights*, in A. An-Na'im and F. Deng, eds., HUMAN RIGHTS IN AFRICA: CROSS-CULTURAL PERSPECTIVES (1980).
17 PEARS CYCLOPEDIA (1998-1999), p. J36.
18 *See*: J. Locke, THE SECOND TREATISE OF GOVERNMENT, in particular arts. 22, 77, 87, 89 and 99 (reproduced in 1963); and J.-J. Rousseau, DU CONTRAT SOCIAL, in particular Livres Premier, Deuxième and Quatrième (reproduced in 1978).

importance.[19] Their texts were to become fundamental contributions of thought on the need for, and formulation of, civil and political rights. Generally speaking, their arguments inform our contemporary understanding of the quintessential formula that since human dignity is grounded in human nature and one's nature is inalienable, it logically follows that human dignity is inalienable.

When natural law was dethroned,[20] the secular and positivist approach entered.[21] Beginning with Hume (1711-1776), and extrapolated to greater depths by Bentham (1748-1832),[22] the utilitarian approach saw rights as a manufactured concept. In simple terms, the *principle of utility* was advanced as a universal moral principle. Reflecting the new theories taking place in science at the time (in particular those of Newton), this principle advanced and calculated the notion of the greatest happiness of the greatest number of persons. 'Happiness' could be weighed by certain quantitative tests in order to ascertain what utility needed.[23] Hume conveyed the relativist logic in simple terms: 'In each city, the rites of that city.'[24] A similar counter-movement came from the theological perspective. Protestant thinkers, such as Berth and Niebuhr, contested the notion of natural law. Niebuhr, in particular, pointed out that there was no law that could be regarded as 'natural' for all men at all times, nor did all men possess the sensibility and reason to discern natural law.[25]

Rawls reclaimed Locke, Rousseau and Kant's theories on natural law and introduced his basic theory of justice[26] – *justice as fairness*. He rejected the utilitarian viewpoint because it did not allow for rational choice. Treating the good as the attainment of the greatest measure of satisfaction (expressed in the form of pleasure and happiness) was unsatisfactory. In contrast, justice as fairness gave priority to inviolable rights or freedoms which could not be overborne by a principle of 'greater good shared by others.'[27] Rawls' theory is deeply rooted in the libertarian attitudes of his time, but his emphasis on individual liberty and freedom has been a distinctive

---

19 *See* A.H. Robertson, HUMAN RIGHTS IN THE WORLD (1996), p. 335. He asserts that Locke and Rousseau were the first to recognize the political aspects of human rights.
20 *See* H.L.A. Hart, *Are there any natural rights?*, The Philosophical Review, Vol. 65 (1955).
21 *See* L. Lloyd of Hampstead, INTRODUCTION TO JURISPRUDENCE (1979), especially pp. 170-177.
22 *See*: H.L.A. Hart, *Bentham on legal rights*, in A.W.B. Simpson, ed., OXFORD ESSAYS IN JURISPRUDENCE (1973); or J. Bentham, in J.H. Burns and H.L.A. Hart, eds., AN INTRODUCTION TO THE PRINCIPLES OF MORALS AND LEGISLATION (1970).
23 *See* Lloyd of Hampstead, *supra*, n. 21, p. 172.
24 As cited in E. Gellner, LEGITIMISATION OF BELIEF (1974), pp. 47-48.
25 *See* PEARS CYCLOPEDIA, *supra*, n. 17, p. J36.
26 J. Rawls, A THEORY OF JUSTICE (1972).
27 As discussed by Lloyd of Hampstead, *supra*, n. 21, pp. 96-97.

feature of Western political and legal philosophy since the seventeenth century, associated particularly with the doctrine of natural rights.[28]

2.3 Contemporary Relativist Arguments

The contemporary doctrine of cultural relativism asserts that rules about morality vary from place to place, depending on the cultural context. Since the world is a plurality of cultures there can be no universal morality. 'Radical cultural relativists'[29] or 'cultural absolutists' maintain that different cultures are not comparable, but all cultures are morally equal. Attempts to assert universality, as a criterion of all morality, are viewed as a well-disguised imperial routine of trying to make the values of a particular culture general.[30] Cultural relativists also maintain, *grosso modo*, that each culture has its own indigenous concept of human rights. Some argue more pointedly that human rights are a notion culturally specific to the Western World and are not relevant to cultures that do not share 'Western' customs, norms, beliefs and values. The language of international human rights law is therefore regarded as a reflection of Western values which cannot be translated into non-Western law, religion or culture. Some further argue that these values issue from Western criteria which they do not wish to emulate, gender equality among them. Of specific relevance to our study, a number of leading African politicians (notably male) have been reported as denouncing internationally established norms of gender equality rights as 'un-African' and claiming that 'phenomena such as authority and equality for women are alien to African cultures'.[31]

Dichotomies between the universalists and relativists are perhaps nowhere more apparent than when addressing the issue of the human rights of women and the socially, culturally and religiously prescribed and adhered roles of men and women. The critique of universality is particularly vociferous when it comes to women's human rights and specifically human rights relevant to sexuality and reproduction. The criticism of the Western foundation of the reproductive rights framework, for instance, draws upon a cultural relativist position that, as summarized by one scholar, 'emphasizes the different cultural and moral patterns prevailing in distinct cultures, and

---

28 His *First Principle* alone reflects one of the fundamental premises of existing human rights treaties: *Each person is to have an equal right to the most extensive total system of equal basic liberties compatible with a similar system of liberty for all.*
29 The term was coined and defined by J. Donnelly in UNIVERSAL HUMAN RIGHTS IN THEORY AND PRACTICE (1989), p. 106. It has essentially the same meaning as Howard's term *cultural absolutism*, as described generally in R.E. Howard, HUMAN RIGHTS AND THE SEARCH FOR COMMUNITY (1995), pp. 50-74, and R.E. Howard, *Cultural Absolutism and the Nostalgia for Community*, Human Rights Quarterly, Vol. 15 (1993).
30 *See* A. Bozeman, THE FUTURE OF LAW IN A MULTICULTURAL WORLD (1977), p. 183.
31 *See* M. Jensen and K. Poulsen, HUMAN RIGHTS AND CULTURAL CHANGE: WOMEN IN AFRICA (1993), p. 6.

challenges the concept of [reproductive] rights as a new form of imperialism.'[32] More specifically, individualism and possession of one's own body, as well as the power dimension implied in a concept of autonomous control (and, therefore, individual choice) are criticized as culturally biased notions inappropriate for many Southern women, particularly in Asia and Africa.[33] Such criticisms give rise to further debates over the non-applicability of 'global' feminism. Elements of this controversy are further addressed in Chapter VI.

Disagreements between universalists and relativists regarding socially and culturally differentiating customs focus mainly on the justification given for the differentiation in question, and more precisely on the community policies which regulate the moral and legal rationales for these – rationales which are usually gender-based, favouring men over women.[34] Ultimately, the protection and continuation of harmful traditional practices on the grounds of cultural relativism is unacceptable to persons who simply *believe* in the universality of human rights, including a particular understanding of the well-being of women. Few universalists would deny that sub-Saharan Africa remains largely *traditional* (arguably because of the strong attachment of individuals to their rural roots, traditional belief systems and traditional styles of living) and rich in socio-cultural norms and customs. Yet, it is precisely these special social and cultural structures which maintain harmful traditional practices that are cited by relativists in support of their arguments. As such, whatever convincing arguments universalists put forth, relativists can always play the trump card of culture. This validates the argument that the discussion is closed because it is culture or tradition which is fundamentally at issue. However, irrespective of the validity of the cultural argument *per se*, such arguments at a minimum deny the reality of naturally occurring evolution.

3 OTHER FACTORS INFLUENCING RELATIVISM

The brief review of theories from Antiquity, the Enlightenment and the present day illustrates two important points. The first is that fundamental disagreements on the absolute or relative nature of 'truth', dignity and morality have long existed and remain at the heart of the universalist/relativist debate. This complex subject cannot be further

---

32 S. Correa, POPULATION AND REPRODUCTIVE RIGHTS (1994), p. 78.
33 For further description of cultural relativist argumentation with regard to women's rights and reproductive rights *see generally*: Correa, *id.*; and M.J. Perry, *Are Human Rights Universal? The Relativist Challenge and Related Matters*, Human Rights Quarterly, Vol. 19 (1997), especially with regard to female circumcision at pp. 487-496.
34 As summarized by Burns Weston, who examines cultural practices that privilege one group of people over another, such as patriarchy, and the ability of human rights to eliminate this privilege; *see Human Rights in a Mulitcultured World*, in B.H. Weston and S.P. Marks, eds., THE FUTURE OF INTERNATIONAL HUMAN RIGHTS (2000), particularly at pp. 84ff.

considered or resolved within the limited parameters of this study. However, it is submitted that strong arguments in favour of a pluralist form of universalism as advanced by numerous contemporary commentators are highly persuasive and accommodating of various relativist concerns, as described below. The second important point to be derived from this review of theories is that popular views on rights, morality and even customs have long been, and continue to be, greatly influenced by the events of the time and experiences lived by philosophers and social commentators. For example, many of the contributions during the Enlightenment accompanied social transformations, including revolutions. It informs us that any issue, even a debate on the circumcision of young women's genitalia among persons from different cultures, is also a matter of politics. The key factors informing views and conditioning the debate today are particular to our time. I suggest that there have been principally three factors and that these overlap.

The first factor was the end of colonialism and imperialism and the consequent effort by many Africans to reject any endeavours or language which may be disguised as neo-colonialism or neo-imperialism. Vincent aptly notes '[t]he doctrine of cultural relativism was not invented by nationalists throwing off the yoke of the empire, but its popularity has been sustained by these movements.'[35] Ojo similarly surmises that

> ... the experience of colonialism... has had a visible psychological impact on Africans. Since independence, there has been a very strong desire to emphasize the 'Africanness,' or put an African imprint on whatever ... programs they [Africans] embark.[36]

In certain instances, therefore, a significant attraction of the doctrine of cultural relativism is that it provides a form of protest against imperialism. Beyond this attraction lie serious considerations. Let us not forget that when the Universal Declaration of Human Rights was formulated, most African countries remained under colonial rule. Although most of these countries gained independence in the 1960s, the dominance of the West was still apparent.[37] The reality of the period, with European democracies proclaiming the rights of individuals against the State while simultaneously holding most of the peoples of Asia and Africa under their dominion by means of oppressive rule, was fraught with contradictions.[38] Even if African States believed in the ideological foundations of human rights, the political reality of the times was such that they

---

35 R.J. Vincent, HUMAN RIGHTS AND INTERNATIONAL RELATIONS (1986), p. 37.
36 O. Ojo, *Understanding Human Rights in Africa*, in J. Berting *et al.*, eds., HUMAN RIGHTS IN A PLURALIST WORLD (1990), p. 117.
37 *See* V. Leary, *The Effect of Western Perspectives on International Human Rights* in HUMAN RIGHTS IN AFRICA, *supra*, n. 16, p. 17.
38 *See* Richard Falk addresses this point in history and its implications today in *A Half Century of Human Rights: Geopolitics and Values* in THE FUTURE OF INTERNATIONAL HUMAN RIGHTS, *supra*, n. 34, pp. 2-3.

were seeking independence from the West in all its forms, ideological independence included. Hence, for much of the decades which followed the formulation of the earlier human rights instruments, Africa sought to situate its own position. For some – but certainly not for all, and admittedly only to a certain degree – the relativist stance may have been (and continues to be) necessary as a strategy to break away from the colonial yoke which bound them so long. There is certainly a broad belief that colonialism had a direct negative impact on human rights, most notably in destroying traditional institutions and relationships that protected people and constrained power.[39] The authoritarian governments which are still in place in many Africa countries and which have reduced the rights exercised by individuals are also considered a product of colonial rule.[40] In this light, African nation-building and the potential of human rights have not yet recovered.

The second factor is the extreme poverty, and the political and economic instability, that characterizes the African region. This phenomenon is commonly blamed on poor and coercive IMF and World Bank (i.e. Western and neo-colonialist) policies, as well as the lasting impact of colonialism.[41] It feeds skepticism of any policy supported by the West and contempt of moral judgements against African ways. For some, the stark realities of Africa (e.g. the need for nation-building, the maintenance and intensification of parochial and tribal identities, and ill-structured economies) do not admit the 'luxury' of human rights.[42] There is a well-established debate regarding the economic cost of ensuring human rights, in particular social and cultural rights. Whatever point of view one takes, however, the freedom of a woman not to have her genitalia cut or not to abide by dietary taboos during pregnancy are without economic cost.[43]

The third significant factor is the reaffirmation of Africa's cultural and religious roots. As noted by Vincent, the emergence of a good part of the world from the

---

39 See, e.g.: B.L. Shadle, *Changing Traditions to Meet Current Altering Conditions: Customary law, African Courts and the rejection of codification in Kenya, 1930-60*, Journal of African History, Vol. 40 (1999); O.O. Taiwo, *Traditional Versus Modern Judicial Practices: A Comparative Analysis of Dispute Resolution among the Yoruba of South-West Nigeria*, Africa Development, Vol. XXIII (1998); and A. Li, *Asafo and destoolment in colonial southern Ghana, 1900-1953*, International Journal of African Historical Studies, Vol. 28 (1995). These authors describe a number of specific attributes of customary law which were diminished by colonizers. For instance, attempts to codify customary law hampered the fluid and evolutionary nature of such law. The benefits of customary law (such as mediation and easy access for all to some form of justice) were discarded along with the drawbacks. Traditional methods of balancing the powers of chiefs were damaged owing to the ignorance of colonizers who believed empowering chiefs was a way to show cultural respect.
40 See J. Silk, *Traditional Culture and Human Rights* in HUMAN RIGHTS IN AFRICA, *supra*, n. 16, particularly at p. 293.
41 See Ojo, *supra*, n. 36, pp. 116-117.
42 Silk summarizes these arguments from a variety of literature; *see supra*, n. 40, pp. 292-302.
43 While it is contended that all human rights entail some costs (but likewise contribute to a system of social development which includes economic gains), the point here is only that the traditional prctices in question, should they be ended, entail no economic loss.

dominance of European imperialism has carried with it a new emphasis throughout Africa on the plurality of values and on the rediscovery of the deep roots of indigenous culture. The phenomenon has been characterized in some parts of Africa by a strengthening movement of Islamization.[44] In other pockets of Africa it has been characterized by the firm rejection of foreign (in particular European) religions altogether and the reaffirmation of traditional ones.[45] In much of the African continent, religious and customary law maintains a stronghold in areas relating to family. As observed by Idowu, African traditional religion and customary laws take precedence in strictly personal matters relating to the passages of life, even among Africans who declare themselves practicing Christians.[46] He adds that, while most Africans may wish to be regarded as connected with one of the two 'fashionable' religions, most are at heart still attached to their own indigenous beliefs, effectively contributing to divided loyalties, particularly where generational practices are concerned.[47] There are numerous stories, for instance, of missionaries succeeding to convert worshipers of traditional African religions to the European religions, although having to turn a blind eye to the continuation of African traditional practices, such as female circumcision. Among the Abagusii of Kenya, for instance, Christian hymns are sung during circumcision ceremonies in place of traditional clitoridectomy songs and references are made to the Bible.[48] Hosken reports with regard to Kenya that although in the past some of the Protestant missionaries were strongly opposed to female genital operations, little or nothing is said against them now; Roman Catholic missionaries in the region condoned female circumcision of the children of their converts because they feared their Catholic community would diminish if men refused to marry because the girls were not excised.[49] In a similar vein, it is largely regarded that the African continent is moving actively and purposefully to recover its traditional roots through the

---

44 Samuel Huntington, in his book THE CLASH OF THE CIVILIZATIONS (1996), hypothesizes that a core geo-political divide has already begun and will only become stronger between Islam and the 'West.' Presumably, the universal ideology of human rights will subsequently suffer further erosion. As a contrasting view, Huliaras argues that the increasing influence of Islam is not primarily due to a religious renaissance in reaction to processes of Westernization, but a response of people looking for answers in an era of economic decline and political disillusionment during a period of ideological vacuum; A.C. Huliaras, *Islam: promise or peril*, THE WORLD TODAY, Vol. 51 (1995), pp. 242-245.
45 See A.E. Barnes, *Evangelization where it is not wanted: colonial administrators and missionaries in Northern Nigeria*, Journal of Religion in Africa, Vol. 25 (1995).
46 E.B. Idowu, AFRICAN TRADITIONAL RELIGION: A DEFINITION (1973), p. 206.
47 *See*: *Id.*, p. 205; and H. Aguessy, *Traditional African views and apperceptions*, in A.I. Sow *et al.*, eds., INTRODUCTION TO AFRICAN CULTURE: GENERAL ASPECTS (1979), p. 112.
48 *See* E. Gwako, *Continuity and Change in the Practice of Clitoridectomy in Kenya*, Journal of Modern African Studies, Vol. 33, p. 335. For other examples of conflicts regarding practices, *see* M. Gilbert, *The Christian executioner: Christianity and chieftancy as rivals*, Journal of Religion in Africa, Vol. 25 (1995).
49 F.P. Hosken, STOP FEMALE GENITAL MUTILATION (1995), p. 23.

'Africanization' of Islam and Christianity.[50] There are attempts, for instance, at the indigenization of the Christian church, the founding of churches by charismatic Christian African leaders and the establishment of splinters from the European-dominated churches[51] as separate churches completely free from foreign intervention.[52] The Islam of sub-Saharan Africa is similarly mixed with pre-Islamic African religions, resulting in a fusion of new beliefs and old practices.[53]

While all three factors may not be determinative of the relativist ideology regarding human rights, they contribute to the rejection, or at least suspicion, of what is considered a foreign (and especially Western) concept. It is by no far stretch of the imagination that one can see that, owing to events experienced by contemporary Africa, sensitivities in Africa are raw not only regarding Western concepts and ideologies filtering into or imposed on Africa, but also regarding condemnation of African concepts, philosophies or customs.[54] One may wonder, as has Leary in surveying criticisms of this kind, whether the objection is not so much to the concept of universality as it is to the simple fact that the international standards are strongly advocated by the West; this has manifested itself as Africans and others questioning the universality of these norms and their suitability in non-Western cultures.[55] One should also question the possibility of 'mixed motives' of proponents of relativism[56] – not ruling out that among the motives for the relativist positions are the material as well as ideological interests of men in power to continue women's subordination[57] and to retain the immaterial benefits of the superior status claimed by men.

---

50 Again, colonialism has had a role to play. It ended the religious authority of kings and the power exercised by priests. Christianity and Islam both spread rapidly under colonial rule and afterwards. Traditional beliefs, however, have generally remained intact. See under 'Religion' in AFRICA TODAY: PART I (1996), pp.10-11.
51 See, e.g., B. Sackey, *Spiritual churches in Kumasi 1920-1986: some observations*, Africana Marburgensia, Vol. 24 (1991).
52 *See generally*: Idowu, *supra*, n. 46, p. 206; and A. Shorter, AFRICAN CULTURE AND THE CHRISTIAN CHURCH (1973), especially Chapter 6: Christianizing African Marriage and Family Life. The latter makes the argument that the Christian perception of the family as the cell of society has never been reconciled with traditional perceptions of kinship throughout Africa. Christian marriage has also not taken indigenous social facts and institutions sufficiently into account.
53 *See* Huliaras, *supra*, n. 44.
54 Even if such condemnation comes from all parts of the world (Asia and Latin America included) and from all religions, it is interpreted, whether deservedly so or not, by many Africans to be Western-dominated or led. This, again, reflects the fundamental politics involved, even at the level of practices harming women's reproductive health.
55 Leary, *supra*, n. 37, p. 15.
56 *See* A. An-Na'im and F. Deng, *Introduction*, in HUMAN RIGHTS IN AFRICA, *supra*, n. 16, p. 1.
57 As proposed by R. Howard, *Women's Rights in English-speaking Sub-Saharan Africa*, in C.E. Welch, Jr. and R.I. Meltzer, eds., HUMAN RIGHTS AND DEVELOPMENT IN AFRICA (1986), p. 46.

4 RESOLVING THE DIFFERENCES

In addressing cultural relativism or cross-cultural perspectives on human rights it is difficult to avoid normative ambiguity. Consensus, for instance, appears to be lacking on fundamental concepts, such as *universal human dignity* and *universal morality* as well as the fundamental relationship between these and human rights and between human rights and religious principles.[58] C.S. Lewis, for example, argued that although religious traditions differ considerably in what he refered to as 'surface teachings,' there remains an underlying 'deep structure' of religious moral reason and common values;[59] despite the diversity of religious faiths and their expressions, the basic process of both religious and moral reasoning is the same in all.[60] 'Specific moral norms are the complex *outcome* [emphasis in the original] of this process after it has been applied to different circumstances in different contexts, and for this reason specific norms can differ. But the underlying method of decision and judgement is the same everywhere.'[61] Still some refute even this notion: even the inherent dignity of the human being, they claim, does not enjoy sacred support. Inasmuch as the assertion of universal human dignity is the cornerstone of universal human rights, they logically conclude that human rights cannot be claimed as universal.[62] Indeed, the use of international law, and specifically human rights law, as a representation of commonality among religions is not acceptable to all. Some have based this conclusion on an absence of a common 'social ethic'[63] while others have referred to an absence of understanding of the concept of human dignity.[64]

---

[58] Howard, for instance, suggests that human dignity and human rights are not coterminous and that the African concept of human rights is actually a concept of human dignity; *see*: R. Howard, *Group versus Individual Dignity in the African Debate on Human Rights*, in HUMAN RIGHTS IN AFRICA, *supra*, n. 16; and Howard, HUMAN RIGHTS IN COMMONWEALTH AFRICA (1986).

[59] Lewis surveyed the major religions and found common values in them; *see generally* THE ABOLITION OF MAN (1943).

[60] *See* R.M. Green, RELIGION AND MORAL REASON: A NEW METHOD FOR COMPARATIVE STUDY (1988). For the views of other scholars and their conclusions on different faiths in relation to human rights, *see generally* A.A. An-Na'im *et al.*, eds., HUMAN RIGHTS AND RELIGIOUS VALUES: AN UNEASY RELATIONSHIP? (1995).

[61] *Id.*, p. xii.

[62] Perry, for example, argues, *supra*, n. 33, p. 462, that 'neither any religious nor any secular support for the claim that any human being (much less every human being) is sacred is persuasive… even if *arguendo* every human being is sacred, it does not follow and in fact is not true that there are things that ought not to be done to *any* human being or things that ought to be done for *every* human being.' Donnelly is of the same opinion and describes the lack of collusion as stemming from discrepancies in the conception of human dignity; *see* J. Donnelly, *Human Rights and Human Dignity: An Analytic Critique of Non-Western Conceptions of Human Rights*, The American Political Science Review, Vol. 76 (1982).

[63] As described by G.L. Dorsey, *Towards World Perspectives*, in S.A. Vojcanin, ed., LAW, CULTURE AND VALUES (1990), pp. 5-28.

[64] As proposed, for example, by Donnelly, *Human Rights and Human Dignity, supra*, n. 62.

Cultural relativism and *universalism* also have no single canonical meaning. For instance, some positions that go by the name of relativism are not convincingly relativist.[65] The point here is not to choose a term which suitably waters down universalism so as to make it acceptable to more, but to choose a term which best defines an approach to universalism, while respecting its boundaries. With this in mind, it is submitted that many relativist concerns could be laid to rest by a pluralist understanding of universality. Perry describes such a pluralist conception as follows:

> To say that human beings *are* all alike in at least some respects such that some things are good and some things are bad for *every* human being is not to deny that human beings are *not* all alike in many other respects; it is not to deny that some things are good and some things are bad for *some* human beings *but not for others* [emphasis in original].[66]

Hence, human beings overwhelmingly make similar assessments in some respects (such that some things good for some human beings are good for every human being and some things bad for some human beings are bad for every human being). Take as an example a woman who is having difficulty in childbirth. Should she be left to suffer and possibly die if there is a medically trained professional nearby? Most of us, regardless of our religion or culture, would agree that denying her this attention would be a bad thing, that ultimately, barring all issues of facilitating the intervention, she should be given the health care of which she has need. Killing an innocent person and thereby depriving her or him of the right to life is also seen as something bad by most human beings. In this respect, universalism about human good and bad is evident.[67] But pluralism about human good and bad is also evident, acknowledging that human beings are not all *exactly* alike (such that some things good for some people may not be good for every human being and some things bad for some people may not be bad for every human being).[68] Divided views on whether female circumcision (or any other harmful traditional practice) is a good or bad thing certainly appears to be a contemporary example of this. For instance, some individuals may believe that girls must feel the pain of circumcision without anaesthetic and survive the ordeal in order to prove their womanhood. Thus, such a ritual is viewed as 'good,' whereas many others may consider it barbaric and inherently 'bad.' Indeed, it is because of this very discrepancy in views (which may only lead to an impasse) that circumcision should not solely, or even mainly, be evaluated as something *good* or *bad* in metaphysical terms, but as

---

65 For example, various elements of Donnelly's 'weak cultural relativism' could easily be represented as 'liberal universalism.'
66 Perry, *supra*, n. 33, pp. 471-472.
67 Note that Perry, Putnam and Hampshire address the issue of universality from the perspective of philosophy and therefore use the term 'human good' as congruent to 'human dignity.'
68 As advanced by H. Putnam, REASON, TRUTH AND HISTORY (1981), cited in Perry, *supra*, n. 33, p. 473.

something *harmful* or *not harmful* to a woman's health. In this sense, the physical evidence against female circumcision would outweigh the metaphysical evidence. But in keeping here with the metaphysical evaluation of traditional practices, it is submitted in Section 6 below that human rights discourses enable us to question – and importantly to deduce – whether a practice in a given community is good or bad according to universal standards. Such a discourse, it is hoped, may be a catalyst for internal critique and, eventually, may lead to the abandonment of the practice.

4.1 The Pluralist Perspective

The pluralist vision of universality has been advanced under various aliases and across various disciplines – philosophy, law and political science included. Putnam, for instance (who like Perry is a philosopher), suggests that a conception of human good can be, and should be, universalist as well as pluralist: it can acknowledge sameness as well as difference, commonality as well as variety.[69] From the perspective of law (specifically in relation to African culture) An-Na'im and Deng's compilation of cross-cultural perspectives on human rights similarly points in favour of a pluralist approach,[70] fundamentally reaffirming the pluralist view of human good where difference as well as sameness is acknowledged. As a political scientist, Donnelly suggests a similar approach – one he calls 'weak cultural relativism' – recognizing that culture may be an important source of the validity of a moral right or rule which allows occasional and strictly local variations and exceptions.[71]

Donnelly's standpoint is not necessarily one that strong universalists like to hear. In his conception there is a certain, albeit weak, degree of cultural relativity which is acceptable and does not pose a threat to the legitimacy of internationally recognized human rights standards. Some of the rights recognized by the UDHR and the two covenants may be viewed as 'interpretations' or 'forms' with which some cultures may differ without necessarily denying universal human rights.[72] We may, for instance, all agree that the right to freedom from discrimination is of fundamental importance to all human beings and thus agree on the universality of the principle of non-discrimination. But our culture may influence what we may or may not consider to be discriminatory. Take the example of men making whistling calls at women. Our view on whether this is acceptable flirting or unacceptable harassment will be significantly influenced by our cultural upbringing. Our understanding of what does or does not comprise violence may also be influenced by our culture; hence the long-standing and still unresolved

---

69 *See* S. Hampshire, TWO THEORIES OF MORALITY (1977), cited in Perry, *supra*, n. 33, p. 473.
70 Although it is expressed in terms of a 'contextual cultural approach' by An-Na'im and Deng, *Introduction, supra*, n. 56, p. 1. Most authors in the compilation agree that this approach is the appropriate means by which to promote universal recognition of the concept of human rights.
71 Donnelly, UNIVERSAL HUMAN RIGHTS IN THEORY AND PRACTICE, *supra*, n. 29, p. 110.
72 *Id.*

debate over the spanking of misbehaved children. In this respect, *weak cultural relativism* may be justified at the level of form and interpretation, without violating the essential universality of human rights. In other words, the fact that human rights are universally accepted does not mean that they must be uniformly applied.[73] Rather, they must be applied as is possible and warranted within a given social, cultural and economic context. Argued from the other side of the coin, 'cultural relativism does not necessarily require allowing cultures total autonomy in accepting a given right as culturally legitimate or rejecting it as culturally illegitimate.'[74]

Admittedly, the pluralist approach to universality may also not rest well with activists against harmful traditional practices in Africa. Certainly, this approach does not negate the applicability and suitability of human rights vis-a-vis practices and values characteristic of traditional African societies. However, it does admit that we are still in the process of establishing inter-culturally whether harmful traditional practices are perceived as universally bad. Still, as suggested in Section 6 below, the framework of universal human rights remains extremely useful in that it enables this process to take place, since it allows us to ask whether our judgement of a practice is valid for everyone.[75]

5 HAVE WE OVER-THEORIZED?

Are we any nearer to resolving the difference between the relativity and universality of human rights with respect to harmful traditional practices affecting women in sub-Saharan Africa? Ronald Dworkin draws a tempting conclusion where rights are concerned, noting that:

> It is wiser and more realistic to concede that though some answers may be plainly wrong, and some arguments plainly bad, there is nevertheless a set of answers and arguments that must be acknowledged to be, from any objective or neutral standpoint, equally good.[76]

However, as Dworkin goes on to admit, the role of the scholar is to make a decision forced by reason. Following the arguments summarized in the previous section, the more convincing position is that of the universalists, tempered by a pluralist perspective. While numerous relativist claims are valid, they do not undermine the univer-

---

73 *See* The Netherlands Advisory Council on International Affairs (AIV), UNIVERSALITY OF HUMAN RIGHTS AND CULTURAL DIVERSITY (1998), pp. 10 and 34.
74 A. An-Na'im, *Problems of Universal Cultural Legitimacy*, in HUMAN RIGHTS IN AFRICA, *supra*, n. 16, p. 343.
75 *See*: M. Nussbaum, *Human Functioning and Social Justice: In Defense of Aristotelian Essentialism*, Political Theory, Vol. 20 (1992), p. 224; and K. Wiredu, CULTURAL UNIVERSALS AND PARTICULARS: AN AFRICAN PERSPECTIVE (1996), especially Chapters 3 and 6.
76 R. Dworkin, TAKING RIGHTS SERIOUSLY (1977), p. 279.

salist-pluralist perspective on human rights. It is true that morality, as a whole, varies from society to society. It is also true that culture is an important source of moral values. But while the plurality of cultures implies that some norms may not be universal, it does not mean that no norms are universal. The *minimum* standards of international human rights law arguably fall into this category. In so doing, they admit to degrees of variation (to borrow from the European Court of Human Rights, they include 'margins of appreciation')[77] which sustains the universal essence of the norm but incorporates the plurality of forms. Further, from the perspective of positive law, relativist claims that human rights are a notion culturally specific to the West must confront the obvious fact that the African region has its own 'home-grown' human rights instrument and that this instrument proclaims the universality of human rights in trumps and spades.[78]

I also join scholars, such as Ibhawoh, who follow An-Na'im, Donnelly and Howard[79] (among others) in subscribing to the theory that relativist arguments are often advanced as a smokescreen for political, religious or sexist motivations. Ibhawoh does not mince words, arguing that the relativist stance

> ... has been dominated by urban-based male elites whose perceptions of 'cultural legitimacy' focuses on the idealised and invented traditions of collectivism, definitive gender roles, and conservative male dominance and interpretation of moral values. These patriarchal notions of cultural legitimacy contrast significantly with those of rural and urban women's groups and non-governmental organisations working for women and minority rights. These latter groups argue for the implicit individualism of human rights and reject a notion of cultural legitimacy that promotes culture-based gender inequalities.[80]

There are further weaknesses or flaws in the relativist argument. For instance, the belief of cultural relativists that universal human rights do not allow for the existence of varied cultures, social practices and customs is (as indicated above) unfounded.[81] Universal human rights do not impose one cultural standard, but rather one *legal* standard of minimum protection necessary for human dignity. Out of the international

---

77 For details on the notion of margin of appreciation, *see generally* P. van Dijk and G.J.H. van Hoof, THEORY AND PRACTICE OF THE EUROPEAN CONVENTION ON HUMAN RIGHTS (1998), pp. 82-95.
78 *See* Chapter V for further discussion.
79 *See* Howard's comments in this regard, particularly in *Women's Rights in English-speaking Sub-Saharan Africa, supra,* n. 57.
80 B. Ibhawoh, *Cultural Relativism and Human Rights: Reconsidering the Africanist Discourse*, Netherlands Quarterly of Human Rights, Vol. 19 (2001), p. 56. *See also* Ibhawoh's article *Between Culture and Constitution: Evaluating the Cultural Legitimacy of Human Rights in the African State*, Human Rights Quarterly, Vol. 22 (2000).
81 *See,* e.g., Howard, *Cultural Absolutism, supra,* n. 29.

standard-setting process, universal human rights emerge with sufficient flexibility to respect and protect cultural diversity and integrity.

Furthermore, it should be recognized, for the sake of argumentation at the very least, that relativism, as a normative approach to how we should make moral judgements, is conceptually flawed. As Martha Nussbaum notes,

> ... normative relativism is self-subverting; for, in asking us to defer to local norms, it asks us to defer to norms that in most cases are strongly non-relativistic. Most local traditions take themselves to be absolutely, not relatively true. So, in asking us to follow the local, relativism asks us not to follow relativism.[82]

Moreover, the relativist argument is often advanced by the elite, and without specification. Surely, when talking about grass-roots implementation of human rights, we should be inquiring to micro-cultures of villages or communities. Should we not, after all, be asking our target audiences – African women in villages, adolescents, village leaders, etc. – what they believe the value and relativity of human rights discourses to be? The number of local African NGOs employing human rights discourses in their campaign to improve women's lives generally or to end harmful traditional practices specifically at the grassroots level attests to the fact that at least some Africans believe the discourse of human rights to be of some positive value and as relevant to them as to the next person.[83] Would it not be more appropriate to ask the people who convey and receive human rights discourses at the African grassroots level whether they see these rights as clashing with their values or as not representative of African morality or of the African conception of dignity?[84]

6 CROSS-CULTURAL NORMATIVE JUDGEMENTS

Universalists maintain that the universal application of human rights reflects a universal need for protection. As such, they argue that most, if not all, individuals would prefer to have the protections which human rights offer.[85] Without human rights law,

---

82 M.C. Nussbaum, WOMEN AND HUMAN DEVELOPMENT: THE CAPABILITIES APPROACH, as cited by Weston, *Human Rights in a Mulitcultured World, supra*, n. 34, p. 73.
83 This view has been formed by the author after many informal discussions with African NGOs working on women's rights and following five years of inquiry into human rights and harmful traditional practices. Several formal interviews with African NGOs working specifically with human rights and harmful traditional practices at the grassroots level have also been conducted. These include interviews with Dr. Irene Thomas, IAC, Lagos (1 August 2000 in Lagos), Mr. Zegeye Asfaw of HUNDEE, Addis Ababa (5 October 2000 in The Hague) and Ms. Helen Seifu, Ethiopian Women Lawyers Association, Addis Ababa (24 February 2001 in Banjul, The Gambia).
84 Akwasi Aidoo notes why the universalist/relativist discourse with regard to Africa is no longer practical; *African: Democracy Without Human Rights*, Human Rights Quarterly, Vol. 15 (1993).
85 *See* Howard, *Cultural Absolutism, supra*, n. 29, pp. 315-316.

individuals would be vulnerable to severe abuses in the name of a collectivity or the community.[86] An-Na'im describes the commitment to the universality of human rights as premised on a *shared consciousness of vulnerability*:

> [A]ll human beings should endeavour to achieve the universal acceptance and practical implementation of international standards of human rights simply because we all need their protection as potential, if not actual, victims of the violation of our rights. In my view, this understanding of the universality of human rights affirms the belief that they are matters of immediate relevance to our own personal situations, wherever we happen to live, instead of assuming that human rights are secure in our societies and threatened in other places.[87]

It is this shared consciousness of vulnerability, An-Na'im further remarks, which enables us to overcome indifference to the suffering of others (in fact, we are acting in our own self-interest when we resist the violation of the rights of others).[88] Others go further to assert that 'the good of other human beings is an end worth pursuing in its own right.'[89] In other words, it is more than a consciousness of vulnerability which makes us want to support human rights; it is also compassion for our fellow human beings. This compassion, some maintain, is an innate feature of the human being.[90] For persons within a culture where harmful traditions are practiced, the need to evaluate these may be based on both the principles of shared vulnerability and compassion. For those outside the culture, evaluating these practices is mostly based on compassion (since most of us outside the culture do not fear that we, too, may one day suffer female circumcision or be exchanged into religious bondage).

6.1 Inevitable Cultural Evaluations

While many of us would accept either premise of vulnerability or compassion, there still remains one important question: How do we know which 'good' or 'bad' is universal for *every* human being, and which therefore should be acted upon from the perspective of human rights? When a traditional norm or practice is condemned

---

86 A discussion of social justice usually accompanies any arguments for or against universalism. For examples, *see* R. Howard, *Dignity, Community and Human Rights*, in A. An-Na'im, ed., HUMAN RIGHTS IN CROSS-CULTURAL PERSPECTIVE (1992).
87 A. An-Na'im, *The Position of Islamic States Regarding the Universal Declaration of Human Rights*, in P. Baehr *et al.*, eds., INNOVATION AND INSPIRATION: FIFTY YEARS OF THE UNIVERSAL DECLARATION OF HUMAN RIGHTS (1999), p. 177.
88 R.M. Hare provides the connection of this principle with philosophy; *see* MORAL THINKING (1981), in particular Chapter 5: Another's Sorrow.
89 As proposed by M.C. Nussbaum, *Skepticism about Practical Reason in Literature and the Law*, Harvard Law Review, Vol. 107 (1994), pp. 714-718.
90 Nussbaum suggests 'it seems to be a mark of the human being to care for others and feel disturbance when bad things happen to them' in *Compassion: The Basic Social Emotion*, Social Philosophy and Policy, Vol. 27 (1996).

internationally as an abuse of human rights, appeals are inevitably made to 'culture'. The argument is made that an observer cannot adequately judge a society's cultural practices from outside the culture because he or she is not capable of fully understanding the practices unique to it. Implied in such assertions is the impossibility of judging another society's peculiar practices as good or bad precisely because they are peculiar to a foreign culture.

An-Na'im and Donnelly respond by proposing that is it exactly the universal character of human rights that enables mankind to assess, even across cultures, what *does* or *does not* constitute a violation of human rights. An-Na'im suggests that:

> ... cross-cultural evaluations, which are unavoidable for any international effort to protect and promote human rights, are most effective when based on universal human values. The more it can be shown that a particular human right is based on a value or norm accepted by the widest range of cultural traditions, the less our efforts to protect and promote that right will be open to charges of ethnocentricity or cultural imperialism.[91]

It follows from this logic that a cross-cultural evaluation can identify values and norms which are *not* accepted by the widest range of cultural traditions and which are contrary to human rights. For instance, it is within this context that discussions surrounding the death penalty take place and in which the USA is ultimately criticized as violating human rights. Customs and practices that are unnecessarily harmful to the health of individuals and are preventable also arguably fall within this realm. Ultimately, a value judgement is being made by the 'international community'. Donnelly comes to the same conclusion that a moral evaluation, a judgement, must ultimately be made, as follows:

> ... our moral precepts are *our* moral precepts. As such, they demand obedience of us. To refuse to act on our own precepts simply because others reject them is to fail to give proper weight to our own moral beliefs, at least in the case of central moral precepts, such as the equality of all human beings and the protection of innocents. And no matter how firmly someone else, or even a whole culture, believes differently, at some point we simply must say that those contrary beliefs are wrong. Negative external judgements may be problematic, but in some cases at least they seem not only permissible but also demanded.[92]

Perry provides a similarly simple and convincing argument by analogy:

> ... Even if by the standards of *his* culture the person standing on my neck, or on my neighbour's neck, or on the neck of a member of his own culture, has a right to do so, that does not mean that by the standards of *our* culture – by the standards *we* accept as correct – we

---

91 An-Na'im, *Problems of Universal Cultural Legitimacy*, in HUMAN RIGHTS IN AFRICA, *supra*, n. 16, p. 343.
92 Donnelly, UNIVERSAL HUMAN RIGHTS IN THEORY AND PRACTICE, *supra*, n. 29, p. 116.

Chapter IV

ought to tolerate his doing so; to the contrary, we might be obligated, by our own standards, to do what we can to remove his foot even from the neck of a member of his own culture.[93] [emphasis in the original]

In the light of such argumentation, it is not supremacist to criticize the death sentence in the USA; it is at least compassionate. The international community is speaking out against a practice which many of its members consider morally abhorrent. Nor is it imperialist to condemn police brutality in Brazil; it is our vulnerability and/or compassion speaking. The international community is admonishing a practice that must be condemned for fear that it will become tolerated... and because it is abhorrent. So why, in this context, is the international community's condemnation of harmful traditional practices in Africa immediately branded imperialist, supremacist or colonialist?

6.2 A Model for Understanding

Three questions merit further consideration:
1. Why and how does a norm or practice become ripe for international scrutiny and condemnation?
2. Is it possible to distinguish condemnation based on imperialist disdain from genuine international moral scrutiny?
3. How is moral scrutiny and condemnation expected to impact upon behaviour?

In response to the first question, it is important to understand how a practice comes to be condemned internationally. Donnelly provides a good model by which to understand the evaluative process.[94] The model pits judgements of a local (internal) community against those of the international (external) community and factors in the moral importance attributed to the practice in question.[95] An internal judgement asks whether a practice is defensible within the fundamental value framework of that society, whereas the external judgement asks the same of the international community.

---

93 Perry, *supra*, n. 33, p. 499.
94 Donnelly, UNIVERSAL HUMAN RIGHTS IN THEORY AND PRACTICE, *supra*, n. 29, pp. 114-115.
95 The grid below is an adaptation of Donnelly's model in *id*.

Figure III
How Practices Become Targeted for Global Human Rights Action

		Internal community condones practice...	
		but judges it morally unimportant	*and judges it morally very important*
External community disapproves of practice...	*but judges it morally unimportant*	**CASE I** – Neck elongation?	**CASE II** – Mourning practices – Scarification – Male circumcision
	and judges it morally very important	**CASE III** – Incisions during pregnancy – Dietary taboos – Birthing practices	**CASE IV** – Female circumcision – Early pregnancy – Religious bondage

Consider the convergence of judgements, as follows:

CASE I (Example: neck elongation).
In this scenario, a practice is condoned by one or more communities yet frowned upon by others. The fact that neither opposing side considers the issue morally important means that little condemnation is likely to occur. The scenario is therefore of little interest. It is difficult to offer an example of this without conducting a survey of what practices some African communities continue but consider of little social significance. For the sake of argumentation, therefore, I have chosen neck elongation, where metal rings are placed around the necks, typically of girls, so as to forcibly stretch the neck and thereby enhance their beauty.

Chapter IV

CASE II (Examples: mourning practices for widows, facial scarification and male circumcision).
Externally unimportant but internally very important. This is equally uninteresting from the perspective of determining a human rights violation since the international community is not interested in condemning the practice as a violation. An example would be the many forms of rituals widows practice to mourn their dead husbands. In Northern Nigeria, for instance, a widow is expected to wail loudly for several hours during the period of mourning, be fully stripped of her clothing by her sisters-in-law, be poorly fed, appear unkempt, drink the water used to bathe her husband's corpse and remain completely ostracized during the pre-burial period.[96] While the external community may believe this practice to be psychologically degrading and unhealthy for the widow, it is not considered so morally important as to condemn it. Nor is there a strong basis under international human rights law to categorize it as a violation. Another example would be the practice of facial scarification, a ritual among various African peoples. The circumcision of boys by numerous religious communities the world over could also arguably be placed within this box. Those communities which practice male circumcision maintain it to be morally imperative (usually because it is believed to be prescribed by religion). Those communities which disapprove of the practice, however, do not attribute it moral importance to the degree that it should be condemned as a violation of a boy's human rights.

CASE III (Examples: incisions, dietary taboos and some traditional birthing practices). Morally unimportant for the local community, but morally very important for the international community. This serves as the best environment to change a practice. Because the issue is of great moral significance to the external evaluator (international community) and of little moral importance internally, external pressure is less likely to be resented and most likely to be effective, so long, warns Donnelly, as the argument against the practice is made with tact and cultural awareness. Reductions in numbers of polygamous marriages may have resulted from such a process. I would also argue that some of the harmful traditional practices focused upon in this study, such as incisions in pregnant women, dietary taboos during pregnancy and lactation and possibly even some traditional birthing practices, could be placed under this category. This follows from the fact that 'moral' arguments are rarely given for their practice or continuation, but rather arguments of superstition (arguably based on ignorance).

---

96 Reported in Inter-African Committee on Traditional Practices Affecting the Health of Women and Children (IAC), RIGHTS AND WIDOWHOOD RITES IN NIGERIA (2000), p. 63.

CASE IV (Examples: female circumcision, early marriage and religious bondage). In this scenario, it is considered internally morally very important that a certain practice be maintained and externally morally very important that the practice be stopped. This is the most difficult case to handle. It is also the situation where arguments for cultural relativism are rife. Numerous harmful traditional practices could be placed within this category, including early marriage, female circumcision and religious bondage.

Through the use of this grid, the question of why and how a practice comes to be earmarked for international scrutiny and condemnation has been answered. We thus turn to the second question of whether it is possible to establish whether condemnation is rooted in some form of cultural imperialism or based in genuine international moral scrutiny. Here, again, it is submitted that the language and approach of international human rights law has been appropriately formulated, namely in the provision of a process to establish consensus. If there is consensus within an intercultural forum such as the United Nations (which includes official voices from Africa) that, e.g., child marriage denies a girl the right to dignity, to security, to health and/or to choose one's spouse, then condemnation of such a practice is legitimate. Any practice in any culture can be challenged in this way. Following the universalist approach, social and cultural norms and practices do not have complete legitimacy simply because they exist and are maintained within the socio-cultural context of a specific community. They must be able to withstand the challenge of universally expressed values, including international human rights standards.

An-Na'im provides us with the answer to the third question in asking why a proponent of one cultural view would accept a judgement of the majority of other cultures. Acceptance can be particularly difficult in light of the fact that the more strongly one adheres to one's values, the less likely one is to concede to the values of others. However, as he explains,

> ... there appears to be a universal rational principle to the effect that strong evidence of a contrary view should induce a person to reexamine her or his position. In my own culture of northern Sudan, this notion is expressed in this maxim: if two people tell you that your head is missing, you better check and see if it is still there. In other words, the more widely our positions are challenged by others, the more likely we are to reconsider those positions.[97]

In order to better understand this process let us examine more closely the example of the traditional practice of female circumcision, which, it is often claimed by cultural relativists, precisely confirms the inability to apply human rights norms between cultures.[98] Female circumcision is widely evaluated (by many cultures, including non-

---

97 An-Na'im, *Problems of Universal Cultural Legitimacy*, *supra*, n. 74, p. 341.
98 Perry, *supra*, n. 33, similarly considers this practice, *modis arguendo*, at length from the perspective of the universalist/relativist dichotomy, pp. 487-490.

circumcising African ones) to be a horrific practice; it is morally abhorrent to those for whom the practice is alien to their culture (and to some from within the culture where it is practiced). However, in the view of some, if not most, people in the cultures which practice it, female circumcision is morally proper. They may suggest that the practice is a matter of cultural preference and that persons who are not of that culture would not understand it and have no right to impose their views: You may find it abhorrent but another finds it ennobling. The question then is whether this is simply a matter of conflicting cultural values or a violation of international human rights. The task at hand, if it has not yet been accomplished, is to examine our position by taking a rational self-critical look at the practice, the forms it takes, the reasons why it is performed, and the conditions under which it occurs and test these against the standards of positive international law.

As a result of this exercise, the external community deems female circumcision to be a violation, *inter alia*, of a woman's right to dignity, integrity and health. The practice, we believe, subjects a woman to cruel and inhuman treatment and is a form of gender-based violence against which human rights protects. We call upon provisions in the Universal Declaration of Human Rights, the International Covenant on Economic, Social and Cultural Rights, the Convention on the Elimination of All Forms of Discrimination against Women, and also non-binding documents, notably the Declaration on the Elimination of Violence against Women which expressly condemns 'female genital mutilation.' The expectation now is that a significant number of members from the cultural communities who maintain the practice come to accept the view that the practice violates a woman's rights and change their behaviour accordingly. This is not an unrealistic expectation because of the ever-changing and pluralist nature of culture. Even traditional or communal African culture is morally pluralistic[99] – not all believe female circumcision is morally just (as is readily evident in asylum cases where women have fled their country to escape the procedure). It is therefore likely that at least some members of that culture might be brought to share, or share already, the external consensus view that the practice is wrong, violative of rights and ought not be performed. In short, any external critique will necessarily generate an internal critique, which will place a moral challenge before the culture which practices female circumcision, and may well change the moral perceptions of at least a few. In this sense, a proponent of one cultural view does not accept *the judgement* of the majority of other cultures, but accepts *the challenge* that judgement poses to their own perceptions. Relativists who reject the right of other cultures to take a critical look at a practice and challenge it on the basis of moral evaluations effectively reject the freedom of indivi-

---

99 As emphasized by N. Kim, *Toward a Feminist Theory of Human Rights: Straddling the Fence between Western Imperialism and Uncritical Absolutism*, Columbia Human Rights Law Review, Vol. 25 (1993), pp. 88-90.

duals to form an opinion and express it.[100] This is arguably because they fear the consequences of the challenge rather than the premises on which it is made.

A similar approach of cross-cultural evaluation[101] has been formulated and advanced by Weston with respect to cultural practices, an approach he refers to as a *methodology of respect* according to which competing relativist-universalist claims can be assessed more objectively. Employing different terminology but conveying the same message, he suggests that a high priority be given to *persuasion* rather than *coercion* in the communication of all-important values.[102] According to Weston, one should take an observational standpoint when making a choice about the abusive or non-abusive nature of a cultural practice. The standpoint requires *rational* persons of *diverse identity* (creed, gender, race, etc.) acting privately (e.g. outside of State or religious interests) to assess a practice relative to how they believe world public order is defined. This standpoint, he concedes, is extremely difficult to achieve. Whatever one may conclude about the effect of Western influence upon the observational standpoint, 'the perspective of free and rational persons acting in their own self-interest in an "initial position" of equality behind a "veil of ignorance" as to the precise terms of their societal circumstance… is most likely impossible.'[103] No social psychologist, he adds, would vouchsafe an individual's capacity for complete objectivity in legal and moral thinking, no matter how open-minded he or she may be.[104] The standpoint is nonetheless recommended by Weston because it remains the most impartial of perspectives.

7 CLOSING THE CIRCLE

We have thus come full circle to Rawls' initial premise of man's capacity to rationalize the universal values of what is good and bad – that the true principles of justice are those of fairness which free and rational persons are able to decipher. At the same time, we have also come full circle to Antiquity's School of Skeptics, in particular Herodotus' claim (meriting repetition) that 'if one were to put before all men the suggestion that out of all customs they should choose the best, each people would examine them and then pick their own; so accustomed are they to think that their own customs are far the best.'[105] Some 2,000 years later, this observation remains valid and powerful.

However, two elements are lacking in Herodotus' and Weston's conclusions. In the case of Herodotus, he ignores the fact that customs do change and he fails to inquire

---

100 For discussion, *see* Howard, *Cultural Absolutism*, *supra*, n. 29.
101 Various scholars from different fields (e.g. law, sociology, psychology and philosophy) have considered the process of 'rationalizing,' but have expressed it in different manners. From philosophy, for example, Hare, *supra*, n. 88, employs the term 'critical thinking' to convey the same meaning.
102 Weston, *supra*, n. 34, p. 81.
103 *Id.*, p. 79.
104 *Id.*
105 Herodotus, *supra*, n. 14, para. 38.

why. Change must have come from internal or external prompts as surmised by Donnelly above. Weston, on the other hand, has drawn a correct conclusion, but has failed to recognize that evaluations of practices (or at least ones which are serious and respectful) should take place through a process of cross-cultural consultation in order to gain the widest possible consensus taking into account variations in religious, cultural, economic, and political perspectives. This process of consensus, as suggested by An-Na'im, should reduce to a minimum, if not remove entirely, the biases we have regarding social precepts and with which any human being would engage in such an evaluation.

Following from these conclusions on cross-cultural evaluations of cultural practices, it must be recognized that no lasting change is possible without an initial process of internal critique, self-evaluation and, ultimately, persuasion. Human rights norms provide the means by which to jump-start the crucial process of change in traditions, by legitimizing external challenges and judgements of certain harmful practices. Naturally, this does not exclude the possibility of internal critique occurring without prompting – a process which is constant in every society. African women and men are challenging harmful traditional practices in their communities every day. For them, human rights discourses may lend additional legitimacy to their challenges.

CHAPTER V
ASSESSING THE AFRICAN CHARTER AS A TOOL FOR SOCIAL CHANGE

1 INTRODUCTION

As the primary human rights instrument in the region, the African Charter on Human and Peoples' Rights[1] (hereafter 'African Charter' or simply 'Charter')[2] and its Commission should be the first port of call for the protection and fulfillment of rights in the region. The intention in this chapter is to establish whether this human rights system unique to Africa sufficiently equips Africans to challenge the harmful traditions in question which are equally unique to African culture.

The special protection of the rights of women is addressed in a solitary, but broad, provision in the African Charter: Article 18, paragraph 3, which reads as follows:

> The State shall ensure the elimination of every discrimination against women and also ensure the protection of the rights of the woman and the child as stipulated in international declarations and conventions.

While this provision appears to offer sufficient protection against harmful traditional practices, the presence of other clauses in the Charter (calling for the protection of the family and traditional values) raises significant ambiguity, and thus is a source of concern. More specifically, these clauses are regarded by a number of scholars and human rights advocates as obstacles to women's full enjoyment of their rights[3] and roadblocks to the challenge of harmful cultural practices rooted in African traditions. The case is made that these clauses should better be regarded as red herrings. Support for this conclusion is drawn from the informal *travaux préparatoires* (working drafts) of the Charter, the interpretations and general application of the clauses by the Commission, and a comparison with the African Charter on the Rights and Welfare of the Child. Scholarly arguments regarding their interpretation are also examined. In analyzing specific clauses outside of the context of their provision, and indeed the larger context of the Charter, we risk misinterpreting their intended meaning. Special

---

1 The African Charter on Human and Peoples' Rights (African Charter). Concluded: 26 June 1981, entered into force: 21 October 1986. International Legal Materials, Vol. 21 (1982), from p. 59.
2 Also referred to by other commentators as the 'Banjul Charter'.
3 Howard, for instance, suggests that '[w]hile the rights of women are... specifically protected, their inclusion within the protection of the family could result in ambiguities when the individual woman comes into conflict with family norms or with her husband's wishes.' R.E. Howard, HUMAN RIGHTS IN COMMONWEALTH AFRICA (1986), p. 186.

measures recently adopted by the Commission to improve the protection of African women's rights are also examined for their potential to assist in the challenge of harmful traditions and practices. The conclusion is made that the Charter can be an effective tool to stimulate changes in traditional practices and behaviours harmful to women's health.

2 DERIVING INSIGHT FROM THE *TRAVAUX PRÉPARATOIRES*

No formal records of the *travaux préparatoires* of the African Charter exist. However, one of the participants in the drafting sessions of Parts II and III (Articles 30-68) of the African Commission (establishing this body and its principles) has published informal records of these.[4] During the *travaux préparatoires* of these parts of the Charter the issue of African practices and customs did briefly surface and was the source of some discussion. It was noticed in an earlier working draft of the Charter that the language of then Article 3 (later to become Article 61 of the Charter) was unsatisfactory. The draft article read:

> The Commission shall also have regard to other international conventions, whether general or particular, establishing rules expressly recognized by the States Members of the OAU; African practices evidencing customs generally accepted as law; the general principles of law recognized by nations...

The portion of this Article which gave rise to discussion was the clause concerning '*African practices evidencing customs generally accepted as law.*' Members of the Working Group, in particular Mr. Mohamadou M'Backé of Senegal, reacted strongly against the concept affirmed in this provision. As explained by Ramcharan, the drafters did not wish to consecrate all of the customs within Africa and wanted to make sure that only those customs were retained by the Commission as were consistent with internationally recognized standards of human rights. Accordingly, the provision was revised in a later draft to provide for '*African practices consistent with international human rights standards evidencing customs generally accepted as law.*' The final language of this provision in Article 61 of the Charter reads only somewhat differently: '*African practices consistent with international norms on human and peoples' rights, customs generally accepted as law...*'

---

4   *See* B.G. Ramcharan, *The Travaux Préparatoires of the African Commission on Human and Peoples' Rights*, Human Rights Law Journal, Vol. 13 (1992), pp. 308-309. For more detail on the drafting and contents of the Charter, *see* E. Kodjo, *The African Charter on Human and Peoples' Rights*, Human Rights Law Journal, Vol. 11 (1990), p. 271.

3 Deriving Insight from the African Commission

Emmanuel Bello, a Commissioner in the early years of the Commission and a scholar on the African Charter, has expressed his views, presumably influenced by his work in the Commission, on the situation of women's rights within the Charter. He notes:

> One issue which the Council of Ministers did not deal with in great depth is that relating to African women. The subject is treated like a sketch-map, roughly drawn with few details. Article 18, paragraph 3, of the Charter merely indicates that the State 'shall ensure the elimination of every discrimination against women and also ensure the protection of the rights of the woman and child…'. No effort was made to draw up a list, at least, that highlights a few women's problems which African governments should endeavour to consider with due diligence, such as the prohibition of forced circumcision and the rights of unmarried mothers. Some form of positive discrimination in favour of women should have been included in the Charter. But, of course, one must remember that all the members of the delegations who drafted the African Charter were men… There are other important omissions in the Charter. But the future will take care of them. These include… the right to free choice of a marriage partner.[5]

Interestingly, Bello does not recount any discussions or thoughts on the scope and implications of the clauses in question. This presses home the point that the inclusion of language referring to the culture of African civilizations and traditional values to be upheld by both the State and the family was not believed to be contentious. Rather, discussion on the poor status of women and harmful practices related to this status, according to Bello, was more likely to have arisen under the context of Article 5, indirectly revealing this provision to serve as the stronger weapon against harmful traditions and practices. Article 5 of the Charter provides that:

> Every individual shall have the right to the respect of the dignity inherent in a human being and to the recognition of his legal status. All forms of exploitation and degradation of man particularly slavery, slave trade, torture, cruel, inhuman or degrading punishment and treatment shall be prohibited.

Bello's remarks on this provision merit repetition with some abridgment. He states:

> The content of Article 5 of the Charter points to the very core of human exploitation and the zenith of man's inhumanity to man. It also contains almost all the evil so easily identified with many African States… It is disturbing to learn that some African parents give away their children in return for money so that the basic necessities of life can be obtained. Young girls have been forced into marriage so that the dowry paid by their husbands can be used

---

5   E.G. Bello, *The African Charter on Human and Peoples' Rights: A Legal Analysis*, Académie de Droit International: Recueil des Cours, Vol. 194 (1985), p. 183.

for the maintenance of their families. The outcome of such phenomena is that some men virtually claim that they own their spouses, just as a man would claim a piece of furniture as his own. Furthermore, whatever material benefits are derived from the personal endeavours of some married African women they devolve automatically on their husbands. The latter derive their legal authority from the effective payment of a 'bride price'.

Customary law and African traditions place considerable strain on women in some African States. Superstitious practices also offer much comfort to these tenets. Men are usually the main defender of many of these traditions. If men so desire they can marry as many wives as they choose. Adultery on the part of a husband is not a legal ground for divorce under such conditions. The customary belief is that men are free to practice polygamy. Adultery on the part of the married woman, on the other hand, is an offence and ground for divorce, except in certain permitted cases. The barrenness of a married African woman, under customary law, is sufficient ground for dissolving a marriage in some African countries..."[6]

Umozurike, who similarly has served as a Commissioner[7] and is an acknowledged scholar on the African Charter, has noted that the principal aim of the inclusion of the provision in Article 5 on women's rights is intended to grant an element of special protection and support.[8]

But what conclusion can we derive from the practice of the Commission over the last dozen years? In light of accusations of purposefully intended omissions and ambiguities with regard to women's rights and the protection of the family and African traditional values within the Charter, it is evident that a large duty of interpretation falls on the shoulders of the Commission. Aside from this duty, the Commission also ultimately holds the tasks of monitoring whether the domestic legislation of any State Party limits or prohibits the exercise of the rights as stipulated in the Charter, and of establishing whether the rights of individuals are being violated. In order to help them carry out these tasks, the Commission has issued guidelines on reporting procedures for States Parties.[9] These guidelines are intended to assist States in drafting their reports to the Commission. With regard to women, States are specifically required to report on measures they have adopted to ensure equal treatment of men and women and on measures to empower women and to eliminate the obstacles (including social, cultural and religious ones) which remain. State reports should also include remedies made available to women who have suffered discrimination.[10] However, despite these guidelines, the quality and actual submission of reports leaves much to be desired. Some States and scholars of the Charter criticize the guidelines as too complex and

---

6 *Id.*, p. 154.
7 Serving since 1989 and re-elected 1992-1997.
8 U.O. Umozurike, *The African Charter on Human and Peoples' Rights*, American Journal of International Law, Vol. 77 (1983), p. 905.
9 For more information and a critical analysis of the content of the guidelines, *see* E.A. Ankumah, THE AFRICAN COMMISSION ON HUMAN AND PEOPLES' RIGHTS: PRACTICES AND PROCEDURES (1996), pp. 82-89.
10 Guidelines VII

demanding.[11] A greater problem lies in the fact that State reports often are kept confidential, as are the Commission's observations on them. It is therefore very difficult to establish whether States are reporting on harmful traditional practices and, if so, whether the Commission is reacting to this information. This makes the challenge of eliminating harmful traditions on the basis of human rights all the more difficult since it is difficult to establish whether any precedents have been set.

According to close observers of the Commission, however, the Commission has been consistently liberal in its interpretation of the vague but potentially powerful provisions.[12] Moreover, rather than concerning itself with establishing whether domestic legislation or cultural practices exist which are contrary to women's rights, the Commission is more likely to make a pre-emptive move, calling upon all States to ensure that the rights set forth in the Charter are not limited on the grounds of culture, religion, or domestic or customary laws.

As a further consolation, four of the total eleven Commissioners in the first session of the African Commission in the new millennium were women.[13] In this light, it could be said that the Commission is becoming balanced on the basis of gender. This is the greatest female representation ever in the Commission. Indeed, until its 14th session in June 1993, when NGO demands for female representation were finally met with the appointment of Ms. Vera Duarte Martins of Cape Verde, all eleven Commissioners were male. Now a fashionable concept, establishing a fair representation of both sexes in any human rights body is intended to ensure that the concerns of both are more adequately addressed. Of course, the mere presence of women as Commissioners does not mean that the special needs and violations suffered by African women will, on the basis of their presence, be addressed, or be addressed better than by any sympathetic male Commissioner. Beyond the sex of the Commissioner, what really matters are the personalities and commitments of the Commissioners. In the case at hand, all four women have an impressive track record in the advancement of human rights – two of them specifically in the advancement of the human rights of women.[14] Ms. Chirwa has the unique distinction as the only Commissioner with the experience of an aggrieved

---

11 *See* Ankumah, *supra*, n. 9.
12 *See* T. Nhlapo, *The African Charter and Women's Human Rights: What Next?*, African Legal Aid Quarterly, July-Sept. 1996, p. 11.
13 They were:
Ms. Florence Butegwa (Uganda): Term of office in the Commission: 1999-2005.
Ms. Vera Mlanguzwa Chirwa (Malawi): 1999-2005.
Ms. Jainaba Johm (The Gambia): 1999-2005.
Dr. Angela Melo (Mozambique): 2001-2007, replacing Ms. Julienne Ondziel-Gnelenga (Republic of Congo): 1995-2001.
14 Ms. Ondziel-Gnelenga served the Commission her full term. She has been an active member in numerous women's and human rights organisations, such as Femmes Africa Solidarité (a women's NGO aimed at conflict prevention, management and resolution in Africa) and the International Federation of Women in Legal Careers. Ms. Butegwa is former Executive Director of Women in Law and Development in Africa (WILDAF) and author of numerous commentaries on African women's rights, some of which are cited in this study.

party. Some years before she was appointed as Commissioner she petitioned the Commission alleging the violation of her and her husband's human rights.[15]

4 DERIVING IINSIGHT FROM THE AFRICAN CHARTER ON THE RIGHTS AND WELFARE OF THE CHILD

Given the controversial nature of the clauses in question, it may be useful to turn to another, more recent African human rights instrument, to establish whether greater clarification has been established. The African Charter on the Rights and Welfare of the Child (hereafter the African Charter on Children's Rights) was adopted in 1990 and entered into force at the end of 1999.[16] This Charter includes clauses similar to the Banjul Charter regarding culture. For instance, Preambular paragraph 7 uses nearly identical language, urging States to consider 'the virtues of their cultural heritage, historical background and the values of the African civilization which should inspire and characterize their reflection on the concept of the rights and welfare of the child'. Article 11 reiterates the need to preserve and strengthen positive African morals, traditional values and cultures within the context of a child's education. Yet Preambular paragraph 4 conveys a stronger message, noting that 'the situation of most African children remains critical due to the unique factors of their ... cultural, traditional and developmental circumstances...' This seems to suggest that culture and tradition must be recognized as sometimes responsible for the poor treatment or low status of many African children. However, this does not provide sufficient insight on the intended meaning of the controversial terms.

Of greater import is the presence of near-to-identical 'controversial' language together with a new, and very revealing, provision. This new provision calls for the protection of the child against harmful social and cultural practices (Article 21). Specifically, the provision calls for the elimination of socio-cultural customs and practices harmful to health or discriminatory to the child. Moreover, it prohibits child marriage and the betrothal of girls. States are required to take all appropriate measures to ensure the elimination of these practices, including (but not exclusively) by adopting legislation. The language of this provision is clear, simple and strong.

In this light, the African Charter on Children's Rights reinforces the view that the clauses in contention in the African Charter were not intended to accommodate traditional customs and practices which are in any way harmful. This is because the African Charter on Children's Rights precisely prohibits those very customs and practices while calling for the preservation of positive African morals and traditional

---

15 For a summary of the case, *see* R. Murray, *Decisions and Reports of the African Commission on Human and Peoples' Rights, Banjul*, Human Rights Law Journal, Vol. 18 (1997), p. 29.
16 As at 19 February 2001, 21 States were party to the African Charter on Children's Rights which entered into force on 29 November 1999, upon its 15th ratification.

values. Clearly *positive* morals and traditional values were not understood or intended to preserve *harmful* traditional customs and practices.

5 DERIVING INSIGHT FROM SCHOLARLY ARGUMENTATION AND INTERPRETATION

5.1 The General Situation of Women's Rights

At first glance, Article 18 (3) providing for the elimination of discrimination against women represents an open canvas for the promotion and protection of women's rights. The provision's call to protect women's rights as stipulated in *all* human rights instruments is significant. Through this provision, the African Charter makes an explicit commitment to provide protection equal in scope to that required by 'international declarations and conventions.' By including 'declarations' among the list of international instruments to be consulted, the African Charter grants an even greater legal scope of protection than is to be found under the systems where these instruments originate. Moreover, international declarations (owing to the fact that they commonly issue out of a political process and are not binding upon States) often suggest a broader selection of rights and scope of protection. A good example of this would be the recognition of 'reproductive rights' in the Beijing Declaration and Platform for Action.[17] Another declaration significant to any effort to end harmful traditions would be the 1993 UN Declaration on the Elimination of Violence against Women. In opting for the term '*international* conventions' (in lieu of '*universal* conventions', or even more specifically '*universal human rights* conventions'), our palette of choices is further enlarged to include provisions stipulated in other regional human rights instruments and international conventions of other UN bodies. This is confirmed under Articles 60 and 61(Principles Applicable to the Commission) of the Charter which identify some of these instruments specifically and call more broadly upon 'the provisions of various instruments adopted within the Specialized Agencies of the United Nations of which the parties of the present Charter are members.'[18] In short, Article 18 ensures that States will *act* to protect the rights of women as stipulated in a broad spectrum of instruments, preambular paragraph 9 affirms that States shall *adhere* to the principles they set forth, and Articles 60 and 61 declare that the Commission shall *draw inspiration* from these in all their deliberations.

The overlap of protection offered between the various declarations and conventions strengthens the claims African women may make in order to challenge, modify or eliminate harmful traditional practices. In this respect, Article 18 of the African Charter

---

[17] Although it is noted that the Universal Declaration of Human Rights is the only Declaration expressly listed in the Preamble and Article 60 of the African Charter.

[18] Preambular paragraph 9 testifies to the recognition of human rights principles to be adhered by OAU Member States, this time as contained in the 'declarations, conventions and other instruments adopted by the Organization of African Unity, the Movement of Non-Aligned Countries and the United Nations.'

is remarkable in its scope, allowing a claimant to pick and choose from those instruments and provisions which most strongly make the case that practices harmful to reproductive health are contrary to human rights law and thereby represent violations of her human rights and those of other women.

Some commentators, however, argue that, because the Charter has only one provision on women's rights, it gives insufficient direct attention to women as a group[19] and thereby skillfully avoids dealing with the rights of women and the forms of violations they may disproportionately suffer because of their gender. It is true that a simple reading of the African Charter gives one little information as to the specific rights women may claim and States must ensure. Filling this gap requires the thorough knowledge and consultation of many instruments by all parties concerned: individuals, human rights activists, the Commission and the States alike. This is a principal reason for the adoption of special measures by the Commission (see Section 7 below).

For some, the Charter also fails sufficiently to engage States to alter the traditional roles of men and women in the family and society to achieve sexual equality.[20] Ankumah, for instance, notes that such an omission may be indicative of the drafters' 'intention not to deviate from customary practices relating to women in general and with respect to marriage in particular.'[21] Nhlapo reasons that this omission may have arisen out of the need to exclude sensitive issues which risked compromising the adoption of the Charter by some Organization of African Unity (OAU) Member States.[22] There may be seeds of truth in both of these views. However, these omissions are more likely a result of two mutually enforcing considerations: the simple lack of awareness by the drafters that women's rights and needs required special focus; and their belief that further specificity was unnecessary in light of Article 18(3).

5.2 Clauses Protecting the African Family, Morals and Traditional Values

It is not only what *is not* in the Charter that worries some people, but what *is included* in the Charter. A controversial issue which is significant to the subject of this study is the placement of the only non-discrimination clause aimed at women as a group (in paragraph 3 of Article 18) within a strongly worded article which further calls for the protection of the family, morals and traditional values (in paragraphs 1 and 2). Similar

---

19 See, e.g., E.V.O. Dankwa, active Chair and longstanding Commissioner of the African Commission, who suggests: 'Women should not only serve as Commissioners, but their rights should receive more serious elaboration and guarantee than what obtains under the present Charter.' *Conference on regional systems of human rights protection in Africa, the Americas and Europe*, Human Rights Law Journal, Vol. 13 (1992), p. 315; and C.E. Welch Jr., *Human Rights and African Women: A Comparison of Protection Under Two Major Treaties*, Human Rights Quarterly, Vol. 15 (1993), p. 554.
20 See, e.g., Ankumah, *supra*, n. 9, p. 156.
21 *Id.*
22 T. Nhlapo, *International Protection of Human Rights and the Family: African Variations on a Common Theme*, International Journal of Law and the Family, Vol. 3 (1989), p. 14.

references throughout the Charter call for the consideration, preservation and strengthening of these values. The ambiguity of these terms, and the intended message such ambiguity conveys, leaves some observers 'uncomfortable.'[23] Those with more extreme views believe the presence of these terms is specifically intended to introduce a duality of norms which inherently place restrictions on women's rights for the good of the family and community. Given that the practices harmful to the reproductive health of women are precisely maintained by the traditions and values upheld by African communities, one understandably approaches these clauses with trepidation. Clearly, it is imperative to shed some light on possible interpretations of notions of family, African culture and traditional values since these are the same notions to be reckoned with in challenging practices and behaviours harmful to women's reproductive health.

5.2.1 Clauses on the Protection of the Family

Three significant clauses in the Charter address the protection and preservation of the family as a duty to be fulfilled by both the State and the individual. Article 18(1) provides that '[t]he family shall be the natural unit and basis of society.' Under Chapter II (Duties), the Charter also stipulates in Article 27 that

> Every individual shall have duties towards his family and society, the State and other legally recognized communities and the international community.

It is further stated in Article 29(1) of the Charter that the individual shall have the duty:

> To preserve the harmonious development of the family and to work for the cohesion and respect of the family; to respect his parents at all times, to maintain them in case of need.

These three provisions point out what we already know to be matters of relative importance in African society, notably:
1. That family (in its nuclear and extended forms) is a significant social unit, carrying important values;[24]
2. That the elderly generally hold a privileged position and must be respected;[25]
3. That, in the event of problems or disputes, solutions should be sought protecting the unity of the family where possible.

---

23 *See*, e.g., T. Nhlapo, *The African Charter and Women's Human Rights: What Next?*, African Legal Aid Quarterly, July-September 1996.
24 *See* C. Bradley and T.S. Weisner, *Introduction: Crisis in the African Family*, in T.S. Weisner *et al.*, AFRICAN FAMILIES AND THE CRISIS OF SOCIAL CHANGE (1997), p. xxvi.
25 For discussion on this subject, *see*, e.g.: C. Meillassoux, *La conquête de l'aînesse [trans: The conquest of the older]*, in C. Attias-Donfut et L. Rosenmayr, eds., VIEILLIER EN AFRIQUE (1994); and L.V. Thomas, *Vieillesse et mort en Afrique [trans: Aging and death in Africa]*, in *id.*

Regarding the first point, the protection of the family is well established in international human rights law. Article 16(3) of the UDHR provides that '[t]he family is the natural and fundamental group unit of society and is entitled to protection by society and the State.' Article 10(1) of the CESCR similarly provides that '[t]he widest possible protection and assistance should be accorded to the family, which is the natural and fundamental group unit of society, particularly… while it is responsible for the care and education of dependent children…' Given that the protection of the family is so well established in numerous human rights instruments and without controversy, the same clause could hardly be brought into doubt in the context of an African human rights instrument.

For some critics, it is the specific framing of the promotion and preservation of the family as a *duty* of the individual which raises concern.[26] Yet the concept of a duty to one's fellow human being is also not estranged from fundamental universal human rights instruments, as demonstrated in the ultimate paragraph of the CESCR's preamble which reads as follows:

> *Realizing* that the individual, having duties to other individuals and to the community to which he belongs, is under the responsibility to strive for the promotion and observance of the rights recognized in the present Covenant.

Indeed, without the fulfilment of such duties, the UDHR suggests the individual is unable to flourish, stating in Article 29 that '[e]veryone has duties to the community in which alone the free and full development of his personality is possible'.

There is nothing inherently contradictory between an individual's duty to preserve and respect his family and others in society, and his own human rights.[27] Nor is there an inevitable conflict between points 2 and 3 above and human rights law. Individuals every day in every society balance without conflict their duties to their family and society with their rights and freedoms.[28] Of course, from the perspective of the African woman, these duties may be interpreted in another manner. For instance, they may support her parents' claim that she must respect their wishes and undergo female

---

26 For a variety of views on the duties conferred on individuals in the African Charter, *see*: Bello, *supra*, n. 5; W. Benedek, *Peoples' Rights and Individuals' Duties as Special Features of the African Charter*, in P. Kunig *et al.*, eds., REGIONAL PROTECTION OF HUMAN RIGHTS BY INTERNATIONAL LAW: THE EMERGING AFRICAN SYSTEM (1985); K. Mbaye, LES DROITS DE L'HOMME EN AFRIQUE (1992); and generally M. Wa Mutua, *The Banjul Charter and the African Cultural Fingerprint: An Evaluation of the Language of Duties*, Virginia Journal of International Law, Vol. 35 (1995).
27 Indeed, C.S. Lewis demonstrated the commonality of duties to parents, elders and ancestors by listing the religious sources of these, including Hindu, Ancient Jewish, Ancient Egyptian and Ancient Chinese scriptures. See C.S. Lewis, THE ABOLITION OF MAN (1943), pp. 53-54.
28 For example, a woman may have to leave her job to help her aging mother or care for her small children. A man may feel it his duty to defend his country in times of war.

circumcision. They may also be used to support her husband's demands not to use protection during intercourse and her duty to maintain harmony within the family.

From this perspective, it is true that such clauses do not offer solace. But interpretations limiting a woman's rights and freedom would clearly contradict a number of rights provided in the Charter, notably to: freedom from discrimination (Article 2); life (Article 4); dignity and freedom from cruel or degrading treatment (Article 5); express her views (Article 9); and the best attainable state of physical and mental health (Article 16). If a woman alleged contradictions within the Charter on this basis, it should at a minimum be easily argued that her duties must be balanced with her rights. Nowhere is it stipulated in the Charter that, in the event of a conflict, duties for the preservation of the family (or indeed any other duties it sets forth) are to take precedence over rights. Rather, the philosophy of human rights law would be strongly averse to such a conclusion since a restrictive interpretation of the controversial clauses[29] and the relationship between rights and duties would be contrary to the Vienna Convention on the Law of Treaties.[30] This conclusion is rationalized on a spectrum of probability:

1. It seems highly unlikely that discrimination and violence against women as condoned by the family, and as a result of a woman's duty to respect her parents and promote harmonious family relations, were directly or indirectly intended to be provided in a treaty defending human rights;
2. It seems more likely from the ordinary meaning of these clauses as parts of a larger provision (in the case of Article 27) that these duties were to be interpreted in a broader sense as obligations to others and respect for the laws of relations among individuals, and between individuals and the State. The fact that the provision which follows further elaborates upon this very notion[31] and that similar language is present in the CESCR supports this logic;
3. It seems more likely from the ordinary meaning of these clauses as parts of a larger provision (in the case of Article 29) that this provision should be understood in the sense of taking care of one's fellow human beings (especially those for whom one is responsible), as conveyed in the secondary clause of the provision. The primordial place of the elderly in African society is deeply embedded in its culture, in keeping with tradition and customary law. To have denied this fact would have contributed to a Charter without cultural basis and, therefore, without broad popular support.

---

29 *See generally*, e.g., A. Clapham, HUMAN RIGHTS IN THE PRIVATE SPHERE (1993) and other discussions on acceptable limitations on rights, such as in M. Nowak, U.N. COVENANT ON CIVIL AND POLITICAL RIGHTS: CCPR COMMENTARY (1993).
30 In particular Article 18 on the obligation not to defeat the object and purpose of a treaty and Article 31(1) which states that 'a treaty shall be interpreted in good faith in accordance with the ordinary meaning to be given to the terms of the treaty in their context and in the light of its object and purpose.'
31 Article 28 reads: 'Every individual shall have the duty to respect and consider his fellow beings without discrimination, and to maintain relations aimed at promoting, safeguarding and reinforcing mutual respect and tolerance.'

5.2.2 Clauses on the Protection of African Morals and Traditional Values

There are four other clauses which commentators argue support the cultural subjugation of African women and continuation of discriminatory or harmful traditions. One commentator sums up the concerns as follows:

> The primary problem with the Charter's mechanisms for the protection of women's human rights is that those protections are located in the context of the family... the high level of standard of equality required by Article 16 of CEDAW, to the extent that this article is incorporated by Article 18(3) and the duty to be conscious of 'the values of African civilization', is not easily reconcilable with the African traditional values that exist in African marriage law... [I]t is not really necessary to rehash the standard debate over the problems posed for women by traditional values in general and customary marriage law in particular. It should suffice simply to post a reminder about the notion of patriarchy that permeates the whole of traditional law, and the stifling aspects of this notion when it is translated into practices which treat women as inferior to men... These factors render the protection of women under the Charter weak and ambiguous.[32]

The specific clauses and language of concern here are as follows:

1. Preambular paragraph 4
   It reminds States parties to the Charter that they must always take into consideration '... the virtues of their historical tradition and the values of African civilization which should inspire and characterize their reflection on the concept of human and peoples' rights.'
2. Article 17(3)
   It notes, in relation to education and the individual's freedom to take part in the cultural life of his community, that '[t]he promotion and protection of morals and traditional values recognized by the community shall be the duty of the State.'
3. Article 18(1) and (2)
   While stipulating the State's duty to protect the family, the State is also called upon in paragraph 1 to '... take care of its [the family's] physical health and morals.' The State is obliged to assist the family... 'which is the custodian of morals and traditional values recognized by the community.'
4. Article 29(7)
   It affirms that every individual also has a duty '[t]o preserve and strengthen positive African cultural values in his relations with other members of the society, in the spirit of tolerance, dialogue and consultation and, in general, to contribute to the promotion of the moral well being of society.'

If we were not considering these clauses specifically with the knowledge that some traditions may harm the health and lives of African women (and must therefore be

---

32 Nhlapo, *supra*, n. 12, p. 12.

loosened from, rather than protected by, the grip of culture), obligations to preserve positive cultural values, promote the moral well being of society and protect traditional values would be viewed as highly desirable in most societies. For example, most of us would believe a relative teaching one's children how to properly behave in public would be acting responsibly. A teacher stopping a fight during school hours or confiscating a pornographic magazine from a group of boys in the schoolyard would be acting similarly in a responsible way – a positive trait of a healthy society. A woman taking care of her children or a son caring for his elderly parents would be viewed as individuals taking on their responsibilities. They would be fulfilling their obligations towards the promotion and protection of a healthy, moral society. As in the case of the previous clauses in contention regarding the protection of the family, it seems far more likely that these clauses were never intended to maintain the cultural subjugation of women but simply to convey the idealism with which the drafters forged the Charter. Indeed, given the historical framework which inspired the drafting of the African Charter (see Section 6 below), this conclusion is very probable.

Much as the duty to preserve and protect the family is placed within the hands of the State and the individual, the obligation to protect the morals and values of African society is similarly dispersed among the State (preamble and Article 18(1)), the family (Article 18(2))[33], and the individual (Article 29(7)). This is very much in keeping with African culture since African women are seen, and sometimes consider themselves, as the custodians and defenders of culture and cultural values. For instance, at the first African Indigenous Women's Conference held in Morocco in April 1998, one of the central issues women addressed was their role as treasurers of the cultural heritage of their people.[34] Even modern African music continues to project the idealistic image of the woman as the symbol of family stability and the moral fibre of the whole nation.[35] Viewed from this perspective, Article 18(2) strongly underlines the point that women and their families are among the principal *conveyors* of tradition. No issue can be taken in this regard with the Charter's provision. The crux of the problem regarding harmful traditions lies in the fact that women have little power to *formulate* or *change* traditions. In other words, they are recognised in the Charter as the messenger and not the creator of socio-cultural values.

Another controversial clause involves the obligation to protect the health and *morals* of individuals and the community. Once again, this obligation is not foreign to

---

33 The family is recognized as the '*custodian* of morals and traditional values recognized by the community' (emphasis added). The role of the State here is simply to assist the family in its custodial role. The definition of a *custodian* is 'a guardian or keeper', and a *guardian* is defined as 'a defender, protector, or keeper;' THE CONCISE OXFORD DICTIONARY (1990).
34 *See generally* A. van Achterberg, ed., OUT OF THE SHADOWS: THE FIRST AFRICAN INDIGENOUS WOMEN'S CONFERENCE (1998).
35 *See*, e.g., H. Chimhundu, *Sexuality and Socialisation in Shona Praises and Lyrics*, in G. Furniss and L. Gunner, eds., POWER, MARGINALITY AND AFRICAN ORAL LITERATURE (1995).

the philosophy of human rights. Article 19(3) of the CCPR, Article 13(3) of the CESCR, Articles 9(2) and 10(2) of the European Convention on Human Rights, and Article 13(2) and (4) of the American Convention on Human Rights call upon the same language of duties to protect public health and morals. While there has been substantial discussion regarding the point at which such a limitation should come into order, there is broad understanding that it is required. Yet, when the same clause appears in the African Charter, suspicions arise. Of course, the question will naturally arise (in Africa, as elsewhere) regarding the acceptable grounds for such limitations, such as in restricting the right to freedom of information in an attempt to 'protect morals'. For example, efforts to eliminate sacrosanct customs harmful to women's reproductive health, such as an education campaign aimed at adolescents to delay, or practice safe, sex (admissible under Articles 17(1) and 18(3)) could conflict with governmental, religious or other efforts to protect morality (admissible under Articles 17(3) and 18(2)). It is then the work of a court of law or the African Commission to determine whether the State censoring the campaign has overstepped its bounds. In the case of the example at hand, the State's ban on such a campaign would be held as unreasonable on numerous accounts.[36]

The same double standard can be said to exist when the presence of nearly identical language in the 1989 Convention on the Rights of the Child has similarly gone unnoticed or at least without criticism. To be more precise, the penultimate paragraph of the Convention on the Rights of the Child requires that States parties take due account of '… the importance of the traditions and cultural values of each people for the protection of the harmonious development of the child.'

The presence of identical terms such as *people* and *harmonious development*, never mind the repetition of the same basic concept of recognizing the role of *traditions* and *cultural values*, are uncanny. Why are these terms perfectly acceptable in a universal human rights instrument but not in an African regional instrument? In this light, Western criticisms of the African Charter as overly accommodating and protective of culture appear unfounded. Moreover, such double standards enhance African claims of cultural elitism.[37]

A final observation supports the view that we are making a mountain out of a molehill when it comes to the clauses protecting traditional values in the Charter. Specifically, the qualification that the cultural values to be promoted and strengthened should be 'positive' ones supports the rejection of 'oppressive' cultural values, such as the inferiority or subjugation of women.[38] The provision protecting against harmful traditions and practices in the African Charter on Children's Rights underlines this point, notably that female circumcision, early marriage or enforced marriage are in no

---

36 *See* arguments presented in C. Packer, THE RIGHT TO REPRODUCTIVE CHOICE (1996), pp. 65-69.
37 Wa Mutua being the most vocal critic in this regard; *see generally supra*, n. 26.
38 Although Nhlapo believes the adjective 'positive' does not really address the matter; *see supra*, n. 12, p. 12.

way to be construed as positive and virtuous values protected by the African human rights instruments.

6 DERIVING INSIGHT FROM THE UNIQUE HISTORY AND OUTLOOK OF THE AFRICAN REGION

The African Charter is intended to be a 'home grown' instrument responsive to African concerns, traditions and values. These can be said to be reflected in its inclusion of collective (or peoples') rights, the new generation of rights to development, clean environment and peace, and the concept of duties to be paired with the individual's rights. No matter what our views may be on the scope or justiciability of these rights, it cannot be denied that the drafters of the African Charter took a refreshingly bold approach to this instrument, with no nuancing of the historical facts which formed the continent into what it was in the late 1960s and 1970s. Words such as *foreign domination, colonialism, dispossessed* and *oppressed peoples* found scattered throughout the document, betray the realities which weighed heavily on the minds of the drafters (and the greater public) during their negotiations on the provisions and wording of the treaty. Preoccupations lay in resurrecting or reclaiming respect for the status of traditional religion,[39] traditional (customary) law,[40] traditional leadership,[41] pastoral traditions,[42] African culture,[43] etc. which colonialism, Christianity and capitalism were widely criticized for having suppressed or destroyed. Hence, to say that the minds of the drafters were on matters other than the particular situation of women would be an understatement.

7 SPECIAL MEASURES TO IMPROVE THE PROTECTION OF WOMEN'S RIGHTS

Two significant measures have been introduced to improve the protection of the human rights of African women. The first is aimed at improving the scope of protection offered by the African Charter by means of an additional protocol on the rights of women in Africa, still in draft form. The second, the appointment of a Special Rappor-

---

39 *See*, e.g.: A. Barnes, *Evangelization where it is not wanted*, Journal of Religion in Africa, Vol. 25 (1995).
40 *See*, e.g.: B.L. Shadle, *Changing Traditions to Meet Current Altering Conditions*, Journal of African History, No. 40 (1999).
41 *See*, e.g.: M. Gilbert, *The Christian executioner: Christianity and chieftancy as rivals*, Journal of African Religion, Vol. 25 (1995); and, A. Li, *Asafo and destoolment in colonial southern Ghana, 1900-1953*, International Journal of African Historical Studies, Vol. 28 (1995).
42 *See*, e.g.: N.J. Migere, *Rural-urban migration and urbanization in Zambia during the colonial and postcolonial periods*, in E. Kalipeni, ed., POPULATION GROWTH AND ENVIRONMENTAL DEGRADATION IN SOUTHERN AFRICA (1994).
43 *See*, e.g.: H. Aguessy, *Traditional African Views and Apperceptions*, in A.I. Sow *et al.*, eds., INTRODUCTION TO AFRICAN CULTURE: GENERAL ASPECTS (1979); and A.B. Stahl, *Valuing the past, envisioning the future: local perspectives on environmental and cultural heritage in Ghana*, in I. Serageldin and J. Taboroff, eds., CULTURE AND DEVELOPMENT IN AFRICA (1994).

teur on the Rights of African Women, is intended to improve the African Commission's monitoring of women's rights. Interestingly, both these measures closely mimic those adopted to complement another regional mechanism: the Inter-American system.[44] Their actual creation and possible impact on women's rights and the elimination of traditions harmful to reproductive health merit closer scrutiny.

7.1 Draft Additional Protocol on Women's Rights

The impetus for such an instrument came largely from NGOs, specifically the International Commission of Jurists (ICJ) and Women in Law and Development in Africa (WILDAF). A seminar was held in Lomé, Togo, in March 1995 to discuss the need for an additional instrument and whether this was the best means by which to promote the rights of women. Participants decided in favour of an additional protocol to the African Charter and recommended that the protocol provide clear guidelines as to the way in which the Charter's concern with cultural relevance should be understood. It would address specifically the perennial problems in the lives of women by listing them. The Draft Additional Protocol to the African Charter on the Rights of Women in Africa was prepared by a group of experts meeting prior to the 21st Ordinary Session of the African Commission in April 1997 in Nouakchott, Mauritania, and was discussed during the Session. The document was prepared together with current Vice Chairman Dankwa (whose views on the inadequacy of the African Charter with regard to women's rights are on record), then Vice Chairperson Ms. Vera Duarte, and Commissioner Ondziel-Gnelenga. The draft continued to be discussed at subsequent ordinary sessions of the Commission, for which purpose a working group was created. A new draft protocol was introduced at the third meeting of the working group, held in Kigali from 30-31 October 1999, presided over by Commissioner Dankwa with the additional participation of Commissioners Ondziel-Gnelenga and Jainaba Johm. Revisions were made and the resulting text was termed the 'Kigali Draft Protocol.' In its Decision on the Draft Protocol to the African Charter on Human and Peoples' Rights Relating to the Rights of Women in Africa,[45] the Council of Ministers of the OAU invited States to ensure participation in a further expert meeting.

In its current form, the twenty-three-article draft contains two basic types of provisions. The first type is intended to introduce a gender perspective into rights. Some of these rights have already been stipulated in the African Charter (e.g. the right to development) and are therefore given more specificity in relation to women, while others are wholly new (e.g. reproductive rights, widow's rights, and rights to informa-

---

44 Notably through the adoption of the 1994 Inter-American Convention on Violence against Women and the appointment of a Special Rapporteur of the Rights of Women within the OAS.
45 Decision adopted at the 74th Session of the Council of Ministers, held in Lusaka, Zambia, 2-11 July 2001; OAU doc. CM/Dec. 618 (LXXIV).

tion and legal aid). The second type of provision is issue-based with titles such as 'Marriage' and 'Violence against Women.' These provisions in particular carry recommendations for appropriate measures to be taken by States Parties. For instance, Article 13 (Violence against Women) stipulates that States Parties shall take all appropriate measures to identify the root causes of violence against women, punish perpetrators of such violence and provide for the rehabilitation and reparation of victims of such violence.

The Kigali Draft Protocol includes both express and implied provisions against harmful traditional practices. Article 5 (Right to Physical Security) offers the widest and most demanding protection. It stipulates that:

In conformity with Articles 4 and 5 of the African Charter,[46] States Parties... shall:
...
e) prohibit all traditional and cultural practices which are physically and/or morally harmful to women and girls and which are against recognized international norms such as force-feeding and female genital mutilation;
f) develop policies to protect the physical health of women and young girls particularly with regard to practices mentioned in e) above.

Article 19 (Cultural Practices) also includes express protection against harmful traditional practices in providing as follows:

1. Women shall have the right to live in a positive cultural environment and to participate at al levels in the determination of cultural policies.
2. States Parties to the Protocol shall take all appropriate measures to protect women and society from the harmful effects of all forms of intolerance and from any other cultural or religious practices.
3. The States Parties will take all appropriate measures to:
   a) favour the participation of women in the determination of cultural politics at all levels;
   b) protect women and society against all forms of intolerance and repugnant cultural and religious practices.

In qualifying in paragraph 1 that the cultural environment in which women in Africa live shall be 'positive,' the draft Protocol echoes clauses of the African Charter. This 'positive cultural environment' is to be free from the 'harmful effects of... cultural or religious practices.' Although the notion 'positive' is undefined in its content, it is placed expressly in contradistinction to harmful cultural practices. It remains unclear in the text whether the latter comprise also what are known as 'harmful traditional practices.' While the intention of the draft and its history would suggest these are

---

46 Article 4 provides for the right of the individual to respect for his life and the integrity of his person and Article 5 for the right to dignity and freedom from slavery, torture, and cruel, inhuman and degrading treatment.

included, it is unclear how this would then differ from the scope of Article 5 other than the express reference in Article 19 to the religious source of some practices. It is also unclear, and of uncertain value, what is comprised under the notion of 'repugnant' found in paragraph 3 b) of Article 19; the notions of 'harmful' or 'discriminatory' would be both clearer and more consistent with human rights norms. Nonetheless, Articles 5 and 19 are both strong provisions which may be used effectively to protect women against harmful traditional practices.

Other provisions offer implicit protection. Article 7 (Marriage) implicitly addresses the widespread custom of early marriage by providing in paragraph 3 that the minimum age of marriage for men and women shall be 18. Article 9 on Widows' Rights stipulates:

1. It shall be prohibited to subject widows to inhuman, humiliating and degrading treatment.
2. After the death of the husband, the widow shall be by law the guardian of the children.
3. A widow shall have the right to marry a person of her choice.
4. A widow shall have the right to inherit her husband's property.
5. In the event of the death of her husband the widow has the right, whatever the matrimonial regime, to continue to live in the matrimonial house.

All of these clauses, and paragraph 3 in particular, can be interpreted as providing protection against the practice of levirate marriage

Many women's rights activists are very eager to see the draft Protocol adopted, particularly with provisions specifically condemning harmful traditional practices in some shape or form.[47] But expectations and enthusiasm appear too high at the moment. There are three reasons for this. First, the Protocol to date has been drafted and discussed only by non-governmental organisations and some sympathetic Commissioners. Aside from the decision of the Council of Ministers to continue the process, there is little indication that African States will take up the project in earnest and bring the drafting to the inter-governmental level. Second, if the draft were to reach the inter-governmental level, it is less certain that all clauses would remain, including especially sensitive and problematic ones such as those relating to harmful traditional practices. Finally, even if these clauses remained, there would still be the considerable hurdle of ratification, not to mention the challenge of effective implementation.

---

47 E.g. Ankumah, Nhlapo and Welch (as cited above) are strongly in favour of such an instrument and its address of discriminatory or harmful customs and practices suffered by women under the veil of culture.

7.2 Special Rapporteur on the Rights of Women

In a closed session in 1998, the African Commission appointed Ms. Julienne Ondziel-Gnelega of the Republic of Congo as its first Special Rapporteur on the Rights of African Women.[48] The appointment of Ms. Ondziel-Gnelega as Special Rapporteur, who was herself one of the 11 Commissioners of the African Commission, was warmly welcomed by human rights activists because of her solid track record in the promotion and protection of human rights. As a seasoned Commissioner with some five years under her belt,[49] she was also elected Vice Chairman of the Commission in 1999.[50] As such, she was aware of the procedures and possibilities of the Commission and was considered by women's rights advocates as key to the advancement of African women's rights and issues in the African human rights system. Ms. Ondziel-Gnelega completed her term as Commissioner in 2001 and was replaced by a newly appointed Commissioner, Ms. Angela Melo of Mozambique, who was also appointed Special Rapporteur on the Rights of Women. Ms. Ondziel-Gnelega had limited her missions and reports largely to prison conditions for women. It will have to be seen whether Ms. Melo will expand the rapporteurship and, more particularly, will consider the issue of harmful traditional practices affecting African women.

7.3 Considering Alternative Measures

Additional interpretative measures to the African Charter would improve the protection of African women's rights. Those in favour of an Additional Protocol as a solution believe, as summarised by one commentator, that '... if you treat two situations alike when they are unalike, you put the weaker group in an even weaker position.'[51] But is an Additional Protocol really the best way to strengthen the positions of the weaker group – in this case, women? Would one consider the same solution for other 'disadvantaged' groups in weak positions, such as the disabled, the elderly, or the poor? Relating this more specifically to the African context, the creation of a protocol addressing women specifically presents a dilemma in risking further ghettoizing women's rights on numerous accounts. First, it has been established that the status of women in Africa is inferior to that of men and that women's concerns are easily ignored. Placing the rights of women within the scope of an instrument aimed solely

---

48 Appointed at the Commission's 23rd Ordinary Session in April 1998.
49 Appointed as Commissioner at the 18th Ordinary Session in October 1995.
50 Elected as Vice-Chairman of the Commission at the 26th Ordinary Session: term of office as Vice-Chairman: 1999-2001. The Chairman and Vice Chairman are elected by the members of the Commission by secret ballot for a period of two years and are eligible for re-election (Article 42) and Rule 17 of the (Revised) Rules of Procedure of the African Commission adopted on 6 October 1995.
51 As reported by A.H. de Wolf, *Panel Discussion: Implementing Women's Rights at the National, Regional and International Levels*, Africa Legal Aid Quarterly, Oct.-Dec. 1997, p. 34.

at them could make it easier to dedicate less attention to African women overall. Second, because the African Commission's capacity to perform its functions is already crippled by the sheer volume of work and inadequate resources,[52] the monitoring of an Additional Protocol would further over-extend the Commission with the Additional Protocol likely receiving the shortest end of the stick. Thirdly, the forms of discrimination African women suffer and women's rights which are meant to be included in the final draft of the protocol risk being less specific or comprehensive than those already acknowledged in the universal human rights instruments and the Beijing Declaration and Platform for Action. In such an outcome, it is unclear what added value would be brought by a protocol. Finally, should the Protocol only muster a few ratifications (and possibly never enter into force), this would represent a serious setback to the advancement of African women's rights, with very little way forward.

While none of these problems is insurmountable, alone or together they present substantial challenges. In light of the possible problems involving an Additional Protocol of the rights of African women, other measures could be undertaken to protect women's rights in general and challenge harmful traditional practices in particular. A General Comment by the African Commission on Articles 4 and/or 5 would be one such measure. Women and the special needs they have could thereby be addressed within the African Charter's scope of protection. Moreover, the Commission could adopt such a Comment independently without consulting or seeking the approval of all the Members of the OAU. While the Commission has never issued a General Comment, it is not precluded. A request for such an interpretation would be required from a State party, an institution of the OAU or an African organisation recognized by the OAU.[53] Alternatively, the Commission could act on its own volition to adopt a resolution on this specific provision, as it has done in the past with regard to ambiguous provisions in the Charter, in order to give the Article clarity and give the Charter its maximum effect.[54]

While the appointment of a special rapporteur on women's rights is helpful, it should only be seen as a temporary measure to address women's special needs and identify the forms of violations women may suffer because of their sex or gender. As Butegwa notes, limiting the duration of the appointment of such a rapporteur would drive home the point that 'otherwise, the entire African Commission should be promoting and protecting the human rights of women in Africa.'[55]

---

[52] For greater discussion on broader weaknesses diminishing the Commission's capacity to perform, *see generally*: Ankumah, *supra*, n. 9; E.G. Bello, *The Mandate of the African Commission on Human and Peoples' Rights*, African Journal of International Law, Vol. 1 (1988); *Interights Bulletin*, Vol. 8 (1994); and C.E. Welch, Jr., *The African Commission on Human and Peoples' Rights: A Five-Year Report and Assessment*, Human Rights Quarterly, Vol. 14 (1992).
[53] As per Article 45(3).
[54] The same is suggested generally by Ankumah, although she adds that even some of these resolutions are no more clearer than the provisions they seek to clarify, in *supra*, n. 9, p. 26.
[55] *See* E. Ankumah, *Interview with Florence Butegwa*, Africa Legal Aid Quarterly, Jan.-Mar. 1996, p. 23.

8 THE VERDICT

Concerns over clauses and terms (both present and absent) in the African Charter have sounded a cautionary note and raised doubts as to whether the instrument is not overly accommodating of culture and tradition. These are believed by some to have potentially serious implications on women's rights and the challenge and elimination of traditional practices harmful to women's health. I have endeavoured to establish that the informal *travaux préparatoires* of the Charter, the practice of the Commission, and interpretations of the clear meaning of these clauses (with due regard to the object and purpose of the Charter), should lay these concerns to rest.

Bearing in mind the social, political and economic realities at the time of drafting the Charter, it is little surprising that women's rights (as a partciular set of rights) were allotted only one provision. Yet, this provision is sufficient for our purposes, particularly in its stipulation that women's rights be protected to the extent provided in all international human rights instruments. As such, far from being a hindrance, the Charter can be an effective tool for social change.

The adoption of an Additional Protocol on African Women's Rights may pose greater problems than provide solutions. Rather, the African Commission, women and the campaign to eliminate harmful traditional practices would be better served by the adoption of General Comments on Articles 2, 3, 5 and/or 18, or a resolution regarding the ordinary meaning of specific notions, such as the 'protection of the family,' 'duties' or the 'protection of traditional values.'

Chapter VI
Practical Limitations on the Human Rights Approach

1 Introduction

It has already been submitted that human rights, *in theory*, have a *universal validity* and *applicability* regardless of communalist sentiments in African society, gender roles in African families, African traditions or any other religiously, socially or culturally inspired factors. Ultimately, the young Ghanaian girl handed into sexual bondage to the deity for the sins of her brother understands that her fate is unjust, even if she does not understand her fate in terms of violations of her 'rights' to dignity and freedom. Similarly, the young Togolese woman who flees her country because she is vehemently opposed to being forcibly circumcised has an instinctive knowledge that such an act represents an affront to her basic dignity and constitutes reprehensible violence. Although both women may never have heard of the Universal Declaration of Human Rights, they have natural fundamental needs and desires for basic respect, safety and personal security. As such, even if unknown to them, 'human rights' remain a valid expression of their basic needs and desires. Odinkalu, a leading African human rights activist, sums up this sentiment otherwise, observing that '[a]lthough in some African languages there is no direct equivalent to the phrase "human rights," neither the notion of justice that underlies human rights nor the experience of struggle to realize these rights is unknown in Africa.'[1] In short, 'people are acutely aware of the injustices inflicted upon them.'[2] This should not, however, diminish the assertion by other commentators that there remains an entire other segment of the female population in Africa who have yet to obtain 'the deep-rooted knowledge and conviction that they are human beings' or to seek, much less gain, 'effective control over their own bodies.'[3]

Accepting, nonetheless, that human rights have a theoretical validity for most in the context of sub-Saharan Africa, it is submitted that, *in practice*, human rights have little *utility* as a means to challenge harmful traditional practices or, indeed, other forms of gender violence and discrimination. In other words, even if the Ghanaian and Togolese women did know of their human rights and how to seek their enforcement, this

---

[1] C.A. Odinkalu, *Why More Africans Don't Use Human Rights Language*, Human Rights Dialogue, Winter 2000, p. 4.
[2] *Id.*
[3] R. Olawale, *Held down by taboos, ravaged by HIV/AIDS*, The Guardian (leading Nigerian daily), 31 July 2000, p. 19.

knowledge would be of limited use to them[4] – certainly considerably less than to their Western counterparts. The situation should therefore be tackled with the understanding that even women who may be aware of their rights and accept their theoretical validity remain unable – and/or unwilling – to exercise them. It is also posited that the manners in which we encourage and expect African women to use human rights are largely untenable within the particular context of sub-Saharan Africa.

The aims of this Chapter therefore are threefold:
- to examine theories on consciousness-raising and empowerment as the means by which human rights are expected to enable individuals, notably women, to challenge harmful traditional practices specifically, and other human rights abuses generally;
- to identify the various strategies widely espoused to date as facilitating these means; and
- to analyze the practical limitations of these strategies in the context of sub-Saharan Africa and their real potential to bring about change.

2 COMMONLY RECOMMENDED STRATEGIES AND THEIR PRESUMED INFLUENCE

Various strategies have been advanced to confront not only harmful traditional practices but also general barriers to the improved legal and socio-cultural status of women. Heralded in the international consensus documents on equality, development, women, human rights, etc., they include the formation and support of women's groups,[5] improved opportunities for general education for the girl child,[6] and legal reform (i.e. the adoption or amendment of relevant legislation).[7] These strategies are commonly situated within a framework of human rights. Our understanding of the relationship between human rights and each strategy is relatively straightforward. Through wo-

---

4   The fact that many African women clearly accept harmful traditional practices means that they are ready to forgive or live with a certain amount of violence – not unlimited, but to the limit of endurance. However, it may be deduced from the arguments of Aida Seif El Dawla that most women in such situations would likely choose otherwise if given a meaningful alternative, i.e. any alternative must be within their socio-cultural context. See A. Seif El Dawla, *Reproductive Rights of Egyptian Women: Issues for Debate*, Reproductive Health Matters, Vol. 8 (2000), p. 49.
5   *See*, e.g.: CEDAW's General Recommendation No. 14, a.ii) (Annex A.I); Declaration of Mexico, Principle 28 (Annex B.I); ICPD, paragraph 4.12 (Annex B.V); and BDPA, paragraphs 107 a) and 108 j) (Annex B.VII).
6   *See*, e.g.: Nairobi Forward-Looking Strategies, paragraph 56 (Annex B.II); ICPD, Chapter IV (Annex B.V); Copenhagen Declaration, Commitment 6 (Annex B.VI); and BDPA, paragraphs 71 and 107 a) (Annex B.VII).
7   *See*, e.g.: Nairobi Forward-Looking Strategies, paragraphs 51 and 56 (Annex B.II); VDPA, paragraph 49 (Annex B.III); Declaration on the Elimination of Violence against Women, Article 4 c) (Annex B.IV); Copenhagen Declaration, Commitment 5 (Annex B.VI); and BDPA, paragraphs 107 d), 108 b) and 124 i) (Annex B.VII).

men's groups, women can identify their needs, make themselves heard and demand their fulfillment on the basis of human rights. With better education (particularly for the girl child), women will act to defend their rights, notably by challenging oppressive societal norms and practices.[8] Through legal reform (demanded on the basis of human rights claims), discriminatory norms and practices will be eliminated and the human rights of women will be respected and protected. Human rights education is seen as a factor facilitating these measures and empowerment as the by-product of human rights education and these measures (schematically displayed in Figure IV). In analogous terms, knowledge of human rights is considered the spark, women's groups, law and formal education the coals, and women's empowerment the fire which ultimately destroys the harmful attitudes and stereotypes which maintain harmful practices insulated by tradition.

Figure IV The Framework of Relations among Strategies

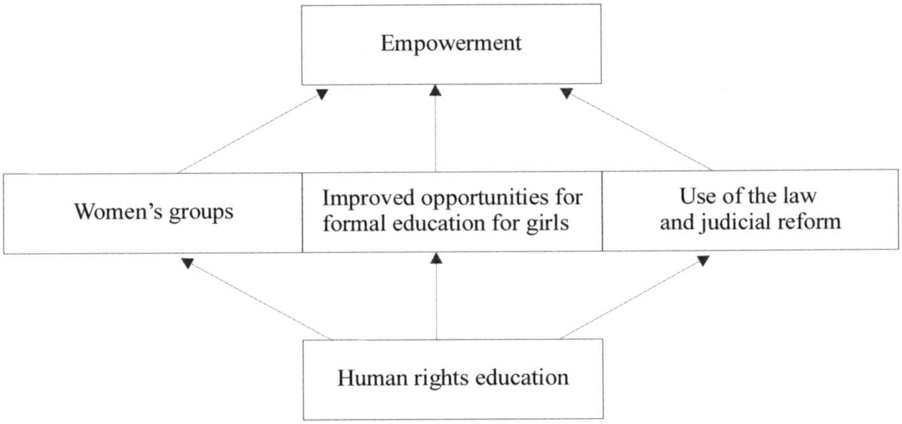

```
                        ┌──────────────┐
                        │ Empowerment  │
                        └──────────────┘
                         ▼     ▲     ▼
  ┌─────────────┐  ┌──────────────────────┐  ┌──────────────┐
  │  Women's    │  │ Improved opportunities│  │ Use of the law│
  │   groups    │  │ for formal education  │  │ and judicial  │
  │             │  │       for girls       │  │    reform     │
  └─────────────┘  └──────────────────────┘  └──────────────┘
                         ▼     ▲     ▼
                        ┌──────────────────┐
                        │ Human rights     │
                        │ education        │
                        └──────────────────┘
```

This framework of understanding is typical of the bottom-up (or grassroots) approach to human rights enforcement. The approach conventionally presumes that consciousness-raising and the empowerment of women will bring about the social and cultural changes needed to improve the status of women and end harmful traditional practices.

---

8   The 'economic' and 'political' arguments are related to better schooling, i.e. with higher education it is believed that women are more likely to obtain gainful employment, be financially independent and more politically involved. Under these conditions, women are more likely to speak out and act forcefully against patterns of gender discrimination and violence. *See*, e.g.: Nairobi Forward-Looking Strategies, paragraph 51 (Annex B.II.); Chapter IV of the ICPD (Annex B.V); and Copenhagen Declaration, Commitment 5 (Annex B.VI). It is also recognised that economic pressures help perpetuate harmful practices and violence against women. *See*, e.g., CEDAW's General Recommendations Nos. 14 and 21 in Annex A.I and A.III, respectively.

Although this approach is strongly supported by the women's rights and wider international human rights communities, evidence suggests that African women face significant constraints on empowerment. Even in cases of success, it is arguably fragile. This appears to be largely because the grassroots empowerment approach alone is unable to challenge obstacles within the law, justice and police, to alter women's power of negotiation, or to engrain, on a popular scale, attitudes against harmful traditional practices.

3 RE-EVALUATING THE IMPACT OF HUMAN RIGHTS EDUCATION

The importance of human rights education and the obligation of the State to educate individuals about their human rights has been stressed in the Preamble of the Universal Declaration of Human Rights.[9] The Vienna Declaration and Programme of Action and its +5 Final Document remind us of the same.[10] Indeed, an entire decade (1995-2004) has been proclaimed the UN Decade of Human Rights Education.[11]

Legal literacy, including literacy in human rights, is understood to be a necessary condition 'for the ability of individuals to apply them in practice, address their violations, restore justice through proper legal proceedings, and demand compensation for damage whenever it occurs.'[12] Greater popular awareness, it is hoped, will lead to demands for respect for human rights and fulfillment of the conditions for their respect. With this understanding in mind, human rights NGOs, women's organisations and development groups in Africa and elsewhere are emphasizing popular human rights education.[13]

---

9 It proclaims that ' ... every individual and every organ of society... shall strive by teaching and education to promote respect for these rights and freedoms... to secure their universal and effective recognition and observance.'
10 *See*, e.g., VDPA+5 Final Docuwment, p. 5.
11 General Assembly Resolution 49/184 which states that 'human rights education constitutes an important vehicle for the elimination of gender-based discrimination... through the promotion and protection of the human rights of women.'
12 D. Gierycz, *Education on the Human Rights of Women as a Vehicle for Change*, in G.J. Andreopoulus and R.P. Claude, eds., HUMAN RIGHTS EDUCATION FOR THE TWENTY-FIRST CENTURY (1997), p. 96.
13 *See* J.P. Martin *et al.*, *Promoting Human Rights Education in a Marginalized Africa*, in *id.*

Table V The Legal Literacy Paradigm[14]

LEGAL LITERACY IS AN EDUCATIONAL PROCESS TO:	
PROMOTE CAPACITIES TO:	BY DEVELOPING KNOWLEDGE AND SKILLS ABOUT:
• critically assess the law and meaning of rights	• gender roles and status and how the law defines them • the meaning of fundamental rights, the content of specific law and their relevancy to life
• assert rights	• the content and relevancy of laws • how to exercise the rights defined (where to go, what to do) • how to get moral and technical support
• mobilize for change	• what needs to be changed • how and where to participate in actions for change • organizing, strategizing, communicating

In the table above the process of legal literacy is deconstructed to demonstrate how women can become empowered and bring about change by learning about the law (in its generic sense). While different analysts use different terms (e.g. consciousness-raising, leading to emancipation, resulting in change as opposed to critical assessment, leading to assertion of rights, resulting in mobilization for change), the process of human rights education is generally described to work in the same manner.[15] Accordingly, human rights education enables women to assess the meaning human rights has for them, assert their rights (e.g. demand their fulfillment, bring complaints to the police or seek redress though the judicial system) and bring about social, cultural, political or other forms of change. We are all aware of this process working with respect to some matters in some countries. However, it is a much more problematic process with regard to harmful traditional practices in sub-Saharan Africa. Despite this, proponents of this process believe that women in African (and most other) societies are operating from a position of such great disadvantage and that the human rights discourse is the only one to offer a recognized vocabulary to frame these disadvantages.[16]

---

14 Reproduced from M. Schuler and S.K. Rajasingham, *Legal Literacy*, in M. Schuler and S.K. Rajasingham, LEGAL LITERACY: A TOOL FOR WOMEN'S EMPOWERMENT (1992), p. 49.
15 *See*, e.g.: G. Meintjes, *Human Rights Education as Empowerment: Reflections on Pedagogy*, in HUMAN RIGHTS EDUCATION, *supra*, n. 12; and Gierycz, *supra*, n. 12.
16 *See*, e.g., H. Charlesworth, *What are 'Women's International Human Rights'*, in R.J. Cook, ed., HUMAN RIGHTS OF WOMEN (1994), p. 61.

It follows that framing one's claims in terms of rights gives them a political force and legitimacy. Human rights education ostensibly enables individuals to acquire the knowledge and critical awareness they need to understand and question oppressive social, political and economic norms and organisation.[17] It is therefore reasoned that when women are aware of the rights they possess they are more likely to act in favour of their protection. It is hoped that, at the grassroots level, this knowledge is translated into action to:

a) seek and obtain justice in an individual case, such as by obtaining a court order against a family member so that one is not forcibly circumcised or married off;
b) convince local populations that certain harmful practices are against women's rights and should therefore be stopped; or
c) convince governments of their obligations to eliminate gender-based violence and discrimination in general, and harmful traditional practices in particular.

Since women have been brought up to believe that harmful traditional practices are the natural order of things and since they are the victims of these practices, it is generally held that women, first and foremost, should receive human rights education. Grassroots women's groups and associations are often advanced as the ideal forum for such education.

While this process seems reasonable and expectations from it logical, it is submitted that, for the most part, human rights education has not led African women to assert their rights and mobilise in favour of change successfully, especially where harmful traditional practices and gender discrimination are concerned. Women who are aware that their husbands, by law, should not beat them, rarely take individual or group action to stop them.[18] Women who know that their right to health allows them to insist that their HIV-infected partners wear condoms, do not.[19] Women in societies with strict codes against pre-marital sex have been made painfully aware that it is only they who will be punished, regardless of equality laws.[20] Women who know that female circum-

---

17 *See* Meintjes, *supra*, n. 15, p. 66.
18 *See*, e.g., A. Armstrong, CULTURE AND CHOICE: LESSONS FROM SURVIVORS OF GENDER VIOLENCE IN ZIMBABWE (1998).
19 *See*, e.g., A.A. Bawah *et al.*, *Women's Fears and Men's Anxieties*, Studies in Family Planning, Vol. 30 (1999).
20 For instance, a teenage mother in the northern Nigerian State of Zamfara received 100 lashes on 19 January 2000. She had told the Higher Sharia Court that she was pregnant as a result of being coerced by her father into having sexual intercourse with three men to whom he was indebted. The men denied the accusation and her evidence was discounted. For a summary of the case, *see* News Reports, *Whipping of Nigerian Teenage Girl Condemned*, Reproductive Health Matters, Vol. 9 (2001), p. 224.

cision is prohibited in their countries by law also know that courts and police, much less their neighbours, will rarely act to protect them.[21]

As Odinkalu notes with regard to human rights education and Africans in general, knowledge of the content of human rights instruments has hardly advanced the condition of Africans.[22] For the overwhelming majority of Africans, the language of human rights has not become the channel through which it was hoped demands would be articulated and responses evoked. Other commentators speak of the inability of human rights language to mobilise the vast majority of people.[23] The fact that sociocultural change in Africa has been extremely slow following some 30 years of human rights education and women's grassroots efforts must be addressed. In this light, analysing the processes through which women's empowerment has been expected to come forth, as well as our understanding of what 'women's empowerment' consists in an African context, would seem a useful exercise.

4 QUESTIONING THE EMPOWERING FORCE OF HUMAN RIGHTS

As already noted above, a key value we generally ascribe to human rights education is its potential to empower and emancipate. Empowerment has been defined as 'a process through which people and/or communities increase their control or mastery of their own lives and the decisions that affect their lives.'[24] It should enable women to analyze their own situation, decide their priorities, develop solutions to their problems, and take collective action to improve various aspects of their lives.[25] The empowerment approach generally maintains that human rights discourses will lead to consciousness-raising which, in turn, will support the growth of women's organisations, leading to political mobilization, improved education opportunities for women and other conditions which are necessary for significant and durable social change.[26] Women are thus

---

21 For instance, for many years female circumcision may be considered a criminal action pursuant to any one of the provisions of the Kenyan Penal Code that bar assault or the infliction of bodily harm to any person. It has also long been possible to bring such a civil action under tort law. However, it was not before December 2000 that a court used its powers to stop a circumcision. In this historic ruling, the court issued an order preventing a father from forcing his daughters, aged 15 and 17, to undergo circumcision. While this case is significant, it is to be noted that it was won on the basis of the magistrate's discretion rather than on the basis of law. For a summary of the case, see A. Baleta, WOMEN'S GROUPS IN KENYA WIN SMALL VICTORY AGAINST FEMALE CIRCUMCISION, 2001 on website: http://thelancet.com/search/search/isa. Also reported in Robinson, Simon, *The Last Rites*, Time Magazine, 3 December 2001, pp. 70-71.
22 Odinkalu, *supra*, n. 1, p. 4.
23 *See*, e.g., observations made generally throughout the Winter 2000 issue of the Carnegie Foundation's regular newsletter 'Human Rights Dialogue'.
24 Meintjes, *supra*, n. 15, p. 65.
25 *See*, e.g.: UNDP, HUMAN DEVELOPMENT REPORT (1997); and, G. Sen *et al.*, POPULATION POLICIES RECONSIDERED: HEALTH, EMPOWERMENT AND RIGHTS (1994).
26 *See* J.C. Mosse, HALF THE WORLD, HALF A CHANCE (1993), as cited in E.D. Naggita, *Why Men Come Out Ahead: The Legal Regime and the Protection and Realization of Women's Rights in Uganda*, East African Journal of Peace and Human Rights, Vol. 6 (2000), p. 60.

viewed as potential positive agents of change rather than pawns of society.[27] The approach was strongly endorsed by the UN population and development conference (ICPD) in Cairo and remains today a strong rallying point of feminists and human rights activists alike.[28]

However, as some commentators (African feminists among them) have already reminded us, learning one's rights and recognizing one's entitlement to a particular right does not necessarily lead to the enjoyment of that right or even an attempt to exercise it, especially if other significant interests and concerns are involved.[29] Rather, a woman's exercise of a particular right will depend largely on her social status, her psychological, social and economic resources and the social costs of entering into conflict for that claim as opposed to the benefits it would bring. In sub-Saharan Africa these considerations arguably hold much sway in a woman's assessment of her own power and even her calculation of the value of mobilization to this end. For example, a woman in Senegal knows that it is her right to seek a divorce if her husband is adulterous. However, her awareness of her rights in such a case does not on its own help her to overcome the scandal, isolation, and loss of family support which are likely consequences of an assertion of her rights in her society. Thus, for the sake of the social acceptance and support that she also needs, she may not exercise her rights, even though they are guaranteed in law. As one commentator has aptly noted,

> [t]he simple need of a woman (or a man) to be part of a family, a marriage, a relationship or a peer group usually entails that they will choose to compromise part of themselves for the sake of this affiliation, which in return provides psychological, social and perhaps economic support. The injustice derives from the inequality of the price paid by women and men for this support, in a patriarchal system, which privileges man.[30]

Not surprisingly, findings of one study on reproductive rights (including in some African countries) revealed that women understood their rights perfectly well.[31] The women interviewed in the study thus expressed their wishes (for themselves as well as their daughters) not to be violated sexually or otherwise by their husbands or anybody else, and not to be subjected to abuse or violence. However, many of them also expressed that they were aware that they would not be able to fulfil these wishes in light

---

27 See M. Schuler, *Conceptualizing and Exploring Issues and Strategies*, in M. Schuler, ed., EMPOWERMENT AND THE LAW: STRATEGIES OF THIRD WORLD WOMEN (1986), p. 27.
28 See, e.g.: S. Maddock, CHALLENGING WOMEN: GENDER, CULTURE AND ORGANISATION (1999); H.B. Presser and G. Sen, eds., WOMEN'S EMPOWERMENT AND DEMOGRAPHIC PROCESSES: MOVING BEYOND CAIRO (2000); and J. Mirsky and M. Radlett, eds., NO PARADISE YET: THE WORLD'S WOMEN FACE THE NEW CENTURY (2000).
29 See, e.g., Seif El Dawla, *supra*, n. 4, p. 47.
30 *Id.*, p. 48.
31 See International Reproductive Rights and Research Action Group (IRRRAG), *Women's Wit over Men's*, in R. Petchesky and K. Judd, eds., NEGOTIATING REPRODUCTIVE RIGHTS (1998).

of the scope of choices available to them. When the cards were down, they would consistently choose to subject their lives and their bodies to harmful socio-cultural norms and practices for the sake of the benefits loyalty to these norms would bring.

An important lesson to be learned from this is that trade-offs such as these must be accepted for what they are: the result of the decision of women choosing relationships over the exercise of their rights. All too often such trade-offs are taken to indicate women's lack of any sense of entitlement to their rights, but this is an oversimplification.[32] In fact, what women consider an acceptable trade-off depends on their real alternatives and their negotiating power.[33] The limits of these choices are the limits of their freedom much more so than the limits of the extent of knowledge of their rights.

5 WOMEN'S GROUPS AND POWER

5.1 Theories on Women's Groups and Empowerment

The first step in the process of empowerment is commonly agreed to be the creation of conditions that enable women to imagine and express their demands. This task is perceived to be best carried out by women's organisations which equally often see it as a task to be set for themselves. Empowerment is to be achieved by enabling women to build a positive self-image and self-confidence to develop the ability to think critically, to build group cohesion, to mobilize and to foster decision-making and action.[34] In short, women's groups are believed to constitute a means of instilling and mobilizing autonomy for women and so their formulation and development are supported to this end..

5.2 Some Challenging Evidence

The fostering of women's groups has been a key strategy of the equality agenda since at least 1975[35] and has spilled over onto the human rights agenda regarding harmful traditional practices and violence against women in general.[36] In fact, women's groups existed in many African countries long before this date. Market women were the first to organize themselves into groups in order to claim their rights. These women were used to managing their own affairs, were able to accrue personal savings and lived

---

32 *Id.*
33 Assumptions underlying gender education and empowerment in Africa, Asia and Latin America are strongly and succinctly challenged in C. Heward and S. Bunwaree, eds., GENDER, EDUCATION AND DEVELOPMENT (1999).
34 *See* Young, K., PLANNING DEVELOPMENT WITH WOMEN (1993).
35 1975 was International Women's Year which marked the beginning of the Decade for Women.
36 *See*, e.g.: CEDAW General Recommendation No. 14, paragraph a.ii) (Annex A.I); Declaration of Mexico on the Equality of Women (Annex B.II); and Beijing Platform for Action, paragraph 108 j) (Annex B.VII).

from their trade.[37] But women's groups in Africa have also had their share of problems and failures.[38] Various reasons for this have been suggested. One has been their lack of cohesion for concerted efforts. In numerous instances it has been found that local women's groups operate in isolation, establishing few links with other women's groups or organisations which may offer better access to resources and legitimacy.[39] Commentators have also underlined the constraints women's groups face in changing power relations. While these groups may well be suited to the realization of practical needs (which explains why they have been modestly successful in development projects and highly successful in women's micro-projects) it does not necessarily follow that they can transform underlying gender norms and relations.[40] Those which have attempted such transformation often have had the legitimacy of their aims challenged by men at the village level whose support (or lack thereof) is obviously critical. On these occasions women's groups have typically faced resistance from men, either because they felt left out or threatened.[41] The threat these groups and their message pose to their communities is certainly an issue to be considered. Meintjes surmises that

> ... the threat of empowerment appears to be inversely proportionate to the degree to which a particular regime is willing or able to tolerate or even encourage unconventional ideas and thinking. Put differently, it is those regimes that are inflexible and static, and whose preservation is dependent upon the maintenance of the status quo, that are most likely to resist or repress the efforts of human rights...[42]

This leads to a basic question: in limiting their constituency to women, are women's groups and their legal literacy programmes reducing their chances of success? Butegwa, a Ugandan human rights activist who founded and continues to work with the NGO International Federation of Women Lawyers (FIDA), explains the problem African women's groups may experience in this regard:

> Within the first year of implementing the legal literacy program, it became clear that focusing on women alone as the sole audience served little purpose. Women attending sessions organized by FIDA raised this issue openly. They pointed out that few women could confront their husbands and assert their rights. Which woman was going to tell her husband that he had no right to beat her or to marry another wife? They rightly argued that

---

37 *See* C. Coquery-Vidrovitch, AFRICAN WOMEN: A MODERN HISTORY (1994), pp. 160-161.
38 *See* N. Veerman, *Women's Groups in Africa: Panacea or Problem?*, Vena Journal, Vol. 7 (1995).
39 *See* A. Aidoo, *Africa: Democracy Without Human Rights?*, Human Rights Quarterly, Vol. 15 (1993), p. 714.
40 *See*, e.g.: J. El Bushra, *Economic interest groups and their relevance for women's development*, YEARBOOK OF CO-OPERATIVE ENTERPRISE (1993); and R. Feldman, *Women's groups and women's subordination: An analysis of policies towards rural women in Kenya*, Review of African Political Economy, Nos. 27/28, 1984.
41 *See*, e.g.: M.G. Ntarangwi, *Feminism and Masculinity in an African Capitalist Context: The Case of Kenya*, SAFERE, Vol. 3 (1998), p. 23; and Veerman, *supra*, n. 38, p. 8.
42 Meintjes, *supra*, n. 15, p. 71.

the men themselves should be there to hear what the law stated. The program was amended to reach out to both men and women, but this again raised another problem. Women whose husbands or relatives were in the audience felt unable to participate freely in the discussions for fear of retribution.[43]

Two other factors have led to the weakness of women's groups in Africa: their politicization and their real or perceived elitism (the two often going hand-in-hand). A number of key women's groups in Africa's modern history, many of which survive today, have been formed or led by the wives of political leaders. In much of West Africa, for instance, political parties have encouraged their leaders' wives to gather themselves into women's associations.[44] Although some were truly engaged politically, they did not necessarily seek to promote women's empowerment or the particular rights of concern to local working women. One such example was the national organisation of Tanzanian women. Its mandate was to encourage girls' education and promote their attempts to create micro-enterprises. But during the 1980s it remained essentially conformist, reminding women of their 'domestic duties' by organizing sewing, knitting, and cooking classes and supporting the government's struggle against the 'provocative' wearing of miniskirts.[45] In the summary of her study of politically formed women's groups in Africa, social anthropologist Coquery-Vidrovitch concludes that, with only a few exceptions, the existence of such women's groups 'reveals less emerging consciousness of a liberation struggle than an attempt to adopt the conventions and prejudices of a middle class struggling to preserve its privileges.'[46]

Women's groups suffer from both the presence and the absence of elite and professional women. On the one hand, such women are arguably ideal leaders in the assertion of women's rights, the liberation from Christian and Islamic socialization patterns and the movement for social change.[47] Yet the fact that they are wealthy and professional does not necessarily mean that that they are strong-willed or keen to challenge the system in which they have fared well (as described in Section 6.2 below). Indeed, elite women may enjoy prestige but remain silent. Wealthy Muslim women in Northern Nigeria are increasingly retreating into *purdah* rather than fighting against it.[48] This is to say nothing of others who are alleged to be more interested in safeguarding their own interests and privileges.[49] Coquery-Vidrovitch, for instance, observes that

---

43 F. Butegwa, *Challenges of Promoting Legal Literacy Among Women in Uganda*, in LEGAL LITERACY, *supra*, n. 14, p. 145.
44 *See* Coquery-Vidrovitch, *supra*, n. 37, pp. 159-183.
45 *Id.*, p. 158.
46 *Id.*
47 *See* R.E. Howard, *Women's Rights and the Right to Development*, in R. Cohen *et al.*, eds., HUMAN RIGHTS AND GOVERNANCE IN AFRICA (1993), p. 126.
48 As summarized from study findings in *id.*
49 *See*, e.g.: C. Itumbi Nyamu, *The International Human Rights Regime and Rural Women in Kenya*, East African Journal of Peace and Human Rights, Vol. 6 (2000), p. 31; and Howard, *supra*, n. 47, pp. 128-129.

women's groups in Africa 'often reflect the narrow-mindedness and elitism of many of their members' and 'have shown themselves to be quite conventional'.[50] She gives the example of the Kenyan women's lobby group *Maendeleo ya Wanawake* (Progress for Women) chaired by a Kenyan Member of Parliament:

> It has branches throughout the country, in both rural and urban areas, and officially promotes women's development. In fact, it is mainly made up of bourgeois women who work in the public sector, the liberal professions, or business and who are often connected by marriage or birth with influential men. Their style… is to organize fashion or craft shows, hold receptions, and do charitable work… These urban elite women are clearly very far from rural and proletarian women, about whom they hold astonishingly antifeminist views.[51]

Feldman, a specialist on women's groups, categorically concludes that the impact of women's groups is 'sparse, uneven and often of dubious value. Seldom indeed do their projects… approach the requirements for fundamentally altering the condition of subordination of rural women.'[52] This conclusion should not surprise us. If the African socialization process deeply enculturates African women and men to believe that women are subordinate, why do we expect women – the most disadvantaged and disempowered group – to break this pattern simply by claiming human rights in greater numbers? Indeed, if we accept that women's consciousness is structured by the socialization process which enculturates the gender ideals of the dominant ideology and pragmatically towards the path of least resistance and hardship, we must equally accept that the barriers to the breakdown of subordination are also doubly fortified. In this light, human rights discourses can have little impact so long as African women are marginalized from the mechanisms and processes by which society defines and defends its norms and values. For the most part, this means religious and customary institutions and laws.

Maintaining the belief that women's empowerment to be achieved through women's group is an adequate solution is problematic. Effectively, it allows States and religious and customary leaders to espouse the rhetoric of gender equality while perpetuating discriminatory gender ideologies and power relations.[53] This being so, should we be celebrating the growth of women's groups in sub-Saharan Africa if these all too frequently have but a symbolic voice and no real power?[54] Surely we are seeking more.

---

50 Coquery-Vidrovitch, *supra*, n. 37, p. 157.
51 *Id.*, p. 158.
52 Feldman, *supra*, n. 40, p. 65.
53 C. Heward, *Introduction: The New Discourses of Gender, Education and Development*, in GENDER, EDUCATION AND DEVELOPMENT, *supra*, n. 33, p. 9.
54 *See* N.P. Stromquist, *Romancing the State: Gender and Power in Education*, Comparative Education Review, Vol. 39 (1995), p. 454.

Of course, the problems encountered by women's groups in the sub-Saharan African region are not unique. They can be witnessed in all regions where the status of women is critically poor.[55] In relation to our particular concern, it is important to stress that while women's groups alone may not be as effective in the challenge of harmful traditional practices as elsewhere, they may promote attitudes of solidarity – attitudes which may be fostered by human rights discourses.[56] Through this solidarity women's groups may at least succeed in placing gender and harmful traditional practices among 'the issues' of broad social and political interest. The mechanisms and individuals capable of negotiating change (notably religious and customary establishments and leaders) must then be persuaded to meet their call and address the issues.

6 FORMAL EDUCATION AND SOCIAL CHANGE

6.1 Theories on Education, Reproductive Health and Empowerment

It is generally held that the higher the woman's education, the more likely she is to have sound reproductive health.[57] Three reasons are commonly given. First, an educated woman is more likely to be informed about the implications of pregnancy and sexual and reproductive behaviour for her health and to seek medical attention.[58] Second, the longer a young woman stays in the educational system, the later in age she is expected to enter into marriage and become pregnant. Third, education is seen as a socialising process that inculcates 'modern' social values, safe sexual practices and behaviours falling within the conception of 'modernity'. Included in this conception of modernity is that educated women will have more egalitarian relationships with their spouses and discuss and decide matters pertaining to sexuality and reproduction with them.[59] Concomitantly, it is considered to improve a woman's ability to resist subjugation and increase her decision-making power.[60] Norms and values supporting the motivation to bear a large number of children are weakened and women are empowered to challenge and reject social, cultural or religious norms and practices harmful to their health.[61]

---

55 *See*, e.g., K. Jayawardene, FEMINISM AND NATIONALISM IN THE THIRD WORLD (1982), pp. 15-17.
56 *See* Meintjes, *supra*, n. 15, p. 69.
57 *See* United Nations, Key Issues in Family Planning, Health and Family Well-Being in the 1990s and Beyond, in United Nations, FAMILY PLANNING, HEALTH AND FAMILY WELL-BEING (1996), p. 32.
58 *See*, e.g., J.C. Caldwell, *Education as a factor in mortality decline: An examination of the Nigerian data*, Population Studies, Vol. 33 (1979), pp. 395-413.
59 *See* S.H. Cochrane, EDUCATION AND FERTILITY: WHAT DO WE REALLY KNOW? (1979).
60 *See*, e.g.: A.J. Gage *et al.*, HOUSEHOLD STRUCTURE, SOCIOECONOMIC LEVEL, AND CHILD HEALTH IN SUB-SAHARAN AFRICA (1996); and K.O. Mason, *The Impact of Women's Social Position on Fertility in Developing Countries*, Sociological Forum, Vol. 2 (1987).
61 *See*, e.g.: J.C. Caldwell, *Mass education as a determinant of the timing of fertility decline*, Population and Development Review, Vol. 6 (1980); Cochrane, *supra*, n. 59; and Mason, *supra*, n. 60.

Chapter VI

This image of the 'rational' educated young woman able to inform herself and take action where fertility and practices impacting on reproductive health are concerned is depicted in a recent Demographic Health Survey, as follows:

> Education can be interpreted as a measure of self-efficacy, of competence and capacity to make informed decisions, and of access to information through print and mass media that may be unavailable to the unschooled. It has been convincingly argued that educated women are less fatalistic and are more attuned to scientific reasoning than the less educated. It is argued that education affects the psyche and shifts allegiance of a person in a developing-country environment from a traditional culture to a modern culture. An educated woman, then, is presented as a shrewd and competent actor who believes that she has the capacity to get the best out of the world without succumbing helplessly to the whims and caprices of nature.[62]

The argument is also made that education offers an alternative means of gaining status and respect in a society where status is highly associated with conformity and acquiescence. For instance, education may make women more interested in, or capable of, using credit, banking, participating in a co-operative, and hiring labourers. Consequently, they may be more autonomous and able, for instance, to delay their daughter's marriage, to insist on using protection during sexual intercourse, to condemn the infidelities of their husbands, or to resist the demands of relatives to have their child circumcised.

6.2 Some Challenging Evidence

Historically in Africa, as elsewhere, girls' education was an apprenticeship in subjugation to male power. Girls were taught never to speak in public and never to speak to a man before being spoken to. Coquery-Vidrovitch describes how this education was not associated with any particular religion in Africa and remains largely intact today:

> Contrary to what might be imagined, this [education] is not limited to Islamic cultures; respectable Hausa and Swahili women are increasingly reticent with strangers, and little Fula girls are trained to these customs from a very young age. These rules are still more strictly observed in central (Zaire, Uganda, Tanzania) and southern Africa, where a convergence of traditional female submission and Christian sexual phobia continues... It would be wrong to attribute women's condition entirely to an indigenous past. But it is clear that among peoples as different as the Kikuyu of Kenya, the Haya of Tanzania, the Tswana of southern Africa, and the Zairean women of Kwilu or Kivu, the rules of female submissive-

---

62 J.A. Adetunji, UNINTENDED CHILDBEARING IN DEVELOPING COUNTRIES: LEVEL, TRENDS AND DETERMINANTS (1998), p. 16.

ness transmitted from generation to generation continue to weigh heavily, especially in the countryside but, ironically, also within the Westernized city-dwelling bourgeoisie.[63]

A number of research findings demonstrate that, in the African model, education has not, at least as of yet, borne a significant impact on traditional norms.[64] For example, although in Nigeria there are more females in school than males, and women are increasingly pursuing university education and professional employment, socio-cultural expectations remain largely unaltered. Even in households where husbands are equally educated and thereby considered 'enlightened,' traditions and expectations remain strong. Although the traditional ceremonies surrounding circumcisions have been greatly simplified, daughters continue to be operated upon. In Mali, Somalia, Nigeria, the Sudan, Kenya and many more countries the operations are now commonly performed in the modern health sector.[65] Whether formally educated or not, women are expected to marry and have children – including at the very least one male child – in order to find fulfilment. They should adhere to these expectations willingly and happily.[66] While in Africa it has generally been educated women who have spoken out against female circumcision, other educated women have undergone the practice voluntarily.[67]

Of course, just because African (or any other) women have a higher education does not necessarily imply that they will challenge traditional norms. Indeed, a woman may use her higher education precisely to fulfil societal norms. Coquery-Vidorvitch observes in this regard that '[r]ather than providing her with independence like her mother, who may have been illiterate but was a competent, working market woman, today's woman will often use her intellectual "worth" to seek a high-level man who will marry her, keep her…'[68] Another study on gender roles and education also found that, contrary to expectation, girls who are better educated are more likely than boys to favour a large age difference between spouses.[69] While spousal age gap is generally viewed as a marker of gender inequality, the researchers carrying out the study speculated from the responses that educated girls tended to have higher material and social aspirations and considered older men economically able to fulfil these desires.

The findings of other studies suggest some reasons why the education-empowerment model may not work as well as expected in the context of sub-Saharan Africa.

---

63 Coquery-Vidrovitch, *supra*, n. 37, p. 56.
64 *See* D.P. Hogan *et al.*, *Household Organisation, Women's Autonomy, and Contraceptive Behaviour in Southern Ethiopia*, Studies in Family Planning, Vol. 30 (1999), p. 304.
65 *See* F.P. Hosken, STOP FEMALE GENITAL MUTILATION: WOMEN SPEAK FACTS AND ACTIONS (1995), p. 18
66 *See* paper presented by Uche Nzewi (University of Nigeria at Nsukka), *The Impact of Education on Nigerian Women's Decision-Making on Reproductive Health*, Indiana University, Indianapolis (1998).
67 *See* R.E. Howard, HUMAN RIGHTS IN COMMONWEALTH AFRICA (1986), p. 204.
68 Coquery-Vidrovitch, *supra*, n. 37, p. 157.
69 [No author], *Gender Roles Sharply Differentiated among Egyptian Youth*, Population Briefs, Vol. 7 (2001), p. 5.

Chapter VI

As a first example, it is widely believed that formal education for women can reduce the likelihood of HIV transmission. This conclusion is largely drawn from behavioural patterns observed in developed countries where one commonly finds lower HIV infection levels in persons with higher literacy rates. While it would appear reasonable to expect that the majority of educated women and men, given the information and expanded choices presented to them, would seize the opportunity to choose safe behaviour and avoid HIV infection, this expectation has failed to apply to the context of sub-Saharan Africa. Why has sub-Saharan Africa deviated from this expectation? More specifically, researchers have had to ask themselves why adults in sub-Saharan Africa with a higher socio-economic status have *higher* HIV infection rates? In rural Rakai District, Uganda, for instance, it was found that household heads with any education were more likely to be infected than those with no schooling. In the Kagera Region of Tanzania, a woman with primary or secondary schooling was more likely to die from AIDS than a woman with no schooling whatsoever.[70] Another study of a large number of pregnant women in Zambia found that, in general, city women who had had a longer formal education were in fact more at risk of contracting HIV than women who had had little or no schooling.[71] The study found that when young girls became sexually active, their education level did not necessarily lead to a status and standard of living that would allow them to adopt less risky behaviour, such as the systematic use of condoms, fidelity or pre-marital abstinence.

Another survey of 14 developing countries found that, in all nine African countries included in the survey, a greater percentage of *educated* men and women reported having had casual sex in the last 12 months.[72] Figures were considerably higher among women and men who had secondary and higher levels of education as compared to those who had primary or no level of education.[73] For instance, in Côte d'Ivoire, 60% of all men and 20% of all women with secondary schooling or higher education reported having had casual sex, as opposed to 29% of all men and 9% of all women with no schooling whatsoever.[74] The trend in sub-Saharan Africa, therefore, appears to be towards a higher prevalence of casual sex with higher educational level. Similar findings arose from analysis of data from WHO sexual behaviour surveys conducted in five African States. The more education a man had, the more he was likely to have higher income which, in turn, made it easier to attract and support additional casual sexual partners. Another finding was that men and women with more education and

---

70 As reported in World Bank, CONFRONTING AIDS (1997), p. 128.
71 As summarized in A. Lawson, *Women and AIDS in Africa: Sociocultural Dimensions of the HIV/AIDS Epidemic*, International Social Science Journal, Vol. 161 (1999), p. 396.
72 Multiple sexual partnerships have been proven to play a significant role in the spread of sexually transmitted diseases, including HIV.
73 *See* M. Caraël, 'Sexual Behaviour', in J. Cleland and B. Ferry, eds., SEXUAL BEHAVIOUR AND AIDS IN THE DEVELOPING WORLD (1995), pp. 113-114.
74 *Id.*

higher incomes were likely to travel more and thus have more opportunities for a variety of sexual contacts.[75]

More evidence that sub-Saharan Africa fails to follow expectations comes from a study on the subject of unintended pregnancy. It concluded that while the normal relationship between female education and unwanted pregnancy is negative (i.e. women with more schooling are less likely to have unwanted children) '[i]n sub-Saharan African countries, there is no clear pattern of association between education and mistimed or unwanted pregnancies...'.[76]

As noted earlier, education, or perhaps more precisely the school environment, is believed to introduce 'modern' values. Young individuals, it is hoped, then may challenge and reject those traditional values and practices which are harmful or discriminatory. It is submitted, however, that schools and their environments throughout sub-Saharan Africa are far from being sufficiently attended, structured or equipped to carry out this function. To begin, girls living in cities are more likely to go to school than girls living in rural areas.[77] But it is precisely in the rural areas that harmful traditional practices are strongly upheld and where the majority of the population of sub-Saharan Africa lives. Second, a significant percentage of girls in sub-Saharan Africa attend sex-segregated schools. While there are many benefits to such a school environment, it is often in these schools (usually run by Catholic missionaries –particularly in the former French, Belgian and Portuguese colonies – or following Islamic teachings) that norms of female inferiority are perpetuated.[78] Moreover, girls' schools tend to be of poorer quality, have fewer amenities, fewer classrooms and higher teacher absenteeism than those only for boys.[79] Where it is more common to go to boarding school for secondary education, girls certainly are more likely to be exposed to modern values of independence and social mobility and are thereby more apt to challenge oppressive traditional norms and practices.[80] The boarding school environment takes adolescents out of their homes and out of the direct influence of their parents.[81] In this environment, girls are more reluctant to observe culturally based values since secondary schools teach self-reliance and 'modern' values in their curricula.[82] However, it should be remembered that few girls in sub-Saharan Africa have the opportunity to

---

75 As summarized in World Bank, *supra*, n. 70, p. 129.
76 Adetunji, *supra*, n. 62, p. 16.
77 Coquery-Vidrovitch, *supra*, n. 37, p. 155.
78 *See id.*
79 *See* [no author], *Would Girls' Schools Help Reduce Fertility?*, Population Briefs, Vol. 6 (2000), p. 4. Absenteeism is explained by the fact that girls'-only schools are commonly staffed by women teachers who tend to have more limited mobility or other demands which interfere with their teaching obligations.
80 *See* K.M. Fallon, *Education and Perceptions of Social Status and Power among Women in Larteh, Ghana*, Africa Today, Vol. 46 (1999).
81 In some sub-Saharan African countries, such as Ghana, the majority of secondary schooling occurs in boarding schools. As reported in *id.*, p. 70.
82 *See* C. Oppong and K. Abu, SEVEN ROLES OF WOMEN: IMPACT OF EDUCATION, MIGRATION AND EMPLOYMENT ON GHANAIAN MOTHERS (1987).

attend a boarding school. Indeed, the portion of girls able to continue their education past the primary level in the regular (public) school system is relatively small,[83] with families typically opting to educate only their sons past the primary level and not their daughters.[84] Yet another number of girls are unable to finish their secondary education because of early pregnancy.[85] Finally, there are also a number of girls who begin secondary schooling but are taken out of school to care for younger siblings or their household.[86]

While no one would assert that formal education is unrelated to many aspects of reproductive health, neither is it the clear-cut solution many would expect or hope it to be. The conclusion is not to discontinue campaigns to increase women's access to education – education for women remains crucial for their fulfilment and development as human beings. But while many demographers and social scientists initially presumed that education would be an engine of social change by increasing girls' autonomy, findings from surveys in sub-Saharan Africa, North Africa and West Asia suggest that the effects of education are more complicated and do not necessarily follow this presumption.[87] Instead, studies demonstrate that gender attitudes may be reinforced rather than challenged by schooling since the curriculum by and large supports stereotypical patterns in the family. While education appears to be central to creating opportunities for young people, it does not always challenge the expression of traditional attitudes or necessarily encourage wider horizons, at least not for girls.[88] No matter how educated women and men become, their environment continues to apply pressures for conformity and limitations on behaviour. Thus, Coquery-Vidrovitch's conclusion rings true that 'we must beware of a Eurocentric belief that would link education to women's emancipation.'[89]

While it is almost never suggested that education alone can empower women and challenge harmful traditions,[90] the conclusions above also suggest that its potential is

---

83   While the gender gap in school enrolment at the primary level is minimal, it increases significantly with each level of education thereafter. For example, in 1990-91 the total enrolment in secondary school in Ghana consisted of 67% boys and 33% girls. As reported by Fallon, *supra*, n. 80, p. 71.
84   *See*, e.g., A. Mutua *et al.*, in A. Hardon and E. Hayes, eds., REPRODUCTIVE RIGHTS IN PRACTICE (1997), p. 62.
85   *See* A. Odaga and W. Heneveld, GIRLS AND SCHOOLS IN SUB-SAHARAN AFRICA: FROM ANALYSIS TO ACTION (1995).
86   Two researchers conclude statistically that with each additional younger sibling, the likelihood of dropping out of school increased for girls by an equal ratio; *see* C. Lloyd and A.J. Gage-Brandon, *Women's Role in Maintaining Households*, Population Studies, Vol. 47. *See also*: Odaga and Heneveld, *supra*, n. 85; and, F. Dolphyne, THE EMANCIPATION OF WOMEN: AN AFRICAN PERSPECTIVE (1991).
87   As concluded, e.g., by: M. Mamdani, BEYOND RIGHTS TALK AND CULTURE TALK (2000), p. 142; and [no author], *supra*, n. 69, p. 5.
88   *See* [no author], *id.*
89   Coquery-Vidrovitch, *supra*, n. 37, p. 156.
90   For instance, in its review of harmful traditional practices, the United Nations has also taken the position that access to education by itself is not enough to eliminate values held by society. *See* United Nations, HARMFUL TRADITIONAL PRACTICES AFFECTING THE HEALTH OF WOMEN AND CHILDREN (1995).

limited even when combined with other strategies. This is particularly true because teachers themselves, even if chosen or instructed by the State to teach 'modern' values, may not be competent or desire to do so, or may lack the legitimacy in the eyes of parents to take on the task of challenging traditional norms and practices. As illustrated in Chapter VII with regard to police and the judiciary, the mere fact that these individuals have special powers and may be entrusted by the State to work against certain harmful practices, they may be reticent to take on this task, either because public opinion or they themselves personally are not convinced of the need for eradication.

7 CRITICAL ASSESSMENTS OF THE VALUE OF LAW AND RIGHTS IN AFRICA

Many Africans have negative attitudes towards the value of state-prescribed law and legal institutions (e.g. courts, administration and law enforcement agencies). African feminist Halim for instance, categorically asserts that '[a]s natural as resorting to the legal system may seem to western women, it is a hateful scandalous process for African Women.'[91] Legal institutions, if not seen as corrupt, are considered a culturally irrelevant relic of colonial rule or a tool meaningful only to the elite.[92] These negative views are reinforced by other structural, cultural and psychological realities, as described next.

7.1 Structural Impediments in the Use of Law

The most obvious structural obstacle to women's use of law is the fact that the judicial system in most of Africa is not easily accessible to women. The principal reasons are:[93]

a) the enormous costs involved;
b) the length of time required to pursue a case to its end;
c) the language of the court;
d) the non-receptive attitude of personnel and officers involved in the administration of justice; and
e) the fact that the courts are few and far between.

Rural populations, and in particular women in these populations, have limited access to legal remedies under the formal legal system. The concentration of legal services and judicial facilities in urban centres reinforces many women's views that law is not tangible and not for them.[94] Moreover, the fact should also be considered that access

---

91 *See* A. Halim, *Tools of Suppression*, in Center for Women's Global Leadership, GENDER VIOLENCE AND WOMEN'S HUMAN RIGHTS IN AFRICA (1994), p. 28.
92 *See* Itumbi Nyamu, *supra*, n. 49.
93 As itemized by Naggita, *supra*, n. 26, p. 59.
94 *See* Itumbi Nyamu, *supra*, n. 49, p. 31.

to law may come too late for the young girl who learns that very morning that she will be circumcised,[95] or that it is extremely difficult to seek and obtain for the young girl about to be married off. In these and many other instances, legal recourse is not a meaningful option.

While these structural obstacles are widely acknowledged, they are rarely given proper consideration when offering human rights education to African women. This simply reinforces the views of some Africans that human rights law is alien to them and their environment, precisely because the solutions it offers are untenable within their realities.[96]

7.2 Cultural Impediments in the Use of Law

At the cultural level, obstacles manifest themselves in many different ways. A number of cultural constraints affect women in particular. Women, for instance, are often found to be reluctant to take public positions on issues that conflict with conservative social and religious values.[97] Those who do, risk paying a high price. Socialization also leads to a certain passivity in confronting injustice in the family sphere. Many feminists from developing countries have noted that most women prefer to lobby or attempt to influence the decisions of their families in a non-adversarial manner; recourse to law is seen as necessarily adversarial and therefore culturally inappropriate.[98]

Recourse to police has commonly not served women well either. Reports illustrate some of the problems women have encountered. According to one story, female circumcision is practised by the Maasai people in a region of Tanzania. At the same time, the Tanzanian Penal Code prohibits female circumcision.[99] According to the Tanzanian Legal and Human Rights Centre, local government officials had issued statements against the practice but had done little to follow-up. The local church intervened in some cases, but even in cases where children bled to death no one was charged. More striking is one particular case in the region where three girls had run away from their father in the summer of 1999 in a desperate effort to save themselves from being circumcised. The girls fled to a local church for protection, whereupon

---

95 Hosken reports that most of the girls circumcised are never informed of what is going to be done to them and have no idea about the real consequences of the operations, let alone the dangers involved. *See supra*, n. 65, p. 58.
96 *See*, e.g.: Itumbi Nyamu, *supra*, n. 49; and A. Ilumoka *African Women's Economic, Social, and Cultural Rights – Toward a Relevant Theory and Practice*, in HUMAN RIGHTS OF WOMEN, *supra*, n. 16.
97 *See* S. Goonesekere, *Legal Status of Women*, in EMPOWERMENT AND THE LAW, *supra* n. 27, p. 56.
98 *See*, e.g.: R. Coomaraswamy, *Ethnicity and Patriarchy in the Third World*, in EMPOWERMENT AND THE LAW, *supra*, n. 27; and Naggita, *supra*, n. 26.
99 Section 169A(1) of the Sexual Offences Special Provisions Act provides that anyone having custody, charge or care of a girl under eighteen years of age who causes her to undergo circumcision commits the offence of cruelty to children. The penalty for this offence is a term of imprisonment from five to fifteen years, a fine of up to 300,000 shillings, or both imprisonment and the fine. The law also provides for the payment of compensation by the prepetrator to the person against whom the offence was committed.

several pastors assisted them and took them to the nearest police station. Rather than protect the girls, the police arrested one of the pastors, as well as his wife, for having taken unlawful custody of minor children. The pastor was severely beaten and asked to confess that he had raped the girls. Fortunately, the girls were taken to the hospital for an examination whereupon it was confirmed that they had not been raped. The girls were then turned over by the police to their father who had them circumcised the next day and married within a month, one as a third wife. The three girls were aged 13 and 14 at the time. One became pregnant a short time after. Although the Legal and Human Rights Centre had submitted its report of the incident to the authorities and was prepared to help the girls prosecute their father, all three said they did not want to pursue prosecution.[100]

Most women will not muster the courage to report any member of their family to the police. Even if a woman manages to get to the police station, she is likely to be told that her complaint is a domestic affair in which the police cannot involve themselves. She will be advised to go back home and work it out with her family.[101] In short, the fact that law enforcement officers and other people who make up the structures of the legal system at this level are as steeped in custom as the women themselves further complicates matters.[102] Hence, even if a young girl dares to report a complaint to the police, there is a real risk that the police will not even register it. The only recourse available to her will thus disappear. Even worse, she will have little choice but to return home and deal with the consequences of her escape to the police. Experience shows that she most likely will be submitted more quickly for circumcision or into marriage.

7.3 Psychological Impediments in the Use of Law

In order to seek fulfilment, an individual must first have faith that human rights are meaningful and demand respect. A woman must, as Bay suggests, 'begin to trust the strength of her mind, built up through experience in discussion in dialogue... sufficiently to enable her to choose her own answers to all the searching questions, regardless of the pressures of conventional wisdom.'[103] Human rights education essentially should create the conditions for critical awareness, wherein individuals feel strong or

---

100 As reported in Equality Now Newsletter June 2001 (Women's Action 20.1).
101 *See* Naggita, *supra*, n. 26, p. 50.
102 *See* F. Butegwa, *Challenges of Promoting Legal Literacy Among Women in Uganda*, in LEGAL LITERACY, *supra*, n. 14, p. 142.
103 C. Bay, STRATEGIES OF POLITICAL EMANCIPATION (1981), p. 77.

Chapter VI

'empowered' enough to ask not only what are the reasons behind traditional practices but to challenge these reasons and thereby seek fulfilment of their human rights.[104]

Yet very few African women or men seem to have passed this threshold where they begin to believe that human rights discourses and law can make a difference in their lives (even if they may believe they suffer injustices and violations). Even fewer have passed the next threshold of seeking to put the law into practice. The stretch between consciousness-raising and action is therefore substantial and its bridging will remain slow-going and be unlikely to improve if our own expectations of human rights as the 'solution' do not change. An-Na'im correctly points out in this regard that

> [t]here is a mistaken impression that all we need to have is a rights paradigm or a system of rights. The issue is not simply a question of rights, it is a question of ability to use rights, to the extent that rights can make any difference anyway. Beyond legal and rights paradigms, there is a whole world of women and men and social, cultural and religious activities, which are deeply rooted and very inaccessible.[105]

The observation should also be made that in sub-Saharan Africa there is suspicion and at times even hostility directed towards any struggle that is framed in terms of rights.[106] Law and rights are perceived as being part of the problem – an instrument of the elite and of the West, not of disadvantaged women and men in Africa. The initial task of educators, therefore, is to get rural women to appreciate a system with which they do not identify.[107] In this connection, Illumoka notes that the assertion of rights presumes their existing and probable violation, and a desire to remedy or prevent violation. Yet, in the case of harmful traditional practices in African communities, both the presumption and the desire are often lacking.

Numerous commentators have also stressed that for the large majority of women in Africa the problem of poverty and under-development are considered a priority over all others.[108] In stressing health, harmful traditional practices, or more significantly gender-based violence as the focus of human rights education and empowerment, one risks in effect reinforcing their belief that such campaigns project the concerns of privileged (and often foreign) women who are able make their voices and interests heard. These may well be viewed as out of touch with the pressing realities of everyday-survival for the average African woman. They also conceive of African women

---

104 This reflects the theory of Immanuel Kant, who believed every individual was an autonomous moral agent able to govern his actions by reason. In this conception, responsible, rational men and women would base their actions on universally valid laws which they would have accepted only through reasoning. *See* GROUNDWORK OF THE METAPHYSIC OF MORALS (reproduced in 1948).
105 A. An-Na'im, *Remarks (Forum on Religious and Cultural Rights)*, The American University Law Review, Vol. 44 (1995), p. 1384.
106 *See*, e.g.: Itumbi Nyamu, *supra*, n. 49; Naggita, *supra*, n. 26; and Ilumoka, *supra*, n. 96, pp. 319-320.
107 *See* Ilumoka, *id.*
108 As suggested, *inter alia*, by: Itumbi Nyamu, *supra*, n. 49; Naggita, *supra*, n. 26; Ilumoka, *id.*

and their problems (especially female circumcision) as objects for change rather than viewing African women as subjects whose circumstances and views (including customs) are to be respected; such projections hardly inspire the allegiance of African women who in one sense would be expected to act against themselves. This complex psychology must be appreciated in any effort to eradicate harmful traditional practices.

7.4 Recognizing the Limitations of Legislation

As noted earlier, law is frequently under-utilised by African women, even in places and situations where family and personal laws are favourable to them.[109] There are many occasions where laws prohibiting harmful traditional practices exist but are not called upon. For example, the 1995 Constitution of Uganda guarantees equal protection of the law to all persons while prohibiting discrimination on various grounds, including gender.[110] Women and men are guaranteed the right to marry with their free and full consent as of the age of 18 years.[111] It expressly prohibits all 'laws, customs or traditions which are against the dignity, welfare, or interest of women, or which undermine their status.'[112] While these provisions are straightforward, neutral, and fair, practices are different. A girl is unlikely to marry without the consent of her father, brother or other paternal male relative. Indeed, her own consent is not important. Whether she is underage is largely irrelevant.[113]

Reasons for the under-utilization or simple disrespect of law go deep into the cultural norms and traditional gender roles of African society.[114] One must also bear in mind that although laws against harmful traditional practices exist,[115] they may not be considered legitimate. To refer to Western legal thinking, in the Thomist tradition of Natural Law it is generally understood that man-made laws which conflict with a community's perceived principles of morality and justice are not considered valid law: *Lex iniusta non est lex*. Hence, if Africans are to have a sense of moral obligation to uphold a law banning child marriages, they must believe that a law is needed, for which they must first be convinced that the practice is 'wrong'. Even if it is agreed that the practice is 'wrong', there may still be hesitation to remedy it or prevent its further practice. As Shils explains,

---

109 *See* A.A. El Dareer, *Sudan: Custom and Customary Laws*, in EMPOWERMENT AND THE LAW, *supra*, n. 27, p. 137.
110 Article 21.
111 Article 26.
112 Article 33.
113 As reported by Naggita, *supra*, n. 26, p. 43.
114 *See* U. Dow *et al.*, *Women's Empowerment Initiatives from a Grassroots Level*, in HUMAN RIGHTS EDUCATION, *supra*, n. 12.
115 Female circumcision alone is illegal in nine sub-Saharan African countries. As reported in CRLP, FEMALE GENITAL MUTILATION: A GUIDE TO LAWS AND POLICIES WOLRDWIDE (2000).

Human beings become attached to the given. It becomes to them the 'natural way' to do things. Being 'natural' is nearly the same as being normative and obligatory, once a pattern is accepted as 'natural'. Other ways might be rationally recommended or even coercively imposed on persons but attachment to the traditional patterns of acting and believing is not easily dissolved.[116]

In view of this, it is very important that neither the human rights community nor African States narrowly interpret or advance the State's obligation as to adopt legislation, inform individuals of its existence or even punish those who break the law.[117] Rather, the obligation must be interpreted as including duties to explain to individuals why the law exists, why it is just and why it should be respected. In this regard, the Women's Convention is appropriately holistic, defining the obligations as much more far-reaching than the mere adoption of legislation to modify or abolish customs and practices which discriminate against women, but including other measures as well (Article 2 e)). States must equally *act* to modify the social and cultural patterns of conduct of men and women in order to eliminate customary and all other practices which subjugate individuals (Article 5 a)). Harmful or negative stereotypes should be challenged in all forms of education (Article 10 c)). Access to information and education as well as health care to ensure the well-being of families and women's reproductive health must be made available (Articles 10 h) and 14.2 b)).

Certainly, legislation against harmful traditional practices does serve a purpose, not the least of which is to acknowledge that a problem exists.[118] Howard further observes that, while we can 'anticipate quite severe social consequences from attempting to legislate out of existence long-standing practices... legislation can also embody anew ideology which can act as an impetus towards future relaxation of community norms.'[119] However, while reliance on the law provides statutory/theoretical protection, it is in itself not sufficient to achieve the practical realisation of women's rights.[120] The passing of legislation favourable to women has helped women to overcome some of the injustices they face. But it is clear that the real position of women will not be improved until traditional mores and customs are examined and replaced. Only then will women be able to appeal to the law to protect their rights.[121] Ultimately, a legal revolution (e.g. through mass popular human rights awareness and legislative texts

---

116 E. Shils, TRADITION (1981), p. 200.
117 CRLP appropriately warns States to reconsider any application of criminal sanctions for harmful traditional practices, unless these are accompanied by sound and broad governmental initiatives to change individual behaviour and social norms. *See* CRLP, FEMALE GENITAL MUTILATION: A MATTER OF HUMAN RIGHTS (1995), pp. 28-29.
118 As suggested by F.N. Adjetey, *Reclaiming the African Woman's Individuality*, The American University Law Review, Volume 44 (1995), p. 1371.
119 R. Howard, *Human Rights and Personal Law: Women in sub-Saharan Africa*, Issue, Vol. XII (1982), pp. 46 and 48.
120 *See* Naggita, *supra*, n. 26, p. 35.
121 *See* El Dareer, *supra*, n. 109, p. 139.

banning harmful practices) may improve the lives of some women, but if the power and attitudinal relationship between African men and women does not change, such a revolution will have a limited impact.[122] Even if a harmful practice is stopped, there is a real risk of its reappearance if the underlying norms and values which gave rise to it in the first place remain unchanged. The story of the Sabini people of Uganda who succeeded in replacing female circumcision with an alternative ritual of gift-giving for a period of a few short years, only to have the practice return, is a perfect example of this.[123]

For all of these reasons and many more, it becomes obvious that legislation is not enough, and is arguably not a priority, to end harmful traditional practices. Indeed, few solutions to socio-cultural problems are generated by law itself. Law must therefore not be seen as the means for social change, but only a part of the process towards change.[124] Ultimately, programmes and advocacy campaigns need to look beyond law for the solution to the gender dilemma.[125]

8 Conclusions

The empowerment of African women and the challenge of harmful traditional practices cannot take root without certain enabling changes in the basic norms and institutions of society. Yet programme managers, NGO strategists and women's rights activists alike continue to advance empowerment as the means, rather than the end. This phenomenon is criticized in bitingly ironic terms by two researchers: 'If stabilising population or high literacy rates is the objective, empowering women becomes a strategy. Poverty alleviation, public health, drought prevention, employment generation – you name it and hey presto! – empowering women will make it happen.'[126]

Another dilemma is that, all too often, human rights education is just about conveying human rights principles, and not about their feasibility or operationalization. So much emphasis has been placed on entitlement that we have forgotten the complexities of fulfilment in the process.[127] As such, the principles risk being degraded in the absence of real meaning in the lives of those for whom they are intended.

Grassroots (bottom-up) strategies to end harmful traditional practices have received the greatest support and attention. This is not surprising since human rights activism has traditionally targeted the local. For most human rights organisations, the grassroots

---

122 *See* M. Velásquez Toro, *Legal Gains for Women*, in EMPOWERMENT AND THE LAW, *supra*, n. 27, p. 76.
123 *See* CRLP, *supra*, n. 117, p. 41.
124 *See* B. de Gaay Fortman, *The Dialectics of Western Law in a Non-Western World*, in J. Berting *et al.*, eds., HUMAN RIGHTS IN A PLURALIST WORLD: INDIVIDUALS AND COLLECTIVITIES (1990), p. 237.
125 *See* Dow *et al.*, *supra*, n. 114.
126 B. Datta and G. Misra, *Advocacy for Sexual and Reproductive Health: The Challenge in India*, Reproductive Health Matters, Vol. 8 (2000), p. 29.
127 As generally argued by de Gaay Fortman, *supra*, n. 124.

level is where they work best, where their skills are most applicable, and where their ethos is most suited. But ending violence against women in Africa requires multiple strategies, not only educating and empowering women but also coordinating institutional responses, harmonizing media and communication strategies at the national level, encouraging opinion leaders to address the norms at issue, etc. Popular support is important to bring about a successful end to harmful traditional practices but it is not sufficient if it comes from the grassroots population alone. It must also come in various manners and at specific times from health officials, policy-makers, police, judges, the news media, employers, health care providers, and religious and community leaders.[128] The appropriate manners and times of intervention by these actors are considered in Chapters VII and VIII.

Various international plans of action have in fact clearly spelled out that the solution to harmful traditional practices ultimately lies in the integration of strategies at the grassroots and State level.[129] They generally acknowledge that the end to gender violence and harmful traditional practices can only occur when various components are in place: legislation, education, economic stability, and policies and programmes challenging negative attitudes and stereotypes, to be facilitated, *inter alia*, through the collection of data, the use of media and communications. Despite this knowledge, our response has been overwhelmingly one-sided, focused primarily on helping Africans empower themselves at the local level, rather than assisting the State grapple with the nuts and bolts of how effectively to change attitudes. While we may have convinced some individuals that they are sufficiently empowered to seek assistance and redress before the police and the judiciary, the questions of how these and other institutions of the State (e.g. schools, government ministries, government-owned media) should respond and whether they are prepared to do so, have been largely ignored. This has been partly a result of our bias towards grassroots 'empowerment' initiatives, which will be effective only when the systems of police, courts, schools, government administration, etc., work as well. It is therefore proposed that at least *equal* attention should be given to empowerment from the top down. This would include turning our attention to those opinion makers and leaders with the power to change attitudes (village elders, customary chiefs, religious leaders, etc.), individuals who have been largely excluded to date. In the interest of achieving a more holistic, and hopefully more successful, approach, top-down strategies are thus considered in the following chapters.

---

128 As noted in U.D. Upadhyay and B. Robey, WHY FAMILY PLANNING MATTERS (1999), p. 3.
129 *See*, e.g., CEDAW'S General Recommendation No. 14 (Annex A.I).

Chapter VII
Drawing Lessons from Successful and Failed Challenges to Traditional Practices

1 Introduction

All forms of traditional practices are similar in that they are strongly embedded within the culture of a group and have significant cultural meaning. All practices involving women are inextricably linked with notions of womanhood, adulthood, marriage and cultural identity. On the basis of this reasoning, African harmful traditional practices in question in this study resemble other harmful traditional practices justified on cultural grounds in other cultural settings. If all traditional practices harmful to women do indeed have similarities, it may be possible to draw lessons from those that were eradicated. In the first part of this chapter, therefore, two abolished practices – footbinding in China and widow burning (or *sati*) in India – are examined along with the factors which led to their demise. Lessons are drawn from these successes and highlighted.

A number of African States have attempted to abolish female circumcision. All have sought to prohibit circumcision by law, but have otherwise varied in the measures adopted. Three in particular (Egypt, Kenya and the Sudan) have legally prohibited female circumcision for nearly a half century or more. Given this length of time and their failure to challenge the practice to date, the experiences of these countries are also analyzed so that lessons might be drawn.

In the final part of this Chapter, the contextual differences between footbinding/*sati* and the African harmful traditional practices are considered along with the possible implications of these on the success of eradication efforts and the cross-cultural application of the lessons learned.

2 CHINESE FOOTBINDING [1]

2.1 The Practice

Footbinding was the traditional Chinese custom of forcibly stunting the normal growth of a woman's feet. The procedure would deform both the shape and size of the foot.[2] This typically would be done by the mother of the child either by tightly applying bandages around the foot so as to force the young girl's toes inwards, towards the heel, or by breaking the girl's toes, resetting them, and then bandaging them.[3] The girl's foot endured unremitting pressure since the toes were forced to bend under and into the sole, and the sole and the heel were forced as close together as possible.[4] Typically, the procedure was performed on girls between the ages of five and seven, when their pre-pubescent bones were still flexible.[5] Footbinding is documented as having been widely performed by all social classes under the Ming (1384-1644) and Ch'ing (1644-1911) dynasties but is recorded as back far as 1130.[6]

The repercussions faced by Chinese girls whose feet were not bound were severe, resulting in diminished status and social rejection. Women whose feet had not been bound were considered prostitutes and slaves.[7] Binding one's feet thereby upheld, both the girl's and the family's reputation. Footbinding played a large role in identifying a girl as attractive (with beauty lying in the extreme delicacy of physical attributes such as the feet) and ensuring her a respectable husband.[8] Mothers played a significant role in maintaining this belief and prospective mothers-in-law, who had the task of selecting their daughters-in law, often used as a primary criterion the discipline exemplified by their bound feet.[9]

---

1 Much of the information on this practice is summarized from E. Sussman's article *Contending with Culture: An Analysis of the Female Genital Mutilation Act of 1996*, Cornell International Law Journal, Vol. 31 (1998), as well as other secondary (English language) historical sources.
2 See A.R. Drucker, *The Influence of Western Women on the Anti-Footbinding Movement 1840-1911*, in R.W. Guisso and S. Johannesen, eds., WOMEN IN CHINA: CURRENT DIRECTIONS IN HISTORICAL SCHOLARSHIP (1981), p. 179.
3 See H.S. Levy, THE LOTUS LOVERS: THE COMPLETE HISTORY OF THE CURIOUS EROTIC CUSTOM OF FOOTBINDING IN CHINA (1992), pp. 23-26.
4 *Id.*
5 See C.F. Blake, *Foot-Binding in Neo-Confucian China*, Signs, Vol. 9 (1994).
6 See Drucker, *supra*, n. 2.
7 See Levy, *supra*, n. 3, p. 272.
8 See E.A. Ross, THE CHANGING CHINESE (1911), as cited in Sussman, *supra*, n. 1, p. 216.
9 A missionary noted:
It has been said by some one, that before the marriage engagements take place, that parties not bring [sic: being] permitted to see each other, the exact size of the lady's foot is given after the manner of sending photographs sometimes practiced in Europe.
And again, that the small shoe is exhibited to the parents of the bridegroom, as one of the arguments employed in discussing the amount of purchase money, or money to be given in presents, to the bride and her family; which after all looks very much like a business transaction.

A bridegroom who discovered his new bride had 'natural feet' would be justified in canceling the marriage.[10]

2.2 Its Demise

Opposition to the practice of footbinding existed as far back as when the practice began. In records of the Sung dynasty (960-1279) a scribe noted 'I don't know when footbinding began. Children not yet four or five years old, innocent and without crime, are caused to suffer limitless pain. What is the use of binding and restraining!'[11] But no official protest was made until four centuries later, when the Manchus conquered China in the seventeenth century. It was during this, the Manchu, dynasty that penalties were first issued for those who bound their feet: binding the feet of any daughters born after 1662 was sanctioned by penalties upon the father.[12] But these laws did very little to change people's behaviour. Indeed, Manchu women and even women within the Manchurian court began to bind their feet.[13]

In the 18th century, some political activists joined in the campaign against footbinding. By 1894, the Unbound Foot Association was formed at Canton. One of the primary arguments made against the practice by its founder, K'ang Kuang-jen was a foreign relations argument resembling shaming tactics. His argument was that footbinding thwarted China's efforts to appear as a modernizing nation.[14] In contemporary terms, this and some of his other arguments may not be so convincing but they drew popular support in his time. For instance, while he was no doubt right to argue that bound feet impaired women in their performance of menial tasks, it is less convincing that it caused women to bear weak offspring.[15]

His speeches, writings and work with the Unbound Foot Association drew greater attention and the Association grew to have a membership of over ten thousand. Natural foot societies consequently emerged. Members of these societies were required not to

---

Recounted by J. Dudgeon in *The Small Feet of Chinese Women*, The Chinese Recorder and Missionary Journal, Vol. 93 (1869), p. 178, as cited in Sussman, *supra*, n. 1, p. 216.

10 *See* Ross, *supra*, n. 8, p. 178.
11 Penned by Ch'e Jo-Shui, as cited in Levy, *supra*, n. 3, p. 65.
12 *See* Levy, *supra*, n. 3, p. 66.
13 *Id.*, p. 67.
14 On one occasion Kuang-jen argued that:
   [A]ll countries have international relations, so that if one commits the slightest error the others ridicule and look down on it... China is narrow and crowded, has opium addicts and streets lined with beggars. Foreigners laugh at us for those things and criticize us for being barbarians. There is nothing which makes us objects of ridicule so much as footbinding.
   As cited in Levy, *supra*, n. 3, at p. 72.
15 He added that:
   I look at Europeans and Americans, so strong and vigorous because their mothers do not bind feet and therefore have strong offspring. Now that we must compete with other nations, to transmit weak offspring is perilous.
   As cited in *id.*

Chapter VII

bind their daughters' feet and to encourage their sons to marry only women with unbound feet. They held educational meetings, created popular songs on the subject of footbinding and gained the support of public officials.[16] Apart from condemning the unnecessary pain and torture inflicted on girls and women, they told of the greater potential of natural-footed women to help their families and society at large.

The religious crusade against footbinding came on two fronts. On the one side, followers of Confucian doctrine argued that Confucius was clearly against this practice.[17] On the other side, Western missionaries were also opposed and campaigned against the practice.[18] By the 1890s Chinese opinion seemed to be shifting against footbinding and missionaries took to the opportunity offered by this softening to intensify their efforts.

On 2 April 1895, ten Western women of different nationalities established what was to be the highly influential Natural Foot Society (*T'ien tsu hui*). Two important characteristics of the group were that it was nondenominational and that it acted as an umbrella of a number of other concerned organisations. The group's first target was the Chinese elite because they had the most political power and the lower classes would emulate their conduct.[19] The Society thus sent in 1896 an appeal to the Empress Dowager to support the campaign against footbinding. The appeal was rejected, so the Society turned to dedicate itself to change public opinion. Part of this effort targeted influential community leaders in China, particularly officials. Society members spoke at engagements and open meetings and further disseminated its message through pamphlets and newspapers. Finally, after persistent lobbying, the Empress Dowager in 1902 publicly denounced footbinding.[20] This act was to prove a landmark in the anti-footbinding movement. Her decree legitimized the movement and encouraged Chinese to join it. The Natural Foot Society quickly followed suit by sending memorials and letters to Viceroys and independent governors, all of whom responded by issuing proclamations against footbinding, which members of the Society immediately communicated within the streets (such as by placing placards with the proclamations on them).[21] Public denunciation and condemnation by Chinese political leaders followed, as did that of religious figures.[22]

---

16 *Id.*, p. 74.
17 Confucius, they argued, urged people to change wrong to right. Here they implied that Confucius himself considered footbinding to be wrong. *See id.*, p. 75.
18 *See* Drucker, *supra*, n. 2, p. 183.
19 *See id.*, p. 189.
20 *See id.*, pp. 189-190.
21 *See id.*, p. 190
22 For instance, a descendant of Confucius publicly announced that:
I have always had my unquiet thought about footbinding… Yet I could not venture to say so publicly. Now there are wise daughters from foreign lands who have initiated a truly noble enterprise… They aim at extinguishing a pernicious custom.
See id.

Drawing Lessons from Successful and Failed Challenges to Traditional Practices

However, the most effective statement by far (credited as having an awakening influence over China) was the Suifu Appeal. The Suifu Appeal, although it collected the arguments of the missionaries and was largely organised by these, was written by a Chinese man, Mr. Chou. It thereby had the added benefit of situating the campaign against footbinding within the cultural and social context of the Chinese people. The Appeal argued that footbinding was sacrilegious because those who bound their daughter's feet ignored Confucius' teaching that people should respect and never injure their bodies. Chou compared the way women were treated in other countries which China tried to emulate. He criticized the unnecessary pain inflicted, arguing that 'It makes the daughters cry day and night, aching with pain. It is a hundred times as bad a punishment as robbers get.'[23] Parents should teach girls about womanly virtues instead of torturing them, he suggested.[24] The Appeal denounced tradition as a basis for the continuation of footbinding. Lastly, it argued practical economic advantages to be derived from its abolition, arguing that stronger women made for a more productive nation.[25]

By 1911, public support for the anti-footbinding campaign reached such a pitch the government officially banned the practice.[26] This time the law, widely supported by the Chinese people, was wholly successful. The role of men in the cultural shift was clearly significant. Increasingly, young men rejected the practice their fathers had so revered. Many would not consent to marry a girl with bound feet. Western-influenced education[27] and the power of the printing press were key in prompting social change.

3 *SATI* (WIDOW BURNING) IN INDIA

3.1 The Practice

Sati was the Hindu practice whereby a living widow would sacrifice herself by joining in the flames of the funeral pyre of her dead husband – hence the term 'widow burning.'[28] Indian mythology tells the story of Sati, granddaughter of Brahma who was the creator of the universe. One day her father performed a grand sacrificial ceremony and invited everyone except his son-in-law, Sati's husband. Outraged by this act of humiliation, she invoked a yogic fire in which she was burned to ashes.[29] Over the years, this act came to be interpreted as a divine act of wifely devotion. Gradually, it evolved into

---

23 *Id.*.
24 *Id.*
25 *Id.*
26 *Id.*, p. 198.
27 Indeed, some missionary schools went so far as to deny admission to their schools to girls whose feet were bound. *See* M.N. Gamewell, NEW LIFE CURRENTS IN CHINA (1919).
28 *See* L. Mani, CONTENTIOUS TRADITIONS: THE DEBATE ON SATI IN COLONIAL INDIA (1998), p. 16.
29 *See* S. Narasimhan, SATI: WIDOW BURNING IN INDIA (1990), p. 11

Chapter VII

a belief that any woman who emulated Sati by sacrificing her own body to honour her husband would be venerated.[30]

Because Hinduism is based on a collection of scriptures spanning over four thousand years, there were great discrepancies which allowed widow burning to be both exalted and condemned in the name of the same religion.[31] *Sati* was first mentioned in Hindu scriptures during the *Vishnusmriti* period. Although the texts did not mandate the practice, it recognized celibacy and immolation as two available options for a Hindu widow. Later, the *Nirnayasindu* declared *sati* to be the widow's essential duty.[32] The *Puranas*, which were a set of scriptures dating as early as the sixth century, also ordered *sati*.[33] The texts even went so far as to describe in great detail how it was to be performed.[34] Eventually, religious leaders and their followers came to deify those women who became *satis*.

Whatever the religious interpretation, the practice became embedded into Indian culture presenting another significant barrier to its eradication. Intertwined with the practice was the social value attributed to widows: perceived as worthless, these women had extremely low social status. Life as an Indian widow was therefore almost unbearable. Even if widows rejected social pressures and did not want to burn themselves, relatives and on-lookers sometimes were found to have coerced, threatened and physically forced them onto the pyre. For instance, in one account, a policeman whose role it was to ensure that the widow was not forced unto the pyre, raised his sword to strike a widow as she attempted to leave the fire. The woman shrank back into the flames.[35] There were also common reports of widows being given mind-numbing drugs involuntarily or being forcibly tied down to the pyre.[36] In many cases, male relatives played a significant role in the widow's 'decision' to commit *sati*.[37]

---

30 *See id.*
31 *See id.*, p. 26.
32 *See id.*, pp. 16-18.
33 One passage of the scriptures reads:
    Tell the faithful wife of the greatest duty of women; she is loyal and pure who burns herself with her husband's corpse... [h]olding his sandals to her breast let her pass into the flames.
    Id., p. 21.
34 According to the Puranas, after having bathed, the widow should dress herself in clean clothing, sip water from her hands, and look eastward and westward while Brahmins chanted. The widow should then bow to one of the gods, recite a prayer and, after circling the pyre three times, ascend it. Another Hindu law-maker stated that:
    She should go near the husband's pyre, with flowers, fruit, etc., give the symbols of her fortunate marital status to other fortunate women then placing a pearl in her mouth, should pray to Agni, the fire god, and enter the flames. At the moment of entering the fire, the Brahmins should chant mantras, to the effect that this woman who is entering the flames should be awarded with entry into heaven via her husband's pyre.
    As described in *id.*, pp. 21-22.
35 *Id.*, p. 79.
36 *Id.*, p. 80.
37 For example, in 1824 a court found that male relatives of the widow had coerced her to commit *sati* in order to gain her husband's property. *See* A. Isaiah, *Lord William Cavendish Bentinck and the Abolition of Suttee*, Journal of Indian History, Vol. 64 (1986), pp. 231-233, as cited in Sussman, *supra*, n. 1, p. 228.

3.2 Its Demise

The British colonizing forces had largely refrained from interfering with Indian culture. They rarely sought to enforce change in Hindu or Muslim religious customs, laws or traditions.[38] In the early 19th century, however, the Governor-General of India raised the issue of whether the government should adopt measures to eradicate *sati*. The cleric entrusted with the question replied that the matter was deeply embedded in Indian culture and should not be interfered with. In 1812, however, the government adopted a law which distinguished between illegal *sati* (e.g. where women were to commit *sati* under force, when drugged or intoxicated, when pregnant or where there were young children in their care).[39] Police were instructed to arrest individuals who sought to commit illegal *sati*, aided in its commitment or forced a woman into the act.[40] The law, however, was overwhelmingly a failure. Rarely could the police or the courts establish whether *sati* had been committed under the defined terms of illegality. Moreover, the presence of police at the site of a *sati* (required in order to establish whether the *sati* was legal or not) was perceived as acquiescence and endorsement. The courts even reported a rise in the practice following the enactment of the law.[41] Five years later, the order was revised so as to require all widows contemplating *sati* to report to the police prior to committing the act. Widows who failed to report would be fined or imprisoned. However, few widows reported their intention and few magistrates sought to punish this failure. The police were equally unmotivated to comply with the order for two reasons. First of all, there was no risk of sanctions upon them if they failed to enforce the law. Second of all, many officers were Hindu themselves and still believed the practice to be honourable and within the edicts of Hinduism. As a result, very few intervened to stop *satis*.[42]

It was around the same time that Rammohun Roy, a Bengali Brahmin intellectual, began his campaign against *sati*.[43] Roy had witnessed his sister-in-law sacrifice herself by *sati* upon the death of his brother. Appalled by this act, he published pamphlets arguing against the practice. In an attempt to dispel the misguided myth of the ritual, he cited thirteen verses from the *Bhagavadgita* (Hindu scriptures) which prohibited any actions that were based entirely upon the expectation of future rewards.[44] He argued that the religious texts in favour of *sati* were in fact contrary to Hinduism and challenged supporters of the practice to open debates on the terms of their religious beliefs

---

38 *See* V.N. Datta, A HISTORICAL, SOCIAL AND PHILOSOPHICAL ENQUIRY INTO THE HINDU RITE OF WIDOW BURNING (1988), p. 21.
39 *See id.*, p. 25.
40 *Id.*
41 *See* Narasimhan, *supra*, n. 29, p. 62
42 *See id.*, p. 65.
43 *See*: A. Sharma, SATI: HISTORICAL AND PHENOMENOLOGICAL ESSAYS (1988), pp. 31-41; and Narasimhan, *supra*, n. 29, p. 68.
44 *See* Sharma, *id.*

Chapter VII

and cultural understandings. In short, he provided a sound alternative interpretation of religious principles requiring *sati*.[45] His efforts were mirrored by those of Baptist missionaries in the region who gathered statistics and reported eye-witness accounts of the practice. Aside from this information, which served as an important tool in the anti-*sati* campaign, the missionaries also actively petitioned the government to abandon their policy of non-intervention.[46]

Through his writings and speeches the anti-*sati* campaign drew greater public support.[47] It was the success of his efforts that prompted in 1829 a new anti-*sati* legislation by then Governor-General, Lord Bentinck. Bentinck cleverly explained his decision to seek an end to *sati* by legislation by arguing that it was an inevitable reaction to popular opinion – as though he was simply responding to the demands of the Indian people to adopt such legislation. The legislation flatly declared *sati* illegal and punishable by the criminal courts, regardless of whether it was voluntary.[48] A group of orthodox Hindus challenged the regulation on the grounds that it constituted unjustifiable religious interference but the case was dismissed. In 1857, a nationalist movement campaigned against the legislation arguing that it was an imperialistic attempt to destroy Indian culture.[49] Despite these appeals and a few random cases of *sati* between 1829 and the end of the century, the practice appeared to have come to an end just as soon as the regulation was adopted.[50]

Of contemporary concern, however, is the resurgence of a few cases of *sati* in the last quarter of the 20th century. The case which has drawn the most attention is that of a young and educated widow, Roop Kanwar, who committed *sati* on 1 September 1987. In response to the avalanche of criticism from women's rights groups, a stream of Hindus defended the incident on the grounds of culture.[51] In the days that followed, pilgrims came to Kanwar's home in the thousands to honour her sacrifice. On the first anniversary of her immolation, a celebration was organized which drew 4,000 people,

---

45 *See* Narasimhan, *supra*, n. 29, p. 68.
46 For instance, they cleverly reasoned that the Government had already 'intervened' with respect to other cultural practices such as infanticide and capital punishment, and therefore were unjustified in maintaining the argument of 'non-interference' with respect to *sati*. *See* Datta, *supra*, n. 38, p. 77.
47 His powerful impact on the practice was widely recognised. In one article of the *Indian Gazette*, it was noted that '... Rammohun Roy's writings have been the means of saving some lives. We understand that there are now many respectable natives convinced by his arguments'. Cited in *id.*, p. 126.
48 *See* Sati Regulation XVII, A.D. 1829 of the Bengal Code, 4 December 1829, as cited in Narasimhan, *supra*, n. 29, p. 69-71.
49 *See* Datta, *supra*, n. 38, p. 147.
50 *See* Narasimhan, *supra*, n. 29, pp. 71-73.
51 One editorial describes the sentiments:
    Roop Kanwar did not become a *sati* because someone threatened her... [S]he purposefully followed the tradition of *sati* which is found in the Rajput families of Rajasthan... It is quite natural that her self-sacrifice should become the centre of reverence and worship. This therefore cannot be called a question of women's civil rights or sexual discrimination. It is a matter of a society's religious and social beliefs.
    As cited in V.T. Oldenburg, *The Roop Kanwar Case: Femininst Responses*, in J.S. Hawley, ed., SATI, THE BLESSING AND THE CURSE: THE BURNING OF WIVES IN INDIA (1994), p. 101.

half of whom were women.⁵² Thus, although the practice is all but completely eradicated, there is evidence enough that its grip remains culturally strong.

4 SOME AFRICAN STATE INITIATIVES TO END FEMALE CIRCUMCISION

4.1 Egypt

According to medical researchers, female circumcision has been practiced in Egypt for more than 2000 years. Archaeologists have discovered that some female mummies they had found had been excised,⁵³ hence the term 'pharonic circumcision' sometimes used. In 1959, following a resolution by the Minister of Public Health, a committee was formed to investigate the matter of female circumcision in Egypt. In its resolution, the committee recommended that only partial clitoridectomy be permitted and only with the consent of a physician.⁵⁴ The resolution went largely unheeded. It was not before another twenty years that the Egyptian government tried to address the issue again by issuing a report (submitted to the 1979 World Health Organization Seminar in Khartoum, Sudan) which recommended further that circumcision be performed only by a physician. The 1959 resolution was thus supplemented and remains the legislation on circumcision in Egypt. According to all accounts, however, it has largely failed to curtail the numbers of illegal circumcisions performed.⁵⁵ A significant problem reportedly lies in the commitment of physicians and the police. Very few doctors, for instance, file reports with the police when they have had to treat hemorrhaging children owing to circumcision by a non-physician. Even when they have, the police have seldom investigated the case, never mind pressed charges. At best, parents are scolded by the police and the case is closed.⁵⁶

4.2 Kenya

In Kenya, the first attempt to legally prohibit circumcision occurred in 1906, in the early days of British colonial rule.⁵⁷ The ban was reportedly perceived by some communities in Kenya as a coercive intrusion into their customs and prompted a firmer attachment to the practice.⁵⁸ Parents sought to have their daughters circumcised at any cost and by whatever means.⁵⁹ In 1915, the Church of Scotland in Kenya further

---

52 *See* Datta, *supra*, n. 38, p. 234.
53 *See* F.P. Hosken, STOP FEMALE GENITAL MUTILATION (1995), p. 55.
54 *See* F.P. Hosken, THE HOSKEN REPORT (1993), p. 131.
55 *See id.*, p. 132.
56 *Id.*
57 A. Slack, *Female Circumcision: A Critical Appraisal*, Human Rights Quarterly, Vol. 10 (1988), p. 477.
58 *See* O.L. Amede, *Bridges and Barricades: Rethinking Polemics and Intransigence in the Campaign against Female Circumcision*, Case Western Reserve Law Review, Vol. 47 (1996), p. 331.
59 *See* J. Kenyatta, FACING MOUNT KENYA: THE TRIBAL LIFE OF THE GIKUYU (1953).

forbade the circumcision of schoolgirls. Girls who had been removed from colonial schools in order to be circumcised were banned from returning to these establishments for 18 months.[60] One response to this was the creation of indigenous and independent schools. Missionaries also took up the crusade against circumcision with zeal. By 1930, it was evident that the two camps were at loggerheads. Opposition to eradication campaigns had intensified. Campaigns were accused of being racially spurred by the colonizers and an interference with the beliefs and culture of the communities within Kenya.[61] A political group was formed (the Kikuyu Central Association) with the express mission to fight for the continuation of female circumcision.[62] It was not long before this fight was joined with the fight for independence from colonial rule. When Jomo Kenyatta came into presidency immediately after the end of colonial rule, he charged that the British were out to destroy Kenyan people by trying to save girls from the practice.[63] He distinguished himself with the statement 'No Kikuyu will ever marry a woman who is not circumcised,' and claimed that female circumcision was essential for his people to flourish: anyone attacking the practice was undermining the social viability of Kenyan society.[64] He further fueled opposition to any legislation against circumcision by expressly citing the practice as one which unified the Kikuyu people (the Kikuyu being the largest ethnic group within Kenya).

When Daniel Arap Moi (who remains the President of Kenya today) was elected upon Keyatta's death, the stance of the Kenyan Government on female circumcision changed. Moi vocalized his opposition to female circumcision in an official statement following the death of over a dozen girls from circumcision in a rural area where he had recently gone to visit and speak.[65] In 1982 (three years before Kenya was to host the UN Decade Conference for Women), Moi categorically prohibited FGM all over Kenya.[66] The police was instructed to pursue murder charges against people who carried out the procedure with fatal results. A formal proclamation was released by the Ministry of Health which ordered health officials in government and missionary hospitals not to carry out the procedure without specific permission.[67] In December 1989 he demanded all communities still practicing female circumcision to stop immediately and six months later declared it officially banned. Despite the commitment of the executive branch of the Government, the legislature has not been forthcoming with any legislation banning the practice. In 1995, a proposal was specifically defeated

---

60 See L.P. Sanderson, AGAINST THE MUTILATION OF WOMEN (1981), p. 65.
61 See Amede, *supra*, n. 58, p. 59.
62 See Kenyatta, *supra*, n. 59, p. 67.
63 See Hosken, *supra*, n. 53, p. 109.
64 As cited in *id.*
65 See *id.* and CRLP, WOMEN OF THE WORLD: LAWS AND POLICIES AFFECTING THEIR REPRODUCTIVE LIVES (1997), p. 69.
66 See Hosken, *supra*, n. 53, p. 109.
67 *Id.*, p. 110.

and has not been attempted again since then.⁶⁸ Few efforts to raise awareness of the harmful effects of the practice have ever been undertaken by the Government.⁶⁹

Some NGOs in Kenya have taken on the campaign against female circumcision. Two such organisations, the Kenyan Family Planning Association⁷⁰ and *Maendeleo Ya Wanawake*, have proceeded with initiatives in this area (see Chapter VIII, Section 3.2.1). Reports of success vary widely from source to source. One report estimates that the practice is still as prevalent in Kenya as it was at the beginning of the century.⁷¹ Another suggests that there has been a 13 per cent decrease in female circumcision from 1995-2000.⁷² Yet another reports a reduction in incidence by up to 15 per cent in some parts of the country.⁷³

4.3 The Sudan

In 1924, the colonial Government of the Sudan issued an 'informal' circular at the request of the Director of Medical Services. The leader of the Islamic Court similarly proposed that a *fatwa* (religious decree) be ordered banning circumcision. However other religious leaders were firmly against such a decree and so ultimately none was issued. Ironically, their argument against such a decree was that Muslims were already aware that circumcision was contrary to Islamic teachings and that it was, therefore, unnecessary to condemn it by religious law.⁷⁴

The question of female circumcision was further considered by the colonial administration in the Sudan in the late 1930s.⁷⁵ While Members of Parliament back in Britain urged the administration to outlaw the practice, it hesitated to do so for two reasons. First, it feared the Sudanese would interpret such legislation as an act against their culture. Second, such interpretation would risk diminishing indigenous support for other social and political reforms, considered to be more important. The administration hesitated long and it was not until 1946 that it amended the Sudanese Penal Code such that only *sunna* type circumcision (which consists of removing only part of the clitoris) would be legal. Anyone committing any other form of female circumcision would be fined and/or be sentenced up to five years in prison.⁷⁶ The reaction of the

---

68 *See* CRLP, *supra*, n. 65.
69 *See* Hosken, *supra*, n. 53.
70 *See* Baleta, A., *Women's groups in Kenya win small victory against female circumcision*, Lancet. Searched http://thelancet.com/search/search/isa, 28 July 2001.
71 CRLP, *supra*, n. 65.
72 Baleta, *supra*, n. 70.
73 Simon Robinson, *The Last Rites*, Time Magazine, 3 December 2001, pp. 70-71.
74 *See* A. El Dareer, WOMAN, WHY DO YOU WEEP? CIRCUMCISION AND ITS CONSEQUENCES (1982), pp. 92-93.
75 *See id.*, p. 93.
76 The law provided as follows:
    Whoever voluntarily causes hurt to the external genital organs of a woman is said... to commit unlawful circumcision... It is not an offense against this section merely to remove the free and projecting part of the

Sudanese people was overwhelmingly negative. Many individuals sought to have the procedure done in secret. Stories abounded of parents bringing their daughters to midwives in the dead of night to be circumcised in a group, in the absence of any celebration or ceremony. Even individuals who were popularly known as proponents of women's equal rights or publicly known as opponents of circumcision refused to support the law because they saw it first and foremost as a covert attempt to rob the Sudanese people of their culture and heritage.[77] While cases of illegal circumcision were reported with some regularity immediately following the adoption of the law, enforcement efforts ceased soon thereafter. Penalties became lax (for instance, a midwife who had committed illegal circumcision would merely be issued a warning from the Health Authority). Indeed cases became so rare that the amendment truly became a 'paper law.'[78] The amendment was eventually abolished in 1983 and although a new Penal Code was adopted in 1991, female circumcision was omitted. Today there is no law in the Sudan specifically banning female circumcision.[79]

Since the early 1990s the IAC has enjoyed the support of the medical faculty and profession. However, given the very strained economic and political situation in the country and the Government's strong support of Islamic tradition, few initiatives to radically change ideas and convictions have seen success. While there is an educated elite, including a large number of physicians, which is well aware of the immediate health and medical problems involved in female circumcision, the practice continues to be performed. Some doctors, for whom the operation is very lucrative,[80] have even been reported as stating that the practice reduces infections.

5 LESSONS DRAWN

5.1 Positive Lessons

5.1.1 The Importance of Local Leadership and Support of Opinion Leaders

The influences of Chou's Suifu Appeal against footbinding and Rammohun Roy's campaign against *sati* were truly catalytic. As natives of the affected culture, Chou and Roy were able to frame the campaign within these cultural contexts. They were able to identify the factors blocking eradication and structure their messages in response to

---

clitoris.
Sudan Penal Code of 1925 § 284-A(1). As cited in *id.*, p. 95.
77 See A.M. A'Haleem, *Claiming Our Bodies and Our Rights: Exploring Female Circumcision as an Act of Violence in Africa*, in M. Schuler, ed., FREEDOM FROM VIOLENCE: WOMEN'S STRATEGIES FROM AROUND THE WORLD (1992), p. 152.
78 *See* El Dareer, *supra*, n. 74, p. 96.
79 *See* N. Toubia, FEMALE GENITAL MUTILATION: A CALL FOR GLOBAL ACTION (1993), p. 45.
80 As reported in Hosken, *supra*, n. 53, p. 106.

the circumstances. Their position was credible and enabled them to engage proponents of the practices in discussions and counter their arguments on the same basis of culture and religion. Both proceeded with intensive education programmes at the community level to challenge public attitudes. Regardless of whether the justifications were based on religion, tradition, marriageability or beauty, they were not insurmountable.

Following from this, the successful challenge of footbinding and *sati* also demonstrated the unequivocal importance of directly addressing the practice in terms of religion, *whether harmful traditions were rooted in religion or not*. Hence, while religious doctrine was not a justification for footbinding, opponents cited Confucian doctrine as supporting their call for its eradication. By drawing upon his scholarly knowledge of the Hindu texts, Roy countered religious justifications in favour of the practice with alternative scriptures and interpretations against it. His actions proved that the only way to fight religious justifications (which ultimately would end in indisputable 'truisms') is with the same weapon, religion itself piercing its own armour.[81] Along with the support of local religious leadership, the support of other key opinion leaders, such as the Empress Dowager, politicians or the Chinese elite was also highly significant.

5.1.2 Gaining Public Support for Eradication as the Primary Measure

In every instance recounted above, efforts to abolish the practices only became successful once the attitude of the general public changed against the practices. As the African Centre for Women has asserted, '[w]hat may be needed is a critical mass – a large enough number of people willing to reject harmful practices – in order to encourage others to follow suit.'[82]

The lack of adequate public support for the end of a particular practice is a significant explanation for the failure of efforts to date in Africa, especially with regards to legislation. Whenever the public was not convinced of the need to abandon a practice, legislation, punishment, or alternatives were simply judged irrelevant and efforts for eradication of the harmful practice proved futile. A crucial lesson has been a common omission: failing to address the police, judiciary and health officials. These individuals, who after all are equally members of the affected culture, are often entrusted with enforcing the eradication of a practice. Yet the experiences related above (and also visited in Chapter VI) demonstrate that the attitudes of these individuals towards the practice must be antithetical and truly committed to eradication before pursuing any strategy which involves them as conduits of change.

---

[81] Refer to Chapter VIII for more discussion.
[82] African Centre for Women, TRADITIONAL AND CULTURAL PRACTICES HARMFUL TO THE GIRL-CHILD (1997), p. 2.

5.1.3 The Role of Outsiders

It is worthwhile to note that where successes have been registered, outsiders to the culture (such as the missionaries with *sati* and the association of western women with footbinding) played an initial role of challenge to the tradition but only a supporting role at the pivotal point of change. In this secondary role, their tasks were those of assistance in the gathering of evidence and dissemination of information rather than the direct challenge or formation of opinions at the local level. This observation confirms the lesson drawn in 5.1.1 above, demonstrating the catalytic influence of local leadership.

5.2 Negative lessons

5.2.1 Prioritizing Legislation as a Measure

Consistent patterns in the examples above have emerged indicating the wisdom of introducing legislation against a practice only *after* public sentiments favouring its eradication are sufficiently widespread. In all instances, legislation prohibiting or criminalizing a practice in the absence of popular consent for its eradication failed to have any significant impact in the long run (further confirming the experiences and views described in Chapter VI). In some cases, fears of punishment slowed the regularity of the practice, but only for a short while. In other cases, these fears forced the practice underground placing the girls at even greater risk of ill-health or death. In all cases,[83] the introduction of legislation against the practices without the public's support awakened suspicions and allegations of interference with the indigenous culture and the cultural over-lording of the colonizers. The inevitable result was a clash and polarization of cultures which in many instances led to a firmer entrenchment of the practice. It was also apparent that both sides could politicize the practice. Hence, since colonial governments were perceived by the colonized as oppressive and invasive, practices became more closely identified with the culture of the colonized and the continuance of the practice was seen as a means of resistance against political as well as cultural domination. Nationalism deepened the cultural significance of the practice.

Although African States are no longer under colonial rule, this does not diminish the anger of some States at receiving criticism against their culture from their former colonizers. More importantly, many feel a new form of colonization in their midst: that of the Western hegemony.[84] This confirms the need for global consensus, among Western and non-Western cultures, on the status of harmful traditional practices as a form of human rights violation (as discussed in Chapter IV).

---

83 China experienced its own unique form of colonization with the passage of each dynasty.
84 Refer to Chapter V for discussion.

To conclude, Sussman convincingly warns that 'If the reassertion of culture is the explanation for the recent resurgence of *sati*, then legal coercion imposed by outside nations may only result in disaster.'[85] The insistence of human rights activists that domestic legislation against harmful traditional practices be adopted is understandable, given that most activists are: a) lawyers (familiar with the tool of law as a means of justice); and, b) acting from outside African States (in which case urging a foreign State to undertake legislative reform is a relatively 'easy' action). However, experience has shown that there is a time and a place for law; notably, after educational efforts designed by and for members of the affected culture have been underway and the tide of public opinion has turned against these practices.

5.2.2 Admissibility under Certain Forms or Circumstances

From the stories of success and failure we may draw the lesson that differentiating between legal and illegal forms of a practice potentially carries greater drawbacks than strengths. Distinctions between legal and illegal *sati*, between medicalized or non-medicalized female circumcision,[86] or between permissible and non-permissible forms of circumcision were easily blurred and abused, usually by the parties wanting to commit or facilitate the practice, but also by the police, judiciary or medical officers unsympathetic to the prohibition of the practice or the role they were forced to play in its eradication. Moreover, inherent in allowing these practices in certain forms or under certain conditions was the perception that the practice, in general, was acceptable.

The issue of differentiation under various guises is indeed a subject of great controversy still today. Proponents and opponents of female circumcision, for instance, teeter on both sides of the issue of consent (e.g. whether a girl or woman should be able to seek circumcision if she is informed of the consequences and freely consents to it).[87] They also teeter on both sides of the issue of medicalizing circumcision (e.g. opponents themselves may argue that admitting circumcision under these circumstances would at least serve as a practical stop-gap measure, allowing time for attitudes to change and saving the lives of girls in the meantime).[88] Judging from the experiences above, however, such differentiation never proved beneficial. Distinguishing between legal and illegal *sati* was practically impossible, with the consent of the

---

85 Sussman, *supra*, n. 1, p. 236.
86 In Egypt, for instance, *dayas* (traditional midwives) are precluded from performing circumcisions but medical practitioners are not. The medicalization of the procedure has not diminished the incidence of the practice as some would have hoped, even though doctors are aware of the medical problems arising from it. The fee received by doctors for the procedure is said to be a substantial reason why they continue to perform it. *See* Hosken, *supra*, n. 53, p. 55.
87 Refer to Chapter III for more discussion.
88 A measure the World Health Organization, in a sense the global health watchdog, is firmly set against. *See* World Health Organization, FEMALE GENITAL MUTILATION: INFORMATION KIT (1994).

woman easily forced by influential persons or external factors (e.g. the bleakness of her future as a widow). Consent to circumcision would be no different. Bending the rules to allow early marriage under certain circumstances or accepting abduction and impregnation in certain instances would introduce difficulties of delineation. Could some girls be sufficiently psychologically and physically mature to marry at an early age? Should the economic circumstances of her family be reason enough to have her married young? Could a young girl have in some way condoned or enticed a man to abduct her? Perhaps she was not really 'raped'? Defining such differences would be an arduous task and, whatever the delineation derived, proponents of the practice would be sure to mold them to their advantage. There would, of course, also be the question of who defines these differentiations. Furthermore, from the experience in the Sudan, we have learned that allowing one form of a practice to be performed and not others, will simply drive those desiring to commit illegal forms to do so in hiding, often under conditions more perilous to the girl.

As already noted, prior to enforcing any legal ban of a harmful traditional practice, there must first be a clear popular opinion in favour of such a ban. Once this has occurred, the lesson drawn here is that the ban must be categorical, prohibiting the practice in toto, in all its forms and under all circumstances. Allowing exceptions as a means of progressive eradication appears to have never improved the chances of campaign's success. Hence, no 'milder' form of circumcision should be allowed, even if it is performed by a trained medical professional or within a hospital setting. Grey areas would certainly arise. For instance, should a trained midwife be allowed to perform a circumcision if the State allows it to be performed by 'medical professionals'? If only allowed in hospitals, can a clinic in a rural area perform a circumcision on the basis of the argument that there is no hospital accessible to the local population? Aside from introducing uncertainty in the interpretation of admissibility, exceptions would present the message that the practice was ultimately acceptable.

5.2.3 Penalizing those Already Penalized

Aside from the fact that refusing the admission or return of schoolgirls who had been circumcised or banning footbound women from the royal court were wholly ineffective strategies, such punitive actions doubly penalized the 'victim.' In contemporary terms, such measures would likely be considered ethically improper and a violation of human rights.

5.2.4 The Persistent Potential of Regression

The reappearance of some cases of *sati* in India, much like female circumcision among the Sabini in Uganda,[89] illustrates a need for sustained pressure and information over the long term. While the efforts of the past were thought to have sufficiently guaranteed total eradication in the cases discussed, their return demonstrates that continual efforts are needed to prevent deeply ingrained cultural beliefs from re-emerging.

6 SOME KEY DIFFERENCES AND THEIR POSSIBLE IMPLICATIONS

There are at least three significant differences between footbinding, *sati* and African harmful traditional practices that should be addressed. These involve the timeframe and the form of practices in consideration.

In the first case, challenges to end harmful traditional practices in Africa have occurred mainly in the last century. This period has coincided with the end of the era of the mass colonization and, eventually, the withdrawal of colonial Governments. This is important for a number of reasons. First of all, as noted in the experience of Kenya, these practices could be politicized by indigenous leaders. Kenyatta used the cultural practice of female circumcision as an emblem of his country's culture, demonstrating its strength in the face of colonialism. Of course, the successful challenge of *sati* took place during a period of colonization in India's history. This leads one to wonder if the form of colonization which took place in Africa also had an impact. For instance, the entire continent of Africa was colonized, borders were redefined which separated tribes and families, and customary leaderships were challenged.

There is also a difference in the longevity of campaigns: campaigns to end harmful practices in Africa date no more than 100 years as compared to millennia in the case of footbinding. However, *sati* was ended relatively quickly by comparison (within thirty years). In my own view, the duration of a campaign has little to do with its success or lack thereof: if the challenge strikes at the right tone, at the right individuals, and at the right time, eradication may occur relatively quickly.

Perhaps the more substantial issue is the justifications for the practices in Africa and the widespread nature of these practices. For instance, it is soundly logical that for a campaign to be successful a great deal more people in Djibouti (where 98 per cent of the female population is cut) must change their attitudes towards circumcision than do people in India towards *sati*.[90] In this example, the near universal nature of the practice of female circumcision implies greater difficulty in finding leadership from within the communities and establishing a strong minority view against it. No doubt

---

89   *See* Chapter VI for greater detail.
90   Records on *sati* kept between 1815 and 1829 (when the practice was largely stopped) showed a total of 7,941 widows burned in the region of Bengal. *See* Narasimhan, *supra*, n. 29, p. 70.

more significant than this, are the justifications behind the African practices. They are not so much for reasons of beauty or subservience (as in the case of footbinding), nor always for reasons of honour (such as in the case of *sati*), but also for more mundane reasons of control over sexuality and progeny (as in the case of circumcision) and economic derivations (such as in the case of early marriage, brideprice and levirate marriage). Hence, while opponents of these practices may convince the affected culture that circumcision and early marriage are bad for health and harsh on women, these arguments may insufficiently address the greater issues of monetary gain and ensuring one's child is one's own.

All this being said, however, the lessons drawn are still very much applicable to contemporary Africa. Legislation, for instance, will still remain ineffective without popular support, and popular support will not be gained without more local initiatives and the input of key opinion leaders. The differences discussed above, however, imply that any effort to eradicate harmful traditional practices in Africa may indeed be more complicated than with footbinding and *sati*.

CHAPTER VIII
KEY AGENTS OF CHANGE AND THE ROLE OF THE AFRICAN STATE

1 INTRODUCTION

Harmful traditional practices have been identified as possibly constituting violations of one or more human rights. By its very nature, international human rights law places duties squarely on the shoulders of the State to respect, ensure and fulfill the human rights of all men, women and children within its jurisdiction. Most African States have ratified one or more human rights treaties which provide for rights which are violated by harmful traditional practices. To the extent a State permits, tolerates or facilitates such practices, it has failed to respect, ensure or fulfill its legal obligations.

The purpose of this Chapter is generally to appraise the role of the African State in light of existing treaty obligations. Acts and omissions of some of these States are reviewed demonstrating a significant level of disparity between their actions and their duties. This continues with a discussion on the role of the State in the socialization of norms in which it is observed that States are not particularly influential agents. From this conclusion, it is suggested that the African State should seek to fulfill its legal obligations by facilitating other mechanisms which are culturally more relevant and, consequently, more influential and likely to succeed in achieving change. The mechanisms which are deemed to be best suited in this regard are religious and traditional institutions. The media, because of its reach and popularity, also has a special role to play. The roles of other possible agents of change are also considered along with their relationship to the State. Box III relates the story of an attempt by a foreign organisation to introduce traditional birth attendants in rural Ghana in order to end women practicing harmful birthing techniques. It illustrates the interdependent roles of these key agents and some of the problems one may encounter if these are not appropriately considered and engaged in an eradication initiative.

2 DETERMINING THE MOST APPROPRIATE ROLE FOR THE STATE

There are some African States which are making serious efforts to eliminate threats to women's health and well-being. These efforts are usually legislative (including adoption of governmental decrees or amendments to Constitutions)[1] or administrative (such

---

[1] *See*, e.g., the report of the Central African Republic to the Committee on the Rights of the Child, 9 October 2000, reproduced (in part) in Annex C.

as through the creation of national commissions, ministerial departments or task forces).² Others States, however, while recognizing the problem of harmful traditional practices and pledging their commitment to end these, do little to translate this commitment into positive action.³ Take, for instance, the Government of Liberia: although it has publicly proclaimed its commitment to end the practice of female circumcision and more generally to protect the human rights of women, circumcisers (most of whom are women) continue to enjoy government patronage.⁴ Despite calls to the Government of Liberia by local health and women's rights groups to address circumcisers and possibly install punitive measures against those who continue to circumcise, no effort has been made at the State level to encourage or coerce them to stop their practice. Because of their protection under the State, and the amount of money and prestige they obtain from circumcising girls, few circumcisers agree to participate in the initiatives of women's rights groups to end female circumcision or to work actively against these.⁵

Another example comes from the Government of Kenya. While President Moi has verbally condemned female circumcision, his Government has failed to adopt any formal measures to combat the practice.⁶ His words and actions on other issues of sexuality demonstrate a serious level of ignorance on matters of health and an open disregard for human rights. This ignorance and disregard is consequently reflected in Kenya's policies and laws. For instance, in early 2000, Moi declared AIDS a national disaster. While this is commendable, his firm ban on condom use is likely to limit the gains which could be made from some of his Government's efforts, such as the allocation of free radio and television time to AIDS awareness.⁷ In July 2001 Moi further pursued this ill-conceived approach by calling on all Kenyans to refrain from having sex for two years as a means of slowing down and possibly eradicating AIDS.⁸

In an attempt to fight the massive problem of AIDS in Swaziland where twenty-five per cent of the population is estimated to be HIV-positive, King Mswati III of Swaziland endorsed a similar plan of action in October 2001.⁹ Reportedly, young women

---

2 Within the Government of Nigeria, for instance, the Ministry of Women Affairs and Social Development created instructional manuals on women and human rights and on controlling violence against women in 1996 and 1997 respectively. The Ministry also funds legal aid centres for women.
3 *See* IAC, ACTIVITY REPORT 1999 (1999), particularly p. 25.
4 *Id.* Of course, what some interpret as government patronage may simply be quiet acquiescence or fear by some leaders to get involved in cultural practices. The latter may occur, for instance, in African States which comprise various communities and various faiths. Where leaders are of a minority tribe or faith, or where inter-ethic and religious rivalry is high, leaders may judge it to be politically unwise to address harmful customs practiced by these groups.
5 *Id.*
6 For details, refer to Chapter VII, Section 4.2.
7 [No author], *Kenya calls AIDS national disaster, bars condoms*, SAfAIDS News, as cited in the section 'Law and Policy' in Reproductive Health Matters, Vol. 8 (2000), p. 178.
8 [No author], *No Sex for Two Years, Moi Urges Kenyan People* on website http://dailynews.yahoo.com/h/nm/20010712/hl/sex_3.html. Searched on 18 July 2001.
9 [No author], *Freeze on Sex in Swaziland*, International Herald Tribune, 1 October 2001, p. 5.

who are virgins now must follow a rite of chastity which requires them to abstain from having sex for the next five years. Breaking the ban will incur a fine: offenders are to pay the fine by giving an animal, such as a cow, or paying about US$160. In order to help girls refrain from having sex, they have been forbidden to wear long pants and miniskirts (symbols of Western culture and promiscuity) and are to wear a bundle of bright traditional tassels, known as an *umcwasho*, as a sign of their celibacy. Confirming the folly of this plan, the King of Swaziland himself, under pressure from angry young women, had to fine himself a cow for violating the very chastity law he imposed on his country no less than one month earlier.[10]

Another dubious effort of the Swazi Government is its proposed legislation on sterilization.[11] If the bill is adopted, it would mean the mandatory sterilization of all HIV-positive citizens. Those tabling the bill have argued that some HIV-infected persons are intentionally infecting others. Aside from the obvious fact that sterilization would not stop or reduce the virus from being transmitted (and would therefore take on a purely punitive character), the individual's rights to private family life, dignity and physical security arguably would be violated. Moreover, the fear of certain sterilization would likely lead individuals not to seek medical attention when they believe they may be HIV-positive. These individuals would therefore remain untreated and, if indeed HIV-positive, would potentially further transmit the virus.

Questionable State measures such as these (which then require our time and attention to criticize and dismantle) illustrate that some African leaders must be placed first in line for health education. The measures also put into question the good faith with which some States have engaged themselves in the fight against harmful practices and the spread of HIV, and indeed freely consented to be bound under human rights treaties. The inadequate funding typically given by States to endeavours to combat harmful traditional practices also raises considerable doubt about their good faith. There is no denying that African States are poor. However, challenging the norms maintaining harmful traditional practices or eradicating harmful traditional practices need not be costly. Indeed, respecting, ensuring and fulfilling the human rights of women which may be violated by such traditional practices is inexpensive compared to the price paid by their families and the wider society when a woman loses her life or is incapacitated by such practices.[12] And yet, economic constraints are usually among the first reasons given by African countries for not taking steps to tackle

---

10 Resentment towards the ban grew when it became known that the King's fiancée was only 17 years old and was living with him; *see* H. Andersson, *Sex-ban Swazi king pays fine*, BBC News on website: http://news.bbc.co.uk/hi/english/...africa/newsid_1651000/1651154.stm.
11 *See* K. Ahmad, *Swaziland debates sterilisation of HIV patients*, Lancet, Vol. 356 (2001).
12 Hosken suggests in this regard that computing the real costs of female circumcision is long overdue. Such statistics that translate the practice into economic costs (including hospitalization and treatment) which are paid by the government may be more convincing to governments and international donors than any other form of campaigning for eradication of the practice; *see* STOP FEMALE GENITAL MUTILATION (1995), p. 114.

harmful traditional practices or other threats to the well-being of women and addressing their human rights.[13]

Excuses of poverty usually hide other realities, notably that African leaders prefer to concentrate their attention and resources in other fields they consider greater priorities. These usually involve urban areas while those in rural areas are left to their own devices.[14] In large part, these rural areas are content with the lack of involvement of their government, particularly to the extent their societies operate according to entirely different logic underpinned by indigenous social organisations, self-help groups, affective networks, local and foreign NGOs and customary law.[15] An inquiry into the maintenance of law and order in the rural areas of African polities raises doubt about the status of the African government in rural areas. Commentators note that the role and capacity of the African State in maintaining law and order has often been overestimated, especially in rural areas, where Government and the State are viewed as being 'political' (in the pejorative sense) and authoritarian and consequently as distant and dissociated from daily life.[16]

Setting aside questions of good and bad faith, and capacity or incompetence, there remains, in my view, an even more fundamental question: the ability (i.e. potential effectiveness) of the State to change attitudes and behaviour. On this note, Emile Durkheim categorically rejected the possible influence of the State in this regard, arguing "... the State is to remote from individuals; its relations with them too external and intermittent to penetrate deeply into individual consciences and socialize them within."[17] While the role of the State in ensuring *public health* (such as by providing clean water, removal of waste and the containment and eradication of infectious diseases) is certainly an obvious and important one, the question arises whether the State is capable or best suited to influence *attitudes* and *behaviour*? Despite sound arguments in favour of the State (e.g., the State's capacity to influence behaviour by legal prescriptions and proscriptions, the scope of its legal authority over the entire populace, its institutional reach, its duty to maintain the welfare of its population, or the weakness of African civil society), these do little to convince us that in *practical* terms it is the African State which is capable or best suited to alter the socio-cultural norms

---

13 To confirm this, one need only peruse the reports submitted to the treaty bodies monitoring the Children's and Women's Conventions; *see*, e.g., the initial report of Malawi (June 2001) under the Children's Convention, where the Government argues that:
Key constraints to the survival of children include lack of financial resources and capacity to implement health programmes, cultural practices and the HIV/AIDS pandemic. These problems are compounded by the pervasive poverty.
UN doc. CRC/C/8/Add.43 of 26 June 2001, at para. 246.
14 *See* A. Anangwe, *Maintenance of Law and Order in Western Kenya*, in J. Semboja and O. Therkildsen, eds., SERVICE PROVISION UNDER STRESS IN EAST AFRICA (1995), p. 106.
15 *Id.*
16 *See id.*, p. 105.
17 E. Durkheim, THE DIVISION OF LABOR IN SOCIETY (1933), p. 28.

which inspire and direct harmful traditional practices, especially where these are rooted firmly in culture and/or religion. For such sensitive matters, moral and social authority is more important than legal authority, and socio-cultural and religious institutions are normally much closer to the population, especially in sub-Saharan Africa.

In a recent and highly acclaimed book on the domestication of human rights norms, Risse and Sikkink have developed a model to demonstrate how the global human rights 'polity' can influence the socialization of new norms of behaviour and thus become the causal mechanism by which international norms affect domestic structural change.[18] By their definition of what this 'polity' consists – international organisations involved with human rights, and domestic and national human rights NGOs – the role of the State in the socialization of new norms is rather minimal. Risse and Sikkink further identify a number of types of socialization processes which are necessary for enduring change: moral consciousness-raising; shaming; argumentation; dialogue and persuasion; adaptation; institutionalization and habitualization.[19] The only process identified within this model to be associated *prima facie* with the State is the institutionalization of new norms – to the extent that the State provides the framework for relevant institutions such as required by, e.g., the rule of law. It is arguable that all other processes are ideally to be undertaken by the polity described by Risse and Sikkink or other non-State actors, such as village elders and spiritual leaders. Even the process of institutionalization may be better achieved by local or traditional institutions where the State is weak, such as in sub-Saharan Africa.

This being said, the State is ultimately the party responsible under international law (and in most cases, if not all, under its Constitution) for the promotion, protection and fulfillment of human rights and should be held so. Effective measures to end harmful traditional practices should, however, not engage States as the *only* or even *principal* actor, but as the structural framework facilitating and supporting initiatives by other actors with greater influence in making and breaking socio-cultural norms and practices. Thus, alternative means should be sought to involve governments while bringing in those with the real power to change traditions. With this aim, it is submitted that two groups in particular should be drawn into the centre of the eradication equation. The first is the media, an institution frequently recognized for its potential to change behaviours and norms. The second group – religious and traditional leaders and their institutional structures – must also be engaged by those who seek change. While rarely considered an appropriate or capable partner for government (especially under the modern concept of separation of Church and State), it is submitted that, with regard to the matter at hand, their role is critical. At least, in the light of the failure of the African

---

18 T. Risse and K. Sikkink, *The Socialization of Human Rights Norms*, in T. Risse *et al.*, eds., THE POWER OF HUMAN RIGHTS: INTERNATIONAL NORMS AND DOMESTIC CHANGE (1999), p. 11.
19 The ideal type differs according to their underlying logic or mode of social action, although they may, and often do, take place simultaneously; *see id.*

Chapter VIII

State acting alone to change behaviours and norms, there is considerable merit in attempting to engage these leaders and their indigenous mechanisms. Both groups (religious and traditional leadership and the media) are therefore next examined along with their relationship with the State. The potentially influential roles of treaty monitoring bodies, donors, the legal profession, local awareness-raising groups, and men (ordinary fathers, brothers and husbands) are also considered in brief.

3 INDIGENOUS MECHANISMS

3.1 Customary (Family) Law

Most States in Africa have adopted a formal system of common or civil law, following the European legal traditions. However, throughout much of the region, the existence of such formal systems does not preclude the application of indigenous customary laws. For instance, in anglophone African countries which adopted English common law (such as Ghana, Kenya, Nigeria, Tanzania, and Zimbabwe), family law has been specifically excluded from this realm.[20] Rather, domestic courts upholding customary law commonly have jurisdiction *inter alia* over cases regarding marriage, divorce, and family relationships – areas relevant to traditional norms and practices. The application of customary legal principles is often complicated by the existence of numerous customary law regimes of different groups. Moreover, most customary law remains uncodified, and therefore open to interpretation. This is not necessarily a bad thing, so long as the 'guardians' of the law apply it in a progressive rather than conservative fashion (such as in a manner in conformity with human rights).

There is no doubt that a people's laws and legal system qualify as an important part of a people's cultural package.[21] Nhlapo observes that '[t]his is probably even more so of indigenous systems of law, which are sometimes so intertwined with other cultural and social institutions as to be indistinguishable as separate entities.'[22] He provides us with a description of the meaning of customary law in Africa:

> The African customary law of the family is the outward and visible sign of a very deep and all-pervasive conception of the world and the meaning of life. It is a view of the world as a place where life's imperatives are survival and security, values which have spawned a maze of elaborate mechanisms for their achievement. By far the most central and durable of these is kinship and the institution of the family.[23]

---

20 African customary laws and religious laws based on Islamic and Hindu principles applied in lieu. *See id.*, p. 154.
21 *See* T.W. Bennett, HUMAN RIGHTS AND AFRICAN CUSTOMARY LAW (1995).
22 T. Nhlapo, *The African Customary Law of Marriage and the Rights Conundrum*, in M. Mamdani, ed., BEYOND RIGHTS TALK AND CULTURE TALK (2000), p. 141.
23 *Id.*, p. 142.

Customary law is therefore the centerpiece of African culture. Unfortunately, it is also the source of women's disempowerment. It is therefore often seen as innately antithetic to women's human rights and their fulfillment. As such, it is a legal system often challenged by human rights defenders.[24] And yet, because customary law and order within African society is so central, such law is defended fiercely in case of attack.[25]

Ultimately, the facts to be borne in mind are that, although customary law is typically patriarchal, it is often the system most readily available and acceptable to women in order to seek justice and change. For most women, especially the large proportion of women who live in rural areas, customary laws may also be the only laws they know. Traditional courts are likely the only courts they can access, which speak their language and work within their social and cultural environment.[26]

What can be done in such cases? Certainly, simply banning the application of customary law is not the answer. Indeed, banning a system of law which is as long-standing and socially-embedded as is customary law would be near to impossible. More importantly, it is not customary law *as a whole* which is inherently discriminatory or contrary to the human rights of women, but *elements* of it within certain contexts. Doing away with customary law entirely would mean that the beneficial aspects of the law would be thrown out along with the bad. Rather, those elements conducive to progressive change should be seized. Kishwar makes an important observation in this regard, noting that:

> Our cultural traditions have tremendous potential within them to combat reactionary and anti-woman ideas; if we can identify their points of strength and use them creatively, the rejection of the harmful is easier than attempts to overthrow traditions totally or attack them arrogantly from the outside. We must realize that if we fail to acknowledge and help reinvigorate the deeply human portions of our heritage, none of our other efforts are likely to succeed.[27]

Bearing this in mind, the beneficial characteristics of customary law and leadership should be nurtured and used to help change harmful traditions. For instance, chiefs with customary powers could be made aware of the harmful elements of some traditional practices and engaged to campaign against these. In some instances the chiefs

---

24 *Id.* He critically observes further that:
   With the exception of a few scholars to whom a deep understanding of the African value system seems important, much of the condemnation appears to come from people with little real understanding of African culture and, sadly, with no intention of attaining such understanding.
   Nhalpo connects this view to a comment made to him by a fellow African that 'I cannot be told how to marry and found a family by someone who does not consider his grandmother's sister to be a close relative'; p. 143.
25 *Id.*, p. 142.
26 *See* O. Ojo, *Understanding Human Rights in Africa*, in HUMAN RIGHTS IN A PLURALIST WORLD (1990), p. 118.
27 M. Kishwar, *Introduction*, in M. Kishwar and R. Vanita, eds., IN SEARCH OF ANSWERS (1984), p. 14.

themselves may be women.[28] As women, they may be more amenable or, at the very least, more comfortable and sensitive in addressing concerns about women's reproductive health. Another strategy could be to target Queenmothers. Queenmothers are generally the female partners of chiefs (such as in the Asante community of Ghana). Traditionally, Queenmothers give advice to chiefs not only on political and administrative matters but also on matters relating to women. As such, they have been known to infuse a feminist perspective into judgements of cases before customary courts.[29] There have also been cases of Queenmothers themselves attending workshops and taking the lead and speaking out against harmful traditional practices; the respect other African women participants gave to these women and their views was serious indeed.[30]

Another positive example of this potential can be found in Ghana among the Akan chiefs. As early as in 1938 the Confederation of Akan Chiefs proclaimed the situation of widows as most tragic. It was thus decided by them that widows and their children would thereafter inherit one-third of the deceased's assets.[31] In 1981 the chiefs further recognized that women who divorced, became pregnant without being married, or were neglected in polygamous unions were also vulnerable and had no legal way to demand assistance (such as receiving child support from their husbands). As a result, the chiefs acted to enable women facing such situations to bring family-related problems to special family courts. It is observed that the economic depression of the 1980s in Ghana (as for the greater African region) hastened this evolution. In any event, while it was formerly unthinkable to talk about domestic problems outside the lineage, such trials are now not only possible but have increased in recent years.[32] The legal system's effects, concludes sociologist Coquery-Vidrovitch, go much farther than simple measures: they are changing the whole society.[33]

3.2 Religion and Traditional Indigenous Belief Systems

Religious beliefs in Africa, as in any other region of the world, reinforce norms of patriarchy. These norms are supported in African society by the combined concepts of

---

28 There is a tradition of women chiefs particularly in West Africa, Cameroon, Senegal and Sierra Leone. For instance, between 1914 and 1970, 7.5 per cent of the 146 chiefs recognized in Sierra Leone were women, despite an ancient, fairly patrilineal tradition; as reported in C. Coquery-Vidrovitch, AFRICAN WOMEN: A MODERN HISTORY (1994), p. 35.
29 As described by F.N. Adjetey in *Reclaiming the African Woman's Individuality*, The American University Law Review, Vol. 44 (1995), p. 1367.
30 Observation of the author at Second International Conference on Women in Africa and the African Diaspora (WAAD): Health and Human Rights, Indiana University, Indianapolis, USA, 23-27 October 1998.
31 Ironically, it took ten years for the Akan chiefs to enforce this law because the British Governor at the time would not co-sign the proposal; reported in Coquery-Vidrovitch, *supra*, n. 28, p. 84.
32 Almost half the women who use the courts are employed in the informal sector and 20 per cent are unemployed. They have typically won cases for child support, help with school fees or assistance in the case of illness. *See id.*, p. 84.
33 *Id.*, p. 85.

traditional principles of male superiority, of common law with Christian principles of female inferiority and Islamic tenets of female domesticity and incapacity. Moreover, religion often reinforces notions of fatalism or spiritualism. Hence, in many societies, God or destiny is thought to predetermine the fate of a young woman suffering the ill-effects of a difficult pregnancy or botched circumcision.

But while religious and indigenous beliefs systems have contributed to the subordination of women, religious and traditional leaders nevertheless can be extremely useful. This is because they can easily reach where the State cannot – within the confines of the home. Such leaders should therefore be considered a vital component of any effort to eradicate harmful traditional practices. Since the very nature of their work allows them to address intimate family matters and their views on practices and behaviour carry much weight before their followers, they and their establishments could serve as significant avenues for change.

Perhaps even more than Christianity and traditional religions and institutions of Africa, Islamic law and culture has been positioned (at least in Western media) as being at odds with some human rights values, and in particular women's human rights. There are many observations to be made on this point. To begin, it is to be noted that, unlike in North Africa where Islam was introduced through military conquest, Islam spread across sub-Saharan Africa through discourse and preaching. In the course of its spread, Islam has interacted and coexisted with traditional African religions for many centuries.[34] Traditionally, Islam in sub-Saharan Africa tended to be more social than political, and more tolerant and accommodating of other religions. These historical features have led to the characterization of Islam in sub-Saharan Africa as a tolerant religion,[35] a religion which one could imagine to be supportive of positive change. Hence, while Islam can be presented and practiced as a totalitarian political ideology which oppresses and excludes (which further complicates the task of human rights advocates[36]), there are in fact very few African States which have adopted strict codes of Islamic *Sharia* law.[37]

In short, there are at least three significant reasons why Islam, Christianity and African traditional religions merit serious attention. First, it is precisely in those societies which adhere to these faiths that norms and practices remain highly influential in daily life. Many norms and traditions which thrive today largely derive their source (or at least are believed by Africans to derive their source) from the belief systems of

---

34 *See* L.M. Lewis, *Introduction*, in L.M. Lewis, ed., ISLAM IN TROPICAL AFRICA (1966).
35 *See* A. An-Na'im, *Cross-Cultural Support for Equitable Participation in sub-Saharan Africa*, in K.E. Mahoney and P. Mahoney, eds., HUMAN RIGHTS IN THE TWENTY-FIRST CENTURY: A GLOBAL CHALLENGE (1993), pp. 137-138.
36 *See id.*, p. 137.
37 Indeed, even where *Sharia* law is enforced, it may not always be State tyranny which drives its interpretations, but patriarchy. The title of one article sums up this notion: *see* Seth Mydans, *Blame Men, Not Allah, Islamic Feminists Say*, New York Times, 10 October 1996, p. A4.

these religions. Hence, where individuals no longer actively practice or adhere to a particular religion or belief system, they both consciously and unconsciously remain influenced by its precepts, if not by the mere fact that the community in which they live (and by whose societal rules they must abide) may still have remnants of religiously-inspired codes of personal and social conduct.

Second, some Muslim and Christian feminist scholars have argued that female submissiveness and patriarchy as expressed in all their forms are strongly rooted in religious norms which have been maintained over centuries.[38] In this light, religious faith must always be contended with,[39] regardless of education, urbanization or any other 'enlightening' processes.

Third, it is important to bear in mind that religious and cultural beliefs are often so closely linked as to become indistinguishable. This is particularly so when the institutions of government and religion combine. In this case, vestiges of cultural and religiously prescribed or proscribed behaviour are inherent in societal expectations, and reinforced by the policies and institutions of government.

A viable solution proposed by An-Na'im is that women's rights advocates should see religion and culture as a medium and vehicle for change rather than antagonistic to reproductive rights and the rights of women.[40] From another perspective, Weston argues that the onus is on the human rights advocate to provide a reasoned, intelligent and respectful response to edicts that are believed to maintain harmful traditional practices.[41] Such approaches invite thinkers and advocates to act both internally and externally to eliminate conflicts by offering new interpretations and shaping a modern, practical philosophy of rights. To this end, there are serious efforts and important discussions underway with a view to redefining or interpreting the normative content of religion and culture.[42]

As already noted in Chapter VII, the successful eradication of harmful traditional practices in other parts of the world strongly confirms the importance of local leader-

---

38 *See*, e.g.: F. Kissling, *The Challenge of Christianity (Forum on Religious and Cultural Rights)*, American University Law Review, Vol. 44 (1995); C.W. Howland, *The Challenge of Religious Fundamentalism to the Liberty and Equality of Women: An Analysis under the United Nations Charter*, Columbia Journal of Transnational Law, Vol. 35 (1997); and S.D. Rose, *Christian Fundamentalism: Patriarchy, Sexuality, and Human Rights*, in C.W. Howland, ed., RELIGIOUS FUNDAMENTALISM AND THE HUMAN RIGHTS OF WOMEN (1999).
39 As reported by Uche Nzewi, *The Impact of Education on Nigerian Women's Decision Making on Reproductive Health* (lecture). Second International Conference on Women in Africa and the African Diaspora (WAAD): Health and Human Rights, Indiana University, October 23-27, 1998.
40 A. An-Na'im, *Remarks (Forum on Religious and Cultural Rights)*, The American University Law Review, Vol. 44 (1995).
41 B.H. Weston, *Human Rights in a Multicultured World*, in B.H. Weston and S.P. Marks, eds., THE FUTURE OF INTERNATIONAL HUMAN RIGHTS (2000), p. 76.
42 *See*, e.g., An-Na'im who has elaborated a methodological approach to Islamic Reformation sensitive to the context of Africa in his book TOWARD AN ISLAMIC REFORMATION: CIVIL LIBERTIES, HUMAN RIGHTS, AND INTERNATIONAL LAW (1990).

ship and the support of key local opinion formers, including spiritual leaders. The eradication of footbinding in China and *sati* in India offered good illustrations of the catalytic potential of these actors, precisely because they were able to frame the campaigns within their cultural and religious contexts. Both demonstrated the importance of directly addressing harmful practices on the terms of religion, whether the harmful traditions were rooted in religion or not.[43] For example, while religious doctrine was not a justification for footbinding, opponents cited Confucian doctrine as supporting their call for its eradication. By drawing upon his scholarly knowledge of the Hindu texts, Roy countered religious justifications in favour of *sati* with alternative scriptures and interpretations against it. His actions proved that the only way to fight religious justifications (which would often end in indisputable 'truisms') is with the same weapon – with religion piercing its own armor. Along with the support of local religious leadership, the support of other key opinion leaders, such as the Empress Dowager in China, politicians or the elite was also highly significant. The same can be pursued throughout Africa with regard to harmful traditional practices. If eradication and human rights campaigns are to be successful, it is important to look at the community itself as a resource. In any community, key individuals and institutions can be identified and employed. These will no doubt vary, with different figures and institutions (elders, traditional leaders, village councils, etc.) providing the resource in different situations. As an example, Box II below illustrates the hazards of carrying out initiatives to change a tradition (here childbirthing practices) without the appropriate involvement of traditional healers (and men) who hold much power.

The IAC, the prominent NGO working on the matter of harmful traditional practices in sub-Saharan Africa, has given serious attention to this strategy. Over half of the organisation's 26 branches now seek specifically to sensitize and inform diverse but powerful groups such as religious organisations and leaders,[44] village chiefs and matrons,[45] first ladies,[46] and traditional leaders.[47] Certainly, organizing, and securing participation and 'training' of these individuals is one matter – a matter in which the IAC claims to have been very successful. However, there then remains the question of whether these individuals actually use this information and follow-up with efforts to change attitudes in their communities. Only in a few regions (notably in Kilimanjaro (Tanzania), Komba (Niger) and some villages in Mali) have the leadership been reported to have moved to the next step of applying their training to educate their communi-

---

43   With regard to female circumcision in particular, it is perhaps useful to repeat at this time that the practice is only in some places justified by religious belief and that it is prevalent among Christians, Muslims, Ethiopian Jews and Animists alike throughout Africa.
44   Such as in the Central River region of the Gambia, the Dodma and Kilimanjaro regions of Tanzania, and in Nouakchott, Mauritania.
45   Such as is the Komba region of Niger.
46   Such as in Mali.
47   Such as in parts of Benin and in Montserrado County, Liberia.

ties about the hazards of certain practices. This may largely be due to the fact that the training missions were only recently carried out and the IAC has yet to conduct follow-up studies on their impact.[48]

3.2.1 Alternative Initiation Rites and the Role of Ceremonial Leaders

Most female circumcisions, including those done in seclusion such as in the 'bush schools,' are accompanied by ritual ceremonies. The ceremony and the circumcision are known as rites of passage, acknowledging the girl's entry into adulthood. Some organisations, and most particularly the IAC, have taken these rites and attempted to replace them with alternative initiation rites, culminating in the offering of gifts to the young woman instead of circumcision. One such initiative which has been well-documented is the initiative of the indigenous NGO *Maendeleo Ya Wanawake Organisation* in Kenya. The NGO introduced the new initiation rite following sensitization efforts with the community, and equally as important with the circumcisers who traditionally coordinate the ceremonies. The NGO found, in doing research in specific communities, that key aspects of the rite were the status of the family and the initiate in holding the special ceremony, the dancing and festivities surrounding it, and the teaching of family life education to the girls. These were all maintained, with the assistance of appointed godmothers to support the girls and guide them through the alternative rite and the presentation of gifts to the initiates as new rituals within the ceremony. It was found to be extremely important to maintain the involvement of the traditional circumcisers within the ceremony and to provide them with alternative income to replace that lost for performing the cutting.[49] The circumcisers hold great influence within the communities they serve and there have been many reports acknowledging the failure to gain their support to modify the initiation right as underlying failed attempts to end the practice.[50] It has also been reported that circumcisers are typically reluctant to stop circumcisions, even if they have alternative sources of income, because of their strong belief in the need for the cricumcision of girls and the status garnered from their role as circumcisers.[51]

It is said that a number of parents in the communities targeted in Kenya have adopted the new rite, although no figures are provided as evidence. A lesson learned from the Sabini experience in Uganda, however, is that the adoption of alternative rites may only be sustained for a limited period of time if sensitization campaigns and pressure

---

48 Refer generally to IAC, *supra*, n. 3.
49 Reported in IAC, FOURTH REGIONAL CONFERENCE/GENERAL ASSEMBLY (1997), pp. 151-153.
50 *Id.*
51 Women who circumcise often come from a family of women circumcisers; as reported by Sarah Longwe, Chairperson of Africa Women's Development and Communications Network (FEMNET), in an interview with the author on 21 April 2001, Tripoli, Libya.

is not maintained. Ceremonial circumcisers and religious and traditional leaders with influence in communities could fulfill this role.

BOX II   Lessons from Rural Ghana

Difficulties in Introducing Birth Attendants in Rural Ghana[52]

In the remote and highly dispersed rural region of Kassena Nankana District of Northern Ghana, women have traditionally given birth alone or attended by kinswomen. The philosophy underlying the Safe Motherhood Initiative set up by the WHO relies on trained traditional birth attendants (TBAs). As there were no TBAs in the region, a training programme set out to identify, train and eventually observe the new skills acquired by 30 women. The elders from the villages in the area were approached and asked to nominate the women to be trained. The elders were also told that the community would have to negotiate remuneration with the women once they were trained.

The elders had difficulty choosing the women, one reason being that there was no tradition of one experienced woman serving a whole village or a collection of villages. The *tindana*, male traditional healers who manage complicated deliveries, were considered inappropriate by the elders since this was essentially a woman's responsibility.

30 women were eventually chosen, trained and began work but problems were soon visible. The *tindana*, although consulted at the beginning, complained that they had not been invited to play a role in the TBA training programme, as they had expected. As such, they were not as supportive of the use of TBAs as had been hoped. Considering the importance of these men within the community, and their potential role in rallying the villagers' support for this new effort, this was an important failure. Of the pregnant women in the study, only 22 of the 137 women who gave birth at home called upon a trained attendant. These tended to be women with access to household finances who could therefore afford to pay for the services by their own means. In a similar vein, the decision whether or not to use a TBA was not usually the woman's to make. It depended on her husband or compound head. Husbands often did not pay for the TBA's service, and the women, fearing this to be a source of embarrassment, preferred not to call the trained attendant. Many women responded that they were reluctant to call trained attendants out during the night because the attendants were older women and they considered it disrespectful to disturb their sleep. A further reason given for not using a TBA was that pregnant women were expected to be prepared for the delivery by purchasing their own razors, soap and cotton wool, yet there was a widespread taboo in the community against it: this would be seen as testing the gods before one had given birth.

52   Summarized from P. Allotey, *Where There's No Tradition of Traditional Birth Attendants: Kassena Nankana District, Northern Ghana*, Reproductive Health Matters, Special Issue, 1999.

3.3 The Relationship between the State and Indigenous Mechanisms

Should the State fail to garner the support of indigenous leaders, official State directives on the eradication of harmful traditional practices risk becoming meaningless. One could therefore have a situation where the Government has good intentions to tackle harmful practices but faces local intransigence. An example of this, although relating to another matter, occurred in Kenya when President Moi directed provincial administrations (consisting of community chiefs) to stamp out illicit brews. Chiefs knew who the local brewers were but took no measures to implement the presidential directive because the local brews were popular in the rural areas and were also the main source of income for some families. Many chiefs and their assistants were accused by the Government of incompetence and threatened with dismissal. But no dismissals occurred since ultimately the chiefs had the support of the populations in their care. In refusing to implement the directive, the chiefs had also considered the fact that they had been elected to their position by their communities and had to be seen to be sensitive to their wishes.[53] The same would no doubt occur if a Governmental directive were to be issued with regard to traditional practices. Bearing this in mind, States should not seek to enforce social change by using indigenous mechanisms as merely their instruments of voice. Rather, the role of the State should be to encourage and facilitate dialogue among and between local leadership and concerned groups on the issue of traditional practices harmful to women, or indeed the health and status of women in general. Furthermore, as established in previous chapters, States should only adopt legislation and seek its implementation *after* public opinion is sufficiently mobilized in favour of eradication.

It is disappointing to see little encouragement given at the international level to States to seek the participation of religious and traditional leaders and institutions in order to resolve the problem of harmful traditional practices. Two notable exceptions are CEDAW's General Recommendation No. 14[54] and the African Declaration on Violence against Women,[55] which make reference, albeit very briefly, to these. In recent times, although sporadically, the Committee on the Rights of the Child has called attention to the role of local leaders and mechanisms in the protection of children's rights. For instance, the Committee in 2001 briefly questioned the Government of Ethiopia with regard to whether 'tribal religious leaders were involved in the information campaigns' undertaken by the Government with respect to children's rights.[56] A more substantial suggestion to involve traditional leaders and institutions

---

53 As reported in Anangwe, *supra*, n. 14, p. 108.
54 *See* paragraph a) iii, Annex A.I.
55 *See* paragraph 2 c), Annex B.VIII.
56 United Nations, Committee on the Rights of the Child, CONSIDERATION OF REPORTS BY STATE PARTIES: SECOND PERIODIC REPORT OF ETHIOPIA, CRC/C/SR.675, 15 November 2001, paragraph 17.

was made by the Committee to the Government of the Central African Republic in the year 2000.[57] This development is promising and should be emulated by other treaty bodies and in other international plans for action (such as in the next periodical assessment of the Beijing Platform for Action).

4 THE MEDIA AND OTHER MECHANISMS OF COMMUNICATION

The use of popular media to influence behaviour has been recommended by various important bodies (such as CEDAW's General Recommendations concerning Harmful Traditional Practices[58] and on Violence against Women)[59] and in international plans of action (such as the Nairobi Forward-Looking Strategies for the Advancement of Women[60] and the Beijing Platform for Action.)[61] Specifically with regard to sub-Saharan Africa, mass media (e.g. soap operas, advertising, music, and news) has been found to have a consistent and frequently strong impact on attitudes and behaviour, independent of residence, education or economic situation.[62] While both public education and mass media inform and educate individuals, open minds to modern ideas, and legitimise attitudes and values derived from modern cultures, media exposure appears to have the strongest and most consistent impact. There are two possible explanations for this. The first is the sheer number of people of all ages and status whom the media reaches with the same message (e.g. village elders and teens are exposed to the same message in the same environment). The second is that mass media is popular culture, capable of competing with traditional beliefs.[63] Findings in this regard note that '…the social network interactions that are stimulated by the media… in turn, may increase media exposure and impact. These networks undoubtedly can communicate, popularise, and reinforce ideas from the media.'[64]

A real example of the positive influence of the media on individual behaviour can be found in a radio soap opera in Tanzania which had immediate effects on the use of family planning in the country. Listeners were found to be twice as likely as non-listeners to discuss family planning with their spouses and a family planning clinic in one region found that the soap opera was the source of referral for 41 per cent of all its new clients. A similar programme sponsored by the same production group (which was further responsible for a successful radio drama in Kenya) led residents in an

---

57 *See* paragraph 59, Annex C.
58 *See* paragraph a.iii), Annex A.I.
59 *See* paragraph 24 d), Annex A.II.
60 *See* paragraph 56, Annex B.II.
61 *See* paragraph 129 d), Annex B.VII.
62 *See* C.F. Westoff and A. Bankole, MASS MEDIA AND REPRODUCTIVE BEHAVIOUR IN AFRICA (1997). The findings were based on surveys conducted in 6 sub-Saharan countries: Burkina Faso, Ghana, Kenya, Madagascar, Namibia and Zambia.
63 *Id.*, p. ix.
64 *Id.*, p. 5.

Indian village to sign pledges that they would not give or receive dowries and that they would educate their daughters as well as their sons. It is important to acknowledge that this production group was funded by a major donor organisation, underlining the significant role these can play in challenging harmful traditional practices.[65]

The strong positive association between mass media exposure and changes in attitudes and behaviour confirms that, if we wish to improve significantly reproductive health in sub-Saharan Africa, we must increase the attention paid by the media to issues of harmful traditional practices and allocate sufficient financial support for such media. The State as well as various other actors can assist with one or both of these measures. As suggestions, the initiative of President Moi granting free airtime for messages on AIDS prevention is a good example of a State facilitating public dialogue and education. This is especially true where the media are mainly government-owned or subject to considerable government influence.[66] Where the media is privately owned and run, the State may also take measures such as regulating against incitement to uphold harmful practices, or requiring that a minimum amount of air time be allotted to health messages.[67] Such regulatory regimes are normally controlled through licensing. Local awareness-raising groups concerned with the eradication of harmful traditional practices could also seek out and offer relevant information to radio, performance groups or the press and suggest that they take on the issue. These groups (with the help of international partners) could even develop progamming to be offered for broadcast or seek financing to purchase broadcasting time for such purposes. Lawyers and health professionals could offer free advice through the media, such as on the legislation protecting women from harmful traditional practices and the steps individuals could take to prevent women becoming victims.

5 THE ROLES OF OTHER ACTORS

5.1 Local Interest Groups and Concerned NGOs

As noted earlier, so far the main advocacy work on all harmful traditional practices, but especially female circumcision, has been predominantly done by non-domestic groups; mostly by non-African NGOs and by agencies in the United Nations system.[68]

---

65 As reported in K. Henderson, *Hope from Soaps*, Ford Foundation Report, Fall 2000.
66 *See* CRLP, FEMALE GENITAL MUTILATION: A MATTER OF HUMAN RIGHTS (1995).
67 The Government of Gambia reportedly acted precisely to the contrary in 1997 when it banned radio stations from airing information on the harmful effects of female circumcision. *See* Equality Now, *The Gambia: government censorship of campaign to stop female genital mutilation*, Women's Action Newsletter, July 1997.
68 Observed by Miriam K. Were, Director, UNFPA/CSTAA, in her opening statement to the Symposium for Legislators on the Drafting of an African Declaration on Violence against Women, 10-12 September 1997, Addis Ababa, Ethiopia; *see* IAC, SYMPOSIUM FOR LEGISLATORS ON THE DRAFTING OF AN AFRICAN DECLARATION ON VIOLENCE AGAINST WOMEN (1997), pp. 24-25.

Were notes that, while this was an important starting point in order to gain international consensus and support,

> ...we need to also know that there has been a price to this. And this price is that within many African countries, people think that efforts to ban FGM is a foreign idea aimed at embarrassing Africa... Therefore, we need to carefully look at what *we* are going to do to ensure that we communicate the difficulties caused by harmful practices to our people.[69]

Local NGOs and concerned groups have the advantage of authenticity, fostering legitimacy, within their own cultural environments. They are also well placed to identify those elements in society which are favourable to change and carry the authority or legitimacy to engage in dialogue and campaign for the eradication of harmful practices. Moreover, because they are situated at the community level and are generally non-political, they are capable of building broad coalitions between, *inter alia*, human rights groups, youth groups, women, village leaders, religious communities and government. The fact that the IAC has been able to link up specifically with all of these and many other such groups shows that such a network can successfully be established and operate.

Aside from the fact that such organisations should be better funded, they should also be permitted to organize and operate without interference. Donor and other organisations concerned with improving women's health and ending harmful traditional practices should target funds to the activities of these local groups.

5.2 Ordinary Men

Given that most African societies are patriarchal, all men – husbands, fathers, brothers and especially adolescent boys – should be among the first targets of awareness-raising initiatives. Ultimately, men have more power than women to deviate from the norm and set trends in a different direction. If they are convinced of the ill-effects of early pregnancy, fathers more than mothers may insist that their daughters marry at a later age and young men may seek to marry girls only past the age of puberty.[70] Young men could also insist on marrying solely uncircumcised girls (as occurred in China where young men insisted on marrying only girls with unbound feet). Furthermore, men in African society will incur less negative social repercussions if they deviate from the

---

69 *Id.*, p. 24.
70 Within Africa itself, men are recognized as a critical factor in HIV/AIDS prevention and control because they remain largely the opinion leaders, taboo breakers and law makers. Their own change in behaviour is vital for broader societal change. Reported in R. Olawale, *Held down by taboos, ravaged by HIV/AIDS*, The Guardian (Nigerian leading daily), 31 July 2000, p. 19.

norm. Fathers and grandfathers can voice their criticism against female circumcision more forcefully than mothers and grandmothers and others in the community.[71]

Recognizing men as an important group for change is a natural conclusion in light of the fact that African women tend to have very little authority and decision-making power to change norms and customs. Even if women are convinced of their rights to health and life and that they should not submit to a traditional practice, few will succeed to secure their rights if the decision-makers within their families and communities are not sensitized and in agreement. For example, even if all the women in a community were convinced of the need to stop female circumcision, men, too, would have to be convinced; if men were not, they could seek wives in other communities where circumcision was still practiced or simply insist that their fiancées be circumcised if they were to marry them.[72] The likelihood of women's successful resistance against the tradition surviving under such circumstances would be little to none. Ultimately, men maintain control over much of the practices in question: it is they who typically pay for their daughters to be circumcised, they who negotiate the marriages of their daughters and they who receive the brideprice.[73] It is also they who control the purse strings and often refuse to pay a skilled medical practitioner to assist their wives to give birth (see Box II above). Until they are convinced to act otherwise, women will continue to have little effective say on matters of circumcision, marriage and birthing practices

African feminist, Halim, brings these examples to life in her recount of how men in her native country of the Sudan were the driving force behind eradicating facial scarification:

> I have seen traditions change during my lifetime. The change was so easy and smooth when the men took the initiative. Change, however, requires a lot of pain and hard work when it is initiated by women. A clear example of this, in my own country, the Sudan, is the quick disappearance of face marks (a mutilation women and some men endured because it is considered a sign of beauty to cut longitudinal or horizontal marks on the face of the woman; it was also a tribal identification for both women and men). When men decided that it was a tradition with no value and that they preferred women without face marks, there was a whole new attitude that affected the change. Suddenly, love songs were describing a

---

[71] In her book, in which she relates her experience in Togo with forced marriage and forced circumcision, Fauyiza Kassindja depicts this very well. Because her father was sternly against the circumcision of his daughters, none of them underwent the operation, despite strong and persistent protest from her father's brother and other members of his family and the community. For her story, see DO THEY HEAR YOU WHEN YOU CRY? (1998).

[72] Kassindja relates this dilemma in which she found herself. When her father passed away and her uncle arranged that she be married, her fiancé demanded that she first be circumcised. Her mother's opinion was completely disregarded. Despite the fact that she was already 17 years old, fully knowledgeable of what was to happen and expressed her rejection of both the marriage and the circumcision, she was given no other choice. *Id.*

[73] *See* F.P. Hosken, STOP FEMALE MUTILATION (1995), p. 18.

woman with a smooth face and women without face marks having a better chance of getting married. Whether women understood the change in attitude or whether they saw themselves as prettier without the marks did not seem to have any weight in getting rid of the tradition – it was the change in attitude of the men.[74]

Hosken, a long-standing and well-respected anti-circumcision campaigner opens her most recent study on female circumcision by indicating in bold and capital letters that the 'next critical issue that needs to be examined is the responsibility of [female circumcision] by men'; men, she affirms, 'are in control of everything in Africa, especially women and children… [female circumcision] is a marriage requirement demanded by men, therefore the practice continues. It is as simple as that.'[75] She then, much like her activist counterpart Halim, categorically concludes that '[i]f tomorrow African men were to publicly declare they will not marry [circumcised] girls, it would stop.'[76]

With a view to greatest effect, different age categories must be targeted: older men who may have influence on matters of the community; husbands with young families whose acceptance of change in traditions could have an immediate impact on this generation of young girls; and boys who can potentially reshape the norms and traditions of the next generation. It is this last strategy which the IAC has embarked upon. Representatives of this NGO working to end female circumcision go into schools and provide 'family life education' consisting of discussions about relationships, marriage, sexuality, pregnancy and female circumcision. In order to keep these issues in the limelight after IAC trainers have left the school, peer educators (adolescent boys and girls) are appointed and trained to continue awareness raising inside and outside school.[77] The IAC claims youth programmes are successful, the organisation of a youth forum on the issue of harmful traditional practices culminating with the 'African Youth Declaration on Harmful Traditional Practices' being one proof of this.[78] It is still too early to tell if adolescents benefitting from such awareness-raising schemes have changed their behaviour and reject these practices when it comes to their own personal situations. No figures, for instance, have been compiled or reported by the IAC on the numbers of individuals who have married at a later age or delayed pregnancy since the generation of youth exposed to the education campaigns has yet to mature. But this will become apparent in dues course. In the meantime, initiatives such as these should be supported and followed-up.

---

74 A.M.A. Halim, *Tools of Suppression*, in Center for Women's Global Leadership, GENDER VIOLENCE AND WOMEN'S HUMAN RIGHTS IN AFRICA (1994), p. 22.
75 Hosken, *supra*, n. 73, p. 3.
76 *Id.*
77 Reported generally in the efforts of national branches; see IAC, FOURTH REGIONAL, *supra*, n. 49.
78 Organised by the IAC in Addis Ababa, Ethiopia, 25-27 April 2000.

5.3 The Monitoring Bodies of the International Human Rights Treaties

In light of the fact that the eradication of harmful traditional practices hinges on fundamental changes in attitudes, treaty bodies should aim to review what measures are being taken specifically to change socio-cultural attitudes and behaviours which support harmful traditional practices. This could be done by:
   a) requesting States to include information on harmful traditional practices in their reports;
   b) inquiring into their actions to end these practices;
   c) offering recommendations and practical suggestions to challenge attitudes and behaviours; and
   d) following-up on the measures States have undertaken or committed to adopt as a consequence.

The initial report of the Central African Republic to the Committee on the Rights of the Child[79] offers a good example of what a cooperative and informed country representative and Committee can do to serve the goal of socio-cultural change. Relevant excerpts of the report are reproduced in Annex C. It is impressive and encouraging that the Central African Republic recognizes from the start (i.e. in its initial report) that if children's human rights are to have any meaning, changes in those traditional attitudes and practices which cause harm or discriminate must occur. Moreover, the Government of the Central African Republic seems to recognize its part in assuring such a change.

5.4 Donors

The glossy covers of the year 2000 reports of the Ford Foundation, as one of the major donors in the field of human rights, attest to the support donors are prepared to give to foster fundamental changes in attitudes and behaviours. The cover story of the Summer report, for instance, explains how one theater project is challenging cultural orthodox beliefs in Egypt. The theatre group uses traditional performance arts (including shadow puppetry, story-telling and religious chanting) with modern twists and messages. The Fall cover story relates how radio dramas in Kenya are altering behaviours and promoting reproductive health.

'Placing their money where their mouth is,' some donors have been increasingly ready to fund awareness-raising activities likely to have an influence on beliefs and behavioural change. In the case of the Ford Foundation, two units (Human Development and Reproductive Health, and Media, Art and Culture) are geared to fund efforts to highlight the dynamic contexts in the family and society that influence people's

---

79 United Nations, Committee on the Rights of the Child, INITIAL REPORT OF THE CENTRAL AFRICAN REPUBLIC, CRC/C/SR.657, 9 October 2000.

health and well-being. Donor States have also been funneling money into reproductive health projects in sub-Saharan Africa. The goal is to see that these projects contribute to improve reproductive health in the immediacy while simultaneously confronting the factors (including harmful traditional practices) which contributed to ill-health in the first place. In other words, some external donors aim beyond localized project efforts to help provide the material foundation for widespread change in the status of women. Without prejudice to the validity of such aims, they merit serious consideration insofar as they contain cultural biases which should be attuned to the culture of the recipient communities. According to Bryceson, the handling of women's issues by donor agencies is

> ... an obvious example of the impossibility of external funding agencies' cultural neutrality. Because the role of women has been so hotly contested in their own societies, external agencies are under pressure to promote a normative notion of what activities women in recipient countries should be pursuing to gain gender equality.[80]

Similar concern has been raised with regard to various related issues within this thesis. As already argued, normative notions (e.g., what constitutes gender equality, assuming that the Western feminist project can be simply transferred across all cultures as a necessary strategy to advance the status of women) may not be the same across all cultures and economic categories. We thus come again to the suggestion that Western models and assumptions are not necessarily always transferable to projects in Africa, or at least not if the immediate aims of these projects are to be achieved. Donors themselves must define their policies on this issue and should allow the means deemed most culturally suitable and effective to challenge harmful traditional practices to emanate mainly from African communities themselves.

5.5 Women's Rights Advocates, Legal Aid and the Legal Profession

As another measure, women's rights advocates could bring test cases in the local courts, opposing traditional practices that impinge on women's rights, in order to obtain court judgements and orders. Such actions would not only contribute effectively to outlaw these practices, but more importantly send a strong message as to how seriously the State considers their abolition. Additionally, activists could appeal decisions from customary courts that had failed to protect women. One successful example of this comes from Ghana, in the case of *Akoringa v. Akawagre*. The appellant (A) appealed the decision of the Chief of Yorugu, awarding damages against A for failing to hand over his adult daughter to the Respondent (R). The case thus involved a classic

---

80 D.F. Bryceson, *Wishful Thinking: Theory and Practice of Western Donor Efforts to Raise Women's Status in Rural Africa*, in D. F. Bryceson, ed., WOMEN WIELDING THE HOE (1995), p. 203.

example of widow inheritance. R had brought this action, claiming that A's daughter, who was the widow of R's deceased older brother, was now his wife under customary law. The Court of Appeals of Ghana held that damages should not have been awarded because the woman was an independent person with rights equal to R and that R's stance was blatantly discriminatory against women and could not under modern conditions be considered part of the customary law of the country.[81]

The campaign for the eradication of harmful traditional practices also could be assisted by well-focused *amicus curiae* submissions from independent non-governmental organisations in novel and important cases where international and comparative law and practice might be relevant.[82]

An obvious measure which could be taken by the State would be to make legal aid more accessible to vulnerable and poor women who wish to access legal advice, bring a case to trial or challenge decisions of customary courts. Finally, human rights should be included in legal education in formal professional teaching and other training activities. Judges, lawyers, litigants and others should be made aware of applicable human rights standards as stated in international instruments and national constitutions and laws.[83] Articles 25 and 26 of the African Charter expressly stress this. States could support such human rights education.

6 CONCLUSIONS

Bearing in mind that the ultimate goal is to reduce and eventually eradicate harmful traditional practices through the use of human rights discourses, one should consider which groups in African communities are the influential decision-makers and opinion leaders. African Governments, in most cases, would not be the first actors to come to mind. Certainly, ending violence against women requires multiple strategies, including: raising the costs to abusers, coordinating institutional responses, involving youth, reaching out to men, and changing community norms. But this Chapter has argued that one should also be strategic about where one starts, with those mechanisms that can mold attitudes and have legitimacy within the culture given priority.

It was already well known that the media, donors, treaty bodies, local NGOs and interest groups, and legal aid can play important roles in defending human rights and changing the *status quo* so that all individuals may live the most dignified, healthy and

---

81 1987-1988 Ghana L. Rep. Dig. 101 (June 23, 1998) as cited in Adjetey, *supra*, n. 29.
82 For discussion, *see* [no author], *The Banjul Affirmation: African Judges Adopt Human Rights Principles*, Interights Bulletin, Vol. 5 (1990).
83 Indeed, the Universal Declaration of Human Rights proclaims in the ultimate paragraph of the Preamble that Member States of the United Nations 'shall strive by teaching and education to promote respect for... rights and freedoms.' Adopted by United Nations General Assembly resolution 217 A (III) of 10 December 1948; full text in United Nations, HUMAN RIGHTS, A COMPILATION OF INTERNATIONAL INSTRUMENTS; VOLUME I (FIRST PART), UNIVERSAL INSTRUMENTS (1994), pp. 1-7.

secure life they can. The purpose of this chapter was therefore not to reiterate the roles of these mechanisms and institutions, but to clarify how they can help to end harmful traditional practices specifically, and how the African State can act to support them. Numerous surveys and reports confirm just how significant their role has been to date. However, much less attention and faith has been given to religious and indigenous mechanisms and their potentially critical role in ending harmful traditional practices. Finally, but not least importantly, a plea has been made in favour of including into the equation ordinary men – fathers, brothers and husbands – who clearly also have much to say in the norms and customs of society.

CHAPTER IX
SUMMARY AND CONCLUSIONS

1 SUMMARY

The challenge of eradicating harmful traditional practices, pursued principally through sensitization campaigns at the grass-roots level and calls for legislation against such practices, has seen steady but slow progress. Generally speaking, the number of circumcisions performed on girls appears to have diminished only slightly. Unprotected sex and childbearing at a young age, commonly resulting from marriage or other forms of unions in adolescence, continue to be very much the norm for African girls. Certain other traditional practices, and the harm they may cause, have only recently gained attention at the international level. These practices carry significant risks to the reproductive health of girls and women, particularly by increasing their exposure to HIV/AIDS and the risk of complications in childbirth, both of which substantially raise the odds of untimely, and yet preventable, death. In the more typical, less dramatic, instances, they are the source of short- or long-term reproductive ill-health in girls and women – ill-health sustained largely for the sake of 'tradition' and maintained for reasons of cohesion and harmony within the family and the community at large.

An initial task of this study was simply to review the existing literature on traditional practices and human rights violations. This literature proved to be misleading at times, particularly the Western feminist literature and its categorical description of all harmful traditional practices as forms of violence against women, a basis on which it is then claimed that women suffer violations of their human rights. Exactly which express rights these may be, and how particular practices constitute their violation, have been scarcely and, even then, poorly established to date. This has arguably contributed to concern among some individuals (particularly non-Westerners) who see the discourse on harmful traditional practices as having been largely led and in some cases 'hijacked' by well-intentioned foreign feminist activists who have failed to connect it with the realities of African women. These sentiments have been reinforced by the fact that the discourse of human rights on the subject has often been joined with a discourse of gender and feminism which, arguably more than the former, is considered a foreign, even neo-colonialist, discourse with little applicability to the lives of the ordinary African woman. The African women's rights activist, Abena Busia, sums it up best in stating that

> African women are not simply waiting to be 'rescued' by outside feminists and practitioners... [O]ne of the more tortured aspects of the feminist praxis in the west is the authority

of their theoretical paradigms in the face of other systems of thought, and other modes of practice and negotiation...[1]

In light of the paucity of detailed analysis, this study has sought in part to inform and develop the prevailing international human rights discourse by establishing how harmful traditional practices violate, or do not violate, specific rights (beyond those that protect freedom from violence), notably the right to health. The successful initiatives of Tostan and IAC demonstrate precisely that it is the negative consequences of these practices on women's (and men's) health which lead communities to discuss and unite to change or end harmful practices. It is therefore in the right to health that the strength of the human rights approach to ending harmful traditional practices lies.

In the hopes of further clarifying matters, I have sought to establish whether and how particular practices termed 'harmful' and 'traditional' may violate a woman's human rights and, if so, which rights specifically. To this end, it was incumbent to establish the reasons generally given for these practices to be carried out and the ways in which they could cause harm, mainly to the reproductive health of a girl or woman. In carrying out this exercise, it became apparent that harmful traditional practices do not necessarily or always constitute human rights violations. Various scenarios call into question claims to the contrary. A fully informed and freely consenting woman who is offered access to a trained and properly equipped traditional birth attendant but refuses because she wants to give birth in a manner (potentially more harmful though it may be) which is traditional in her community can hardly be said to have her rights violated. Similarly problematic is the woman who is knowledgeable of the harmful effects of female circumcision and willingly undergoes the procedure. Such a situation highlights the issue of tacit consent. These scenarios tend to be forgotten or ignored, possibly because they complicate what is otherwise emphatically presented as a clear-cut matter of violation. In fact, there are indications that numerous African girls and women who undergo these practices are aware of their potential harm and nonetheless accept this risk. Moreover, many, if not most, consent without coercion. They have sat in the 'bush school' with other young village girls and have been taught that a virtuous girl should be circumcised, and have accepted this to be true in the face of evident social reinforcement. They may even have been informed by a nurse at the maternity clinic that they should eat plenty of foods rich in essential nutrients when pregnant or breastfeeding, but still choose to follow the traditional taboo against such foods.

It is precisely because African women continue to uphold harmful traditional practices, despite their general awareness of potential harm and their theoretical ability to reject these traditions, that we must look beyond to the customs and norms which bolster such traditions and the actors in their societies who can effectively challenge

---

[1] A.P.A. Busia, *Foreword*, in Centre for Women's Global Leadership, GENDER VIOLENCE AND WOMEN'S HUMAN RIGHTS IN AFRICA (1994), pp. iii-iv.

them. With regard to the former, I have highlighted a selection of customs and norms and attempted to explain their relationship to the harmful traditional practices in question in Chapter II. In Chapter III, notably in Table IV, the express treaty obligations on States to modify or eliminate these have been emphasized. It must remain foremost in our minds that the elimination of harmful traditional practices ultimately requires addressing these customs, norms and beliefs.

The language of the universality of human rights conveys a sense of global social and moral justice which can be very useful in addressing harmful traditional practices across cultural and religious divides. The concept of human rights as universal to all cultures, religions and economic groupings, however, has had its share of criticism. Rejecting the universal nature of human rights would have serious implications for the global campaign to end harmful traditional practices and for the lives of African women since it would imply that culture could be argued as conditioning our notions, *inter alia*, of justice and human dignity. Justice and dignity for women, most activists fear, would be the first casualties of such a position. In light of this real risk, Chapter IV endeavoured to survey the arguments in favour and against the universality of human rights and the basis for these arguments. The exercise revealed that, particularly with regard to Africa, views against the universality of human rights may be influenced by the colonial history and poverty of the region. Unease with the discourse of human rights (and particularly such a gendered discourse which largely excludes similar violations suffered by men) may relate to the sense of need by Africans to reject any discourse thought to be dressed in neo-colonialist clothing and, concomitantly, their strong desire to 'emphasize the 'Africanness' or put an African imprint on whatever… they embark upon.'[2] This is precisely why the African Charter on Human and Peoples' Rights must be placed at the forefront. And it is similarly precisely because of the importance of this treaty in the protection and promotion of human rights in sub-Saharan Africa that clauses thought to be problematic for African women and their equal rights were addressed, and the concerns put to rest, in Chapter V of this study. In this regard, it will be interesting to see what the special measures available to the African Commission at present, and under negotiation for the future, will bring in the way of effective challenges to harmful traditional practices. So far, the Commission's Special Rapporteur on the Rights of Women has reported only generally on the status of African women and limited specific studies to the situation of women in prison in various African countries. It is also to be seen if the Draft Protocol to the African Charter on Human and Peoples' Rights Relating to the Rights of Women will be accepted in its present form, revised or ever adopted, not to mention ratified and fully implemented. The document, I have argued, has not been appropriately formulated as a treaty; it is too lengthy, overly descriptive and in parts repetitive, and would better

---

2   O. Ojo, *Understanding Human Rights in Africa*, in J. Berting *et al.*, eds., HUMAN RIGHTS IN A PLURALIST WORLD (1990), p. 117.

be used as guidelines. Rather, the Commission could consider transforming the document into what would be its first General Comment or Recommendation. In this case, it would avoid the process of approval by the Council of Ministers of the OAU/African Union, an approval which risks taking a long time to obtain and is far from guaranteed.

In terms of the 'universality' of rights, it is evident that differences in opinion on notions of universal justice, equality among all human beings, and moral right and wrong pre-date modern international human rights law nearly 2,500 years. The Ancient Greek philosopher, Herodotus, encapsulated a fundamental concern of the contemporary relativist school of thought when he stated

> ...if one were to put before all men the suggestion that out of all customs they should choose the best, each people would examine them and then pick their own; so accustomed are they to think that their own customs are far the best.[3]

But times have changed since Herodotus. The notion of human rights, and determinations of what constitutes their violation, have become truly global and culturally and religiously pluralistic in influence, thus reducing bias in such determinations. This process of evaluation was explained in Chapter IV. Examples of various customs, both chosen and rejected for inspection under the human rights microscope, illustrate how the human rights approach can work with regard to cultural practices.

In Chapter VI, the argument has been made (and supported by commentaries largely from African or other developing world researchers) that human rights offer a limited degree of empowerment to African women at the grassroots level. An appeal is therefore made to place less emphasis on the bottom-up approach to the implementation of human rights, especially where fundamental attitudinal changes in African society are concerned. This approach generally purports that the empowerment of women (through human rights education, the formation of women's groups and increased access to schooling) will bring about the social and cultural changes needed to improve the status of women and thereby end harmful traditional practices. Although this approach is widely supported by women's rights advocates and the international human rights community (and works effectively in numerous environments), evidence strongly suggests that African women face too many obstacles and constraints to make this approach effective. This is especially so for the rural poor of sub-Saharan Africa and their unique social and political environment. For instance, women's groups tend to face numerous problems internally (e.g. politicization and elitism among the upper ranks) and externally (particularly in the way of doubts as to the legitimacy and importance of their work on the part of men in positions of power). The conclusion of anthropologist Coquery-Vidrovitch that women's groups in Africa reveal

---

3 Herodotus, THE HISTORIES, Book III (1954), para. 38.

'less emerging consciousness of a liberation struggle than an attempt to adopt the conventions and prejudices of a middle class struggling to preserve its privileges'[4] is perhaps over-stated but should temper our expectations from such groups. With regard to schooling, evidence shows that education has not yet had an impact on traditional norms and attitudes. Until many significant elements change (e.g. enrolment of girls in schools increases, contents of teaching materials are altered, attitudes of teachers change, and the norms and beliefs of communities are modified) schooling will have a minor influence on the empowerment of girls.

Numerous structural, cultural and psychological impediments to the use of law also have been identified as reducing the likelihood of women using their knowledge of human rights to challenge discriminatory norms in general or harmful traditional practices in particular. The impediments which seem to be particularly difficult to surmount relate to the socio-cultural environment of the region. Notably, human rights education typically encourages African women to seek to have their rights protected, ultimately through the use of the legal system (i.e. by lodging complaints with the police, seeking injunctions against parties and pursuing claims in court). Yet research demonstrates that African women, largely because of their socialization, are adverse to using the law in this way, preferring to influence the decisions of their families in a non-adversarial way. Numerous stories of women courageous enough to seek recourse to the police have ended in tragedy as the police, in turn, failed to protect them. Such stories demonstrate how deep we must dig to unveil the roots of socialization in upholding traditions, in this case requiring attitudinal change in the police as well. However, this does not imply that women have no social or legal mechanisms to which they can turn to promote and protect their rights. Research shows that women are more comfortable with, and can better access, traditional mechanisms of conflict resolution. Indeed, family disputes, particularly in the rural areas of the region, are typically brought before customary courts or traditional dispute mechanisms. Although these courts and mechanisms (and the men controlling them) are commonly reported to be antagonistic towards women's rights, their potential positive influence (should they be brought on board), could be immense and determinative. It is therefore surprising, and somewhat worrying, to see that apart from Tostan in Senegal and a few national branches of the IAC few other groups sought to include traditional leaders and mechanisms – leaders and mechanisms which hold real authority in Africa and which women can and do access – in human rights education exercises or campaigns against harmful traditional practices.

The review of harmful traditional practices which have been successfully eradicated in other regions of the world confirms the importance of local leadership and the support of key local opinion leaders. The eradication of footbinding in China and *sati* in India offer good illustrations of this. In both cases the influence of native individuals

---

4   C. Coquery-Vidrovitch, AFRICAN WOMEN: A MODERN HISTORY (1994), p. 158.

on abandonment were catalytic. As natives of the affected culture, Chou and Roy were able to tailor their campaign to their cultural contexts. They were able to identify the factors blocking eradication and structure their messages in response to these. Their position was credible and enabled them to engage proponents of the practices in discussions and counter their arguments on the same basis of culture and religion. Both proceeded with intensive education programmes at the community level to challenge public attitudes. As pointed out in the introduction to this study, such grassroots activism has been long underway and continues strong today in sub-Saharan Africa. These findings from China and India are therefore comforting, confirming the effectiveness of strategies employed to date, but they offer little in the way of new lessons we can adapt to the campaign against harmful traditional practice in sub-Saharan Africa. Still, additional lessons were extracted. Two of these, in my view, are particularly significant. The first is that adopting and seeking to enforce legislation banning traditional practices in the absence of widespread popular support for such a ban is likely to be futile. Indeed, in some cases it has raised public fury against State intervention in 'private' matters and entrenched loyalty to the practice. This has proved to be the experience in Egypt, Kenya and the Sudan with regard to female circumcision. In this light, and from the findings of Chapter VI which demonstrate that legislation is rarely heeded and that police fail to protect women from these practices even when outlawed, the emphasis activists today place on legislative reform in African States seems misplaced. Much more effort must be channeled into changing public opinion on these practices prior to adopting proscriptive legislation and expecting health professionals, the police and other authorities, never mind the common person, to uphold it. The second notable lesson learned is that legislation, such as against the circumcision of girls or against the marriage of girls under the age of 18 years, must simultaneously ban *all* forms of the practice. Allowing certain 'softer' forms or exceptions to remain in the hope that even these will by themselves be gradually abandoned has never proved successful. Rather, such action only confirmed the State's tacit acceptance of the practices and, more importantly, the rationales behind them.

Following from the findings on the bottom-up approach toward women's empowerment, it has become clear that our energies should at least equally be placed on the top-down approach to empowerment. The means by which we may succeed in this effort were therefore the subject of Chapter VIII. In international human rights law it is the State which is obligated to respect, ensure and fulfill the human rights provided in the instruments to which it has become a party. However, this does not imply that it is the State alone which must carry out activities to fulfill these obligations. To the contrary, I have argued that it is not realistic to expect that even the most committed and diligent of African States can, through its agents, end harmful traditional practices, even if they had adequate financial and technical resources. This is, in short, because, barring a few exceptions, it is not African States *per se* which carry out or uphold these practices. Indeed, it is not the State which is responsible for our socialization (and, this, arguably more so in Africa than in the West). Rather, socialization occurs in the community, in village meetings, through religious institutions and, most importantly, in the home. The power to change therefore lies with the social and religious institutions, the media and men. Yet programme managers, NGO strategists and women's rights activists alike tend to overlook, reject or condemn these very institutions and actors. An appeal is therefore made for their inclusion.

2 CONCLUSIONS

2.1 The Utility and Effectiveness of the Human Rights Approach

We are still in the process of discerning the most effective strategies to challenge harmful traditional practices. To this end, it is important to examine the strengths and weaknesses of our approaches and strategies to face this challenge in the specific context of sub-Saharan Africa.

The first step of consciousness-raising or sensitization with regard to harmful traditional practices is well underway at the grassroots level and is steadily growing. Individuals have been trained to proceed with sensitization programmes at the community level, with other awareness-raising activities, such as in schools and government, being carried out in various parts of sub-Saharan Africa. However, while not wanting to diminish the excellent work achieved in this regard, these activities do not necessarily mean that harmful traditional practices are being eliminated, as some activists and organisations claim. More time is needed to see if these claims are true, and why so or not. In the absence of comprehensive social science research clarifying this matter, an inductive approach assessing the appropriateness of the international human rights discourse – emphazing law and empowerment of African women – has been followed.

In her article *Compassion: The Basic Social Emotion*,[5] Nussbaum has touched the nerve behind the global human rights campaign against harmful traditional practices, particularly against female circumcision. It is in our human nature, she submits, to feel compassion for others when suffering. This compassion may be heightened when a harmful practice such as female circumcision is so far removed from the traditions of one's own society, such as in the West, and is therefore all the more incomprehensible, or indeed reprehensible. Other reasons may motivate our 'intervention' to stop these traditional practices. For instance, it may be argued that modes of HIV transmission are the concern of the entire international community. Female circumcision, early marriage, incisions in pregnancy and some traditional birthing practices all introduce a risk of such transmission. Infection and ill-health (limiting women's potential and

---

5   M.C. Nussbaum, *Compassion: The Basic Social Emotion*, Journal of Social Philosophy and Policy, Vol. 13, No. 1, 1996.

dignity) and premature death (leaving children orphaned, family structures in tatters and family incomes reduced) are also arguably the concern of a caring world community.

But the argument of global well-being need not be the only basis for condemnation of harmful traditional practices and intervention. We can also legitimately channel our compassion and concern through the human rights paradigm because the traditions have been established as negatively affecting women's health, threatening their lives, discriminating, interfering with their freedom of thought and belief, or diminishing their right to pursue education – all violations of their universally protected human rights. By 'processing' this concern through multiple international (i.e. culturally and religiously pluralistic) human rights plenaries we can seek to assure that criticisms are based on valid and universally accepted principles and not merely a reflection of our fear and ignorance of others or, worse yet, sentiments of cultural superiority. The fact that much criticism and condemnation of harmful traditional practices has come from within the African continent and that the human rights treaty specific to the region supports such a stance confirms the validity of condemnation of harmful traditional practices on the basis of *universal* human rights.

This partly answers the question posed in the introduction to this study asking why we have turned to the human rights approach as a means of eliminating harmful traditional practices. Importantly, it legitimises our concern for the health and status of African women and criticism of these practices, both of which could easily be construed negatively as neo-colonialism, cultural elitism or plain and simple racism. In effect, the language and discourse of human rights empowers those eager to see the eradication of harmful traditional practices and protects and reinforces their views. This partly explains why we have seen the health professions, development agencies and even economic institutions such as the World Bank employ the language of human rights in their conventional work – human rights essentially providing them added protection and ammunition.

A second reason for using the human rights approach has emerged in this study. Human rights treaties demonstrate the interconnected nature of the family of human rights and establish how discriminatory patterns of conduct bolster prejudicial practices. The fact that these treaties are instruments of law places an obligation on States (African and all others) to act toward their elimination. Moreover, some of these instruments actually provide strong recommendations on how to do so. For instance, the Women's Convention encourages the revision of school textbooks to ensure the elimination of stereotyped negative roles for women. Human rights law, and activists and organisations seeking enforcement of these rights, have further spawned a multitude of plans of action filled with recommendations as to how States and various partners in civil society can work to eliminate violence and discrimination against women, including harmful traditional practices as forms of these. These recommendations have been highlighted in Annexes A through C. Importantly, the international standards have also inspired a wide variety of programmes doing practical work.

While the human rights approach has empowered us to challenge harmful traditional practices in sub-Saharan Africa from outside the cultre, it has yet to succeed in its ultimate goal to empower those from within. Few African women are able to assert their rights within the framework of social and cultural norms which influence their daily lives. For the most part, women, even if knowledgeable of their human rights, are not able to negotiate real or perceived opposition of parents, husbands, male figureheads, religious authorities and influential members of their communities when it comes to harmful traditional practices, or many other injustices for that matter. In addition it must be kept in mind that not all African women, not even those who are knowledgeable of their human rights, necessarily view harmful traditional practices as violating their rights or as needing to be abandoned. Thus, unfortunately, the answer to the second question posed in the introduction to this study – *whether the discourse of human rights has brought meaningful change in the lives of African women and improved reproductive health in the region* – is so far generally 'no'.

While the effort to empower African women as a means, *inter alia*, to end harmful traditional practices has received significant support and attention, it is still weak and, barring rapid and widespread societal change, will remain so for a long time to come. Despite our knowledge of this, our response has been generally one-sided, focusing on helping African women empower themselves at the local level, rather than assisting the State (and broader society) grapple with changing attitudes. It is not surprising, therefore, that while we may have convinced some women to seek assistance and redress before the police and the courts, these institutions have not always responded in a positive manner. This is principally owing to the fact that those opinion makers and leaders with the power to change attitudes (village elders, customary chiefs, religious leaders, etc.) have largely been over-looked or excluded from strategies for change. However, the Tostan experience in Senegal is a wonderful example of how women within a community can work together with indigenous (and largely male) institutions with the cultural authority to make and enforce laws and change social norms. These women may not have been 'empowered' by human rights education or acted to protect their human rights in a conventional sense, i.e. by contesting authority. But, after sharing as a group their concerns about the harmful effects of female circumcision and their doubts on the need for the practice to continue, they sought the help of the village chief and Imam who took on the challenge to end this practice. The chief and Imam did so successfully not only in their village of Malicounda Bambara, but in surrounding ones as well. In this sense, the women of Malicounda Bambara 'empowered' themselves in a manner which was culturally appropriate and effective.

The Draft African Declaration on Violence against Women (reproduced in Annex B.VIII) has set the goal to eradicate female circumcision by the year 2005. Certainly, this goal will not be met. But with some adjusting, the human rights approach can

Chapter IX

eventually pose a formidable challenge to harmful traditional practices in the region and bring positive change to the lives of African women.

2.2 General Recommendations

Challenges to traditional practices harmful to African women posed in the language of human rights could be strengthened in the region of sub-Saharan Africa in various ways. One way would be to increase popular knowledge of the existence of a treaty and mechanism formed uniquely for the promotion and protection of human rights in Africa. States could endeavour to do so, for example, by placing the treaty and human rights education in general on the school curriculum and placing information bites on television, radio and in the press. Knowledge of this 'home-grown' mechanism – created by Africans, situated in Africa, and staffed by Africans – could increase the legitimacy of the human rights discourse in the region, since it could no longer be claimed to be an 'imported good' or imposed body of law.

The African Commission's Special Rapporteur on the Rights of Women should be informed by local NGOs and interest groups of the prevalence of traditional practices harmful to women, how the State is failing to challenge these or is obstructing such challenge, and what improvements could be made. The Rapporteur should follow-up by issuing public reports containing this information and petitioning the State accordingly. These groups could also submit reports directly to the African Commission, perhaps in conjunction with other groups which follow more broadly the status of the rights of women in their countries. At present States rarely submit their mandatory reports on the situation of human rights in their countries in a timely fashion. Indeed, a good number of them have failed ever to submit a report. As a result, the Commission is highly dependent on reports by NGOs and other interest groups to assess the situation in a given country. From a positive perspective, this means that these organisations can make themselves and their concerns heard. Therefore, it would be worth their time and effort to report to the Commission on harmful traditional practices. Similarly, it is vital that the Commission make public and widely disseminate both the reports of States and its own observations on these, which it has been reticent to do until now. Only through such public processes can we establish whether States are cognizant of, and acting upon, their duties in relation to the elimination of harmful traditional practices and devise our own priorities and strategies accordingly. Concomitantly, such processes would heighten awareness of the work of the Commission and the legitimacy of human rights in the region. Of course, the chronic under-funding of the Commission must be addressed if submissions are not to become wasted paper; increased funds must come from African States, non-African States and private donor groups alike. Finally, groups concerned with harmful traditional practices should immediately involve themselves in the process of re-evaluating the Draft Protocol to the African Charter on Human and Peoples' Rights Relating to the Rights of Women

Summary and Conclusions

to ensure that it adequately addresses their concerns and is the type of instrument they can use effectively once adopted.

Beyond improvements in the international human rights discourse and machinery as suggested above, it is a central argument of this study that more important would be to develop and implement strategies and programmes for change through indigenous institutions with social and cultural relevance. Certainly, many sensitization initiatives already have been undertaken to challenge popular beliefs and turn these against harmful traditional practices, and many more must be taken. But the situation is synonymous with many other human rights and welfare projects in Africa: too scattered, inadequately targeted and desperately under-funded. Sub-Saharan Africa is a vast region with many languages and many isolated communities. Organising sensitization efforts and offering human rights education at the micro-village level will be a painfully slow and uncertain process toward the eradication of these practices. For instance, it is difficult to imagine thousands of other villages in Mali following the example of the nine which have been reported as having abandoned female circumcision without the same presence, time and effort invested by the IAC. Moreover, there is no guarantee that once the IAC stops their involvement in these villages the practice will not resurface. It is therefore recommendable to focus sensitization and human rights education programmes on those individuals and institutions which are permanently present in the community, already have well-established channels of communication, and carry authority. It is also easier to keep in touch with and, if necessary return to, this smaller target group. In this regard, the individuals and institutions which are important are both the usual candidates (i.e., government ministries, health professionals, and the media and other popular mechanisms of communication) and the unusual ones (institutions of customary law, village elders and influential men).

Fundamentally, this is a matter of focusing energies and funds into those efforts with the greatest likelihood of sustainable success. It may require concerned NGOs and interest groups combining their work and funds so that they may reach further, a development with which donors may be pleased. Finally, if human rights in general are to gain greater credibility in the region, African States, for their part, will have to clean up and invigorate their own institutions of law and order with a view to treating human rights seriously.

Finally, it may be necessary to reevaluate some of our core assumptions about women's empowerment in terms of the actual roles of formal schooling for girls, human rights education, women's groups and legislation on the elimination of harmful traditional practices in Africa.[6] For instance, it would be helpful to explore our (not so) common definition, and expectations, of women's empowerment and inquire whether these are overly influenced by the culture of, and dependent upon the level of develop-

---

6   All of these being strategies advanced by international human rights treaties and platforms of action for the advancement of women; *see generally* Annexes A and B.

ment in, the Western world (e.g., where the institutions of police, judiciary and State administration are in relatively good working order and comparatively more responsive to the experiences and realities of women, where women have comparatively better access to these, and where they are not culturally precluded from doing so. Similarly, with regard to the formal education of girls, it remains to be proven definitively that increased formal schooling *alone*, even with a 'gendered' curriculum, contributes to an increased level of empowerment for girls. More scientific research is needed in this regard. But, it is possible for instance that the type of schooling a girl's father obtains is more likely to determine whether she is circumcised or her level of autonomy (reflected in her status within the family unit). We may certainly ask ourselves whether the total mean period of schooling of children in sub-Saharan Africa is substantial enough to influence positive norms, attitudes and stereotypes.[7] No doubt, more and better general education would make a positive contribution. However, and more specifically, while according to the Western model co-education *may* be more conducive to fostering equality between the sexes, the research of Heward and Bunwaree suggests this to be precisely the reverse in patriarchal societies.[8] If this is so, we may want to revisit and qualify (e.g through a General Recommendation of CEDAW) Article 10 c) of the Women's Convention, which recommends co-education as a means of eliminating 'any stereotyped concept of the roles of men and women.' In summary, human rights advocates may have succeeded in incorporating a gender perspective into human rights discourses, but there is still much research and work to be done to incorporate a cultural perspective into the use and implementation of human rights standards.

---

7 For instance, the total mean period of schooling for girls and boys in the Sudan and Burkina Faso is 0.8 and 0.9 years, respectively, as compared to 10.1 and 12.4 years in the European Union and North America, respectively; Africa Institute of South Africa, AFRICA AT A GLANCE: 1997/8, pp. 31-32.
8 *See generally* C. Heward and S. Bunwaree, eds., GENDER, EDUCATION AND DEVELOPMENT: BEYOND ACCESS TO POWER (1999).

ANNEXES

Annex A

Relevant Interpretations by Treaty Bodies

I. *CEDAW'S General Recommendation No. 14 concerning Harmful Traditional Practices (1990)*

Noting with satisfaction that Governments, where such practices exist, national women's organizations, non-governmental organizations, specialized agencies, such as the World Health Organization, the United Nations Children's Fund, as well as the Commission on Human Rights and its Sub-Commission on Prevention of Discrimination and Protection of Minorities, remain seized of the issue, having particularly recognized that such traditional practices as female circumcision have serious health and other consequences for women and children,

Noting with grave concern that there are continuing cultural, traditional and economic pressures which help to perpetuate harmful practices, such as female circumcision,

Recommends to State parties:
a) that State parties take appropriate and effective measures with a view to eradicating the practice of female circumcision. Such measures could include:
   i) the collection and dissemination by universities, medical or nursing associations, national women's organizations or other bodies of basic data about traditional practices;
   ii) the support of women's organizations at the national and local levels working for the elimination of female circumcision and other practices harmful to women;
   iii) the encouragement of politicians, professionals, religious and community leaders at all levels including the media and the arts to cooperate in influencing attitudes towards the eradication of female circumcision;
   iv) the introduction of appropriate educational and training programmes and seminars based on research findings about the problems arising from female circumcision;
b) that States parties include in their national health policies appropriate strategies aimed at eradicating female circumcision in public health care. Such strategies could include the special responsibility of health personnel including traditional birth attendants to explain the harmful effects of female circumcision;
c) that State parties invite assistance, information and advice from the appropriate organizations of the United Nations system to support and assist efforts being deployed to eliminate harmful traditional practices;
d) that States parties include in their reports to the Committee under articles 10 and 12 of the Convention on the Elimination of All Forms of Discrimination against Women information about measures taken to eliminate female circumcision.

Annexes

II. CEDAW's General Recommendation No. 19
on Violence against Women (1992)

Background
1. Gender-based violence is a form of discrimination that seriously inhibits women's ability to enjoy rights and freedoms on a basis of equality with men.
...

General Comments
6. The Convention in Article 1 defines discrimination against women. The definition of discrimination includes gender-based violence, that is, violence that is directed against a woman because she is a woman or that affects women disproportionately. It includes acts that inflict physical, mental or sexual harm of suffering, threats of such acts, coercion and other deprivations of liberty...

7. Gender-based violence, which impairs or nullifies the enjoyment by women of human rights and fundamental freedoms under general international law or under human rights conventions, is discrimination within the meaning of Article 1 of the Convention. These rights and freedoms include:
a) the right to life;
b) the right not to be subjected to torture, inhuman or degrading treatment or punishment;
c) the right to equal protection according to humanitarian norms in times of international or internal armed conflict;
d) the right to liberty and security of person;
e) the right to equal protection under the law;
f) the right to equality in the family;
g) the right to the highest standard attainable of physical and mental health;
...

Comments on Specific Articles of the Convention
...

Articles 2(f), 5 and 10(c)
11. Traditional attitudes by which women are regarded as subordinate to men or as having stereotyped roles perpetuate widespread practices involving violence or coercion, such as family violence and abuse, forced marriage, dowry deaths, acid attacks and female circumcision. Such prejudices and practices may justify gender-based violence as a form of protection or control of women. The effect of such violence on the physical and mental integrity of women is to deprive than of the equal enjoyment, exercise and knowledge of human rights and fundamental freedoms. While this comment addresses mainly actual or threatened violence the underlying consequences of these forms of gender-based violence help to maintain women in subordinate roles and contribute to their low level of political participation and to their lower level of education, skills and work opportunities.
...

Article 12
19. States parties are required by article 12 to take measures to ensure equal access to health care. Violence against women puts their health and lives at risk.
20. In some States there are traditional practices perpetuated by culture and tradition that are harmful to the health of women and children. These practices include dietary restrictions for pregnant women, preference for male children and female circumcision or genital mutilation.

Article 14
21. Rural women are at risk of gender-based violence because traditional attitudes regarding the subordinate role of women persist in many communities...
...

Specific Recommendations
24. In light of these comments, the Committee on the Elimination of Discrimination against Women recommends:
a) States parties should take appropriate and effective measures to overcome all forms of gender-based violence, whether by public or private act;
...
c) States parties should encourage the compilation of statistics and research on the extent, causes and effects of violence, and on the effectiveness of measures to prevent and deal with violence;
d) effective measures should be taken to ensure that the media respect and promote respect for women;
e) States parties in their reports should identify the nature and extent of attitudes, customs and practices that perpetuate violence against women, and the kinds of violence that result...
f) effective measures should be taken to overcome these attitudes and practices. States should introduce education and public information programmes to help eliminate prejudices which hinder women's equality (Recommendation No. 3, 1987);
...
l) States parties should take measures to overcome such practices and should take account of the Committee's recommendation on female circumcision (Recommendation No. 14) in reporting on health issues;
...
t) that States parties should take all legal and other measures that are necessary to provide effective protection of women against gender-based violence, including, *inter alia*:
  i. effective legal measures, including penal sanctions, civil remedies and compensatory provisions to protect women against all kinds of violence...
  ii. preventive measures, including public information and education programmes to change attitudes concerning the roles and status of men and women;
...

III. CEDAW's General Recommendation No. 21 regarding Equality in Marriage and Family Relations (1994)

...

Article 16

...

Public and private life

11. Historically, human activity in public and private life has been viewed differently and regulated accordingly. In all societies women who have traditionally performed their roles in the private or domestic sphere have long had those activities treated as inferior.

12. As such activities are invaluable for the survival of society, there can be no justification for applying different and discriminatory laws or customs to them. Reports of State parties disclose that there are still countries where *de jure* equality does not exist. Women are thereby prevented from having equal access to resources and from enjoying equality of status in the family and society. Even where *de jure* equality exists, all societies assign different roles, which are regarded as inferior, to women. In this way, principles of justice and equality contained in particular in article 16 and also in articles 2, 5 and 24 of the Convention are being violated.

...

Article 16(1)(e)

21. The responsibilities that women have to bear and raise children affect their right of access to education, employment and other activities related to their personal development. They also impose inequitable burdens of work on women. The number and spacing of their children have a similar impact on women's lives and also affect their physical and mental health, as well as that of their children. For these reasons, women are entitled to decide on the number and spacing of their children.

22. Some reports disclose coercive practices which have serious consequences for women, such as forced pregnancies, abortion and sterilization. Decisions to have children or not, while preferably made in consultation with spouse or partner, must nevertheless be limited by spouse, parent, partner or Government. In order to make an informed decision about sex and reliable contraceptive measures, women must have information about contraceptive measures and their use, and guaranteed access to sex education and family planning services, as provided in article 10(h) of the Convention.

23. There is general agreement that where there are freely available appropriate measures for the voluntary regulation of fertility, the health, development and well-being of all members of the family improves. Moreover, such services improve the general quality of life and health of the population, and the voluntary regulation of population growth helps preserve the environment and achieve sustainable economic and social development.

...

Annex A

Reservations

41. The Committee has noted with alarm the number of States which have entered reservations to the whole or part of article 16, especially when a reservation has also been entered in article 2, claiming that compliance may conflict with a commonly held vision of the family based, *inter alia*, on cultural and religious beliefs or on the country's economic or political status.

42. Many of these countries hold a belief in the patriarchal structure of a family which places a father, husband or son in a favourable position. In some countries where fundamentalist or other extremist views or economic hardships have encouraged a return to old values and traditions, women's place in the family has deteriorated sharply. In others, where it is has been recognized that a modern society depends for its economic advance and for the general good of the community on involving all adults equally, regardless of gender, these taboos and reactionary or extremist ideas have progressively been discouraged.

43. Consistent with articles 2, 3 and 24 in particular, the Committee requires that all States parties gradually progress to a stage where, by its resolute discouragement of notions of the inequality of women in the home, each country will withdraw its reservations, in particular to articles 9, 15 and 16 of the Convention.

44. States parties should resolutely discourage any notions of inequality of women and men which are affirmed by laws, or by religious or private laws or by custom to the state where reservations, particularly to article 16, will be withdrawn.

45. The Committee noted, on the basis of its examination of initial and subsequent periodic reports, that in some States parties to the Convention that had ratified or acceded without reservation, certain laws, especially those dealing with family, do not actually conform to the provisions of the Convention.

46. Their laws still contain many measures which discriminate against women based on norms, customs and socio-cultural prejudices. These States, because of their specific situation regarding these articles, make it difficult for the Committee to evaluate and understand the status of women.

47. The Committee, in particular on the basis of articles 1 and 2 of the Convention, requests that those States parties make the necessary efforts to examine the *de facto* situation relating to the issues and to introduce the required measures in their national legislation still containing provisions discriminatory to women.

...

Encouraging compliance with the Convention

50. Assisted by the comments ion the present general recommendation, and as required by articles 2, 3 and 24, States parties should introduced measures directed at encouraging full compliance with the principles of the Convention, particularly where religious or private law or custom conflict with those principles.

IV. *Committee on Economic, Social and Cultural Rights' General Comment No. 14 on Health (2000)*

...

'Women and the right to health'

21. To eliminate discrimination against women, there is a need to develop and implement a comprehensive national strategy for promoting women's right to health throughout their life span. Such a strategy should include interventions aimed at the prevention and treatment of diseases affecting women, as well as policies to provide access to a full range of high quality and affordable health care, including sexual and reproductive health services. A major goal should be reducing women's health risks particularly lowering rates of maternal mortality and protecting women from domestic violence. The realization of women's right to health requires the removal of all barriers interfering with access to health services, education and information, including in the area of sexual and reproductive health. It is also important to undertake preventive, promotive and remedial action to shield women from the impact of harmful traditional cultural practices and norms that deny them their full reproductive rights.

...

35. Obligations to protect include, *inter alia*, the duties of States to adopt legislation or to take other measures ensuring equal access to health care and health-related services provided by third parties; to ensure that privatization of the health sector does not constitute a threat to the availability, accessibility, acceptability and quality of health facilities, goods and services; to control the marketing of medical equipment and medicines by third parties; and to ensure that medical practitioners and other health professional meet appropriate standards of education, skill and ethical codes of conduct. States are also obliged to ensure that harmful social or traditional practices do not interfere with access to pre- and post-natal care and family-planning; to prevent third parties from coercing women to undergo traditional practices, e.g. female genital mutilation; and to take measures to protect all vulnerable or marginalized groups of society, in particular women, children, adolescents and older persons, in light of the gender-based expressions of violence. States should also ensure that third parties do not limit people's access to health-related information and services.

ANNEXES

Annex B

Relevant Statements and Strategies from Declaratory Documents

I. *Declaration of Mexico on the Equality of Women*
World Conference on the International Women's Year (United Nations, 1975)
...
Principle 28: Women all over the world should unite to eliminate violations of human rights committed against women and girls such as: rape, prostitution, physical assault, mental cruelty, child marriage, forced marriage and marriage as a commercial transaction.

II. *Nairobi Forward-Looking Strategies for the Advancement of Women*
World Conference on the United Nations Decade for Women
(United Nations, 1985)

A. Obstacles
...
45. One of the fundamental obstacles to women's equality is that *de facto* discrimination and inequality in the status of women and men derive from larger social, economic, political and cultural factors that have been justified on the basis of physiological differences. Although there is no physiological basis for regarding the household and family as essentially the domain of women... the belief that such a basis exists perpetuates inequality and inhibits the structural and attitudinal changes necessary to eliminate such inequality.

...
B. Basic Strategies
51. The political commitment to establish, modify, expand or enforce a comprehensive legal base for the equality of women and men on the basis of human dignity must be strengthened. Legislative changes are most effective when made within a supportive framework promoting simultaneous changes in the economic, social, political and cultural spheres, which can help bring about a social transformation. For true equality to become a reality for women, the sharing of power on equal terms with men must be a major strategy.
...
56. The obstacles to the equality of women created by stereotypes, perceptions of and attitudes towards women should be totally removed. Elimination of these obstacles will require, in addition to legislation, education of the population at large through formal and informal channels,

including the media, non-governmental organizations, political party platforms and executive action.

58. Timely and reliable statistics on the situation of women have an important role to play in the elimination of stereotypes and the movement towards full equality. Governments should help collect statistics and make periodic assessment in identifying stereotypes and inequalities, in providing concrete evidence concerning many of the harmful consequences of unequal laws and practices and in measuring progress in the elimination of inequalities.

III. *Vienna Declaration and Programme of Action World Conference on Human Rights (United Nations, 1993)*

...

38. In particular, the World Conference stresses the importance of working towards the elimination of violence against women in public and private life... and the eradication of any conflicts which may arise between the rights of women and the harmful effects of certain traditional or customary practices, cultural prejudices and religious extremism...

...

48. Exploitation and abuse of children should be actively combated, including by addressing their root causes...

49. ... The World Conference on Human Rights urges States to repeal existing laws and regulations and remove customs and practices which discriminate against and cause harm to the girl child.

IV. *Declaration on the Elimination of Violence against Women (Res. 48/104 of the United Nations General Assembly of 20 December 1993)*

...

Recognizing that violence against women is a manifestation of historically unequal power relations between men and women, which have led to domination over and discrimination against women by men and to the prevention of their full advancement, and that violence against women is one of the crucial social mechanisms by which women are forced into a subordinate position compared with men,

...

Recalling Economic and Social Council resolution 1990/15 of 24 May 1990, in the annex to which it was recognized that violence against women in the family and society was pervasive and cut across lines of income, class and culture, and had to be matched by urgent and effective steps to eliminate its incidence,

...

Article 1
For the purposes of this Declaration, the term violence against women means any act of gender-based violence that results in, or is likely to result in, physical, sexual or psychological harm or

suffering to women, including threats of such acts, coercion or arbitrary deprivation of liberty, whether occurring in public or in private life.

Article 2
Violence against women shall be understood to encompass, but not be limited to, the following:
a) physical, sexual and psychological violence occurring in the family, including battering, sexual abuse of female children in the household, dowry-related violence, marital rape, female genital mutilation and other traditional practices harmful to women...
...
c) physical, sexual and psychological violence perpetrated or condoned by the States, wherever it occurs.
...

Article 4
States should condemn violence against women and should not invoke any custom, tradition or religious consideration to avoid obligations with respect to its elimination. States should pursue by all appropriate means and without delay a policy of eliminating violence against women and, to this end, should:
...
c) exercise due diligence to prevent, investigate and, in accordance with national legislation, punish acts of violence against women, whether those acts are perpetrated by the State of by private persons;
...
e) consider the possibility of developing national plans of action to promote the protection of women against any form of violence, or to include provisions for this purpose in plans already existing, taking into account, as appropriate, such cooperation as can be provided by non-governmental organizations, particularly those concerned with this subject;
...
j) adopt all appropriate measures, especially in the field of education, to modify the social and cultural patterns of conduct of men and women and to eliminate prejudices, customary practices and all other practices based on the idea of the inferiority or superiority of either of the sexes and on stereotyped roles for men and women;
...

V. *Cairo Programme of Action International Conference on Population and Development (United Nations, 1994)*

Chapter IV: Gender Equality, Equity and Empowerment of Women

A. Empowerment and Status of Women
Basis for Action
4.1 The empowerment and autonomy of women and the improvement of their political, social, economic and health status is a highly important end in itself. In addition, it is essential for the achievement of sustainable development. The full participation and partnership of both women and men is required in productive and reproductive life, including shared responsibilities for the

care and nurturing of children and maintenance of the household. In all parts of the world, women are facing threats to their lives, health and wellbeing as a result of being overburdened with work and of their lack of power and influence... The power relations that impede women's attainment of healthy and fulfilling lives operate at many levels of society, from the most personal to the highly public. Achieving change requires policy and programme actions... In addition, improving the status of women also enhances their decision-making capacity at all levels in all spheres of life, especially in the area of sexuality and reproduction.
...

4.2 Education is one of the most important means of empowering women with the knowledge, skills and self-confidence necessary to participate fully in the development process... More than one third of the world's adults, most of them women, have no access to printed knowledge, to new skills or to technologies that would improve the quality of their lives and help them shape and adapt to social and economic change. There are 130 million children who are not enrolled in primary school and 70 per cent of them are girls.

Actions
4.4 Countries should act to empower women and should take steps to eliminate inequalities between men and women as soon as possible by:
a) Establishing mechanisms for women's equal participation and equitable representation at all levels of the political process and public life in each community and society and enabling women to articulate their concerns and needs;
b) Promoting the fulfillment of women's potential through education, skill development and employment, giving paramount importance to the elimination of poverty, illiteracy and ill health among women;
c) Eliminating all practices that discriminate against women; assisting women to establish and realize their rights, including those that relate to reproductive and sexual health;
d) Adopting appropriate measures to improve women's ability to earn income beyond traditional occupations...
e) Eliminating violence against women;
...

4.12 Every effort should be made to encourage the expansion and strengthening of grass-roots, community-based and activist groups for women. Such groups should be the focus of national campaigns to foster women's awareness of the full range of their legal rights, including their rights within the family, and to help women organize to achieve those rights.
...

4.19 Schools, the media and other social institutions should seek to eliminate stereotypes in all types of communication and educational materials that reinforce existing inequities between males and females and undermine girls' self-esteem. Countries must recognize that, in addition to expanding education for girls, teachers' attitudes and practices, school curricula and facilities must also change to reflect a commitment to eliminate all gender bias...
...

4.21 Governments should strictly enforce laws to ensure that marriage is entered into only with the free and full consent of the intending spouses. In addition, Governments should strictly enforce laws concerning the minimum legal age of consent and minimum age at marriage and should raise the minimum age at marriage where necessary. Governments and non-governmental organizations should generate social support for the enforcement of laws on minimum legal age at marriage, in particular by providing educational and employment opportunities
...

Chapter VII: Reproductive Rights and Reproductive Health

...

7.2 Reproductive health is a state of complete physical, mental and social well-being and not merely the absence of disease or infirmity, in all matters relating to the reproductive health system and to its functions and processes. Reproductive health therefore implies that people are able to have a satisfying and safe sex life and that they have the capability to reproduce and the freedom to decide if, when and how often to do so. Implicit in this last condition are the right of men and women to be informed and to access to safe, effective, affordable and acceptable methods of family planning of their choice, as well as other methods of their choice for regulation of fertility which are not against the law, and the right of access to appropriate health-care services that will enable women to go safely through pregnancy and childbirth and provide couples with the best chance of having a healthy infant. In line with the above definition of reproductive health, reproductive health care is defined as the constellation of methods, techniques and services that contribute to reproductive health and well-being by preventing and solving reproductive health problems. It also includes sexual health, the purpose of which is the enhancement of life and personal relations, and not merely counselling and care related to reproductive and sexually transmitted diseases.

7.3 Bearing in mind the above definition, reproductive rights embrace certain human rights that are already recognized in national laws, international human rights documents and other consensus documents. These rights rest on the recognition of the basic right of all couples and individuals to decide freely and responsibly the number, spacing and timing of their children and to have the information and means to do so, and the right to attain the highest standard of sexual and reproductive health. It also include their right to make decisions concerning reproduction free of discrimination, coercion and violence, as expressed in human rights documents... Reproductive health eludes many of the world's people because of such factors as: inadequate levels of knowledge about human sexuality and inappropriate or poor-quality reproductive health information and services, the prevalence of high-risk sexual behaviour; discriminatory social practices; negative attitudes towards women and girls; and the limited power many women and girls have over their sexual and reproductive lives...

Annexes

VI. Copenhagen Declaration
World Summit for Social Development (United Nations, 1995)

...

C. Commitments

...

Commitment 5: We commit ourselves to promoting full respect for human dignity and to achieving equality and equity between women and men and to recognizing and enhancing the participation and leadership roles of women in political, civil, economic, social and cultural life and in development. To this end, at the national level, we will:
a) Promote changes in attitudes, structure, policies, laws and practices in order to eliminate all obstacles to human dignity, equality and equity in the family and in society...

...

Commitment 6: We commit ourselves to promoting and attaining the goals of universal and equitable access to quality education, the highest attainable standard of physical and mental health and the access of all to primary health, making particular efforts to rectify inequalities relating to social conditions.... To this end, at the national level, we will...
y) Intensify and coordinate international support for education and health programmes based on respect for human dignity and focused on the protection of all women and children, especially against... harmful practices such as child prostitution, female genital mutilation and child marriages.

VII. Beijing Declaration and Platform for Action
World Conference on Women (United Nations, 1995)

Global Framework

...

39. ... [T]here exists world-wide evidence that discrimination and violence against girls begin at the earliest stages of life and continue unabated throughout their lives... They are often subject to various forms of... violence and harmful practices such as female infanticide and prenatal sex selection, incest, female genital mutilation and early marriage, including child marriage.

...

Strategic Objectives and Actions

...

B. Education and Training of Women

...

71. Discrimination in girls' access to education persists in many areas, owing to customary attitudes, early marriages and pregnancies, inadequate and gender-biased teaching and educational materials...

72. Creation of an educational and social environment... where educational resources promote non-stereotyped images of women and men would be effective in the elimination of the causes of discrimination against women and inequalities between women and men...

...

74. Curricula and teaching materials remain gender-biased... This reinforces traditional female and male roles that deny women opportunities for full and equal partnership in society...

C. Women and Health
89. ... Women's health is determined by the social, political and economic context of their lives
...
92. ... The prevalence of... negative attitudes towards women and girls... the limited power many women have over their sexual and reproductive lives and lack of influence in decision-making are social realities which have an adverse impact on their health.
...
95. ... Reproductive health eludes many of the world's people because of such factors as: inadequate levels of knowledge about human sexuality and inappropriate or poor-quality reproductive health information and services; the prevalence of high-risk sexual behaviour; discriminatory social practices; negative attitudes towards women and girls; and the limited power many women and girls have over their sexual and reproductive lives...
...
98. HIV/AIDS and other sexually transmitted diseases... have emphasized that social vulnerability and the unequal power relationships between women and men are obstacles to safe sex... and efforts to control the spread of sexually transmitted diseases...
...

Actions to be taken
C.2: Strengthen preventive programmes that promote women's health
107. ...
a) Give priority to both formal and informal educational programmes that support and enable women to develop self-esteem, acquire knowledge, make decisions on and take responsibility for their own health, achieve mutual respect in matters concerning sexuality and fertility and educate men regarding the importance of women's health and well-being, placing special focus on programmes for both men and women that emphasize the elimination of harmful attitudes and practices, including female genital mutilation, son preference (which results in female infanticide and prenatal sex selection), early marriage, including child marriage, violence against women, sexual exploitation, sexual abuse, which at times is conducive to infection with HIV/AIDS and other sexually transmitted diseases, drug abuse, discrimination against girls and women in food allocation and other harmful attitudes and practices related to life, health and well-being of women, and recognizing that some of these practices can be violations of human rights and ethical medical principles;
...
d) Reinforce laws, reform institutions and promote norms and practices that eliminate discrimination against women and encourage both women and men to take responsibility for their sexual and reproductive behaviour; ensure full respect for the integrity of the person, take action to ensure the conditions necessary for women to exercise their reproductive rights and eliminate coercive laws and practices;
...

C.3: Undertake gender-sensitive initiatives that address sexually transmitted diseases HIV/ AIDS, and sexual and reproductive health issues
108. ...
b) Review and amend laws and combat practices, as appropriate, that may contribute to women's susceptibility to HIV infection and other sexually transmitted diseases, including enacting legislation against those socio-cultural practices that contribute to it, and implement legislation, policies and practices to protect women, adolescents and young girls from discrimination related to HIV/AIDS;

....

e) Develop gender sensitive multisectoral programmes and strategies to end social subordination of women and girls and to ensure their social and economic empowerment and equality; facilitate promotion of programmes to educate and enable men to assume their responsibilities to prevent HIV/AIDS and other sexually transmitted diseases;

...

j) Assist women and their formal and informal organizations to establish and expand effective peer education and outreach programmes...

k) Give full attention to the promotion of mutually respectful and equitable gender relations...

D. Violence against Women

...

113. The term 'violence against women' means any act of gender-based violence that results or is likely to result in, physical, sexual or psychological harm or suffering to women, including threats of such acts, coercion or arbitrary deprivation of liberty, whether occurring in public or private life. Accordingly, violence against women encompasses but is not limited to the following:
a) Physical, sexual and psychological violence occurring in the family, including battering, sexual abuse of female children in the household, dowry-related violence, marital rape, female genital mutilation and other traditional practices harmful to women...

...

118. ... Violence against women throughout the life cycle derives essentially from cultural patterns, in particular the harmful effects of certain traditional or customary practices and all acts of extremism... that perpetuate the lower status accorded to women in the family, the workplace, the community and society...

Actions to be taken
D.1: Take integrated measures to prevent and eliminate violence against women

124. ...
a) Condemn violence against women and refrain from invoking any custom, tradition or religious consideration to avoid [State] obligations with respect to its elimination...

i) Enact and enforce legislation against the perpetrators of practices and acts of violence against women, such as female genital mutilation... and give vigorous support to the efforts of non- governmental and community organisations to eliminate such practices;

...

k) Adopt all appropriate measures, especially in the field of education, to modify the social and cultural patterns of conduct of men and women, and to eliminate prejudices, customary practices and all other practices based on the idea of the inferiority or superiority of either of the sexes and on stereotyped roles for men and women;

126. ...
b) Develop programmes and procedures to educate and raise awareness of acts of violence against women that constitute a crime and a violation of the human rights of women.
...

D.2: Study the causes and consequences of violence against women and the effectiveness of preventive measures

129. ...
a) Promote research, collect data and compile statistics... and encourage research into the causes, nature, seriousness and consequences of violence against women and the effectiveness of measures implemented to prevent and redress violence against women.
...
d) Encourage the media to examine the impact of gender role stereotypes... which foster gender-based violence and inequalities...and take measures to eliminate these negative images...

VIII. *Draft Addis Ababa [African] Declaration on Violence against Women (1997)*

We, the representatives of the National Committees of the Inter-African Committee on Traditional Practices Affecting the Health of Women and Children, participating at the Symposium for Legislators held at the headquarters of the Organization of African Unity in Addis Ababa, Ethiopia from 10 to 12 September 1997,

Reaffirming that it is the responsibility of the States and Government to protect their citizens and preserve their fundamental rights,

Painfully aware of the misery and suffering of most women and girl-children of Africa due to violence inflicted on them in the name of custom and tradition,

Considering that violence against women and girl-children can be physical, psychological, sexual and includes female genital mutilation (FGM), early childhood marriages and pregnancy, wife battering, widowhood rites, son preference, scarification, food taboos and rape,

Aware that all violence against women and girls have serious physical and psycho-social consequences which adversely affect their health and quality of life,

Recognizing with satisfaction the progress made in the high-level sensitization, education and information campaigns on the adverse effects of female genital mutilation and other harmful practices on women and girl-children,

Expressing our shame and indignation on the continuation of the degrading and inhuman practice of female genital mutilation and other harmful practices,

Observing that no religion recommends practices that are harmful to the health of women and girl-children,

Further taking into account the extremely high rates of infant and maternal mortality and morbidity in Africa as we enter into the twenty-first Century,

Noting that our States and Governments have signed/ratified/endorsed international instruments, amongst which figure:
  a) The Universal Declaration of Human Rights (1948);
  b) The United Nations Convention on the Elimination of all Forms of Discrimination against Women (1979);
  c) The African Charter on Human and Peoples' Rights (1981);
  d) The Treaty Establishing the African Economic Community (1991);
  e) The Convention on the Rights and Welfare of the Child (1991) [sic];
  f) The Declaration on Violence against Women (1993);
  g) The Vienna Declaration and the Programme of Action of the World Conference on Human Rights (1993);
  h) The Programme of Action of the International Conference on Population and Development (ICPD), Cairo, Egypt (1994);
  i) The African Platform for Action, Dakar, Senegal (1994);
  j) The Resolution passed at the forty-seventh World Health Assembly on Traditional Practices Harmful to Maternal and Child Health (1994);
  k) Platform for Action and the Beijing Declaration (1995);
  l) The International Convention against Torture, Inhuman and Degrading Treatment [sic];

Further noting that in spite of the signature/ratification/endorsement of the said instrument by the African States and Governments, the situation of most African women and girl-children remains grave and vulnerable,

Vividly aware that all efforts to promote peace, equality and development in Africa shall fail without a violence-free environment for women and girl-children,

HEREBY STRONGLY CALL UPON our African Heads of State and Government to:
1. **ADOPT** clear and consistent national policies for the abolition of female genital mutilation and other harmful practices including the enactment of specific national legislation to prohibit FGM and these harmful practices;
2. **ESTABLISH** concrete mechanisms for the implementation of national policies and effective legislative measures for the elimination of all forms of violence against women and girl-children by:
   a) Designating a ministry to coordinate and monitor the implementation of national policies and legislative measures for the elimination of all harmful practices through a multi-sectoral approach;
   b) Strengthening existing structures and creating a conducive environment for the effective enforcement of laws and judicial decisions for the elimination of violence against women and girl-children;
   c) Organizing strong community out-reach education programmes that involve village and religious leaders;
   d) Supporting and encouraging non-governmental organizations particularly women's associations and advocacy groups; and,

    e) Providing protection and security from physical harm for the advocates of the eradication of harmful traditional practices;
3. **PROHIBIT** the medicalization or para-medicalization of all forms of female genital mutilation and other harmful traditional practices;
4. **DESIST** from hindering, in any form, efforts to eradicate the practice of female genital mutilation and other harmful traditional practices;
5. **ENSURE** that by the year 2005 the practice of female genital mutilation will have been completely eradicated or its incidences drastically reduced.

FINALLY CALL UPON the Organization of African Unity to sensitize Member States and Governments and support the implementation of policies and legislations for the elimination of female genital mutilation and all forms of practices affecting the health of women and girl-children and request it to submit the Declaration on Violence against Women to the next session of the Assembly of Heads of State and Government.

ANNEXES

Annex C

Excerpts from the Initial Report of the Central African Republic to the Committee on the Rights of the Child (2000)[1]

...

8. The report's conclusions provided a very objective summary of the implementation of the Convention and the main achievements concerning the rights of the child, together with an outline of the constraints the country faced and the problems which remained despite the Government's efforts... Many traditional attitudes and customs hampered acceptance of the Convention and its principles...

9. Despite those difficulties, the Government has taken positive steps... Assault causing bodily harm against children had been prohibited... and excision, a practice which had also been banned by decree... A Decree had been issued under which it was a punishable offence to prevent a girl from continuing her education...

21. Ms. Karp commended the Central African Republic for its inclusion of some of the Convention's basic principles in the Constitution itself, given the profound contrasts in the country's cultural background, which demonstrated its political will to enhance the exercise of human rights. However, traditions and customs seemed to have pride of place. She asked whether religious and traditional leaders might be encouraged to help change attitudes.

...

26. Ms. Ouedraogo asked whether the fact that education was compulsory for girls up to the age of 21 meant that girls were required to attend school until that age, or whether that was simply a measure for protecting them from early marriage..

...

29. Turning to the definition of the child, she asked whether any campaigns on early marriage had been conducted and how that traditional practice could be reconciled with the legal provision establishing 18 as the age of marriage...

---

[1] United Nations, Committee on the Rights of the Child, INITIAL REPORT OF THE CENTRAL AFRICAN REPUBLIC, CRC/C/SR.657, 9 October 2000.

Annexes

31. Ms. Dea (Central African Republic) said that the Central African Republic was prepared to modify its policies in the area of children's rights… Unfortunately, it was difficult to uproot certain entrenched attitudes and traditions…

32… In reality, the Government's most challenging task was changing mentalities, especially those of people in remote rural areas.
…

50. Mr. Samba (Central African Republic) said that… a commission responsible for monitoring the implementation of the Convention had been created in 1993… A number of private individuals with a particular interest in the rights of children sat on the commission as well.

51. Sub-commissions at the central level specialized in such areas as culture and law… had also been set up…

58. Ms. Dea (Central African Republic), replying to a number of questions said the decree prohibiting girls under the age of 21 from marrying had been established at a time when many girls had been abandoning their studies in order to marry. Its purpose was to protect and promote the rights of girls…

59. Ms. Ouedraogo said it was clear from the report that the population of the Central African Republic tended to adhere to custom and tradition. The Government should consider working with traditional structures, and with traditional communicators, to change attitudes; admittedly, that was a slow process...

SELECTED BIBLIOGRAPHY

Adetunji, Jacob A., UNINTENDED CHILDBEARING IN DEVELOPING COUNTRIES: LEVEL, TRENDS AND DETERMINANTS, Demographic and Health Surveys Analytical Reports, No. 8. (Calverton, Maryland, USA: Macro International Inc., 1998).

Adjetey, Fitnat Naa-Adjeley, *Reclaiming the African Woman's Individuality: The Struggle between Women's Reproductive Autonomy and African Society and Culture*, The American University Law Review, Vol. 44, No. 4, 1995, pp. 1351-1382.

Africa Institute of South Africa, AFRICA AT A GLANCE: FACTS AND FIGURES, QUALITY OF LIFE AND POLITICAL CHANGE, 1997/8, 10th ed. (Pretoria: Africa Institute of South Africa, 1998).

African Centre for Women, TRADITIONAL AND CULTUAL PRACTICES HARMFUL TO THE GIRL-CHILD (UN: Economic Commission for Africa, 1997).

Aguessy, Honorat, *Traditional African views and apperceptions*, in Alpha I. Sow, Ola Balogun, Honorat Aguessy and Pathé Diagne, eds., INTRODUCTION TO AFRICAN CULTURE: GENERAL ASPECTS (Paris: UNESCO, 1979), pp. 83-123.

A'Haleem, Asma Mohammed, *Claiming Our Bodies and Our Rights: Exploring Female Circumcision as an Act of Violence in Africa*, in Margaret Schuler, ed., FREEDOM FROM VIOLENCE: WOMEN'S STRATEGIES FROM AROUND THE WORLD (New York: Widbooks and UNIFEM: 1992), pp. 141-155.

Ahmad, K., *Swaziland debates sterilisation of HIV patients*, Lancet, Vol. 356, 2001, pp. 320-322.

Aidoo, Akwasi, *Africa: Democracy Without Human Rights*, Human Rights Quarterly, Vol. 15, No. 4, 1993, pp. 703-715.

Allotey, Pascale, *Where There's No Tradition of Traditional Birth Attendants: Kassena Nankana District, Northern Ghana*, Reproductive Health Matters (Special Focus: Safe Motherhood Initiatives: Critical Issues), 1999, pp. 147-154.

Althaus, Francis A., *Female Circumcision: Rite of Passage or Violation of Rights?*, International Family Planning Perspectives, Vol. 23, No. 3, 1997, pp. 130-133.

Amede, Obiora L., *Bridges and Barricades: Rethinking Polemics and Intransigence in the Campaign against Female Circumcision*, Case Western Res. Law Review, Vol. 47, 1996, pp. 275-333.

Amin, Sajeda and Cynthia B. Lloyd, WOMEN'S LIVES AND RAPID FERTILITY DECLINE: WORKING PAPER NO. 117 (New York: Population Council, Policy Research Division, 1998).

Anangwe, Amukowa, *Maintenance of Law and Order in Western Kenya*, in Joseph Semboja and Ole Therkildsen, eds., SERVICE PROVISION UNDER STRESS IN EAST AFRICA (London: James Curry, 1995) pp. 105-119.

Andersson, H., *Sex-ban Swazi king pays fine*, BBC News on website: http://news.bbc.co.uk/hi/english/...africa/newsid_1651000/1651154.stm.

Ankomah, Augustine, *Sex, Love, Money and AIDS: The Dynamics of Premarital Sexual Relationships in Ghana*, Sexualities, Vol. 2, No. 3, 1999, pp. 291-308.
Ankrah, E.M., *The impact of HIV/AIDS on the family and other significant relationships: the African clan revisited*, AIDS Care, No. 5, pp. 5-22.
Ankumah, Evelyn A., THE AFRICAN COMMISSION ON HUMAN AND PEOPLES' RIGHTS: PRACTICES AND PROCEDURES (The Hague: Martinus Nijhoff Publishers, 1996).
___, *Interview with Florence Butegwa*, Africa Legal Aid Quarterly, January-March 1996, pp. 22-24.
An-Na'im, Abdullahi, *The Position of Islamic States Regarding the Universal Declaration of Human Rights*, in Peter Baehr, Cees Flinterman and Mignon Senders, eds., INNOVATION AND INSPIRATION: FIFTY YEARS OF THE UNIVERSAL DECLARATION OF HUMAN RIGHTS (Amsterdam: Royal Netherlands Academy of Arts and Sciences, 1999), pp. 177-192.
___, Jerald D. Gort, Henry Jansen and Hendrik M. Vroom, eds., HUMAN RIGHTS AND RELIGIOUS VALUES: AN UNEASY RELATIONSHIP? (Amsterdam: Wm. B. Eerdmans Publishing Co., 1995).
___, *Remarks (Forum on Religious and Cultural Rights)*, The American University Law Review, Vol. 44, No. 4, 1995, pp. 1383-1384.
___, *Cross-Cultural Support for Equitable Participation in sub-Saharan Africa*, in Kathleen E. Mahoney and Paul Mahoney, eds., HUMAN RIGHTS IN THE TWENTY-FIRST CENTURY: A GLOBAL CHALLENGE (Dordrecht: Martinus Nijhoff Publishers, 1993), pp. 133-148.
___, TOWARD AN ISLAMIC REFORMATION: CIVIL LIBERTIES, HUMAN RIGHTS, AND INTERNATIONAL LAW (Syracuse: Syracuse University Press, 1990).
___ and Francis Deng, *Introduction*, in Abdullahi A. An-Na'im and Francis M. Deng, eds., HUMAN RIGHTS IN AFRICA: CROSS-CULTURAL PERSPECTIVES (Washington, D.C.: Brookings Institute, 1990), pp. 1-11.
___, *Problems of Universal Cultural Legitimacy*, in Abdullahi A. An-Na'im and Francis M. Deng, eds., HUMAN RIGHTS IN AFRICA: CROSS-CULTURAL PERSPECTIVES (Washington, D.C.: Brookings Institute, 1990), pp. 331-367.
Armstrong, Alice, CULTURE AND CHOICE: LESSONS FROM SURVIVORS OF GENDER VIOLENCE IN ZIMBABWE (Chapel Hill, NC, USA: AKA, 1998).
Azu-Billa Anaba, Faisal, *Traditional practices, beliefs and taboos that affect the health and nutrition of women and children in the northern sector of Ghana*, in IAC, REPORT ON THE REGIONAL CONFERENCE ON TRADITIONAL PRACTICES AFFECTING THE HEALTH OF WOMEN AND CHILDREN IN AFRICA (Addis Ababa: IAC, 1991), pp. 127-129.
Baleta, A., *Women's Groups in Kenya Win Small Victory against Female Circumcision, 2001* on website: http://thelancet.com/search/search/isa.
Barnes, Andrew E., *Evangelization where it is not wanted: colonial administrators and missionaries in Northern Nigeria*, Journal of Religion in Africa, Vol. 25, Fasc. 4, 1995, pp. 412-441.
Bathily, F., *Combat against traditional practices harmful to the health of the mother and the child: Activity report from the Senegalese Red Cross* in IAC, REPORT ON THE RE-

GIONAL CONFERENCE ON TRADITIONAL PRACTICES AFFECTING THE HEALTH OF WOMEN AND CHILDREN IN AFRICA (Addis Ababa: IAC, 1991), pp. 232-236.

Bawah, Ayaga Agula, Patricia Akweongo, Ruth Simmons and James F. Phillips, *Women's Fears and Men's Anxieties: The Impact of Family Planning on Gender Relations in Northern Ghana*, Studies in Family Planning, Vol. 30, No. 1, 1999, pp. 54-66.

Bay, Christian, STRATEGIES OF POLITICAL EMANCIPATION (South Bend, Indiana: University of Notre Dame Press, 1981).

Bello, Emmanuel G., *The Mandate of the African Commission on Human and Peoples' Rights*, African Journal of International Law, Vol. 1, No. 1, 1988, pp. 31-64.

___, *The African Charter on Human and Peoples' Rights: A Legal Analysis*, Académie de Droit International: Recueil des Cours (Collected Courses), Vol. 194, 1985, pp. 9-268.

Benedek, Wolfgang, *Peoples' Rights and Individuals' Duties as Special Features of the African Charter*, in Philip Kunig, Wolfgang Benedek and Costa Ricky Mahalu, eds., REGIONAL PROTECTION OF HUMAN RIGHTS BY INTERNATIONAL LAW: THE EMERGING AFRICAN SYSTEM (Baden-Baden: Nomos Verlagsgesellschaft, 1985), pp. 59-94.

Bennett, T. W., HUMAN RIGHTS AND AFRICAN CUSTOMARY LAW (Cape Town, South Africa: Juta, 1995).

Bentham, Jeremy, in J.H. Burns and H.L.A. Hart, eds., AN INTRODUCTION TO THE PRINCIPLES OF MORALS AND LEGISLATION (London: Athlone, 1970).

Bhasin, Kamla, WHAT IS PATRIARCHY? (New Delhi: Kali for Women, 1993).

Biddlecom Ann E. and Bolaji M. Fapohunda, *Covert Contraceptive Use: Prevalence, Motivations, and Consequences*, Studies in Family Planning, Vol. 29, No. 4, 1998, pp. 360-372.

Blake, C. Fred, *Foot-Binding in Neo-Confucian China*, Signs, Vol. 9, 1994, pp. 676-681.

Boye, Abdel-el-Kader, Kathleen Hill, Stephen Isaacs, and Deborah Gordis, *Marriage law and practice in the Sahel*, Studies in Family Planning, Vol. 22, No. 6, 1991, pp. 343-349.

Bozeman, Adda, THE FUTURE OF LAW IN A MULTICULTURAL WORLD (Princeton: Princeton University Press, 1977).

Bradley, Candice and Thomas S. Weisner, *Introduction: Crisis in the African Family*, in Thomas S. Weisner, Candice Bradley and Philip L. Kilbride, eds., AFRICAN FAMILIES AND THE CRISIS OF SOCIAL CHANGE (London: Bergin & Garvey, 1997), pp. xix-xxxii.

Bradley, Candice, *Is Fertility Going Down in Margoli*, in Thomas S. Weisner, Candice Bradley and Philip L. Kilbride, eds., AFRICAN FAMILIES AND THE CRISIS OF SOCIAL CHANGE (London: Bergin & Garvey, 1997), pp. 227-252.

Brokensha, D., *Social factors in the transmission and control of AIDS in Africa*, in N. Miller and R.C. Rockwell, eds., AIDS IN AFRICA: THE SOCIAL AND POLICY IMPACT (Lewiston/Queenston: Edwin Mellen Press, 1988), pp. 167-173.

Brownlie, Ian, BASIC DOCUMENTS IN INTERNATIONAL LAW, 5th ed. (Oxford/New York: Oxford University Press, 2002).

Bryceson, Deborah Fahy, *Wishful Thinking: Theory and Practice of Western Donor Efforts to Raise Women's Status in Rural Africa*, in D. F. Bryceson, ed., WOMEN WIELDING THE HOE: LESSON FROM RURAL AFRICA FOR FEMINIST THEORY AND DEVELOPMENT PRACTICE (Oxford, U.K./Washington D.C.: Berg Publishers, 1995), pp. 201-222.

Busia, Abena P. A., *Foreword*, in Center for Women's Global Leadership, GENDER VIOLENCE AND WOMEN'S HUMAN RIGHTS IN AFRICA (New York: Center for Women's Global Leadership, 1994), pp. iii-iv.

Butegwa, Florence, *Challenges of Promoting Legal Literacy Among Women in Uganda*, in Margaret Schuler and Sakuntala Kadirgamar-Rajasingham, eds., LEGAL LITERACY: A TOOL FOR WOMEN'S EMPOWERMENT (New York: UNIFEM/OEF International, 1992), pp. 139-162.

Caldwell, John C., DISASTER IN AN ALTERNATIVE CIVILIZATION: THE SOCIAL DIMENSION OF AIDS IN THE SUB-SAHARAN AFRICA DEMOGRAPHIC CENTRE (Canberra: Health Transition Centre, National Centre for Epidemiology and Population Health, Australian National University 1989).

___, *Mass education as a determinant of the timing of fertility decline*, Population and Development Review, Vol. 6, No. 2, 1980, pp. 225-255.

___, *Education as a factor in mortality decline: An examination of the Nigerian data*, Population Studies, Vol. 33, No. 3, 1979, pp. 395-413.

___, Pat Caldwell, Bruce K. Caldwell and Indrani Pieris, *The Construction of Adolescence in a Changing World: Implications for Sexuality, Reproduction, and Marriage*, Studies in Family Planning, Vol. 29, No. 2, 1998, pp. 137-153.

___, P. Caldwell and P. Quiggin, *The Social Content of AIDS in sub-Saharan Africa*, Population and Development Review, Vol. 15, No. 2, 1989, pp. 185-234.

Caraël, Michael, *Sexual Behaviour*, in John Cleland and Benoît Ferry, eds., SEXUAL BEHAVIOUR AND AIDS IN THE DEVELOPING WORLD (London UK/Bristol, PA: Taylor and Francis, 1995) pp. 75-123.

Castle, Sarah, Mamadou Kani Konaté, Priscilla R. Ulin, and Sarah Martin, *A Qualitative Study of Clandestine Contraceptive Use in Urban Mali*, Studies in Family Planning, Vol. 30, No. 3, 1999, pp. 231-248.

Center for Reproductive Law and Policy (CRLP), FEMAL GENITAL MUTILATION: A GUIDE TO LAWS AND POLICIES WOLRDWIDE (London: Zed Books, 2000).

___, WOMEN OF THE WORLD: LAWS AND POLICIES AFFECTING THEIR REPRODUCTIVE LIVES – ANGLOPOHONE AFRICA (New York: CRLP, 1997).

___, FEMALE GENITAL MUTILATION: A MATTER OF HUMAN RIGHTS (New York: CRLP, 1995).

Charlesworth, Hilary, *What are 'Women's International Human Rights'*, in Rebecca J. Cook, ed., HUMAN RIGHTS OF WOMEN: NATIONAL AND INTERNATIONAL PERSPECTIVES (Philadelphia: University of Pennsylvania Press, 1994), pp. 58-84.

Chelala, Cesar *A critical move against female genital mutilation*, Populi, March/April 1998, pp. 13-15.

Chimhundu, Herbert, *Sexuality and Socialisation in Shona Praises and Lyrics*, in Graham Furniss and Liz Gunner, eds., POWER, MARGINALITY AND AFRICAN ORAL LITERATURE (Cambridge: Cambridge University Press, 1995), pp. 147-161.

Chodorow, Nancy J., FEMINISM AND PSYCHOANALYTIC THEORY (New Haven: Yale University Press, 1989).

Clapham, Andrew, HUMAN RIGHTS IN THE PRIVATE SPHERE (Oxford: Clarendon Press, 1993).

Cleve, M., THE GIANTS OF PRE-SOPHISTIC GREEK PHILOSOPHY, Volume II (The Hague: Martinus Nijhoff, 1969).

Cochrane, Susan Hill, EDUCATION AND FERTILITY: WHAT DO WE REALLY KNOW?, World Bank Occasional Papers, No. 26 (Baltimore: Johns Hopkins University Press, 1979).

Selected Bibliography

Cook, Rebecca J., WOMEN'S HEALTH AND HUMAN RIGHTS (Geneva: World Health Organisation, 1994).

___, *State Accountability under the Convention on the Elimination of All Forms of Discrimination against Women*, in Rebecca J. Cook, ed., HUMAN RIGHTS OF WOMEN: NATIONAL AND INTERNATIONAL PERSPECTIVES (Philadelphia: University of Pennsylvania Press, 1994), pp. 228-257.

Coomaraswamy, Radhika, *Ethnicity and Patriarchy in the Third World*, in Margaret Schuler, ed., EMPOWERMENT AND THE LAW: STRATEGIES OF THIRD WORLD WOMEN (Washington, D.C.: OEF International, 1986), pp. 94-109.

Coquery-Vidrovitch, Catherine, AFRICAN WOMEN: A MODERN HISTORY (Oxford: Westview Press, 1994).

Correa, Sonia, POPULATION AND REPRODUCTIVE RIGHTS: FEMINIST PERSPECTIVES FROM THE SOUTH (London: Zed Books Ltd., 1994).

Dankwa, Victor, Cees Flinterman and Scott Leckie, *Commentary on the Maastricht Guidelines on Violations of Economic, Social and Cultural Rights*, in Theo C. van Boven, Cees Flinterman and Ingrid Westendorp, eds., THE MAASTRICHT GUIDELINES ON VIOLATIONS OF ECONOMIC, SOCIAL AND CULTURAL RIGHTS, SIM Special, No. 20, 1998, pp. 13-34.

Dankwa, E.V.O., *Conference on regional systems of human rights protection in Africa, the Americas and Europe*, Human Rights Law Journal, Vol. 13, Nos. 7-8, 1992, pp. 314-317.

___ and Cees Flinterman, *Commentary by the Rapporteurs on the Nature and Scope of States Parties' Obligations*, Human Rights Quarterly, Vol. 9, No. 2, 1987, pp. 136-146.

Dator, Jim, *Loose Connections: A Vision of a Transformational Society*, in Eleonora Masini, ed., VISIONS OF DESIRABLE SOCIETIES (Oxford: Pergamon Press, 1983), pp. 25-45.

Datta, Bishakha and Geetanjali Misra, *Advocacy for Sexual and Reproductive Health: The Challenge in India*, Reproductive Health Matters, Vol. 8, No. 16, 2000, pp. 24-34.

Datta, Vishwa Nath, A HISTORICAL, SOCIAL AND PHILOSOPHICAL ENQUIRY INTO THE HINDU RITE OF WIDOW BURINING (New Delhi: Manohar, 1988).

de Gaay Fortman, Bastiaan, *The Dialectics of Western Law in a Non-Western World*, in Jan Berting et al., eds., HUMAN RIGHTS IN A PLURALIST WORLD: INDIVIDUALS AND COLLECTIVITIES (Westport and London: Meckler, 1990) pp. 237-250.

de Wolf, Antenor Hallo, *Panel Discussion: Implementing Women's Rights at the National, Regional and International Levels*, Africa Legal Aid Quarterly, October-December 1997, pp.33-35.

Diagne, Sény, *Defending Women's Rights - Facts and Challenges in Francophone Africa*, in J. Kerr, ed., OURS BY RIGHT: WOMEN'S RIGHTS AS HUMAN RIGHTS (London: Zed Books Ltd., 1993), pp. 43-51.

Dorsey, Gray L., *Towards World Perspectives*, in S.A. Vojcanin, ed., LAW, CULTURE AND VALUES (London: Transaction Publishers, 1990), pp. 5-28.

Dolphyne, Florence, THE EMANCIPATION OF WOMEN: AN AFRICAN PERSPECTIVE (Accra: Ghana University Press, 1991).

Donnelly, Jack, UNIVERSAL HUMAN RIGHTS IN THEORY AND PRACTICE (Ithaca: Cornell University Press, 1989).

___, *Human Rights and Human Dignity: An Analytic Critique of Non-Western Conceptions of Human Rights*, The American Political Science Review, Vol. 76, No. 2, 1982, pp. 303-316.

Dow, Unity, Sheryl Stumbras and Sue Tatten, *Women's Empowerment Initiatives from a Grassroots Level*, in George J. Andreopoulus and Richard Pierre Claude, eds., HUMAN RIGHTS EDUCATION FOR THE TWENTY-FIRST CENTURY (Philadelphia: University of Pennsylvania Press, 1997), pp. 455-468.

Drucker, Allison R., *The Influence of Western Women on the Anti-Footbinding Movement 1840-1911*, in Richard W. Guisso & Stanley Johannesen, eds., WOMEN IN CHINA: CURRENT DIRECTIONS IN HISTORICAL SCHOLARSHIP (Youngstown, N.Y.: Philo Press, 1981).

Durkheim, Émile, DE LA DIVISION DU TRAVAIL SOCIAL *[trans. The Division of Labor in Society]* (New York: The Macmillan company, 1933).

Dworkin, Ronald, TAKING RIGHTS SERIOUSLY (London: Duckworth, 1977).

El Bushra, J., *Economic interest groups and their relevance for women's development*, YEARBOOK OF CO-OPERATIVE ENTERPRISE 1993 (London: ACORD, 1993), pp. 185-195.

El Dareer, Asma A., *Sudan: Custom and Customary Laws*, in Margaret Schuler, ed., EMPOWERMENT AND THE LAW: STRATEGIES OF THIRD WORLD WOMEN (Washington, D.C.: OEF International, 1986), pp. 135-139.

___, WOMAN, WHY DO YOU WEEP? CIRCUMCISION AND ITS CONSEQUENCES (London, Zed Press, 1982).

Edwards, Carolyn Pope, *Morality and Change: Family Unity and Paternal Authority among Kipsigis and Abaluyia Elders and Students*, in Thomas S. Weisner, Candice Bradley and Philip L. Kilbride, eds., AFRICAN FAMILIES AND THE CRISIS OF SOCIAL CHANGE (London: Bergin & Garvey, 1997), pp. 51-82.

Eide, Asbjørn, *Realization of Social and Economic Rights and the Minimum Threshold Approach*, Human Rights Law Journal, Vol. 10, Nos. 1-2, 1989, pp. 35-51.

Eliah, Elaine, *REACHing for a Healthier Future*, Populi, March 1996, pp. 12-16.

El-Saadawi, Nawal, THE HIDDEN FACE OF EVE: WOMEN IN THE ARAB WORLD (London: Zed Press, 1980).

Ezeh, Alex Chika, *The influence of spouses over each other's contraceptive attitudes in Ghana*, Studies in Family Planning, Vol. 24, No. 3, 1993, pp. 163-174.

Falk, Richard, *A Half Century of Human Rights: Geopolitics and Values*, in Burns H. Weston and Stephen P. Marks, eds., THE FUTURE OF INTERNATIONAL HUMAN RIGHTS (Ardsley, New York: Transnational Publishers, Inc., 1999), pp. 1-24.

Fallon, Kathleen M., *Education and Perceptions of Social Status and Power among Women in Larteh, Ghana*, Africa Today, Vol. 46, No. 2, 1999, pp. 66-91.

Fapohunda, Eleanor R. and Micheal P. Todaro, *Family structure, implicit contracts, and the demand for children in Southern Nigeria*, Population and Development Review, Vol. 14, No. 4, 1988, pp. 571-594.

Farley, T.M.M., *The WHO Standardized Investigation of the Infertile Couple*, in S. Shan Ratnam et al., eds., INFERTILITY: MALE AND FEMALE - THE PROCEEDINGS OF THE 12TH WORLD CONGRESS ON FERTILITY AND STERILITY, SINGAPORE (Geneva: WHO, 1986), pp. 123-135.

Fathalla, Mahmoud F., *The Impact of Reproductive Subordination on Women's Health*, The American University Law Review, Vol. 44, No. 4, 1995, pp. 1179-1189.

Feldman, Rayah, *Women's groups and women's subordination: An analysis of policies towards rural women in Kenya*, Review of African Political Economy, No. 27/28, 1984, pp. 67-85.

Fitzpatrick, Joan, *The Use of International Human Rights Norms to Combat Violence against Women*, in Rebecca J. Cook, ed., HUMAN RIGHTS OF WOMEN: NATIONAL AND

INTERNATIONAL PERSPECTIVES (Philadelphia: University of Pennsylvania Press, 1994), pp. 532-571.

Freedman, Lynn P. *Reflection on Emerging Frameworks of Health and Human Rights*, in Jonathan M. Mann, Sofia Gruskin, Michael A. Grodin, George J. Annas, HEALTH AND HUMAN RIGHTS: A READER (New York: Routledge, 1999), pp. 227-252.00

Gage, Anastasia J., A. Elisabeth Sommerfelt and Andrea L. Piani, HOUSEHOLD STRUCTURE, SOCIOECONOMIC LEVEL, AND CHILD HEALTH IN SUB-SAHARAN AFRICA, DHS Analytical Reports, No. 1 (Calverton, Maryland: Macro International Inc., 1996).

Gamewell, Mary Ninde, NEW LIFE CURRENTS IN CHINA (New York: Missionary Education Movements of the U.S. and Canada, 1919).

Gellner, Ernest, LEGITIMISATION OF BELIEF (Cambridge, Cambridge University Press, 1974).

Gierycz, Dorota, *Education on the Human Rights of Women as a Vehicle for Change*, in George J. Andreopoulus and Richard Pierre Claude, eds., HUMAN RIGHTS EDUCATION FOR THE TWENTY-FIRST CENTURY (Philadelphia: University of Pennsylvania Press, 1997), pp. 96-118.

Gilbert, Michelle, *The Christian executioner: Christianity and chieftancy as rivals*, Journal of Religion in Africa, Vol. 25, Fasc. 4, 1995, pp. 347-386.

Gillespie, Alexander, *Ideas of Human Rights in Antiquity*, Netherlands Quarterly of Human Rights, Vol. 17, No. 3, 1999, pp. 233-258.

Glendon, Mary Ann, RIGHTS TALK: THE IMPOVERISHMENT OF POLITICAL DISCOURSE (New York: The Free Press, 1991).

Goonesekere, Savitri, *Legal Status of Women*, in Margaret Schuler, ed., EMPOWERMENT AND THE LAW: STRATEGIES OF THIRD WORLD WOMEN (Washington, D.C.: OEF International, 1986), pp. 52-59.

Graham, Wendy J. and Susan F. Murray, *A Question of Survival: A Review of Safe Motherhood in Kenya*, Reproductive Health Matters (Special Issue on Safe Motherhood Initiatives: Critical Issues) 1999, pp. 102-118.

Grant, Judith, ed., FUNDAMENTAL FEMINISM (New York and London: Routledge, 1993).

Green, Ronald M., RELIGION AND MORAL REASON: A NEW METHOD FOR COMPARATIVE STUDY (Oxford: Oxford University Press, 1988).

Gunning, Isabelle, *Arrogant Perception, World Travelling and Multicultural Feminism: The Case of Female Genital Surgeries*, Columbia Human Rights Law Review, Vol. 23, 1991, pp. 238ff.

Gwako, Edwin, *Continuity and Change in the Practice of Clitoridectomy in Kenya*, Journal of Modern African Studies, Vol. 33, No. 2, pp. 333-337.

Hakansson, N. Thomas and Robert A. Le Vine, *Gender and Life-Course Strategies among the Gusii*, in Thomas S. Weisner, Candice Bradley and Philip L. Kilbride, eds., AFRICAN FAMILIES AND THE CRISIS OF SOCIAL CHANGE (London: Bergin & Garvey, 1997), pp. 253-267.

Halim, Asma Mohamed Abdel, *Tools of Suppression*, in Center for Women's Global Leadership, GENDER VIOLENCE AND WOMEN'S HUMAN RIGHTS IN AFRICA (New York: Center for Women's Global Leadership, 1994), pp. 21-29.

Haraway, Donna, *Situated Knowledges in Feminism and the Privilege of the Partial Perspective*, Feminist Studies, Vol. 14, 1988, pp. 575-599.

Harding, Sandra, THE SCIENCE QUESTION IN FEMINISM (Ithaca, N.Y.: Cornell University Press, 1986).
Hare, R. M., MORAL THINKING: ITS LEVELS, METHODS AND POINTS (Oxford: Clarendon Press, 1981).
Hart, H.L.A., *Bentham on Legal Rights*, in A.W.B. Simpson, ed., OXFORD ESSAYS IN JURISPRUDENCE, 2nd series (Oxford: Clarendon Press, 1973).
___, *Are There any Natural Rights?*, The Philosophical Review, Vol. 65, 1955, pp. 175-191.
Henderson, Kathy, *Hope from Soaps*, Ford Foundation Report, Fall 2000, pp. 10-13.
Herkovits, Melville J., CULTURAL RELATIVISM: PERSPECTIVES IN CULTURAL PLURALISM (New York: Vintage, 1973).
Herodotus, THE HISTORIES (Reproduced by Harmondsworth: Penguin Classics, 1954).
Heward, C., *Introduction: The New Discourses of Gender, Education and Development*, in Christine Heward and Sheila Bunwaree, eds., GENDER, EDUCATION AND DEVELOPMENT: BEYOND ACCESS TO POWER (London and New York: Zed Books, 1999), pp. 1-14.
Higgins, Tracy, *Anti-Essentialism, Relativism, and Human Rights*, Harvard Women's Law Journal, Vol. 19, 1996, pp. 89ff.
Hogan, Dennis P., Betemariam Berhanu and Assefa Hailemariam, *Household Organisation, Women's Autonomy, and Contraceptive Behavior in Southern Ethiopia*, Studies in Family Planning, Vol. 30, No. 4, 1999, pp. 302-314.
Hosken, Fran P., STOP FEMALE GENITAL MUTILATION: WOMEN SPEAK FACTS AND ACTIONS (Lexington, MA: Women's International Network News, 1995).
___, THE HOSKEN REPORT, 4th ed. (Lexington, MA: Women's International Network News, 1993).
Howard, Rhoda E., *Women's Rights, Group Rights and the Erosion of Liberalism*, in Cyril Levitt, Scott Davies and Neil McLaughlin, eds., MISTAKEN IDENTITIES (New York: Peter Lang, 1999), pp. 130-144.
___, HUMAN RIGHTS AND THE SEARCH FOR COMMUNITY (Boulder, Colorado: Westview Press, 1995).
___, *Cultural Absolutism and the Nostalgia for Community*, Human Rights Quarterly, Vol. 15, 1993, pp. 315-338.
___, *Women's Rights and the Right to Development*, in Ronald Cohen, Goran Hyden and Winston P. Nagan, eds., HUMAN RIGHTS AND GOVERNANCE IN AFRICA (Gainesville: University Press of Florida, 1993), pp. 111-138.
___, *Dignity, Community and Human Rights*, in A.A. An-Na'im, ed., HUMAN RIGHTS IN CROSS-CULTURAL PERSPECTIVE: A QUEST FOR CONSENSUS (Philadelphia: University of Pennsylvania Press, 1992), pp. 81-102.
___, *Group versus Individual Dignity in the African Debate on Human Rights*, in Abdullahi A. An-Na'im and Francis M. Deng, eds., HUMAN RIGHTS IN AFRICA: CROSS-CULTURAL PERSPECTIVES (Washington, D.C.: Brookings Institute, 1990), pp. 159-183.
___, HUMAN RIGHTS IN COMMONWEALTH AFRICA (Totowa, N.J.: Rowman & Littlefield, 1986).
___, *Women's Rights in English-Speaking Sub-Saharan Africa*, in Claude E. Welch, Jr. and Ronald I. Meltzer, eds., HUMAN RIGHTS AND DEVELOPMENT IN AFRICA (Albany: State University of New York Press, 1986), pp. 46-74.

___, *Human Rights and Personal Law: Women in sub-Saharan Africa*, Issue, Vol. 12, Nos. 1 and 2, 1982, pp. 45-52.

Howland, Courtney W., *The Challenge of Religious Fundamentalism to the Liberty and Equality of Women: An Analysis under the United Nations Charter*, Columbia Journal of International Law, Vol. 35, No. 2, 1997, pp. 271-377.

Huntington, Samuel, THE CLASH OF THE CIVILIZATIONS (London: Simon and Schuster UK Ltd., 1996).

Hyde, Elizabeth, *The African woman and nutrition* in IAC, REPORT ON THE REGIONAL CONFERENCE ON TRADITIONAL PRACTICES AFFECTING THE HEALTH OF WOMEN AND CHILDREN IN AFRICA (Addis Ababa: IAC, 1991), pp. 131-132.

Ibhawoh, Bonny, *Cultural Relativism and Human Rights: Reconsidering the Africanist Discourse*, Netherlands Quarterly of Human Rights, Vol. 19, No. 1, 2001, pp. 43-62.

___, *Between Culture and Constitution: Evaluating the Cultural Legitimacy of Human Rights in the African State*, Human Rights Quarterly, Vol. 22, No. 3, 2000, pp. 838-860.

Idowu, E. Bolaji, AFRICAN TRADITIONAL RELIGION: A DEFINITION (Ibadan, Nigeria: Fountain Press, 1973).

Ilumoka, Adetoun O., *African Women's Economic, Social, and Cultural Rights – Toward a Relevant Theory and Practice*, in Rebecca J. Cook, ed., HUMAN RIGHTS OF WOMEN: NATIONAL AND INTERNATIONAL PERSPECTIVES (Philadelphia: University of Pennsylvania Press, 1994), pp. 307-325.

Inter-African Committee on Traditional Practices Affecting the Health of Women and Children (IAC), RIGHTS AND WIDOWHOOD RITES IN NIGERIA (Lagos: IAC, 2000).

___, FOURTH REGIONAL CONFERENCE/GENERAL ASSEMBLY, 17-21 NOVEMBER, DAKAR, SENEGAL (Addis Ababa: IAC, 1997).

___, SYMPOSIUM FOR LEGISLATORS ON THE DRAFTING OF AN AFRICAN DECLARATION ON VIOLENCE AGAINST WOMEN, 10-12 SEPTERMBER 1997, ADDIS ABABA, ETHIOPIA (Addis Ababa: IAC, 1997).

___, SITUATION OF WOMEN IN AFRICA IN THE CONTEXT OF FAMILY HEALTH (paper delivered to the Fifth Conference of African Ministers of Health (CAMH V), 24-28 April 1995.

___, REPORT OF THE INTER-AFRICAN COMMITTEE ON TRADITIONAL PRACTICES AFFECTING THE HEALTH OF WOMEN AND CHILDREN, (Geneva: IAC, 1994).

___, REPORT ON THE REGIONAL CONFERENCE ON TRADITIONAL PRACTICES AFFECTING THE HEALTH OF WOMEN AND CHILDREN IN AFRICA, 19-24 NOVEMBER 1990, ADDIS ABABA, ETHIOPIA (Addis Ababa: IAC, 1991).

International Reproductive Rights and Research Action Group (IRRRAG), *Women's Wit over Men's* in R. Petchesky and K. Judd, eds., NEGOTIATING REPRODUCTIVE RIGHTS: WOMEN'S PERSPECTIVES ACROSS COUNTRIES AND CULTURES (London: Zed Books, 1998).

Itumbi Nyamu, Celestine, *The International Human Rights Regime and Rural Women in Kenya*, East African Journal of Peace and Human Rights, Vol. 6, No. 1, 2000, pp. 1-33.

Jayawardene, Kumari, FEMINISM AND NATIONALISM IN THE THIRD WORLD (The Hague: ISS, 1982).

Jensen, Marianne and Karin Poulsen, HUMAN RIGHTS AND CULTURAL CHANGE: WOMEN IN AFRICA (Copenhagen: The Danish Centre for Human Rights, 1993).

Jere-Malanda, Regina, *Wife by Abduction*, New Africa, No. 376, July/August 1999, pp. 46-47.

Jowett, B., THE DIALOGUES OF PLATO, Vol. I (Oxford: Oxford University Press, 1931).
Kapinga, Antoinette, *Freedom for African Women?*, The Courier, No. 169, May-June 1998, p. 77.
Kassindja, Fauyiza, DO THEY HEAR YOU WHEN YOU CRY? (New York: Dell Publishing, 1998).
Kenyatta, Jomo, FACING MOUNT KENYA: THE TRIBAL LIFE OF THE GIKUYU (London: Secker and Warburg, 1938, edited and reproduced in 1953).
Kilbride, Philip L. and Janet C. Kilbride, "Stigma Role Overload, and Delocalization among Contemporary Kenyan Women, in Thomas S. Weisner, Candice Bradley and Philip L. Kilbride, eds., AFRICAN FAMILIES AND THE CRISIS OF SOCIAL CHANGE (London: Bergin & Garvey, 1997), pp. 208-225.
Kim, Nancy *Toward a Feminist Theory of Human Rights: Straddling the Fence between Western Imperialism and Uncritical Absolutism*, Columbia Human Rights Law Review, Vol. 25, 1993.
Kishwar, Madhu, *Introduction*, in M. Kishwar and Ruth Vanita, eds., IN SEARCH OF ANSWERS (London: Zed Press, 1984).
Kissling, Frances *The Challenge of Christianity (Forum on Religious and Cultural Rights)*, American University Law Review, Vol. 44, No. 4, 1995, pp. 1345-1350.
Kodjo, Edem, *The African Charter on Human and Peoples' Rights*, Human Rights Law Journal, Vol. 11, Nos. 3-4, 1990, pp. 271-283.
Koso-Thomas, Olayinka, THE CIRCUMCISION OF WOMEN: A STRATEGY FOR ERADICATION (London: Zed Books, 1987).
Lawson, Agathe Latré-Gato, *Women and AIDS in Africa: Sociocultural Dimensions of the HIV/AIDS Epidemic*, International Social Science Journal, Vol. 161, September 1999, pp. 391-400.
Le Vine, Robert A. and Barbara B. Le Vine, NYANSONGO: A GUSII COMMUNITY IN KENYA (New York: Wiley, 1996).
Leary, Virginia, *The Effect of Western Perspectives on International Human Rights*, in Abdullahi A. An-Na'im and Francis M. Deng, eds., HUMAN RIGHTS IN AFRICA: CROSS-CULTURAL PERSPECTIVES (Washington, D.C.: Brookings Institute, 1990), pp. 15-30.
Levy, Howard Seymour, THE LOTUS LOVERS: THE COMPLETE HISTORY OF THE CURIOUS EROTIC CUSTOM OF FOOTBINDING IN CHINA (Buffalo, N.Y.: Prometheus Books, 1992).
Lewis, C.S., THE ABOLITION OF MAN (1943) (reproduced in London: Fount Paperbacks, 1978).
Li, Anshan, *Asafo and destoolment in colonial southern Ghana, 1900-1953*, International Journal of African Historical Studies, Vol. 28, No. 2, 1995, pp. 327-357.
Lima da Costa, Maria, *Activity Report of the Union Démocratique des Femmes Guinéennes* in IAC, REPORT ON THE REGIONAL CONFERENCE ON TRADITIONAL PRACTICES AFFECTING THE HEALTH OF WOMEN AND CHILDREN IN AFRICA (Addis Ababa: IAC, 1991), pp. 214-216.
Lissner, Craig and Eva Weissman, *How much does safe motherhood cost?*, World Health, No. 1 January-February 1998.
Little, David, *A Christian Perspective on Human Rights*, in Abdullahi A. An-Na'im and Francis M. Deng, eds., HUMAN RIGHTS IN AFRICA: CROSS-CULTURAL PERSPECTIVES (Washington, D.C.: Brookings Institute, 1990), pp. 59-103.

Lloyd, Cynthia B. and Anastasia J. Gage-Brandon, *Women's Role in Maintaining Households: Family Welfare and Sexual Equality in Ghana*, Population Studies, Vol. 47, No. 1, pp. 115-131.

Lloyd of Hampstead, Lord, INTRODUCTION TO JURISPRUDENCE, 4th ed. (London: Stevens and Sons, 1979).

Locke, John, THE SECOND TREATISE OF GOVERNMENT (1690) (reproduced with amendments in Cambridge: Cambridge University Press, 1963).

Maddock, Su, CHALLENGING WOMEN: GENDER, CULTURE AND ORGANISATION (London: Sage Publications, 1999).

Mamdani, Mahmood, BEYOND RIGHTS TALK AND CULTURE TALK (Cape Town, South Africa: David Philip Publishers, 2000).

Mani, Lata, CONTENTIOUS TRADITIONS: THE DEBATE ON SATI IN COLONIAL INDIA (Berkeley: University of California Press, 1998).

Mann, Jonathan M., S. Gruskin, M.A. Grodin, G.J. Annas, *Introduction*, in Jonathan M. Mann, Sofia Gruskin, Michael A. Grodin, George J. Annas, HEALTH AND HUMAN RIGHTS: A READER (New York: Routledge, 1999), pp. 1-3.

Martin, J. Paul, Cosmas Gitta and Tokunbo Ige, *Promoting Human Rights Education in a Marginalized Africa*, in George J. Andreopoulus and Richard Pierre Claude, eds., HUMAN RIGHTS EDUCATION FOR THE TWENTY-FIRST CENTURY (Philadelphia: University of Pennsylvania Press, 1997), pp. 436-454.

Mason, Karen Oppenheim, *The Impact of Women's Social Position on Fertility in Developing countries*, Sociological Forum, Vol. 2, No. 4, 1987, pp. 718-745.

Mayambala, Esther, WOMEN AND HIV TRANSMISSION IN UGANDA: AN EVALUATION OF SAFER SEX STRATEGIES (unpublished manuscript). Georgetown University Law Center, Washington D.C., 1994.

Mbaye, Kéba, LES DROITS DE L'HOMME EN AFRIQUE (Paris: Pedone, 1992).

Mckean, Warwick, EQUALITY AND DISCRIMINATION UNDER INTERNATIONAL LAW (Oxford: Clarendon Press, 1983).

Meekers, Dominique and M. Oladosu, *Spousal Communication and Family Planning Decision-Making in Nigeria*, in POPULATION RESEARCH INSTITUTE WORKING PAPERS IN AFRICAN DEMOGRAPHY, NO. AD96-03 (University Park, PA: The Pennsylvania State University, 1996).

Meillassoux, Claude, *La conquête de l'aînesse [trans. The conquest of the older]*, in Claudine Attias-Donfut and Léopold Rosenmayr, eds., VIEILLIR EN AFRIQUE (Paris: Presses universitaires de France, 1994), pp. 49-67.

Meintjes, Garth, *Human Rights Education as Empowerment: Reflections on Pedagogy*, in George J. Andreopoulus and Richard Pierre Claude, eds., HUMAN RIGHTS EDUCATION FOR THE TWENTY-FIRST CENTURY (Philadelphia: University of Pennsylvania Press, 1997), pp. 64-79.

Meintjes, Graeme, *Challenge to Tradition: Medical Complications of Traditional Xhosa Circumcision*, INDICATOR, Vol. 15, No. 13, 1998, pp. 67-73.

Mhloyi, Marvellous, *Sociocultural Milieu, Women's Status and Family Planning*, in United Nations, FAMILY PLANNING, HEALTH AND FAMILY WELL-BEING (New York: United Nations, 1996).

Migere, Nsolo N.J., *Rural-urban migration and urbanization in Zambia during the colonial and postcolonial periods*, in Ezekiel Kalipeni, ed., POPULATION GROWTH AND ENVIRON-

MENTAL DEGRADATION IN SOUTHERN AFRICA (Boulder, Colorado: Lynne Rienner, 1994), pp. 147-177.
Miller, F., *Aristotle and the Origins of Natural Rights*, Review of Metaphysics, Vol. 49, 1996.
Minority Rights Group International, BROKEN BODIES, SHATTERED MINDS: THE TORTURE OF WOMEN WORLDWIDE (London: MRGI, 2001).
Mirsky, Judy and Marty Radlett, eds., NO PARADISE YET: THE WORLD'S WOMEN FACE THE NEW CENTURY (London: Zed Books, 2000).
Murray, Rachel, *Decisions and Reports of the African Commission on Human and Peoples' Rights, Banjul*, Human Rights Law Journal, Vol. 18, Nos. 1-4, 1997, pp. 28-36.
Naggita, Esther Damalie, *Why Men Come Out Ahead: The Legal Regime and the Protection and Realization of Women's Rights in Uganda*, East African Journal of Peace and Human Rights, Vol. 6, No. 1, 2000, pp. 34-65.
Narasimhan, Sakuntala, SATI: WIDOW BURNING IN INDIA (New Delhi: Thousand Oaks/ California: Sage Publications, 1990).
National Research Council, Committee on Population, FACTORS AFFECTING CONTRACEPTIVE USE IN SUB-SAHARAN AFRICA (Washington, D.C.: National Academy Press, 1993).
Netherlands Advisory Council on International Affairs (AIV), UNIVERSALITY OF HUMAN RIGHTS AND CULTURAL DIVERSITY, Series No. 4 (The Hague: AIV, 1998).
Nhlapo, Thandabantu, *The African Customary Law of Marriage and the Rights Conundrum*, in Mahmood Mamdani, ed., BEYOND RIGHTS TALK AND CULTURE TALK (Cape Town, South Africa: David Philip Publishers, 2000), pp. 136-148.
___, *The African Charter and Women's Human Rights: What Next?*, African Legal Aid Quarterly, July-September 1996, pp. 10-13.
___, *International Protection of Human Rights and the Family: African Variations on a Common Theme*, International Journal of Law and the Family, Vol. 3, 1989.
Nichol. J., *The Clitoris Martyr*, World Health, 6 May 1969, pp. 59-65.
Nnaemeka, Obioma, *Introduction: Imag(in)ing Knowledge, Power, and Subversion in the Margins*, in O. Nnaemeka, ed., THE POLITICS OF (M)OTHERING: WOMANHOOD, IDENTITY, AND RESISTANCE IN AFRICAN LITERATURE (London/New York: Routledge, 1997), pp. 1-7.
Nowak, Manfred, U.N. COVENANT ON CIVIL AND POLITICAL RIGHTS: CCPR COMMENTARY (Kehl: N.P. Engel, Publisher, 1993).
Ntarangwi, Mwenda G., *Feminism and Masculinity in an African Capitalist Context: The Case of Kenya*, SAFERE *(South African Feminist Review)*, Vol. 3, No. 1, 1998, pp. 19-31.
Nussbaum, Martha C., WOMEN AND HUMAN DEVELOPMENT: THE CAPABILITIES APPROACH (Cambridge: Cambridge University Press, 2000).
___, *Compassion: The Basic Social Emotion*, Journal of Social Philosophy and Policy, Vol. 13, No. 1, Winter 1996.
___, *Skepticism about Practical Reason in Literature and the Law*, Harvard Law Review, Vol. 107, 1994, pp. 714-728.
___, *Human Functioning and Social Justice: In Defense of Aristotelian Essentialism*, Political Theory, Vol. 20, No. 2, 1992, pp. 202-246.
Nyamongo, Isaac, *Anthropology: A Social Science in the Control of HIV Transmission in Africa*, African Anthropology, Vol. 2, No. 1, 1995, pp. 45-57.

Selected Bibliography

Nzewi, Uche, University of Nigeria at Nsukka, Nigeria, *The Impact of Education on Nigerian Women's Decision Making on Reproductive Health* (lecture presented at Session VI-II: Educating Women for Development and Health Care in Nigeria). Second International Conference on Women in Africa and the African Diaspora: Indiana University, Indianapolis, USA, 23-27 October 1998.

Obbo, Christine, *What Women Can Do: AIDS Crisis Management in Uganda*, ed. Deborah Fahy Bryceson, WOMEN WIELDING THE HOE: LESSONS FROM RURAL AFRICA FOR FEMINIST THEORY AND DEVELOPMENT PRACTICE (Oxford/Washington D.C.: Berg Publishers, 1995), pp. 165-178.

Obermeyer, Carla Makhlouf, *Female Genital Surgeries: The Known, the Unknown, and the Unknowable*, Medical Anthropology Quarterly, Vol. 13, No. 1, 1999, pp. 79-106.

Odaga, Adhiambo and Ward Heneveld, GIRLS AND SCHOOLS IN SUB-SAHARAN AFRICA: FROM ANALYSIS TO ACTION, World Bank Technical Paper No. 298 (Washington, D.C.: World Bank, 1995).

Odinkalu, Chidi Anselm, *Why More Africans Don't Use Human Rights Language*, Human Rights Dialogue, Series 2, No. 1, Winter 2000, pp. 3-4.

Ojo, Olusola, *Understanding Human Rights in Africa*, in Jan Berting et al., eds., HUMAN RIGHTS IN A PLURALIST WORLD (Westport/ London: Meckler, 1990), pp. 115-123.

Oldenburg, Veena Talwar, *The Roop Kanwar Case: Femininst Responses*, in John Stratton Hawley, ed., SATI, THE BLESSING AND THE CURSE: THE BURNING OF WIVES IN INDIA (Oxford: Oxford University Press, 1994).

Oppong, Christine and Katherine Abu, SEVEN ROLES OF WOMEN: IMPACT OF EDUCATION, MIGRATION AND EMPLOYMENT ON GHANAIAN MOTHERS (Geneva: International Labour Office, 1987).

Oueguergouz, Fatsah, LA CHARTE AFRICAINE DES DROITS DE L'HOMME ET DES PEUPLES (Geneva: Institut universitaire des hautes etudes internationals, 1991).

Oyewumi, Oyeronke, THE INVENTION OF WOMEN: MAKING AN AFRICAN SENSE OF WESTERN GENDER DISCOURSES (Minneapolis: University of Minnesota Press, 1997).

Packer, Corinne, *Preventing Adolescent Pregnancy: The Protection Offered by International Human Rights Law*, International Journal of Children's Rights, Vol. 5, No. 1, 1997, pp. 47-76.

___, THE RIGHT TO REPRODUCTIVE CHOICE: A STUDY IN INTERNATIONAL LAW (Åbo/Turku: Institute for Human Rights, Åbo Akademi University, 1996).

Perry, Michael J., *Are Human Rights Universal? The Relativist Challenge and Related Matters*, Human Rights Quarterly, Vol. 19, No. 3, 1997, pp. 461-509.

Population Reference Bureau (PRB), 2001 WORLD POPULATION DATA SHEETS on website: http://www.prb.org/Content/Naviga...1_World_Population_Data_Sheet.html.

Presser, H. B. and G. Sen, eds., WOMEN'S EMPOWERMENT AND DEMOGRAPHIC PROCESSES: MOVING BEYOND CAIRO (Oxford: Oxford University Press, 2000).

Ramcharan, B.G., *The Travaux Préparatoires of the African Commission on Human and Peoples' Rights*, Human Rights Law Journal, Vol. 13, Nos. 7-8, 1992, pp. 307-313.

Rawls, John, A THEORY OF JUSTICE (Oxford: Clarendon Press, 1972).

Risse, Thomas and Kathryn Sikkink, *The Socialization of Human Rights Norms* in Thomas Risse, Stephen C. Ropp and Kathryn Sikkink, eds., THE POWER OF HUMAN RIGHTS: INTERNATIONAL NORMS AND DOMESTIC CHANGE (Cambridge: Cambridge University Press, 1999), pp. 1-38.

Robertson, A. H., HUMAN RIGHTS IN THE WORLD, 4th ed. (Manchester: Manchester University Press, 1996).
Rose, Susan D., *Christian Fundamentalism: Patriarchy, Sexuality, and Human Rights*, in Courtney W. Howland, ed., RELIGIOUS FUNDAMENTALISM AND THE HUMAN RIGHTS OF WOMEN (New York: St. Martin's Press, 1999), pp. 9-20.
Rousseau, Jean-Jacques, DU CONTRAT SOCIAL (1762) (reproduced in Paris: Collection Pluriel, 1978).
Sackey, Brigid, *Spiritual churches in Kumasi 1920-1986: some observations*, Africana Marburgensia, Vol. 24, No. 2, 1991, pp. 32-49.
Salway, Sarah, *How attitudes toward family planning and discussion between wives and husbands affect contraceptive use in Ghana*, International Family Planning Perspectives, Vol. 20, No. 2, 1994, pp. 44-47.
Sanderson, Lillian Passmore, AGAINST THE MUTILATION OF WOMEN: THE STRUGGLE TO END UNNECESSARY SUFFERING (London: Ithaca, 1981).
Sangree, Walter H., *Pronatalism and the Elderly in Tiriki, Kenya*, in Thomas S. Weisner, Candice Bradley and Philip L. Kilbride, eds., AFRICAN FAMILIES AND THE CRISIS OF SOCIAL CHANGE (London: Bergin & Garvey, 1997), pp. 184- 207.
Saunders, J.L., ed., GREEK AND ROMAN PHILOSOPHY AFTER ARISTOTLE: READINGS IN THE HISTORY OF PHILOSOPHY (New York: The Free Press, 1966).
Schoenmaeckers, Ronnie, Iqbal H. Shah, Ronald Lesthaeghe, and Oleko Tambashe, in Hillary Page and Ronald Lesthaeghe, eds., CHILD-SPACING IN TROPICAL AFRICA: TRADITIONS AND CHANGE (London: Academic Press, 1981).
Schuler, Margaret and Sakutala Kadirgamar Rajasingham, *Legal Literacy*, in M. Schuler and S.K. Rajasingham, LEGAL LITERACY: A TOOL FOR WOMEN'S EMPOWERMENT (New York: UNIFEM/OEF International, 1992), pp. 21-72.
Schuler, Margaret, *Conceptualizing and Exploring Issues and Strategies*, in Margaret Schuler, ed., EMPOWERMENT AND THE LAW: STRATEGIES OF THIRD WORLD WOMEN (Washington, D.C.: OEF International, 1986), pp. 13-38.
Sedler, Robert A. *The Role of 'Intent' in Discrimination Analysis*, in Titia Loenen and Peter R. Rodrigues, eds., NON-DISCRIMINATION LAW: COMPARATIVE PERSPECTIVES (The Hague/London/New York: Kluwer Law International, 1999), pp. 91-103.
Seif El Dawla, Aida, *Reproductive Rights of Egyptian Women: Issues for Debate*, Reproductive Health Matters, Vol. 8, No. 16, 2000, pp. 45-54.
Sen, G., A. Germain and L. Chen, POPULATION POLICIES RECONSIDERED: HEALTH, EMPOWERMENT AND RIGHTS (New York: International Women's Health Coalition, Harvard School of Public Health, 1994).
Shadle, Brett L., *Changing Traditions to Meet Current Altering Conditions: Customary law, African Courts and the rejection of codification in Kenya, 1930-60*, Journal of African History, Vol. 40, 1999, pp. 411-431.
Sharma, Arvind, SATI: HISTORICAL AND PHENOMENOLOGICAL ESSAYS (1988).
Shils, Edward, TRADITION (London/Boston: Faber and Faber, 1981).
Shorter, Aylward, AFRICAN CULTURE AND THE CHRISTIAN CHURCH (London: Geoffrey Chapman, 1973).
___, *Concepts of Social Justice in Traditional Africa* in AFRICAN TRADITIONAL RELIGION on website: http://isizoh.net/afrel/atr-socjustice.htm.

Silk, James, *Traditional Culture and Human Rights*, in Abdullahi A. An-Na'im and Francis M. Deng, eds., HUMAN RIGHTS IN AFRICA: CROSS-CULTURAL PERSPECTIVES (Washington, D.C.: Brookings Institute, 1990), pp. 290-330.

Slack, Alison, *Female Circumcision: A Critical Appraisal*, Human Rights Quarterly, Vol. 10, 1988, pp. 437-477.

Stahl, Ann B., *Valuing the past, envisioning the future: local perspectives on environmental and cultural heritage in Ghana*, in Ismail Serageldin and June Taboroff, eds., CULTURE AND DEVELOPMENT IN AFRICA (Washington, D.C.: World Bank, 1994), pp. 411-424.

Steiner, Henry J. and Philip Alston, INTERNATIONAL HUMAN RIGHTS IN CONTEXT: LAW, POLITICS, MORALS, 2nd ed. (Oxford: Oxford University Press, 2000).

Stromquist, Nelly P., *Romancing the State: Gender and Power in Education*, Comparative Education Review, Vol. 39, No. 4, 1995, pp. 423-454.

Sussman, Erica, *Contending with Culture: An Analysis of the Female Genital Mutilation Act of 1996*, Cornell International Law Journal, Vol. 31, No. 1, 1998, pp. 193-250.

Tahzib-Lie, Bahia G., *Dissenting Women, Religion or Belief, and the State: Contemporary Challenges that Require Attention*, in Tore Lindholm, W. Cole Durham Jr., and Bahia G. Tahzib-Lie, eds., FACILITATING FREEDOM OF RELIGION OR BELIEF: A DESK-BOOK (The Hague/London/NewYork: Kluwer Law International, 2002).

Tahzib, Bahia G., FREEDOM OF RELIGION OR BELIEF: ENSURING INTERNATIONAL LEGAL PROTECTION (The Hague/London/NewYork: Kluwer Law International, 1995), pp. 307-370.

Taiwo, Olukayode O., *Traditional Versus Modern Judicial Practices: A Comparative Analysis of Dispute Resolution among the Yoruba of South-West Nigeria*, Africa Development, Vol. XXIII, No. 2, 1998, pp. 209-226.

Thiam, Awa, BLACK SISTERS, SPEAK OUT: FEMINISM AND OPPRESSION IN BLACK AFRICA (London: Pluto Press, 1986).

Thomas, Louis Vincent, *Vieillesse et mort en Afrique [trans: Aging and death in Africa]*, in Claudine Attias-Donfut and Léopold Rosenmayr, eds., VIEILLIR EN AFRIQUE (Paris: Presses universitaires de France, 1994), pp. 149-167.

Toebes, Brigit C.A., THE RIGHT TO HEALTH AS A HUMAN RIGHT IN INTERNATIONAL LAW (Antwerp/Groningen/Oxford: Intersentia-Hart, 1999).

Tomaševski, Katarina, HUMAN RIGHTS IN POPULATION POLICIES (Lund, Sweden: Omslag Alf Dahlberg, 1994).

Tostan, BREAKTHROUGH IN SENEGAL – ENDING FEMALE GENITAL CUTTING (New York: Population Council, 1999).

Toubia, Nahid, FEMALE GENITAL MUTILATION: A CALL FOR GLOBAL ACTION (New York: Women, Ink., 1993).

Umozurike, U.O., *The African Charter on Human and Peoples' Rights*, American Journal of International Law, Vol. 77, 1983, pp. 902-912.

UNAIDS, WORKSHOP REPORT ON HIV/AIDS AND REPRODUCTIVE HEALTH, 9-11 FEBRUARY 1998, HARARE (SAfAIDS: UNAIDS, 1998).

United Nations, HARMFUL TRADITIONAL PRACTICES AFFECTING THE HEALTH OF WOMEN AND CHILDREN, Fact Sheet No. 23 (Geneva: United Nations, 1996).

___, HUMAN RIGHTS, A COMPILATION OF INTERNATIONAL INSTRUMENTS; VOLUME I (FIRST PART), UNIVERSAL INSTRUMENTS (New York: United Nations, 1994).

Selected Bibliography

___, HUMAN RIGHTS, A COMPILATION OF INTERNATIONAL INSTRUMENTS; VOLUME II, REGIONAL INSTRUMENTS (New York: United Nations, 1997).

___, *Key Issues in Family Planning, Health and Family Well-Being in the 1990s and Beyond*, in United Nations, FAMILY PLANNING, HEALTH AND FAMILY WELL-BEING (New York: UN, 1996), pp. 27-58.

___, REPORT OF THE FOURTH WORLD CONFERENCE ON WOMEN, BEIJING, 4-15 SEPTEMBER 1995, UN doc. A/CONF.177/20, 17 October 1995.

___, REPORT OF THE INTERNATIONAL CONFERENCE ON POPULATION AND DEVELOPMENT, CAIRO, 5-13 SEPTEMBER 1994, UN doc. A/CONF.171/3, 18 October 1994.

United Nations, Committee on the Rights of the Child, CONSIDERATION OF REPORTS: INITIAL REPORT OF MALAWI, UN doc. CRC/C/8/Add.43, 26 June 200.

___, SECOND PERIODIC REPORT OF ETHIOPIA, UN doc. CRC/C/SR.675, 15 November 2001.

___, INITIAL REPORT OF THE CENTRAL AFRICAN REPUBLIC, UN doc. CRC/C/SR.657, 9 October 2000.

United Nations, Economic and Social Council, PRELIMINARY REPORT SUBMITTED BY THE SPECIAL RAPPORTEUR ON VIOLENCE AGAINST WOMEN, ITS CAUSES AND CONSEQUENCES, MS. RADHIKA COOMARASWAMY, UN doc. E/CN.4/1995/42, 22 November 1994.

___, OFFICIAL RECORD OF THE ECONOMIC AND SOCIAL COUNCIL, 1998, Supplement No. 7, UN docs. E/1998/27 and E/CN.6/1998/12.

United Nations, General Assembly, TRADITIONAL OR CUSTOMARY PRACTICES AFFECTING THE HEALTH OF WOMEN, UN doc. A/53/354, 10 September 1998.

United Nations Development Programme (UNDP), HUMAN DEVELOPMENT REPORT 1997 (Oxford: Oxford University Press, 1997).

___, HUMAN DEVELOPMENT REPORT 1995 (Oxford: Oxford University Press, 1995).

United Nations Population Fund (UNFPA), ANNUAL REPORT 1996 (New York: UNFPA, 1997).

___, MEETING THE POPULATION CHALLENGE (New York: UNFPA, 1996).

___, MATERNAL MORTALITY UPDATE 1998-1999 on website: http://www.unfpa.org/tpd/mmupdate/hilites.htm.

___, POPULATION ISSUES BRIEFING KIT 2001 on website: http://www.unfpa.org/modules/briefkit/05.htm.

United Nations High Commissioner for Refugees, Office of (UNHCR), HANDBOOK ON REPRODUCTIVE HEALTH IN REFUGEE SITUATIONS (Geneva: UNHCR, 1996).

___, SEXUAL VIOLENCE AGAINST REFUGEES: GUIDELINES ON PREVENTION AND RESPONSE (Geneva: UNHCR, 1995).

Upadhyay, Ushma D. and Bryant Robey, WHY FAMILY PLANNING MATTERS, Population Reports, Series J, No. 49 (Baltimore: Johns Hopkins University School of Public Health, Population Information Program, July 1999).

Van Achtenberg, Angeline, ed., OUT OF THE SHADOWS: THE FIRST AFRICAN INDIGENOUS WOMEN'S CONFERENCE (FAIWC) (Utrecht: International Books, 1998).

van Boven, Theo C., Cees Flinterman and Ingrid Westendorp, *Introduction*, in Theo C. van Boven, Cees Flinterman and Ingrid Westendorp, eds., *The Maastricht Guidelines on Violations of Economic, Social and Cultural Rights*, SIM Special, No. 20, 1998, pp. 1-12.

van Dijk, P. and G.J.H. van Hoof, THEORY AND PRACTICE OF THE EUROPEAN CONVENTION ON HUMAN RIGHTS, 3rd ed. (The Hague/London/Boston: Kluwer Law International, 1998).
Veerman, Nel, *Women's Groups in Africa: Panacea or Problem?*, Vena Journal, Vol. 7, No. 2, 1995, pp. 5-10.
Velásquez Toro, Magdala, *Legal Gains for Women*, in Margaret Schuler, ed., EMPOWERMENT AND THE LAW: STRATEGIES OF THIRD WORLD WOMEN (Washington, D.C.: OEF International, 1986), pp. 71-76.
Vincent, R. J., HUMAN RIGHTS AND INTERNATIONAL RELATIONS (Cambridge: Cambridge University Press, 1986).
Wa Mutua, Makau, *The Banjul Charter and the African Cultural Fingerprint: An Evaluation of the Language of Duties*, Virginia Journal of International Law, Vol. 35, No. 1, 1995, pp. 339-380.
Waite, G., *The politics of disease: The AIDS virus and Africa*, in N. Miller and R.C. Rockwell, eds., AIDS IN AFRICA: THE SOCIAL AND POLICY IMPACT (Lewiston/Queenston: Edwin Mellen Press, 1988), pp. 145-164.
Welch, Claude E. Jr., PROTECTING HUMAN RIGHTS IN AFRICA: STRATEGIES AND ROLES OF NON-GOVERNMENTAL ORGANIZATIONS (Philadelphia: University of Pennsylvania Press, 1995).
___, *Human Rights and African Women: A Comparison of Protection under Two Major Treaties*, Human Rights Quarterly, Vol. 15, No. 3, 1993, pp. 549-574.
___, *The African Commission on Human and Peoples' Rights: A Five-Year Report and Assessment*, Human Rights Quarterly, Vol. 14, No. 1, 1992, pp. 43-61.
Westoff, Charles F. and Akinrinola Bankole, MASS MEDIA AND REPRODUCTIVE BEHAVIOUR IN AFRICA, DHS Analytical Reports No. 2 (Calverton, Maryland: Macro International Inc., 1997).
Weston, Burns H., *Human Rights in a Mulitcultured World*, in Burns H. Weston and Stephen P. Marks, eds., THE FUTURE OF INTERNATIONAL HUMAN RIGHTS (Ardsley, New York: Transnational Publishers, Inc., 1999), pp. 65-99.
Williams, Lindy and Teresa Sobieszczyk, ATTITUDES SURROUNDING THE CONTINUATION OF FEMALE CIRCUMCISION IN THE SUDAN: PASSING THE TRADITION TO THE NEXT GENERATION, Research Report No. 96-366 (Ann Arbor: Population Studies Center, University of Michigan, 1996).
Wiredu, Kwasi, CULTURAL UNIVERSALS AND PARTICULARS: AN AFRICAN PERSPECTIVE (Bloomington: Indiana University Press, 1996).
___, *An Akan Perspective of Human Rights*, in Abdullahi A. An-Na'im. and Francis M. Deng, eds., HUMAN RIGHTS IN AFRICA: CROSS-CULTURAL PERSPECTIVES (Washington, D.C.: Brookings Institute, 1990), pp. 243-260.
World Bank, CONFRONTING AIDS: PUBLIC PRIORITIES IN A GLOBAL EPIDEMIC (Oxford: Oxford University Press, 1997).
World Health Organization (WHO), FEMALE GENITAL MUTILATION: INFORMATION KIT (Geneva: WHO, 1994), WHO/FHE/94.4.
___, REPRODUCTIVE HEALTH: A KEY TO A BRIGHTER FUTURE. BIENNIAL REPORT 1990-1991 (Geneva: WHO, 1992).
Yilla, Sophie, *African (Sierra Leone) Women and Nutrition*, in IAC, REPORT ON THE REGIONAL CONFERENCE ON TRADITIONAL PRACTICES AFFECTING THE

HEALTH OF WOMEN AND CHILDREN IN AFRICA (Addis Ababa: IAC, 1991), pp. 133-135.

Young, K., PLANNING DEVELOPMENT WITH WOMEN: MAKING A WORLD OF A DIFFERENCE (London: MacMillan, 1993).

Zabin, Laurie Schwab and Karungari Kiragu, *The Health Consequences of Adolescent Sexual and Fertility Behaviour in Sub-Saharan Africa*, Studies in Family Planning, Vol. 29, No. 2, 1998, pp. 210-232.

INDEX

Abduction, practice of 42
Abortion 4
Addis Ababa [African] Declaration on Violence against Women (draft) 65, 188, 207
Additional Protocol to the African Charter on Violence against Women (draft) 124-129, 201, 208
African Charter on Human and Peoples' Rights (African Charter) 14, 109-129, 196, 201, 208
African Charter on the Rights and Welfare of Children 54, 77, 114-115, 122
African Commission on Human and Peoples' Rights (African Commission) 109-114, 122-129, 208
African Youth Declaration on Harmful Traditional Practices 193
Akan 182
Amicus curiae 196
Anaemia 1, 28, 45

Beijing Declaration and Platform for Action (BDPA) 56, 115, 128, 189
Benin 9
Brideprice (*bridewealth*) 31, 40-41, 48, 53
Bundu 45
Burkina Faso 9-10
Burundi 7

Central African Republic 39, 189, 194
China 15, 157-161, 185, 191, 203-204
Church of Scotland 165
Christianity 8, 35, 37, 42, 85-86, 92-93, 141, 144, 147, 183-184
Colonialism 123, 173, 201, 206

Congo, the 7
Contraception 4, 6, 45, 47
    (*see also* family planning)
Convention on the Elimination of All Forms of Violence against Women (Women's Convention) 55, 57, 62, 106, 206, 210
Convention on the Rights of the Child (Children's Convention) 55
Cultural relativism (relativity) 88-108
Customary
    Courts 180-182
    law (traditional) 8, 112, 119, 178, 180-182, 208
    leaders (*see* traditional leaders)

Declaration of Mexico on the Equality of Women 57
Declaration on the Elimination of All Forms of Intolerance and of Discrimination Based on Religion or Belief 74
Declaration on the Elimination of Violence against Women 56, 64-65, 106, 115
Democratic Republic of the Congo 7
Dietary (*nutritional*) taboos 1, 13, 28, 31, 35, 58, 60, 62-63, 69, 103-104
Djibouti 19, 173
Donors 194-195, 209
Due diligence 50
Duties (of the State) 49-57, 60-61, 78

Early marriage 13, 25-26, 31, 35, 48, 53, 62, 63, 67-68, 79, 103, 105, 204
    (*see also* early pregnancy)
Early pregnancy 1, 7, 13, 25-27, 36, 58, 68
Egypt 9, 157, 165, 194, 204

249

Education
  formal (schooling) 14, 35, 132, 143-149, 202-203, 209, 210
  human rights 14, 133-137, 151, 155-156, 202, 209
Elders 36, 42-43, 156, 187, 209
Elongation (of neck) 3, 103
Empowerment 15, 133, 137-156, 202, 209
Ethiopia 27, 32-33, 37, 42, 188
Extra-marital sexual activity 38-39, 46

Family law (*see* customary law)
Family planning 4, 6, 32
  (*see also* contraception)
Fanado 45
Female circumcision,
  definition of 18-19
  general 1, 5, 9-12, 15, 17, 31, 33, 47, 51, 58, 50-67, 96, 103-105, 165-168, 171-172, 187, 191-193, 204-205
  health effects 22-24
  reasons for 20-22
Female religious bondage 1, 13, 31, 58-59, 62-63, 67, 79, 103, 105
Feminism 70-74, 79-80
Fertility 35, 42-44, 53
Fistula (obstetric) 23, 27
Footbinding 15, 157-161, 185, 203

Gender (-based) violence 14, 49, 63-70, 152
Gender ideologies (*see* feminism)
General Comment
  No. 14 on Health (Committee on Economic, Social and Cultural Rights) 51, 188
  No. 22 on the Right to Freedom of Religion or Belief (Human Rights Committee) 74
General Recommendation
  No. 14 concerning Harmful Traditional Practices (CEDAW) 56, 58, 189
  No. 19 on Violence against Women (CEDAW) 56, 63, 66, 68, 189

Ghana 9, 13, 25, 29-32, 40, 46, 175, 182, 195
Guinea-Bissau 45
Gusii 36

Hinduism 161-163, 169, 185
HIV/AIDS 1, 5, 7, 27, 39, 46-47, 58-60, 136, 146, 176-177, 190, 199, 205
Horizontal effect (of human rights) 54
Household structure,
  extended-family 32-34, 36
  nuclear 33
  polygamous 31, 47, 48

Incisions (in pregnant women) 1, 13, 58, 60, 62, 103-104
India 15, 157, 161-165, 185, 203-204
Indigenous mechanisms
  (*see* traditional mechanisms)
Infertility 5, 22, 42
Initiation rites 12, 21, 186
Inter-African Committee on Traditional Practices Affecting the Health of Women and Children (IAC) 9-11, 25, 47, 168, 185-186, 191, 193, 200, 203, 209
Inter-American Convention on Violence against Women 54-56
International Conference on Population and Development (ICPD) 6
International Covenant on Civil and Political Rights (CCPR) 74, 122
International Covenant on Economic, Social and Cultural Rights (CESCR) 58, 106, 118-119, 122
Islam 8, 42, 92-93, 141, 183-184

Kasaï 48
Kenya 12, 25, 35-37, 40, 70-71, 92, 144, 157, 165-167, 173, 176, 186, 188-189, 194, 204
Kikuyu 144-145, 166
Kin (*kinship*), influence of 34-35, 40, 42-43

Legal aid 195-196
Lesotho 39
Levirate marriage 31, 41
Liberia 45, 176
Lineage (*see* kin)

Male circumcision 69, 104
Mali 11, 145, 185, 209
Marriage,
   norm of universal 43, 53
   polygamous 36-38
   (*see also* early marriage and extra-marital sexual activity)
Maternal mortality 5-6, 29
Media 189-190, 209
Mozambique 27, 41
Muslim (*see* Islam)

Nairobi Forward-Looking Strategies 58, 189
Nigeria 35, 37, 145

Obligations of States (*see* duties)
Organization for African Unity (OAU) 65, 116, 202

Patriarchy 35, 184
Patrilineal societies 40
Pluralism (of human rights) 96-67
Polygamy (*see* polygyny and household structure)
Polygyny 31, 36-38, 46

Queenmother 182
Qu'ran 11

REACH 12
Reparations 52
Right to
   choose one's spouse 78
   education 77-78
   found a family 78-79
   freedom from discrimination 24, 61-63
   freedom from violence 24, 63
   freedom of expression 74
   freedom of (religion and) belief 69, 74
   freedom of thought 74
   health 24, 58-61, 63
   life 59-60, 63, 65
   physical security 65, 69
Rwanda 7

Sabini 68-69, 173, 186
Safe motherhood 5-6
Sande (bush school) 45
Sati 15, 157, 161-165, 185, 203
Scarification (scarification) 3, 103-104
Senegal 9, 11, 26, 35, 203, 207
Septicaemia 22, 29
Sexually transmitted diseases (STDs) 5, 37, 39, 41, 46, 58
Sharia 183
Sierra Leone 28
Somalia 19, 145
Son preference, norm of 28, 31, 35-36, 53
Special Rapporteur on violence
   against women (UN) 64-66
   the rights of African women 123-124, 127, 201
Sudan, the 19, 145, 157, 167-168, 192, 204
Superstition (superstitious practices) 28-29, 44-45, 47-48, 53, 63, 74
Swaziland 176-177

Taboos 28, 32, 39
   (*see also* dietary taboos)
Tanzania 9, 146, 150, 185, 189
Teenage pregnancy (*see* pregnancy)
Tiriki 35
Tooth-pulling, practice of 68
Tostan 11, 200, 203, 207
Total fertility rate 6, 43
Traditional
   ancestral rites 42
   birth attendants 9, 11, 60-61, 175, 187
   childbirth practices 1, 17, 29-30, 58-59, 62-63, 103-104

institutions 7-8
leaders 3, 34, 42, 156, 169, 173, 180, 184-185, 187-188, 191, 203, 207
mechanisms 180, 185, 188-189, 197, 203
religions 8, 183

Uganda 7, 12, 18, 68, 146, 173, 186
UNFPA 6, 9, 25
Universal Declaration of Human Rights 67, 106, 118, 131, 134
Universalism (universality of human rights) 83-108, 202

Vienna Convention on the Law of Treaties 119
Vienna Declaration and Programme of Action (VDPA) 134
Violence against women
(*see* gender-based violence)
Virgin slave
(*see* female religious bondage)

Widow burning (*see* sati)
Widowhood (mourning) practices 3, 103-104
Wife inheritance
(*see* levirate marriage)
Women's groups 14, 81, 132-133, 139-143, 202
World Bank 39, 206
World Health Organization 6, 9, 63, 146

Xhosa 69

Yorugu 195

Zambia 146
Zimbabwe 37
Zur Zur (*see* incisions)

SAMENVATTING

De campagnes voor het beëindigen van schadelijke traditionele praktijken ('harmful traditional practices'), voornamelijk door voorlichtingscampagnes op 'grass-roots level' en wetgeving tegen dergelijke praktijken, boeken een constante maar langzame vooruitgang. In het algemeen kan worden gezegd dat de besnijdenis van vrouwen slechts een geringe afname vertoont. Onveilig vrijen en het krijgen van kinderen op een jonge leeftijd, als gevolg van het huwen of een andere vorm van samenleven tijdens de adolescentie, zijn nog steeds de norm voor Afrikaanse meisjes. Bepaalde andere traditionele praktijken en de schade die zij kunnen veroorzaken hebben pas recentelijk op internationaal niveau aandacht gekregen. Deze gebruiken vormen echter een groot risico voor de reproductieve gezondheid van vrouwen en meisjes, vooral doordat zij in toenemende mate worden blootgesteld aan HIV/AIDS en het risico op complicaties bij de bevalling. Deze beide gevaren verhogen de kans op voortijdige dood, die echter te voorkomen is. In de meer voorkomende, minder dramatische, gevallen leiden deze praktijken tot kortdurende of langdurige schade voor de reproductieve gezondheid van vrouwen en meisjes. Dit wordt grotendeels in standgehouden omwille van 'traditie,' die in stand wordt gehouden om redenen als sociale cohesie en harmonie binnen de familie en de gemeenschap als zodanig.

Een initieel doel van dit onderzoek was om alleen de bestaande literatuur over traditionele schadelijke praktijken en de mensenrechtenschendingen te onderzoeken. Deze literatuur bleek bij tijd en wijle misleidend te zijn, vooral de Westerse feministische literatuur en diens categorische beschrijving van alle schadelijke traditionele praktijken als vormen van geweld tegen vrouwen, op basis waarvan er wordt gesteld dat vrouwen slachtoffer zijn van deze mensenrechtenschendingen. Welke rechten er nu precies worden geschonden en hoe bepaalde praktijken tot een schending daarvan leiden is echter zelden onderzocht. In die gevallen dat het is onderzocht is dit inadequaat gedaan. Dit heeft in bepaalde gevallen bijgedragen aan de bezorgdheid van vooral niet-westerlingen, volgens wie het discours over schadelijke traditionele praktijken voornamelijk wordt geleid door niet-Afrikaanse feministische activisten met goede bedoelingen, die er echter niet in slagen het te verenigen met de dagelijkse realiteit van Afrikaanse vrouwen. Deze gevoelens worden versterkt door het feit dat het discours van 'gender' en feminisme als een buitenlands, zelfs neo-kolonialistisch, discours wordt beschouwd met beperkte toepasbaarheid op het leven van gewone Afrikaanse vrouwen.

Samenvatting

In het licht van het ontbreken van een gedetailleerde analyse, is het doel van dit onderzoek om het dominante internationale mensenrechtendiscours te deconstrueren en een alternatief te ontwikkelen. Dit wordt gedaan door vast te stellen hoe schadelijke traditionele praktijken specifieke mensenrechten – niet alleen die rechten welke het vrij zijn van geweld beschermen, maar vooral ook het recht op gezondheid – schenden of niet. In de hoop dit verder te verhelderen, heb ik geprobeerd vast te stellen of en hoe bepaalde praktijken, die als 'schadelijk' en 'traditioneel' worden bestempeld, mensenrechten van vrouwen schenden, en zo ja welke precies. Hiervoor was het nodig om de redenen die over het algemeen worden gegeven voor het toepassen van deze praktijken vast te stellen en de manier waarop deze praktijken schade kunnen veroorzaken, vooral voor de reproductieve gezondheid van vrouwen en meisjes. Dit maakte duidelijk dat schadelijke traditionele praktijken niet noodzakelijkerwijs en niet altijd leiden tot een mensenrechtenschending.

Gezien het feit dat het de Afrikaanse vrouwen zelf zijn die de schadelijke traditionele praktijken uitvoeren, ondanks dat zij zich in het algemeen bewust zijn van de mogelijke schade en de theoretische mogelijkheid zich te verzetten tegen deze tradities, dienen we te kijken naar de gewoonten en normen die dergelijke tradities voeden. In hoofdstuk II heb ik er een aantal geselecteerd en geprobeerd hun relatie tot de specifieke schadelijke traditionele praktijk te verklaren. De specifieke verdragsverplichtingen voor staten om deze gewoonten te veranderen of uit te bannen worden in hoofdstuk III, in tabel IV, uitgewerkt.

Het afwijzen van het universele karakter van mensenrechten zou ernstige implicaties hebben voor de wereldwijde campagne om schadelijke traditionele praktijken te beëindigen en voor de levens van de Afrikaanse vrouwen, aangezien dat zou impliceren dat cultuur kan worden beschouwd als iets dat onze noties van, *inter alia*, rechtvaardigheid en menselijke waardigheid, conditioneert. De meeste activisten vrezen dat in dat geval rechtvaardigheid en waardigheid voor vrouwen als eerste zullen sneuvelen. In het licht van dit reële risico is in hoofdstuk IV een overzicht gegeven van de argumenten voor en tegen universaliteit van mensenrechten. Mensenrechten en wat wij als een schending daarvan beschouwen, wordt gedetermineerd door een pluralistisch kader, wat de invloed van culturele of religieuze vooroordelen bij het vaststellen van een schending vermindert. Dit wordt verder toegelicht in hoofdstuk IV. Verscheidene gewoonten worden als hierbij als voorbeeld genomen om te illustreren hoe de mensenrechtenbenadering kan werken ten aanzien van culturele praktijken.
Beide exercities die in hoofdstuk IV zijn ondernomen tonen aan dat, vooral ten aanzien van Afrika, argumenten tegen de universaliteit van mensenrechten beïnvloed kunnen zijn door het koloniale verleden en de armoede in de regio. Een ongemakkelijk gevoel ten aanzien van het mensenrechtendiscours kan verband houden met het gevoel van Afrikanen dat het nodig is elk discours te verwerpen dat geacht wordt neo-kolonialistisch te zijn en met hun sterke wens een stempel te drukken op zaken die betrekking hebben op Afrika. Exact om die redenen is het van belang het Afrikaans Handvest voor

de Rechten van Mensen en Volken op de voorgrond te plaatsten. Gezien het belang van dit verdrag, was het nodig die bepalingen die volgens wetenschappers een bedreiging vormen voor de positie van Afrikaanse vrouwen en hun rechten te bestuderen. In hoofdstuk V worden deze bepalingen besproken en wordt de stelling verdedigd dat deze bepalingen de positie of de rechten van Afrikaanse vrouwen niet aantasten.

In hoofdstuk VI wordt de stelling ingenomen, welke ondersteund wordt door voornamelijk Afrikaanse en andere uit ontwikkelingslanden afkomstige onderzoekers, dat mensenrechten slechts een beperkte bijdrage leveren aan de mate van 'empowerment' van Afrikaanse vrouwen op 'grassroots level.' Er wordt derhalve bepleit minder nadruk te leggen op de 'bottom-up' benadering voor de implementatie van mensenrechtennormen in de regio. Deze benadering claimt dat bewustwording en 'empowerment' van vrouwen – door mensenrechtenonderwijs, voorlichting aan vrouwengroepen en verbeterde toegang tot het onderwijs – zal zorgen voor sociale en culturele veranderingen die nodig zijn om de positie van vrouwen te verbeteren en daardoor het beëindigen van schadelijke traditionele praktijken. Alhoewel deze benadering breed wordt gedragen door vrouwenrechtenactivisten en door de internationale mensenrechtengemeenschap en effectief werkt in talrijke situaties, wordt hier aangetoond hoe Afrikaanse vrouwen met te veel structurele, psychologische en praktische obstakels en beperkingen worden geconfronteerd. Dit is vooral het geval voor de arme rurale vrouwen in sub-Sahara Afrika, gezien hun unieke sociale en politieke omgeving. Vrouwengroepen, bijvoorbeeld, hebben vaak te maken met talrijke interne problemen, zoals politisering en elitevorming binnen de hoogste rangen, en externe problemen, vooral twijfel ten aanzien van de legitimiteit en het belang van hun werk ten overstaan van mannen in machtige posities. Met betrekking tot scholing is aangetoond dat onderwijs nog geen impact heeft gehad op de traditionele stereotypen en normen. Totdat een groot aantal belangrijke elementen veranderen, zoals toename van het aantal meisjes dat toegang heeft tot onderwijs, aanpassing van de inhoud van het onderwijsmateriaal, de houding van docenten en de normen en waarden van de gemeenschap, zal scholing slechts een beperkte invloed hebben op de 'empowerment' van meisjes.

Talrijke belemmeringen bij het toepassen van het recht zijn onderkend die het niet waarschijnlijkheid maken dat vrouwen hun mensenrechtenkennis gebruiken om discriminerende normen in het algemeen, en schadelijke traditionele praktijken in het bijzonder, te bestrijden. Belemmeringen die bijzonder moeilijk zijn te overkomen houden verband met de regionale sociale-culturele context. Dit is met name het geval omdat mensenrechteneducatie er voornamelijk op is gericht Afrikaanse vrouwen aan te moedigen om rechtsbescherming te zoeken door het gebruik van het juridische stelsel, zoals door het indienen van klachten bij de politie en het voor de rechter brengen van een zaak met het oog op gerechtelijke maatregelen. Onderzoek wijst echter uit dat Afrikaanse vrouwen, vooral door hun socialisatie, het recht niet snel op die manier zullen gebruiken. Zij geven er de voorkeur aan de beslissingen van hun familie te beïnvloeden op een niet-confronterende manier. Talrijke verhalen van vrouwen die zo

Samenvatting

moedig zijn om de politie in te schakelen hebben vaak een tragische afloop, omdat de politie op haar beurt faalde hen te beschermen. Dergelijke verhalen tonen aan hoe diep we moeten graven om de wortels van socialisatie, waardoor traditties in stand worden gehouden, bloot te leggen. Echter, dit betekent niet dat vrouwen geen sociale of juridische middelen hebben die zij kunnen gebruiken om hun rechten te verdedigen. Onderzoek wijst uit dat vrouwen zich meer op hun gemak voelen en een betere toegang hebben tot traditionele middelen voor conflictbeheersing. In het geval van conflicten binnen de familie worden, vooral in de rurale gebieden, vaak traditionele rechtbanken die gewoonterecht toepassen ingeschakeld of worden traditionele middelen voor geschilbeslechting gebruikt. Alhoewel deze rechtbanken en deze middelen, en de mannen die ze beheersen, normaal gesproken worden gezien als antagonistisch ten aanzien van rechten van vrouwen, zou hun potentiële positieve invloed, indien zij erbij betrokken worden, enorm en bepalend kunnen zijn.

Het overzicht dat in hoofdstuk VII wordt gegeven van de schadelijke traditionele praktijken die met succes zijn uitgebannen in andere regio's van de wereld, bevestigt het belang van lokale leiders en de steun van belangrijke lokale opinieleiders. De uitbanning van het afbinden van voeten in China en de *sati* in India zijn hier goede voorbeelden van. In beide gevallen werkte de invloed van lokale vertegenwoordigers van de gemeenschap als katalysator bij de uitbanning. Behorende tot de betreffende cultuur, konden de Chou en Roy hun campagne toesnijden op de culturele context. Zij waren in staat de factoren te identificeren die de uitbanning blokkeerden en konden hun campagne daarop richten. Hun boodschap was geloofwaardig en maakte het voor hen mogelijk om met voorstanders van deze praktijken in discussie te treden en tegenargumenten te geven op dezelfde religieuze en culturele basis. Beiden gebruikten intensieve voorlichtingsprogramma's op lokaal niveau om de publieke opinie te beïnvloeden. Zoals is opgemerkt in de inleiding van dit onderzoek, vinden dergelijke 'grassroots' activiteiten al gedurende een langere periode plaats en nemen deze alleen maar toe in het hedendaagse sub-Sahara Afrika. Deze specifieke onderzoeksuitkomsten ten aanzien van China en India zijn derhalve geruststellend, aangezien zij de effectiviteit van de tot op heden gebruikte strategieën bevestigen. Er kunnen echter weinig nieuwe lessen uit worden getrokken waarmee we de campagne tegen schadelijke traditionele praktijken in sub-Sahara Afrika kunnen aanpassen. Wel kan er lering uit worden getrokken. Twee lessen die we ervan kunnen leren zijn in mijn ogen van bijzonder belang. De eerste is dat het aannemen en het proberen af te dwingen van de naleving van wetgeving voor de uitbanning van traditionele praktijken vaak weinig impact heeft indien wijdverspreide steun onder de bevolking ontbreekt voor een dergelijke uitbanning. In sommige gevallen heeft dit zelfs geleid tot publieke woede tegen het overheidsingrijpen in 'privé' zaken en een versterkte loyaliteit aan de praktijk. Dit is althans de ervaring met vrouwenbesnijdenis in Egypte, Kenia en Soedan. In dit licht en in combinatie met de uitkomsten van hoofdstuk VI die aantonen dat wetgeving zelden wordt nageleefd en dat ook de politie vrouwen niet beschermt

Samenvatting

tegen deze praktijken, zelfs wanneer deze praktijken bij wet zijn verboden, lijkt de nadruk die hedendaagse activisten leggen op het aannemen van wetgeving door staten derhalve misplaatst. Veel meer inspanningen dienen te worden gekanaliseerd in het veranderen van de publieke opinie ten aanzien van deze praktijken voordat aanname van wetgeving effectief kan zijn, en medewerkers in de gezondheidszorg, de politie en andere autoriteiten, laat staan de gewone burger, dit kunnen uitvoeren. De tweede belangrijke les die getrokken kan worden is dat wetgeving, zoals die tegen het besnijden van meisjes of tegen het huwen van meisjes jonger dan 18 jaar, alle vormen van deze praktijk tegelijkertijd moet verbieden. Het toestaan van bepaalde 'zachtere' vormen of van uitzonderingen in de hoop dat zelfs deze vanzelf geleidelijk zullen verdwijnen heeft nog nooit succes opgeleverd. Veel meer lijken dergelijke maatregelen de stilzwijgende instemming van de overheid ten aanzien van deze praktijken en, nog belangrijker, de achterliggende ideeën te bevestigen.

Volgend uit de bevindingen van de 'bottom-up' benadering ten aanzien van de 'empowerment' van vrouwen, wordt het duidelijk dat wij onze energie op zijn minst evenveel moeten richten op de 'top-down' benadering ten aanzien van 'empowerment'. In hoofdstuk VIII worden de middelen beschreven waarmee we hierin kunnen slagen. In internationale mensenrechtenverdragen is het de staat die verplicht is de mensenrechten van de verdragen waarbij de staat partij is te respecteren, te verzekeren en te vervullen ('to respect, ensure and fulfill'). Dit houdt echter niet in dat de staat de enige is die activiteiten moet verrichten om aan deze verplichtingen te voldoen. Integendeel, ik heb betoogd dat het niet realistisch is te verwachten dat zelfs de meest gecommitteerde Afrikaanse staten een einde kunnen maken aan schadelijke traditionele praktijken, middels hun overheidsinstanties, zelfs niet als ze de financiële en technische middelen ervoor zouden hebben. Dit komt, kort samengevat, doordat het niet de Afrikaanse staten *per se* zijn die deze praktijken uitvoeren of instandhouden. Immers het is niet de staat die verantwoordelijk is voor onze socialisatie, en men zou kunnen beweren dat dit nog meer het geval is in Afrika dan in het Westen. Veeleer vindt socialisatie plaats binnen de gemeenschap, tijdens dorpsbijeenkomsten, door religieuze instellingen en vooral binnen de familie. Religieuze instellingen, de media en mannen zijn derhalve diegenen die capabel zijn om deze normen en tradities werkelijk te veranderen. Echter projectmanagers, NGO's en vrouwenrechtenactivisten hebben allemaal de neiging precies deze instellingen en actoren te negeren, af te wijzen of te verwerpen. Derhalve pleit ik ervoor om juist deze instellingen en actoren erbij te betrekken.

ABOUT THE AUTHOR

Corinne A.A. Packer (1967) received her Bachelor of Arts, Honours (B.A., Hons.) degree (first class) in French language and literature at the University of Manitoba, Canada, and went on to complete a Master of Arts (M.A.) degree (with distinction) in Applied Population Research at the University of Exeter, England and a Master of Philosophy (M.Phil.) degree in International Relations at the University of Cambridge, England. In 1999 she joined the Netherlands Institute of Human Rights (SIM), University of Utrecht, as a Ph.D. candidate.

Ms. Packer has written and lectured on various topics relating to human reproduction and human rights, including: THE RIGHT TO REPRODUCTIVE CHOICE: A STUDY IN INTERNATIONAL LAW (Åbo Akademi University, Finland, 1996); and *Sex Education: Child's Right, Parent's Choice or State's Obligation?* in E. Heinze, ed., OF INNOCENCE AND AUTONOMY (Dartmouth, U.K.: Ashgate, 2000). She has also contributed articles to the International Journal of Children's Rights, the Nordic Journal of International Law and the European Journal of Health Law. Most recently she has written on the African Union (American Journal of International Law).

She has worked on projects related to family planning/reproductive health with the Office of the United Nations High Commissioner for Refugees and the World Health Organization. In 1997 she was invited by the Council of Europe to speak and write on reproductive trends in Europe. She also has been employed as a researcher/writer by The Netherlands Ministry of Foreign Affairs (on the role of The Netherlands in the United Nations) and The Netherlands Ministry of Social Affairs and Employment (on the subject of women's rights). From 1993 to 2000 she worked for the International Labour Organisation (ILO), Legislative Information Branch, on a database of ILO legislation and jurisprudence.

SCHOOL OF HUMAN RIGHTS RESEARCH SERIES

The School of Human Rights Research is a joint effort by human rights researchers in the Netherlands. Its central research theme is the nature and meaning of international standards in the field of human rights, their application and promotion in the national legal order, their interplay with national standards, and the international supervision of such application. The School of Human Rights Research Series only includes English titles that contribute to a better understanding of the different aspects of human rights.

Editorial Board of the Series: Prof. dr C. Flinterman (Utrecht University),
Prof. dr W.J.M. van Genugten (Tilburg University), Prof. dr A.P. van Goudoever (Utrecht University), Prof. dr M.T. Kamminga (Maastricht University), Prof. dr P.A.M. Mevis (Erasmus University Rotterdam) and dr H. Werdmölder (Utrecht University)

Published titles within the Series:

1. Brigit C.A. Toebes, *The Right to Health as a Human Right in International Law*
   ISBN 90-5095-057-4

2. Ineke Boerefijn, *The Reporting Procedure under the Covenant on Civil and Political Rights. Practice and Procedures of the Human Rights Committee*
   ISBN 90-5095-074-4

3. Kitty Arambulo, *Strengthening the Supervision of the International Covenant on Economic, Social and Cultural Rights. Theoretical and Procedural Aspects*
   ISBN 90-5095-058-2

4. Marlies Glasius, *Foreign Policy on Human Rights. Its Influence on Indonesia under Soeharto*
   ISBN 90-5095-089-2

5. Cornelis D. de Jong, *The Freedom of Thought, Conscience and Religion or Belief in the United Nations (1946-1992)*
   ISBN 90-5095-137-6

6. Heleen Bosma, *Freedom of Expression in England and under the ECHR: in Search of a Common Ground. A Foundation for the Application of the Human Rights Act 1998 in English Law*
   ISBN 90-5095-136-8

7. Mielle Bulterman, *Human Rights in the External Relations of the European Union*
   ISBN 90-5095-164-3

8. Esther M. van den Berg, *The Influence of Domestic NGOs on Dutch Human Rights Policy. Case Studies on South Africa, Namibia, Indonesia and East Timor*
   ISBN 90-5095-159-7

9. Ian Seiderman, *Hierarchy in International Law: the Human Rights Dimension*
   ISBN 90-5095-165-1

10. Anna Meijknecht, *Towards International Personality: the Position of Minorities and Indigenous Peoples in International Law*
    ISBN 90-5095-166-X

11. Mohamed Eltayeb, *A Human Rights Approach to Combating Religious Persecution. Cases from Pakistan, Saudi Arabia and Sudan*
ISBN 90-5095-170-8

12. Machteld Boot, *Genocide, Crimes Against Humanity, War Crimes: Nullum Crimen Sine Lege and the Subject Matter Jurisdiction of the International Criminal Court*
ISBN 90-5095-216-X

13. Corinne Packer, *Using Human Rights to Change Tradition. Traditional Practices Harmful to Women's Reproductive Health in sub-Saharan Africa*
ISBN 90-5095-226-7